6000

Eisenhower Center Studies on War and Peace

Stephen E. Ambrose and Günter Bischof, editors

Cold War Respite

Cold War Respite

The Geneva Summit of 1955

EDITED BY GÜNTER BISCHOF
AND SAKI DOCKRILL

Louisiana State University Press

Baton Rouge

MM

09 08 07 06 05 04 03 02 01 00

5 4 3 2 1

Designer: Erin Kirk New
Typeface: Trump Mediaeval with Frutiger display
Typesetter: Coghill Composition Co.
Printer and binder: Thomson-Shore, Inc.

Library of Congress Cataloging-in-Publication Data:

Cold war respite : the Geneva Summit of 1955 / edited by
Günter Bischof and Saki Dockrill.
    p. cm.—(Eisenhower Center studies on war and peace)
    Based on papers presented at a conference held Oct. 20–22,
1995, New Orleans, La.
    Includes bibliographical references and index.
    ISBN 0-8071-2370-6 (alk. paper)
    1. Geneva Summit (1955)—Congresses.   2. Summit
meetings—Switzerland—Geneva—Congresses.   3. World
politics—1945–1955—Congresses.   4. Eisenhower, Dwight D.
(Dwight David), 1890–1969—Congresses.   5. United
States—Foreign relations—Soviet Union—Congresses.
6. Soviet Union—Foreign relations—United States—
Congresses.   7. United States—Foreign relations—
1945–1989—Congresses.   I. Bischof, Günter, 1953–
II. Dockrill, Saki.   III. Series.

D843 C57735   2000
327.1'09'045—dc21   00-028739

Contents

Illustrations

Acknowledgments

This collection of essays is based upon papers given at the conference "The Geneva Summit, July 1955," held in New Orleans October 20–22, 1995. The conference was sponsored by the Eisenhower Center for American Studies of the University of New Orleans; King's College, London; and the Foreign and Commonwealth Office, London.

John Young's advice and encouragement were crucial at the conceptualizing stage of the project. The editors would also like to thank Robert Dupont, the dean of UNO's Metropolitan College, for his invaluable support in preparing and planning the conference. His assistant Beryl Gauthier was instrumental, as always, in getting things done on time. We also benefitted from the keen advice of Douglas Brinkley, the Eisenhower Center's director, and Stephen E. Ambrose, its founder. Anne O'Herren Jacobs and her dedicated team at the Conference Services of Metropolitan College went out of their way to make the participants' stay in New Orleans as pleasant and memorable as possible. Both Arnold Hirsch, the chairman of UNO's History Department, and Lawrence Freedman, head of the War Studies Programme at King's College, gave us their unstinting support.

We are most grateful to Ernest R. May for delivering the keynote address and for contributing to our discussions until the final day of the conference. Doug Brinkley, Effie Pedaliu, David G. Herrmann, and Geoffrey Warner chaired sessions during the conference and added many valuable insights.

Regarding the preparation of the collection, the editors would like to thank the staffs of the various archives that were consulted. Copyright material from the Public Record Office, Kew, appears by permission of the controller, Her Majesty's Stationery Office.

On behalf of John Young and Saki Dockrill, we would like to thank the British Academy and the British Council for providing funds to enable them to complete their research for this volume. We also wish to thank the Louisiana State University Press reader whose constructive advice helped improve the manuscript. Our warm thanks also go to Maureen Hewitt and Gerry Anders at LSU Press for their work in preparing the manuscript for publication, to Sara Anderson for her superb copy editing, and to Linda Webster for the Index. Two UNO history graduate students were also helpful: Markus Hünemörder, a visiting student from the Amerika Institut of the University of Munich, compiled the bibliography, and Günther Walder, a visiting student from the University of Innsbruck, assisted with some fact checking.

Finally, this volume is the outcome of international collaboration between Britain, Canada, the United States, France, Italy, and Germany. Our letters and drafts and redrafts of chapters crossed and recrossed the Atlantic Ocean and the English Channel on many occasions. The editors would like to thank the contributors for their patient cooperation in answering our incessant queries and demands while we were preparing the manuscript.

Our dear spouses Michael Dockrill and Melanie Boulet gave us their loving support when we needed it most in completing the project.

This volume is dedicated to Steve Ambrose, the founder of the Eisenhower Center, who has been an inspiration for two generations of Eisenhower scholars across the world. His role as a fatherly mentor for Günter Bischof's American career was incalculable. One result of that influence is clear: we are quite sure that President Eisenhower, if he were alive today, would enjoy reading *Cold War Respite*.

Abbreviations

CWIHP	Cold War International History Project, Woodrow Wilson International Center for Scholars
DDEL	Dwight D. Eisenhower Library, Abilene, Kansas
DDF	Ministère des affaires étrangères, *Documents diplomatiques français* (Paris)
FRUS	*Foreign Relations of the United States*. Published by U.S. Department of State, Washington, D.C. Year span and volume number given with each cite.
Geneva Meeting	U.S. State Department, *The Geneva Meeting of Foreign Ministers, October 27–November 16, 1955* (Washington, D.C., 1955)
NA	National Archives, Washington, D.C. Documents are classified by numbered Record Group (RG)
PRO	Public Record Office, Kew, England. Documents are classified as FO (Foreign Office), PREM (Premier), and CAB (Cabinet)

Cold War Respite

Introduction

Geneva: The Fleeting Opportunity for Détente

SAKI DOCKRILL AND GÜNTER BISCHOF

Historical Significance of the Geneva Summit

The end of the cold war has ushered in a period of uncertainty and instability. John Lewis Gaddis once described the cold war as "the long peace," during which a certain degree of stability and prosperity was maintained under the bipolar system despite the enormous accumulation of nuclear weapons and despite numerous regional conflicts and revolutionary movements in Africa, the Middle East, and Southeast Asia.[1] However, the world became bipolar abruptly, even before the postwar peace settlements were completed. By 1955, the Austrian State Treaty remained to be signed, while the date of the final settlement regarding Germany was still uncertain.

According to a recent study by Vladimir O. Pechatnov, in 1944 and 1945 Joseph Stalin and V. M. Molotov, although suspicious about the intentions of the Soviet Union's wartime allies, nevertheless hoped for "continued cooperation with the Western Allies" because they thought it would benefit the Soviet Union in a postwar world.[2] Of course, toward the end of the war, Stalin became more single-minded about obtaining gains to which he thought the Soviet Union was entitled as a victorious power. But Stalin did not seek to destroy the grand alliance in 1945. For Britain, inclusion in the grand alliance helped maintain its image of being a great power rather than a junior partner of a younger

1. John Lewis Gaddis, "The Long Peace: Elements of Stability in the Postwar International System," in *The Long Peace: Inquiries into the History of the Cold War*, ed. John Lewis Gaddis (New York, 1987), 215–6.
2. Vladimir O. Pechatnov, "The Big Three after World War II: New Documents on Soviet Thinking about Post War Relations with the United States and Great Britain," CWIHP Working Paper no. 13 (Washington, D.C., 1995), 22.

yet economically stronger United States.[3] Washington believed that the newly formed United Nations, where the Soviet Union, Britain, the United States, and China were to play major roles, would be sufficient to establish a new peaceful order in the postwar world.

Thus neither Britain nor the United States nor the Soviet Union sought the breakdown of the wartime grand alliance. Nor did they anticipate the development of a cold war that would become the dominant feature of the international system for several decades. The immediate consequences of the cold war (rising tension, rearmament, and fear of another world war) seemed too much for anxious nations who were desperate to recover from the effects of World War II. Logically, then, any opportunity—for instance, in the form of summit conferences—for resolving the cold war would have been viewed as beneficial to the great powers.

Even so, the Geneva summit conference of July 1955 was a unique event in the history of cold war. It was the first and last meeting that brought together the heads of state of the United States, the Soviet Union, Britain, and France. After having been excluded from the Yalta and Potsdam wartime summit conferences, France was invited to Geneva, thus bringing together all four countries occupying Germany. After Geneva, there was a further attempt to convene a four-power summit in Paris in 1960, but the meeting collapsed almost as soon as it opened, ostensibly because of the Soviet shooting down of an American U-2 spy plane. Thereafter, numerous summit talks were held, but only between the United States and the Soviet Union, and dealing chiefly with the control of nuclear weapons.

The main motive for Western attendance at the Geneva summit was the future of Germany. The German question had become the main source of East-West tension after the end of World War II, and it had shaped the nature and scope of the cold war in Europe for the next ten years. The conclusion of the Austrian State Treaty between the four occupying powers in May 1955 also facilitated the convening of the Geneva Conference the following July. The presence of Britain and France at Geneva demonstrated that the two smaller countries were still able to exert some influence on the direction of the cold war.

The second significant aspect of the Geneva summit was its timing.

3. A British school of thought maintains this approach; see, for instance, John Kent and John W. Young, "British Policy Overseas: The 'Third Force' and the Origins of NATO—In Search of a New Perspective," in *Securing Peace in Europe, 1945–1962*, ed. Beatrice Heuser and Robert O'Neill (London, 1992), 41–61.

The conference took place during the "high" cold war—that is, at a time in the 1950s when the cold war had become institutionalized as a central feature of the international system. What were the purposes of the conference? Can it be regarded as a "wartime" conference, like the Allied summits that were a regular feature of World War II? By 1955, the Soviet Union was the sole representative of the Communist camp, facing the three Western capitalist countries (France, Britain, and the United States). Can the Geneva summit be seen as an attempt to resolve the differences between the two sides before the signing of peace accords, as in the case of the conference on Bosnia in Dayton, Ohio, in 1995? If so, how was it possible to hold such a meeting during the height of the cold war, and, given that the meeting did take place, why was the "spirit of Geneva" so short-lived? From the short-term perspective, one could argue that expectations for a détente were raised when Stalin died in March 1953. Why did it then take the four powers two years to agree to hold the conference?

The final feature of the Geneva Conference was that, for all the huge publicity it generated and all the talk of the "spirit of Geneva" as a symbol of the relaxation of international tension, the summit produced few tangible achievements in terms of resolving the crucial issues that separated the two sides. Massimo Magistrati, the director general of political affairs at the Italian foreign ministry, was surprised to see more than "1500 journalists from every country" gathering at Geneva for the summit. Dwight D. Eisenhower, the president of the United States, recalled that on his arrival at Geneva, he was "astonished at the size and enthusiasm of the crowds that gathered at the airfield and in the streets along [the] route to our villa."[4] Yet in the end there was little progress on the future of Germany or on the question of a stable system of European security. Trade and cultural exchanges were discussed and Eisenhower put forward his "Open Skies" proposal to enable the Soviet Union and the United States to inspect each other's military installations by means of aerial reconnaissance, but no firm agreements were reached. The continued lack of agreement on these issues was confirmed at a meeting of the foreign ministers of the four powers later in the year.[5]

4. Brunello Vigezzi, "Italy and the Problems of 'Power Politics' " in *Power in Europe?* ed. Ennio Di Nolfo (New York, 1992), II, 111; Dwight D. Eisenhower, *Mandate for Change: The White House Years, 1953–1956* (New York, 1963), 510.

5. For instance, see Stephen E. Ambrose, *Eisenhower: The President, 1953–1969* (London, 1984); John Lewis Gaddis, *Strategies of Containment: A Critical Appraisal of Postwar American National Security Policy* (New York, 1982); Richard Immerman, ed., *John Foster Dulles and the Diplomacy of the Cold War* (Princeton, 1990).

What went wrong? Were all or any of the players—Britain, France, the Soviet Union, or the United States—responsible for the failure? Or did the Soviet Union and the West simply distrust each other too much for serious negotiations to occur? Did the conference merely follow the classical pattern of arms negotiations between opposing parties who, although agreeing on the need for negotiations, often lack the confidence in each other necessary for the success of such negotiations?

The Geneva summit, therefore, had wide ramifications. Indeed, the conference in New Orleans on which this volume is based raised more questions than were answered.

The Geneva summit has been mentioned in passing by numerous cold-war historians. Although most of the World War II summits have been the subjects of excellent historical treatments, the cold-war summits have not yet been explored in detail.[6] There is a dated study by Keith Eubank and an overview by political scientists.[7] Two recent volumes based on two conferences in Germany analyzed post-Stalin Soviet foreign policy and Western responses to it. *Zwischen Kaltem Krieg und Entspannung* is perhaps one of the first serious attempts at a full historical assessment of the Geneva summit.[8]

The editors hope that this volume will provide a new approach, departing from the traditional assumption that the cold war was chiefly about America's reactions to what it perceived to be a threat from the Communist bloc. Written from various national perspectives, the essays address both the background of the conference and the substantive

6. See, for example, Keith Sainsbury, *The Turning Point: Roosevelt, Stalin, Churchill, and Chiang Kai-Shek, 1943: The Moscow, Cairo, and Teheran Conferences* (Oxford, U.K., 1985); Diane Shaver Clemens, *Yalta* (New York, 1970); Russell D. Buhite, *Decisions at Yalta: An Appraisal of Summit Diplomacy* (Wilmington, Del., 1986); Herbert Feis, *Between War and Peace: The Potsdam Conference* (Princeton, 1960); Robin Edmonds, *The Big Three: Churchill, Roosevelt, and Stalin in Peace and War* (Penguin, 1991); Lloyd C. Gardner, *Spheres of Influence: The Great Powers Partition Europe, from Munich to Yalta* (Chicago, 1993).
7. Keith Eubank, *The Summit Conferences, 1919–1960* (Norman, Okla., 1966), 144–59; Gordon R. Weihmiller with Dusko Doder, *U.S.-Soviet Summits: An Account of East-West Diplomacy at the Top, 1955–1985* (New York, 1986), 16–27; David H. Dunn, ed., *Diplomacy at the Highest Level: The Evolution of International Summitry* (Basingstoke, U.K., 1996).
8. Bruno Thoss and Hans-Erich Volkmann, eds., *Zwischen Kaltem Krieg und Entspannung: Sicherheits- und Deutschlandpolitik der Bundesrepublik im Mächtesystem der Jahre 1953–1956* (Boppard am Rhein, 1988); see also Rolf Steininger et al., eds., *Die doppelte Eindämmung: Europäische Sicherheit und deutsche Frage in den Fünfzigern* (Munich, 1993).

issues dealt with at it. Given limitations of space and time, the focuses are necessarily on the perspectives of those powers chiefly concerned with the Geneva initiative—the United States, Britain, France, Germany, and Russia. In recent years, archives in Central-Eastern Europe have increasingly become available to Western scholars, thereby correcting an obvious lacuna in cold-war research of previous years. Unfortunately, the present volume does not cover Central-Eastern European perspectives. Another international conference is needed to fill that gap.[9]

Background for the Geneva Conference

Winston Churchill, who returned to 10 Downing Street in the autumn of 1951, has been regarded as a major advocate of direct dialogue with Moscow. The newly elected Republican U.S. president was also initially enthusiastic about meeting the Russians. When Churchill met Eisenhower at Bernard Baruch's flat in New York on January 7, 1953, the prime minister was struck by Eisenhower's eagerness to meet Stalin. The president-elect asked Churchill whether, in his upcoming inaugural speech, he should announce that "he [Eisenhower] would go to, say Stockholm, to meet him, if Stalin were willing." Eisenhower also stated that he would have "no objections at all" if Churchill wished to meet with Stalin. (Churchill was opposed to bilateral American-Soviet talks from which Britain would be excluded; he wanted either an informal Anglo-Soviet meeting or a revival of the Big Three summit.) Churchill advised the president-elect to "spend some months learning all the facts

9. Melvyn P. Leffler, "Inside Enemy Archives: The Cold War Reopened," *Foreign Affairs*, LXXV (1996), 120–34; Valur Ingimundarson, "The Eisenhower Administration, the Adenauer Government and the Political Uses of the East German Uprising in 1953" *Diplomatic History*, XX (1996), 381–409; Norman Naimark, *The Russians in Germany: A History of the Soviet Zone of Occupation, 1945–1949* (Cambridge, Mass., 1995). See also a number of working papers published by the Woodrow Wilson International Center in Washington, D.C., under the editorship of James Hershberg: P. J. Simmons, "Archival Research on the Cold War Era: A Report from Budapest, Prague and Warsaw," CWIHP Working Paper no. 2 (1992); James Richter, "Reexamining Soviet Policy towards Germany during the Beria Interregnum," CWIHP Working Paper no. 3 (1992); Hope M. Harrison, "Ulbricht and the Concrete 'Rose': New Archival Evidence on the Dynamics of Soviet–East German Relations and the Berlin Crisis, 1958–1961," CWIHP Working Paper no. 5 (1993); Norman Naimark, " 'To Know Everything and to Report Everything Worth Knowing': Building the East German Police State, 1945–1949," CWIHP Working Paper no. 10 (1994). See also *CWIHP Bulletin*, V (1995).

about the present position before he embarked on such a momentous adventure."[10] By the end of February 1953, Eisenhower's readiness to talk to Stalin became public knowledge.[11]

The death of Stalin put an end to this. His one-man regime in Moscow was replaced by a collective leadership headed by Georgi Malenkov. It is nonetheless remarkable that Churchill and Eisenhower at least agreed on the need for a top-level conference in early 1953, for this was the first and last time that such an agreement existed between the two men. As Antonio Varsori and Richard Immerman point out in this volume, after Stalin's death Churchill, for both political and personal reasons, became even more enthusiastic for a direct dialogue with the new Kremlin leadership, but Eisenhower's initial enthusiasm for a summit meeting was not shared by the State Department, and thereafter the president became reluctant to support Churchill's aspirations.

As it turned out, the death of the Soviet premier and the subsequent efforts by the new Kremlin leaders to create a mood of détente were regarded by Western leaders with considerable suspicion. They did not believe that the Kremlin's new look implied any profound change in Soviet attitudes; in their opinion, it was designed to gain time for the consolidation of the new regime at home and for the normalization of Soviet relations with its satellites. Vladislav Zubok confirms that this Western assumption was broadly correct. Although there was a genuine eagerness on the part of the new Kremlin leaders to soften Stalin's rigid foreign policy and reestablish the image of the Soviet Union as a legitimate international player, those officials in the Politburo who clung to a Stalinist approach became more influential in the formulation of Soviet foreign policy after the fall of Lavrenti Beria.[12]

10. Roger Makins to FO, January 8, 1953, PREM 11/422, PRO; Colville memorandum, January 8, 1953, FO 371/106537, PRO; Jebb (New York) to FO (from Churchill to Eden), January 6, 1953, PREM 11/373, PRO. See also John Colville, *The Fringes of Power: Downing Street Diaries, 1941–April 1955* (London, 1987), 310; Klaus Larres, *Politik der Illusionen: Churchill, Eisenhower und die deutsche Frage, 1945–1955* (Göttingen, 1995), 67–72. For the details of Churchill's summit diplomacy, see John Young, *Winston Churchill's Last Campaign: Britain and the Cold War, 1951–5* (Oxford, U.K., 1996). See also *The Churchill-Eisenhower Correspondence, 1953–1955*, ed. Peter Boyle (Chapel Hill, 1990); Anthony Seldon, *Churchill's Indian Summer: The Conservative Government 1951–1955* (London, 1981); Martin Gilbert, *Never Despair* (London, 1988), Vol. VIII of Randolph S. Churchill and Martin Gilbert, *Winston S. Churchill*.

11. See Saki Dockrill, *Eisenhower's New-Look National Security Policy, 1953–1961* (New York, 1996), 25–9.

12. For insightful recent studies based on extensive Soviet archival evidence, see James G. Richter, *Khrushchev's Double Bind: International Pressures and Domestic Politics* (Baltimore, 1994); Amy Knight, *Beria: Stalin's First Lieutenant* (Princeton, 1993); and Vlad-

It was therefore sensible for the West to adopt caution toward Moscow in the aftermath of Stalin's death. On April 8, 1953, the British foreign office summarized the arguments for this attitude, which was shared by the foreign office's French and American counterparts: "But this change of tactic offers an opportunity to the Western powers, who should meet Soviet conciliatory moves half way with a view to reaching agreement on specific outstanding questions. We must avoid being lulled into a sense of false security and must continue with the essential measures still required to complete the defensive strength of the non-Soviet world."[13] The "specific outstanding questions" included early settlements in Korea and Austria, but not such controversial issues as the future of Germany or of NATO.

For the West, the main task was to complete the integration of West Germany into the Western defense system. The treaty for setting up a supranational European army—the European Defence Community (EDC)—was signed in May 1952 by six European states (France, West Germany, Italy, Belgium, Luxembourg, and the Netherlands). Although the EDC scheme was regarded as the most politically feasible means of rearming the West Germans inside the Western bloc, by 1953 it appeared that it would take some time before the parliaments of the six nations could be persuaded to ratify the treaty. Konrad Adenauer, the West German chancellor, strongly believed that West Germany's integration into the West should have priority over the reunification of Germany on Western terms. The EDC offered an opportunity for such integration in the key area of defense. The new Republican administration under Eisenhower enthusiastically supported the early completion of the EDC project.

Even after Stalin's death, NATO continued to support the EDC, and the NATO Council's ministerial meeting in December 1954 agreed to take account of nuclear weapons in future NATO strategic planning. The West was determined to strengthen its bargaining position vis-à-vis the Soviet Union even though this policy meant widening the division of Europe. Indeed, there appeared to be every disadvantage in negotiating with the Soviet Union over the future of Germany before the West completed the integration of West Germany into its defense network.

---

islav Zubok and Constantine Pleshakov, *Inside the Kremlin's Cold War: From Stalin to Khrushchev* (Cambridge, Mass., 1996). See also Günter Bischof, "Eisenhower, the Summit, and the Austrian Treaty, 1953–1955," in *Eisenhower: A Centenary Assessment*, ed. Günter Bischof and Stephen E. Ambrose (Baton Rouge, 1995), and Larres, *Politik der Illusionen*.

13. Eden to British Embassy (Washington), April 8, 1953, FO 371/106524, PRO.

This apparent Western unity was soon challenged, however, by the collapse of the EDC project and subsequent new Soviet approaches to the West beginning in the autumn of 1954. After long deliberation, France decided not to ratify the EDC treaty, and the alternative put forward by the British foreign secretary, Anthony Eden, culminated in the signature of the Paris agreements of October 1954, which not only restored full West German sovereignty (except over German reunification) but also allowed West Germany to become a full member of NATO and of an enlarged Brussels Treaty Organization.[14]

The Soviet Union's reaction to the Paris agreements was by no means unreasonable. Western Europe had already been strengthened by the creation of NATO with the United States as a full member, bringing America's bases in Europe and its nuclear weapons into the equation. By integrating West German military effectiveness into NATO, the West would further consolidate its sphere of influence in Europe. As West German remilitarization became more certain, Moscow grew more receptive to the idea of delaying such rearmament by reducing tension in Europe. Thus, in the autumn of 1954, the Kremlin renewed its efforts to secure Western agreement to four-power talks. On several occasions the Soviet leaders revealed their motives by insisting on the incompatibility of the Paris agreements with the restoration of Germany as a united country.[15]

France was more receptive than its allies to the Soviet pressure for a four-power meeting. Paris remained uncomfortable with the idea of rearming the West Germans and preferred a four-power conference before the ratification of the Paris agreements. The French faced a difficult situation, since efforts to delay, or even reject, the Paris agreements would further isolate France from the Western alliance. On the other hand, in order to persuade the National Assembly to ratify the agreements, France needed a definitive assurance from its allies that a four-power conference would take place soon. In this volume, Colette Barbier discusses the French dilemma.[16]

14. Saki Dockrill, *Britain's Policy for West German Rearmament, 1950–1955* (Cambridge, U.K., 1991); Thomas Alan Schwartz, *America's Germany: John J. McCloy and the Federal Republic of Germany* (Cambridge, Mass., 1991).

15. See John Van Oudenaren, *Détente in Europe: The Soviet Union and the West since 1953* (Durham, N.C., 1991).

16. Renata Fritsch-Bournazel, "Frankreichs Ost- und Deutschlandpolitik im Zeichen der Genfer Gipfelkonferenz von 1995," in *Zwischen Kaltem Krieg und Entspannung,* ed. Thoss and Volkmann, 71–91.

By January 1955, Churchill was persuaded by the British foreign office to postpone his cherished meeting with the Kremlin leaders until West Germany had been formally admitted to NATO. As a result, Britain and the United States were able to agree that a four-power conference should follow, rather than precede, the ratification of the Paris agreements. For Adenauer, there could be no question of reversing the order of business—the integration of West Germany into the West must come *before* negotiations with the Soviet Union over the reunification of Germany. However, despite Adenauer's publicly stated belief in ultimate reunification, it was clear to other German decision makers that once West Germany's integration with the West was finalized, the division of Europe would harden, providing less scope for West Germany to achieve the reunification on its own terms. Eckart Conze's chapter examines Germany's difficulties in this regard.

France's ratification of the Paris agreements was almost complete by the end of March. At the same time, the new French prime minister, Edgar Faure, who had replaced Pierre Mendès-France in February 1955, demanded a four-power conference immediately after France ratified the agreements. Britain was also keen to see East-West tensions reduced, and now that France was on the point of finalizing the Paris agreements, London's main objection to a four-power conference was removed. All of this, however, coincided with growing discord between Britain and the United States over their approaches to the coming four-power talks. As Varsori and Saki Dockrill write in this volume, Anthony Eden, who took over from Churchill as prime minister in early April 1955, vigorously pushed for a four-power summit at which he was determined to discuss the reunification of Germany. Eden, like Churchill, sought to exploit Russian fears of a rearmed and reunited Germany by presenting a proposal that the Soviet Union would seemingly find attractive, yet which would at the same time enable a reunified Germany to remain in NATO.

Like Britain, the United States became less opposed to four-power talks once the Paris agreements had been ratified by all the powers concerned. By that time, McCarthyism was on the wane and the mood in Congress was more receptive to the Soviet Union.[17] Yet even though

17. For a recent study, see Günter Bischof, "The Politics of Anti-Communism in the Executive Branch during the Early Cold War: Truman, Eisenhower, and McCarthy(ism)," in *Anti-Communism and McCarthyism in the United States (1946–1954)*, ed. A. Kaenel (Paris, 1995), 55–77.

President Eisenhower responded favorably to the growing desire expressed by Britain and France for four-power talks, he remained hesitant about a summit conference, as opposed to four-power foreign ministers' talks. But as Immerman shows in his essay, British and French enthusiasm soon forced the Eisenhower administration to reconsider and agree to a summit.

According to Zubok, Nikita Khrushchev, first secretary of the Central Committee of the Soviet Communist Party, was conscious of the need to respond to Eisenhower's April 1953 "Chance for Peace" speech, in which the president demanded that Moscow demonstrate a willingness to make concrete concessions rather than mere rhetorical flourishes. The Kremlin could thus contend that its new peace offensive following Stalin's death had contributed to the end of the Korean War and to the Indochina settlement. Furthermore, a series of Soviet diplomatic initiatives during the spring of 1955 included the signature of the Austrian State Treaty, high-level talks with Yugoslavia, the formation of the Warsaw Pact, and Moscow's invitation to the Federal Republic for talks on the normalization of relations between the two countries. The Soviet Union also presented a comprehensive disarmament proposal to the UN disarmament subcommittee on May 10. Of all these things, the most dramatic example of the Kremlin's new approach was the conclusion, in May, of the Austrian State Treaty.[18]

Molotov wished to retain the linkage between the solutions of the Austrian and German questions. Khrushchev, however, regarded Austria as (in Zubok's words) an "easy diplomatic target" whose solution had hitherto been prevented by Russia's inability to agree to a few minor points. Backed by a majority in the Politburo, Khrushchev now overruled Molotov's more conservative approach and secured the successful settlement of the Austrian question. Zubok states that this was the first time in the cold war when the Soviet Union agreed to a policy not based on its "strategic or security significance."

The implications of the conclusion of the Austrian State Treaty were complex. Günter Bischof argues in this volume that the Soviet Union offered Austrian neutrality as a means of preventing Western Austria from being rearmed and integrated with the West. In any case, the treaty

18. Nikita Khrushchev, *Khrushchev Remembers: The Glasnost Tapes*, ed. Jerrold L. Schecter and Vyacheslav V. Luchkov (Boston, 1990), 72–80. For Eisenhower's speech, see *Documents on International Affairs, 1953* (London, 1956), 51–7.

appeared to demonstrate that the West could do business with the new leadership in the Kremlin. Of course, the extension of this cooperation to other issues depended on their nature and importance. If Khrushchev, eager to show the Kremlin's newfound flexibility, resolved the Austrian question at the cost of a few minor concessions, that did not mean that the Soviet Union would also give way on Germany, which was of far greater importance to its security. Alternatively, the separation of the Austrian and German questions might mean that the Soviet Union would abandon negotiations with the West over Germany, especially over reunification.[19]

Anthony Eden, in presenting his package proposal on German reunification and European security, relied on the belief that the Kremlin's conversion to greater flexibility was genuine. However, he was well aware that "the Russians probably would not want to discuss the subject," since it was in the "Russian interest to delay a settlement on Germany." Indeed, as this volume demonstrates, none of the four powers, including the Soviet Union, believed that the German question could be resolved at Geneva.

Despite the swift conclusion of the Austrian State Treaty in May, and despite the fact that Germany had now become the main battleground of the cold war in Europe, the objectives of the powers differed substantially prior to the opening of the Geneva summit. With the Paris agreements, West Germany became a sovereign nation and a member of NATO. The West German public expected the next goal to be reunification, but Bonn was by no means enthusiastic about the forthcoming summit. As Conze argues, the Federal Republic was aware of the importance of supporting French and British enthusiasm for détente but accepted that détente could be achieved without resolution of the German question—i.e., that the division of Germany would continue. This meant that the German question could be isolated from the other cold-war problems, thereby hardening the division of Germany.

19. Historians remain divided over the Kremlin's intentions. For instance, Thoss, "Modellfall Österreich? Der österreichische Staatvertrag und die deutsche Frage 1954/55," in *Zwischen Kaltem Krieg und Entspannung*, ed. Thoss and Volkmann, argues that the Kremlin had no intention of using the Austrian solution as a model for Germany, whereas Rolf Steininger, "1955: The Austrian State Treaty and the German Question," *Diplomacy and Statecraft*, III (1992), 494–522, and Michael Gehler, "State Treaty and Neutrality: The Austrian Solution in 1955 As a 'Model' for Germany," in Günter Bischof, Anton Pelinka, and Rolf Steininger, eds., *Austria in the Nineteen Fifties* (New Brunswick, N.J., 1995), 39–78, assert that this was indeed the Soviets' intention.

As Barbier argues in this volume, France was conscious of its isolation from the North Atlantic Alliance, its defeat in Indochina, its growing difficulties in North Africa, and its vulnerability to the newly independent West Germany. It was thus less concerned than its allies about resolving the German question. In an effort to restore its image as a great power, France in December 1954 began serious efforts to develop nuclear weapons, which would strengthen it vis-à-vis West Germany. At the same time, Paris saw participation in the Geneva summit as an opportunity to reassert France's equality with the United States, Britain, and the USSR. France wanted to use the summit "to achieve a psychological and propaganda advantage" in world opinion by assuming the role of a major peacemaker.

To a considerable extent, Britain shared France's desire for a thaw in East-West relations, mainly because both countries felt more vulnerable to the Soviet threat than did the USA. Like France, Britain wanted to seize the initiative at Geneva before the Russians could turn the summit into a propaganda organ. To Britain and France, the American insistence that concrete proposals not be formally considered at Geneva was a serious limitation on their freedom of action. On the other hand, if Eden was to succeed in his bid for German reunification, he needed the support of the United States. Dockrill explains this British dilemma in her essay.

The United States, after agreeing to participate in the Geneva summit, was divided as to what approaches the West should take in the talks. Washington regarded the German question as nonnegotiable: no proposal, regardless of how attractive it might be to Moscow, was acceptable if it undermined the existing arrangements for West Germany. As Immerman and Ronald Pruessen explain, John Foster Dulles, the American secretary of state, suspected that the Soviet Union saw the summit as a chance to enhance its prestige and demonstrate equality with the West. With the conference only days away, Dulles informed congressional leaders about what he thought would be the Soviet tactics. He claimed that the Russians not only wanted to sabotage NATO's collective efforts by creating "an atmosphere of relaxation," but also hoped to secure a "European Security Plan" that was "designed to get the United States out of Europe."[20]

20. See "Bipartisan Legislative Meeting," July 12, 1955, Box 2, Legislative Meetings Series, Ann Whitman File, DDEL.

At a dinner with C. D. Jackson on July 11, thirty-six hours before Dulles left for Geneva, the secretary of state was pessimistic, telling Jackson that "I am terribly worried about this Geneva conference." Dulles was afraid that the French, eager to achieve détente with the Soviet Union, and the British, hoping for German reunification, might be "tricked" by the Russians into agreements contrary to Western interests. Dulles was also concerned that the president, who was "so inclined to be humanly generous," might accept "a promise or a proposition at face value and upset the apple cart." Any Soviet proposal was likely to aim at enhancing Soviet prestige while reducing that of the West. Dulles therefore wanted to avoid discussion of concrete issues at Geneva and concentrate on "principles"—for example, human rights issues in Eastern Europe and condemnation of the activities of the international Communist movement.[21]

The question of arms control most divided the administration, but Eisenhower was perhaps keener than Dulles and the State Department to discover whether the Soviets would agree to slow the escalating nuclear race between the two superpowers. Although the accumulation of nuclear weapons strengthened each power's nuclear deterrence, it also made the world a more dangerous place. The president was well aware of "a universal urge" that "the political leaders of our great countries find a path to peace."[22] Immerman examines the ways in which the United States's approach to Geneva differed from those of its allies, although he stresses that the Eisenhower administration was prepared to accede to the aims of the allies as far as possible. Thus, despite the different objectives of Britain, France, West Germany, and the U.S., these four powers agreed that the solidarity of the Western alliance must be preserved in the face of Soviet attempts to undermine their unity at Geneva. They also agreed that the West, by virtue of its nuclear supremacy and the recent inclusion of West Germany in NATO, was now in a stronger position to deal with Moscow.

As Zubok shows, however, the Kremlin's initiatives, which were designed to be conducive to lessening East-West tensions, helped Khru-

21. Dockrill, *Eisenhower's New-Look National Security Policy*, 139. See also Richard D. Challener, "The Moralist As Pragmatist: John Foster Dulles As Cold War Strategist," in *The Diplomats, 1939–1979*, ed. Gordon A. Craig and Francis L. Loewenheim (Princeton, 1995), 159.

22. Eisenhower's opening speech at Geneva, July 18, 1955, in *Documents on International Affairs, 1955* (London, 1958), 6.

shchev overcome the Soviet Union's inferiority complex. On the eve of the Geneva summit, Khrushchev was reasonably confident that the Russians could negotiate with the West from a position of equality. Like France and Britain, the Soviet Union saw the talks as an opportunity to enhance its international standing. Moreover, just as Eisenhower was anxious to reach agreement on confidence-building measures that would reduce the danger of an accidental nuclear war, Khrushchev regarded nuclear weapons chiefly as a means of deterrence and wanted to find out how serious the Americans were in their talk of nuclear "massive retaliation."

It is clear, therefore, that neither the Soviet Union nor the Western powers went to Geneva with the intention of resolving outstanding issues at the cost of undermining their own interests. They nonetheless hoped that the summit would provide an opportunity to reduce East-West tensions. As Varsori and Barbier discuss, Britain and France were also determined to reassert their world-power status, while the United States and the Soviet Union wanted to show the world that they were global peacemakers and not warmongers. Under these circumstances, there was little incentive to alter the status quo in any major way, especially if doing so would adversely affect East-West equilibrium or the solidarity of the North Atlantic Alliance.

The Summit and After

The Geneva summit soon demonstrated that the Soviet Union's new approach did not extend to the reunification of Germany. This came as no surprise to the West German leaders, who were under no illusion that the Soviet Union could be persuaded to accept a reunified Germany within NATO, as was provided by the Eden plan. In the Soviet view, the Paris agreements and West Germany's subsequent admission to NATO provided sufficient evidence that the West was not interested in reunifying Germany; therefore, Russia could not be blamed for dividing it. The fact that the Kremlin was prepared to deal with two Germanies was clear from its swift creation of the Warsaw Pact and its invitation of Konrad Adenauer to bilateral talks on normalizing Soviet-West German relations.

As Dockrill explains, the core of the Eden plan was first to obtain Soviet agreement to the reunification of Germany, then to work out a common security arrangement among the powers concerned, and finally to secure a reunified Germany that would remain in NATO. The original plan was modeled on the similar plan produced in West Germany (the Heusinger plan), but Britain modified it to make it more attractive to the Soviets. The subsequent responses to the plan from Britain's allies and the Soviet Union demonstrated that the West had limited room for maneuver on the reunification issue.[23]

Moreover, the West could not offer the USSR a neutral united Germany. As Conze emphasizes, Adenauer was adamant on this subject. Neutralization had never been seriously considered by the three Western powers as a practical possibility, and France's opposition was clear beyond doubt to Britain and the United States. A unified and neutral Germany might create a new security problem in Europe—which explains why Stalin's famous note of March 10, 1952, calling for the creation of a just such a nation, had been so poorly received by the West.[24]

The crucial requirement of any Western reunification plan was that it had to be based on the status quo reached by 1955—that is, West Germany's integration into the West, the existence of NATO, and America's defense commitment to Western Europe. Although the Eden proposal (including a security pact, the creation of a demilitarized strip, and a ceiling on military forces in countries bordering Germany) was rewritten many times in order not to undermine this status quo, the changes made the proposal even less attractive to the Soviets than it might originally have been. In any case, the United States regarded it as a hopeless proposition. Nor was there any effective cooperation between the Germans and British before the Geneva summit, so that considerable confusion existed in Bonn and elsewhere regarding the Eden package proposal presented at Geneva (a plan to *reunify* Germany in the wider context of European security) and the British arms-control plan, containing joint inspection zones, which was also put forward at Geneva (on July 21, in response to the Soviet disarmament plan of May 1955). The British prime minister was not in fact greatly interested in the arms-control topic, and Britain's general position at Geneva was that arms-control/disarmament issues need not be discussed in any de-

23. Hermann-Josef Rupieper, "Deutsche Frage und europäische Sicherheit: Politisch-strategische Überlegungen, 1953–1955," in *Zwischen Kaltem Krieg und Entspannung*, ed. Thoss and Volkmann, 179–80. Saki Dockrill and Eckart Conze discuss the Heusinger plan in their essays later in the present volume.

24. For Adenauer's pre-Geneva reactions to a possible neutral Germany, see Hans-Peter Schwarz, *Adenauer: Der Staatsmann, 1952–1967* (Stuttgart, 1991), 183–6.

tail there but should continue to be dealt with by the UN subcommittee on disarmament.

Still, the Eden plan achieved some success on a tactical level. During the conference the Soviet Union made it clear that it had no interest in a plan patently designed to create a reunified Germany that would remain in the West. As Zubok points out, the Eden plan placed the Russians in an invidious position in that Moscow had to explain why it was interested in resolving the German question, the outstanding issue that divided East and West. As a result, the Geneva discussion became bogged down in disputes about the agenda: the Soviets wanted to discuss first an all-European peace settlement, while the three Western powers remained faithful to the Eden proposal—that is, to discussing German reunification before dealing with overall European security. The implications were clear: as long as the Russians refused to cooperate with the West on the creation of a unified Germany, or as long as the West persisted in the idea of reunifying Germany within NATO, there could be no reunification acceptable to both blocs.

During the summit, although the bulk of the discussion was devoted to Germany and European security, the East-West trade question was equally controversial. Just as the European allies were more eager than the United States to discuss the German question at Geneva, they also tended to be more enthusiastic about increasing their trade with the Soviet bloc, since this would benefit their economies. They believed, moreover, that increasing contacts with the Eastern bloc through trade and other means would help to undermine Communist control over Eastern Europe, thereby leading to the resolution of the cold war.

The Americans, especially Congress and hardliners in the Eisenhower administration, were sensitive on this issue. They did not want to facilitate, even indirectly, the growth of the Communist bloc's economies—and hence its military power—by increasing East-West trade. The Soviet Union had begun to exploit its economic policy to the advantage of the Communist bloc, and Khrushchev was particularly keen to use economic weapons (trade and loans) to attract newly emerging third-world countries into the Soviet orbit. Thus the East-West trade question was at the heart of the nonmilitary competition in the cold war. However, at Geneva the West was surprised at how little interest the Soviets evinced in increasing East-West trade. Mark Spaulding discusses this subject extensively. He contends that the reason for Soviet unwillingness to raise the trade issue at Geneva was internal power struggles in the Kremlin. It was not until 1957, after Khrushchev had removed his rivals from the Politburo, that the Soviet Union clarified its foreign economic and trade policies and resumed its interest in increasing trade with the West.

The United States also wanted to discuss the position of the Soviet Union's Eastern European satellites and the activities of international Communism as the main sources of international tension. In his opening speech at Geneva, the president stated that the "American people feel strongly" about "certain peoples of Eastern Europe" who were deprived of "the right of peoples to choose the form of government" they desire. During dinner with the Soviet delegation on July 18, Eisenhower again raised the question of the satellite states. He said that there were "literally millions of Americans who had their roots and origins in Central Europe" and that the "status of the satellites was a matter of very genuine concern to him." Inevitably, the Russians refused to discuss the subject at Geneva, and despite the prevailing mood of détente, the Eisenhower administration could not persuade the Soviet Union to reconsider its policy toward Eastern Europe.[25]

In appraising the summit at a National Security Council meeting on July 28, 1955, Allen Dulles, the director of the CIA, commented on "the effect of the Geneva conference in the European satellites." He stated that " 'run-away' hope before the conference had been followed by a letdown" in the satellites. Here was a dilemma for the United States: If America appeared content with the outcome of the Geneva meetings, the peoples of the satellite countries would suspect that the West might be "preparing to 'sell them down the river' " as part of a general relaxation of tensions. On the other hand, the U.S. could not afford to be seen, "in the eyes of the world," as increasing tension by publicly attacking the Soviet Union's policy toward the satellites. The secretary of state recognized this dilemma and wrote to Eisenhower on August 11, 1955: "The important thing was to make it perfectly clear that we did not identify increased hope of peace with increased solidification of the status quo . . . and that we now expected there to be changes in the European situation . . . as evidenced by . . . greater freedom for the satellites."[26]

25. Dockrill, *Eisenhower's New-Look National Security Policy*, 138, 153. See also "Bipartisan Legislative Meeting," July 28, 1955, NSC Series, Ann Whitman File, DDEL.
26. NSC 256 meeting, July 28, 1955, NSC Series, Ann Whitman File, DDEL; Dulles's special assistant (John Hanes) minute (for Robert Murphy), August 12, 1955, in *FRUS, 1955–1957*, VII, 71.

Another disappointment at Geneva was in the area of arms control and disarmament. Thus far, meaningful progress in East-West arms-control negotiations had been impaired by the question of inspection. Moreover, neither side was willing to compromise at the cost of undermining its military strength. Further, given the imbalance between U.S. military power and that of Western Europe, as well as the different interpretations by America and its European allies of the nature of the nuclear threat, it was difficult to formulate a common arms-control policy within the North Atlantic Alliance. As Barbier argues, France put forward at Geneva a comprehensive and detailed disarmament proposal, but neither Britain nor the United States supported it. At the same time, Britain's inspection plan was viewed with considerable suspicion in the West, especially in West Germany, since acceptance would probably solidify the division of Germany.

Both the fear of a nuclear war with Russia and the dangers of nuclear fallout (as demonstrated by the Bikini incident of 1954) were very much on the mind of the American president. Even if the United States could not put forward an effective disarmament proposal acceptable to its internal agencies and its allies, Eisenhower wanted Geneva to be "a solid beginning towards world disarmament."[27] John Prados explains the difficulties in the formulation of Eisenhower's "Open Skies" policy and Khrushchev's reaction to it at Geneva. As Prados argues, Eisenhower was certain that the Soviet Union would reject the proposal, since accepting it would provide the U.S. with a legitimate means of uncovering Soviet nuclear secrets by overflights. Zubok confirms that the Soviet nuclear deterrent "relied predominantly on the preservation of uncertainty and ignorance in the United States about the true size of the Soviet strategic arsenal." Thus there was no way the Kremlin could have accepted such a proposal.

The Germans were not interested in any détente based on the continued division of their country. Adenauer was certain that "Europe would never find stability" unless Germany was reunited. During the Geneva summit Anthony Eden echoed this view: "Until the security of Germany is restored there can be neither confidence nor security in this continent." Indeed, this conviction gave rise to the Eden package pro-

27. Eisenhower to Churchill, July 15, 1955, *FRUS, 1955–1957*, V, 336; Goodpaster minute, July 12, 1955, ibid., 306; Robert Griffith, ed., *Ike's Letters to a Friend, 1941–1958* (Lawrence, Kans., 1984), 146.

posal. Although the two men never achieved any close meeting of minds, they were both correct in this assertion. The Geneva détente on the basis of the division of Germany was short-lived, and the cold war continued.[28]

However, the Soviet Union's ambitions were frustrated. Adenauer visited Moscow in September, but as a result of his determination to keep Germany with the West, the Soviet–West German normalization talks did not lead to a second Rapallo. The Soviet Union resisted the Eden package proposal but failed to wean West Germany from the North Atlantic Alliance.

Pruessen, whose chapter focuses on John Foster Dulles, notes that prior to the foreign ministers' conference at Geneva in October and November of 1955, Dulles took renewed interest in the possibility of some movement toward German reunification but recognized that the process would be a long one. As it turned out, as John Young points out in his summarizing chapter, the foreign ministers' conference only confirmed that East and West were unable to compromise in any way on the outstanding issues—German reunification and European security, disarmament, and the development of East-West contacts. By the end of 1955, the "Geneva spirit" was largely a matter of history.

Nevertheless, the Geneva Conference took place during the high cold war, and if one looks at it as a wartime conference, the psychological effects of such a gathering were of immense significance to the history of international relations. John Foster Dulles and the British foreign office were skeptical about summit conferences, which they believed "generally create more problems than they solve, largely because they are bad places for the conduct of serious business and always arouse unreasonable expectations." The fact remains that, thanks to the Geneva summit, the world community was relieved that nuclear confrontation between the United States and the Soviet Union had become at least temporarily unlikely. Western Europe, too, appreciated the lessening of the military pressures of the cold war, and in the aftermath of the meeting, none of the European NATO countries was prepared to continue with rearmament at the cost of undermining its own economic and in-

28. For Eden's opening speech at Geneva, July 18, 1955, see *Documents Relating to the Meeting of Heads of Government of France, the United Kingdom, the Soviet Union, and the United States of America*, in Command Papers, no. 9543 (London, 1955), 31. See the "Introduction" in *Diplomats, 1939–1979*, ed. Craig and Loewenheim, 6.

dustrial strength.[29] The Geneva summit at least provided the West with a short-lived respite from the cold war.

Finally, this volume shows how far apart the Western powers (Britain, France, West Germany, and the United States) were in their approaches to the Geneva summit. However, the record of the discussions also shows how united these powers were in dealing with the Soviet Union at that summit. Neither the Geneva Conference nor Adenauer's visit to Moscow split the North Atlantic Alliance. All of this demonstrates the uniqueness of the 1955 summit, signifying the complexity as well as the dynamism of international relations during the cold war.

29. See Saki Dockrill, "Misperceptions and Irreconcilables: Britain, the United States, and Their Troop Deployment in West Germany, 1945–61" in Controversy and Compromise: Alliance Politics between Great Britain, the Federal Republic of Germany, and the United States of America, 1945–1967, ed. Saki Dockrill (Bodenheim, Germany, 1998).

Background

The Early Cold War

ERNEST R. MAY

The Geneva Conference of 1955 marked the midpoint of the high cold war. At the time, according to public opinion polls, most people in North America and Europe thought catastrophic nuclear war almost inevitable. The conference produced a temporary easing of tension, but afterwards, tension began to rise again. During a series of crises beginning in 1958 and culminating in the Caribbean (or Cuban missile) crisis of 1962, it reached almost unbearable levels. As essays in this volume attest, some historians believe that if the opportunity of 1955 had been grasped more eagerly, those later crises might have been averted. Whether or not this is so, it may nevertheless be true that the momentary relaxation in 1955 and on a few later occasions postponed those crises, which might in turn help to explain why they are studied now as examples of crisis management, not of actual nuclear war.

The cold war as a whole ran for just under fifty years—from the closing phase of World War II until the dissolution of the Soviet Union. Some see it starting much earlier, perhaps with the Russian Revolution of 1917, which marked the commencement of Communist-capitalist ideological competition that only intensified after World War II. Some go back even farther, recalling Alexis de Tocqueville's famous observation of 1832 that Russia and America were destined to be the dominant powers of a future era. Regardless of various interpretations, a cold war—in the sense of antagonism threatening to turn into armed combat—definitely set in no later than the final year of World War II, when Soviet armies streamed westward and American, British, and French armies streamed eastward toward a meeting in conquered and devastated Germany.[1]

1. The most informed and up-to-date survey is John Lewis Gaddis, *We Now Know: Re-thinking Cold War History* (New York, 1997). See also Randall B. Woods and Howard Jones, *Dawning of the Cold War: The United States' Quest for World Order* (Chicago, 1991) and

The first battleground of this long, nonshooting war was in Poland. In anticipation of the arrival of Russian troops, Polish underground forces came into the open and attacked the Nazi occupiers of Warsaw. The Red Army, however, stopped in its tracks. The Polish underground was slaughtered. The Americans and British begged Russia's permission to airlift supplies to Warsaw. Soviet generalissimo Joseph Stalin refused. The Polish underground answered to a non-Communist Polish government in exile in London. The result of their being decimated by the Germans was that, when the Red Army finally did march into Warsaw, the Polish Communists who arrived in the Russian train faced little opposition.

From that time on, the Western powers and the Soviet Union quarreled about the degree to which Western-style self-determination should operate in Europe and elsewhere. Other issues arose regarding, among other things, voting powers in the new United Nations organization, the disposition of former Italian colonies, and Soviet claims for reparations based on the undeniable fact that Russian losses in the war had been far greater than those of the Western allies.

The first postwar year, 1946, saw continuous wrangling in meetings of foreign ministers and sessions of the UN. Early in the year Stalin made a speech reasserting the doctrine that Communism and capitalism could not permanently coexist. William O. Douglas, a liberal New Deal jurist, read the speech as threatening World War III. He was not alone. Not long afterward, Winston Churchill, no longer British prime minister, made in Fulton, Missouri, the famous speech asserting: "From Stettin in the Baltic to Trieste in the Adriatic, an iron curtain has descended across the continent." Commenting on these speeches and surrounding events, the columnist Walter Lippmann popularized the term *cold war.* The speeches were not in fact very warlike. Their shock value

---

Melvin Leffler's voluminous *A Preponderance of Power: National Security, the Truman Administration, and the Cold War* (Stanford, Calif., 1992). For the Soviet side, see, in addition to Gaddis: Adam B. Ulam, *The Rivals: America and Russia since World War II* (New York:, 1971); Vojtech Mastny, *Russia's Road to the Cold War: Diplomacy, Warfare, and the Politics of Communism, 1941–1945* (New York, 1979) and *The Cold War and Soviet Insecurity: The Stalin Years* (New York, 1996); William Taubman, *Stalin's American Policy: From Entente to Détente to Cold War* (New York, 1982); and Vladislav Zubok and Constantine Pleshakov, *Inside the Kremlin's Cold War: From Stalin to Khrushchev* (Cambridge, Mass., 1996). For other countries, see David Reynolds, ed., *Origins of the Cold War in Europe: International Perspectives* (New Haven, 1994) and Thomas A. Schwartz, *America's Germany: John J. McCloy and the Federal Republic of West Germany* (Cambridge, Mass., 1991).

arose from their contrast with the "all for one" oratory of the war. Behind closed doors, however, officials in London, Washington, and Moscow were looking at secret documents that speculated about the possibility of West and East being on the road to eventual war.

As late as the summer of 1947, divisions between West and East were still well short of what we now characterize as "cold war." Though continuing to voice criticism, the Western powers accepted as a *fait accompli* Soviet domination of countries behind the "iron curtain." This acceptance was registered in formal peace treaties signed in the spring of 1947. President Truman, to be sure, had already made his ringing "Truman Doctrine" address and secured from Congress appropriations to aid the Greek and Turkish governments in resisting Soviet pressure. But the Marshall Plan, put forward in June 1947, looked toward achieving economic and political stabilization throughout Europe, including portions controlled by the Soviets. And we know, from recently released Russian records, that Stalin's advisers seriously considered participating in the Marshall Plan but then decided to attack and try to frustrate it, hoping thereby to tighten Moscow's control over both Eastern Europe and Communist parties in the West.[2]

In 1948 the West-East relationship became one of political antagonism, plainly deserving a label like "cold war." Communists in Western Europe organized strikes and riots that severely tested the mechanisms of government so recently set up in liberated and occupied nations. In Czechoslovakia, which had theretofore provided an example of the feasibility of Communist/non-Communist collaboration, Communists seized power and reorganized the nation along Soviet lines. In Italy, non-Communist parties, with both open and clandestine support from the United States and Britain, eked out a victory over a Communist Party equally, if not more actively, supported by the Soviet Union. A fissure meanwhile developed within the Soviet bloc, as Yugoslavia declared independence from Moscow, even while remaining Marxist-Leninist in official ideology and Stalinist in political structure. The summer of 1948 then saw West and East in serious conflict over Berlin, with the Soviets shutting off road and rail access to the city and Westerners using a round-the-clock airlift to supply and maintain their zones of occupation.

2. Scott D. Parrish and Mikhail M. Narinsky, "New Evidence on the Soviet Rejection of the Marshall Plan, 1947: Two Reports," CWIHP Working Paper no. 9 (March 1994).

Nor was this cold war confined to Europe. When Secretary of State Marshall visited Bogotá in April 1948, he was confronted by a riot managed, if not instigated, by Communists. Just before that, he had spoken to the Senate Foreign Relations Committee in executive session and had confided his judgment that the Communists in China could not be prevented from defeating Chiang Kai-shek's Nationalists and taking control of all or most of the country. This would in fact occur during subsequent months. So would a de facto partition of Korea, creating a Soviet-backed Communist state north of thirty-eight degrees north latitude and an American-backed non-Communist state south of that line.

The cold war of 1948 to 1950 remained, however, a political contest. General Lucius Clay, who commanded American forces in occupied Germany, suggested testing the Soviet blockade of Berlin by sending in an armored train. Undersecretary of State Robert Lovett cited this recommendation as an example of a military man's trying to come up with a military solution when he knew perfectly well that there was none. General Clay, he observed, was an engineer officer well acquainted with the practicalities of rail transport. Lovett, who in private life had been chief executive officer of the Union Pacific Railroad, claimed that Clay recognized the limitations of an armored train as well as he. Clay understood that it did not take an army to stop such a train—just four strong men: two would lift up track in front of the train; when it stopped, two others would lift up track behind it; and the train would be marooned. Though Soviet fighter planes occasionally buzzed Western transports supplying Berlin, it appears that Stalin and his advisers were equally loath to let the confrontation become one between military forces.

The Western powers did put the Soviets on notice that, in event of such a confrontation, they would unite in armed resistance. The Western European states signed an all-for-one alliance at Brussels in 1948. The United States joined them in 1949 by signing the North Atlantic Treaty—a step intended to create conviction in Moscow that, if another European war commenced, the United States would be a belligerent from the outset, not a latecomer as in 1917 and 1941. But the American commitment was a paper commitment. The United States maintained little ready military force in Europe. The American occupation armies in Germany and Austria and the garrison in Berlin were not combat forces. After the Soviets lifted the blockade of Berlin, the United States pulled back most of the military aircraft it had positioned in Europe. Total American and British military strength dropped below immediate prewar levels, and President Truman announced publicly early in 1950 that he planned still further reductions in spending for military forces.

In the early 1950s, however, the cold war ceased to be primarily political and ideological, becoming instead a confrontation between armed camps poised for instant combat. The Soviet Union had begun urgent preparation for a future war even before World War II was over. Aware of his nation's overall weakness in comparison with the United States, assuming that Britain and the United States were implacably hostile to Communism, and expecting the decade or so after World War II to be simply another interwar era, Stalin gave highest priority to rebuilding and modernizing the Soviet military-industrial complex. Informed by his own physicists of the potentialities of nuclear energy, and having learned through espionage of British, Canadian, French, and American progress toward the atomic bomb, he committed large resources to developing such a bomb of his own.[3] He ordered aircraft designers to develop military aircraft that could fly faster and farther than American aircraft. His first postwar Five-Year Plan, announced in 1946, concentrated investment in plants to produce these aircraft and also to produce new models of tanks, armored personnel carriers, artillery pieces, and rockets, and to mass-produce copies of Nazi Germany's oceangoing submarines.[4]

For a long time, governments in the West were unaware of the extent to which the Soviet Union was building new military strength, since their official representatives were allowed to see very little. Foreign journalists were admitted only if they would report what Soviet authorities wanted them to report. Since Soviet agents like Harold "Kim" Philby dominated analysis of the Soviet Union in the British secret service and since the United States was only beginning to build peacetime intelligence services of its own, clandestinely gathered information did not make up for the lack of other reportage. For practical purposes, Stalin's Soviet Union was, for the West, a closed black box.[5]

Nonetheless, by 1949–1950 Western observers could no longer miss

3. See David Holloway, *Stalin and the Bomb* (New Haven, 1994).
4. See Vojtech Mastny, "Stalin and the Militarization of the Cold War," *International Security*, IX (1984–85), 109–29.
5. See Bruce Page, David Leitch, and Philip Knightley, *Philby: The Spy Who Betrayed a Generation* (London, 1969); John Ranelagh, *The Agency: The Rise and Decline of the CIA* (New York, 1986); and John Prados, *The Soviet Estimate: U.S. Intelligence Analysis and Soviet Strategic Forces*, new ed. (Princeton, 1986).

seeing evidence of the Soviet Union's increasing military strength. In late 1949, U.S. Air Force air sampling off the coast of Siberia detected unmistakable evidence that the Soviets had successfully tested an atomic bomb. In the May Day parade in 1950 and on other occasions, Stalin put on display some of his new military equipment. Westerners saw not only new jet fighters but large numbers of medium-range bombers—TU-4s, which were exact copies of the U.S. B-29—capable of delivering either conventional or atomic bombs against any part of Western Europe, including the United Kingdom and surrounding waters. Westerners saw new model tanks and other equipment deployed along the "iron curtain." On the oceans they encountered Soviet submarines similar to those that had almost severed Atlantic supply and transport routes during World War II.[6]

In London and Washington the Soviet military buildup created alarm, but officials reacted much more strongly than did politicians. Within the diplomatic and military establishments of the two countries, near consensus developed in favor of a well-advertised Western military buildup designed both to deter the Soviets from making use of their growing military power and, if deterrence failed, to counter a Soviet march against Western Europe. In Britain, Clement Attlee and most members of his Labour cabinet gave higher priority to social welfare programs. In the United States, the same was true of Harry Truman, who in 1948 had surprised almost everyone by winning the presidential election. Hoping to revive the New Deal reform agenda that Franklin Roosevelt had ceased pursuing before World War II, Truman called in 1949 for a "Fair Deal." Needing money for this program and being constitutionally opposed to deficit spending, Truman appointed a tough Missouri politician, Louis Johnson, to be secretary of defense and made him his agent for capping and, if possible, squeezing down military spending.

The Soviet atomic-bomb test detected in September 1949 gave officials in Washington an opening for pressing Truman to change his position. Some nuclear physicists had been arguing all along for an effort to develop a hydrogen bomb much more powerful than the atomic bomb. They now contended that such an effort was necessary if the United

6. For details, see Ernest R. May, John D. Steinbruner, and Thomas W. Wolfe, *History of the Strategic Arms Competition, 1945–1972* (Washington, D.C., 1981), declassified with deletions, December 1990, National Security Archive, Washington, D.C.

States were not to fall behind the Soviet Union. Other physicists argued that there was no political, military, or moral justification for a super-bomb. The U.S. Atomic Energy Commission split on the issue. The president had to make a decision. He came down in favor of the "super."[7]

Since most of the prospective spending lay well in the future, this decision did not in itself commit Truman to shelving his Fair Deal. To reassure those with misgivings about too heavy a reliance on nuclear weapons alone, however, Truman agreed that there should be a general review of U.S. national security policy. Secretary of State Dean Acheson and the chief of his Policy Planning Staff, Paul H. Nitze, snatched this opportunity. Both being strongly in favor of crash rearmament by the West, Acheson and Nitze contrived to produce a paper, NSC 68, which made their case in the starkest terms possible. "The issues that face us are momentous," said the document, "involving the fulfillment or destruction not only of this Republic but of civilization itself. . . . A more rapid build-up of political, economic, and military strength . . . is the only course which is consistent with progress toward achieving our fundamental purpose. . . . [T]he survival of the free world is at stake."

By the time Truman saw NSC 68, it had been endorsed by all his senior officials and by a panoply of outsiders eminent in science, the academy, business, or public service. If the president simply rejected the recommendation, he would seem to say that his domestic agenda was more important than saving civilization. He was trapped.[8]

By what seems sheer coincidence, Stalin chose this moment to prod his client regime in northern Korea to launch an all-out military offensive against the American client regime in southern Korea.[9] The result was to change the minds of almost all politicians in both the United States and the United Kingdom. Truman and Attlee alike concluded

7. The best account is still Herbert York, *The Advisers: Oppenheimer, Teller, and the Superbomb*, new ed. (Stanford, 1989).

8. This story is told in some detail in Ernest R. May, *American Cold War Strategy: Interpreting NSC 68* (New York, 1994).

9. Evidence from both China and the former Soviet Union makes it difficult (though demonstrably not impossible) for scholars to continue to question Stalin's dominant role. See Kathryn Weathersby, "New Findings on the Korean War," *CWIHP Bulletin*, issue 3 (Fall 1993); "Response: Korean War Origins," ibid., issue 4 (Fall 1994); and "New Evidence on the Korean War," ibid., issue 6–7 (Winter 1995–6). See also Sergei N. Goncharov, John W. Lewis, and Xue Litai, *Uncertain Partners: Stalin, Mao, and the Korean War* (Stanford: Stanford University Press, 1993).

that their officials had been in the right. Both of them made 180-degree turns. Each became a champion of an urgent military buildup. Truman not only subscribed to NSC 68; he fired Louis Johnson and was soon himself sending notes to his military chiefs chiding them for not asking for more money for their services. Attlee announced a large three-year rearmament program. Truman sent Congress a succession of requests for supplemental funds and ended up quadrupling budgeted expenditures for military forces.

The cold war became a contest between an already-militarized Soviet bloc and a newly militarized Western bloc. Even before Korea, the American Joint Chiefs of Staff had reckoned that Western Europe could be defended only if a German army came back into being. After the Korean War commenced, the United States and Britain stationed combat forces of their own along the frontier between West and East Germany. The two governments worked out with the French and other Europeans a scheme for a European Defence Community (EDC) within which there could be German military units. The long-term safety of the region was assumed to depend on either creation of the EDC or, for an indefinite period, maintenance of large, ready American and British military forces along the East-West boundary.

At Lisbon in the spring of 1952, at a meeting of the North Atlantic Council, the Americans and British found a formula which promised success for the EDC. NATO agreed officially on the forces needed to meet the Soviet threat: twenty-five divisions always at the ready; another sixty-four to sixty-five divisions mobilizable within thirty days; and air and naval forces corresponding in size and levels of readiness.[10] These numbers seemed large enough so that the French and others would recognize not only that they could not fill the void themselves but also that, even if the Germans contributed up to twelve divisions, they would still be outnumbered.

It was soon evident that these Lisbon force goals would not be met. In Britain, many in the Labour government had concluded that funding both social welfare programs and the military buildup required, in the words of Health Minister Aneurin Bevan, "the arithmetic of Bedlam."[11] In October 1951, a general election put the Conservatives back into of-

10. Historical Section, Joint Chiefs of Staff, *The Joint Chiefs of Staff and National Policy*, Walter S. Poole, *1950–1952* (Wilmington, Del., 1979), IV, 289–95.
    11. John Baylis, ed., *British Defence Policy in a Changing World* (London, 1977), 185.

fice, with Churchill again prime minister, and even while the Lisbon conference was sitting, Churchill announced cutbacks both in overall British military spending and in troop deployments abroad.

In the United States, the 1952 election brought a Republican victory. Dwight D. Eisenhower became president, with his party having narrow majorities in both houses of Congress. The victorious commander of Allied forces in World War II, Eisenhower had gone back into uniform in 1950 to be Supreme Allied Commander, Europe (SACEUR) and whip together the American, British, and other NATO forces designed to stem the apprehended Soviet attack on Western Europe. He had been one of the sponsors of the EDC and one of the authors of the Lisbon force goals. As a Republican president, however, taking office in a time of inflation and economic slowdown, he was committed to cutting back on federal spending. Since very little of Truman's Fair Deal had actually been enacted, and much domestic spending was nondiscretionary, this meant that Eisenhower had to trim the greatly expanded defense budget that resulted from Truman's accepting unreservedly the logic of NSC 68. It also meant that he had to find some means of backing away from the Lisbon force goals without either disrupting the Western alliance or jeopardizing European security.

The solution to Eisenhower's dilemma seemed evident. By relying more heavily on nuclear weapons, the West might be able to maintain a barrier against the Soviets without having to field all the divisions and supplementary forces envisioned at Lisbon. Although the United States had collapsed most of its vast World War II atomic bomb project, the successor Atomic Energy Commission had continued to develop nuclear weaponry. Field tests in 1948 had demonstrated that future weapons did not need to be as large or delicate as those used against Japan. They could be produced in a wide variety of sizes and with a variety of yields. And with finds of uranium ore multiplying, they could be mass-produced.[12]

Because of the Soviet atomic bomb, Truman increased the budget of the AEC. When he decided in favor of the hydrogen bomb, he increased its budget still more. After the opening of the Korean War and Truman's endorsement of NSC 68, the AEC, like the armed services, had the wherewithal to develop almost anything it wanted to develop. By the

12. The best account is David Alan Rosenberg, "The Origins of Overkill: Nuclear Weapons and American Strategy, 1945–1960," *International Security*, VII (1983), 3–71.

early Eisenhower administration, the AEC was on its way to having thirteen plutonium production reactors and four gaseous diffusion plants turning out nuclear material, while giant laboratories at Los Alamos, New Mexico, Livermore, California, and elsewhere around the United States hummed away to convert this material into weaponry.

As a result, the U.S. armed services began to have in their supply lines an almost unimaginable array of nuclear weapons. A hydrogen bomb tested in March 1954 had explosive power equal to more than a thousand of the bombs dropped on Nagasaki. Measured in terms of tons of TNT, this bomb had a yield of 15 million tons (or 15 megatons); the Nagasaki bomb had had a yield of about 14 thousand tons (or 14 kilotons). At the other end of the spectrum were nuclear artillery shells and even launchable grenades (the "Davy Crockett") with yields not much greater than the one-ton blockbuster TNT bombs of World War II. In between were 10-megaton bombs for the new intercontinental B-52 bomber, 1-to-3-megaton bombs for medium-range B-47 bombers and for fighter-bombers, both land based and carrier based; warheads of between 10 and 50 kilotons for short- and medium-range guided missiles, again either land based or ship based; and nuclear devices that could be fitted into torpedoes and mines.[13] Although most such weapons were not actually deployed before the later 1950s, the armed services expected them and planned around them.

For the European defense dilemma, nuclear weapons offered two basically different but not necessarily incompatible solutions. First, the West could threaten to respond to a Soviet attack on Europe (or any other part of the "free world") by large-scale strategic bombing. In the words of one U.S. Air Force planner, the operational aim would be to render the Soviet Union "a smoking radiating ruin at the end of two hours."[14] Alternatively, the West could maintain along the East-West frontier in Europe relatively small forces which, if sufficiently strong in "nuclear firepower," could obstruct a forward march by much more numerous Soviet forces. With Britain having developed its own atomic bomb and being on the way to having its own hydrogen bomb, the Brit-

13. See Natural Resources Defense Council, *Nuclear Weapons Databook*, Vol. I: Thomas B. Cochran, William M. Arkin, and Milton M. Hoenig, *U.S. Nuclear Forces and Capabilities* (Cambridge, Mass., 1984).

14. David Alan Rosenberg, " 'A Smoking Radiating Ruin at the End of Two Hours': Documents of American Plans for Nuclear War with the Soviet Union, 1945–1955," *International Security*, VI (1981–82), 3–38.

ish Chiefs of Staff in June 1952 endorsed and shared with their American counterparts a "global strategy paper" urging that defense of Europe be keyed almost entirely to the threat of strategic bombing.[15]

As SACEUR, Eisenhower had heard the British chiefs' argument while it was still in germination. After becoming president, he appointed an entirely new set of American chiefs of staff. Under Eisenhower's guidance, they developed a basic strategy for the United States that had many ingredients taken from the British global strategy paper. Approved by Eisenhower in October 1953 as NSC 162/2, this so-called "New Look" entailed a leveling-off in overall U.S. defense spending, with reduction in allocations to the army, navy, and marines but greater investment in the air force, particularly in the Strategic Air Command. Eisenhower's secretary of state, John Foster Dulles, publicized the new U.S. strategy in a speech in New York. The most memorable line therein said that the administration had made a "basic decision . . . to depend primarily upon a great capacity to retaliate, instantly, by means and at places of our choosing."

Meanwhile, the Eisenhower administration began to decrease ground forces in Europe and to make up for doing so by equipping the remaining forces with tactical nuclear weapons. Under existing U.S. law, neither these weapons nor any information about them could be shared with foreigners—even the British. Nevertheless, Eisenhower and the successor SACEUR, General Alfred Gruenther, had a multinational "New Approach Group" work on doctrine for employing tactical nuclear weapons in actual combat. The foreign officers in the group were given hypothetical data about the characteristics of the weapons.

During the more than two years between Eisenhower's inauguration and the 1955 Geneva conference, three significant developments occurred. First in importance was a leadership change in the Soviet Union. In March 1953 Stalin died. For a time a triumvirate seemed to rule. Its members were Premier Georgi Malenkov, police head Lavrenti Beria, and Moscow party boss Nikita Khrushchev. Beria was soon murdered. In 1954 Malenkov was demoted. Khrushchev eventually emerged as the new number one. Though American intelligence had reported this to Eisenhower, he says in his memoirs that he was not entirely sure of the

15. The paper is discussed in detail in Ian Clark, *The British Origins of Nuclear Strategy, 1945–1955* (Oxford, 1989), and John Baylis, *Ambiguity and Deterrence: British Nuclear Strategy, 1945–1964* (Oxford, 1995). The text of the paper (CAB 131/12, D (52) 26, 17 June 1952) is Appendix 6 in the latter.

information's validity until he actually saw Khrushchev dominating his colleagues at Geneva.[16]

As the reader of this volume will see, the circumstances attending the regime change in the Soviet Union were unclear to Western observers at the time and in many respects remain obscure still, despite the dissolution of the Soviet Union and the opening of some of its archives. Before Stalin's death, the Soviet government had launched a worldwide "peace campaign." Accompanying it had been a proposal for negotiations to complete a peace treaty for all of Germany. Had the Western governments agreed to enter such negotiations, they might have found the Soviets seriously willing to write a treaty, or so some scholars now believe. Or Western governments might have found that they were right in suspecting—as they did—that the Soviets merely meant to disrupt progress toward an EDC and re-creation of a German army. It is not clear that the Soviets themselves knew what would happen, for even though Stalin was still an omnipotent tyrant, his physical and mental powers appear to have been failing, and the outcome of any negotiations about Germany might have depended on the outcome of maneuvers and countermaneuvers among his subordinates and eventual successors.[17] In any case, the black box on the other side of the iron curtain had emitted some signals suggesting at least a possibility of détente.

Very soon after Stalin's death, the North Koreans and Chinese agreed to a truce in the Korean War. We now know that they had long wanted relief from the draining costs of that war, but the terrible old man in the Kremlin had insisted that the fighting continue. Stalin's successors were less obdurate. Perhaps unfortunately, the new Eisenhower administration had circulated some hints that if the Communists did not agree to end the Korean War, the United States might use nuclear weapons, and many in Washington, and the West more generally, attributed the truce to this threat rather than to the death of Stalin. Nevertheless, the Soviet peace offensive, the ending of the Korean War, and rhetoric from Stalin's successors about the mutual destructiveness of conflict all pointed in the same direction—toward a possible turn away from cold war.

16. Dwight D. Eisenhower, *The White House Years*, Vol. II: *Mandate for Change, 1953–1956* (Garden City, N.Y., 1963), 517–22.

17. See Amy Knight, *Beria, Stalin's First Lieutenant* (Princeton, 1993) and Zubok and Pleshakov, *Inside the Kremlin's Cold War*. The clearest summary of a vast controversial literature is Ruud Van Dijk, "The 1952 Stalin Note Debate: Myth or Missed Opportunity for German Unification?" CWIHP Working Paper no. 14 (May 1996).

The second major development was the completion of arrangements to put some Germans back in uniform. After long delays, the proposed EDC came before the French National Assembly. That body voted to kill the scheme. More than three years of bargaining and political maneuver seemed to have gone for nought. But British foreign secretary Anthony Eden, in the only certifiable success of his long diplomatic career, led in developing a new plan, in which the French and other European governments and the Americans all concurred. A West German government which had been groomed to be a partner in the EDC simply became a member of NATO, agreeing to create military forces solely for participation in that organization and effectively forswearing nuclear forces of its own.

Though it would be some time before the virtually sovereign Federal Republic of Germany actually produced soldiers for NATO, these arrangements, combined with the promise that all NATO forces would benefit from U.S. tactical nuclear firepower and, behind that, the threat of "massive retaliation," seemed to promise Western Europe the security it had lacked when the Soviet military threat first became apparent in the late 1940s.

The third major development, occurring at the upper levels of the American and British governments, was a gradual increase in understanding of, and worry about, the nuclear genie released to solve the dilemma created by the gross imbalance in ready power between West and East. From test reports, Eisenhower, Churchill, and their intimates learned just how horribly destructive hydrogen bombs could be. "There is an immense gulf between the atomic and hydrogen bomb," Churchill was to explain to the House of Commons. "The atomic bomb, with all its terrors, did not carry us outside the scope of human control or manageable events in thought or action, in peace or war." With the hydrogen bomb, he said, "the entire foundation of human affairs was revolutionized, and mankind placed in a situation both measureless and laden with doom." And as early as August 1953, Eisenhower and Churchill had learned that the Soviets, too, possessed ability to produce hydrogen bombs.[18]

Meanwhile, members of the New Approach Group and other officers at NATO and in the Pentagon and Whitehall became less and less con-

18. See McGeorge Bundy, *Danger and Survival: Choices about the Bomb in the First Fifty Years* (New York, 1988), and John Lewis Gaddis et al., eds., *Cold War Statesmen Confront the Bomb: Nuclear Diplomacy since 1945* (New York, 1999).

fident of the battlefield utility of nuclear firepower. It proved very hard to figure out how, if nuclear weapons were in play, ground forces could be concentrated so as to form the mass necessary either for defense or for exploitation of an opportunity to commence an offensive. No one was ever to work out a satisfactory answer.[19]

In view of these three developments, members not only of the British and American but of other Western governments turned to mulling whether diplomacy might provide an escape before the prospect of mutual thermonuclear annihilation became a condition of life and before they had to face the possibility that nuclear firepower did not, after all, provide an economical formula for defending Europe without resorting to "massive retaliation." The chapters here describe in fascinating detail how the leaders of these governments, and their counterparts on the other side of the iron curtain, pursued this question and what came of their efforts.

19. See John P. Rose, *The Evolution of U.S. Army Nuclear Doctrine, 1945–1980* (Boulder, Colo., 1980) and contributions by Catherine M. Kelleher and Ernest R. May in Stephen D. Biddle and Peter D. Feaver, eds., *Battlefield Nuclear Weapons* (Cambridge, Mass.: Center for Science and International Affairs, John F. Kennedy School of Government, Harvard University, 1989).

"Trust in the Lord but Keep Your Powder Dry"

American Policy Aims at Geneva

RICHARD H. IMMERMAN

The 1952 presidential campaign was bitter. Having four years earlier abided by the maxim that politics stops at the water's edge—and having lost—the Republicans forswore bipartisanship and came out swinging from the start. Adlai E. Stevenson was Dwight D. Eisenhower's opponent, but Harry S. Truman was his target. The general-cum-candidate exploited the cold-war climate of fear and frustration by indicting the incumbent administration for strategic ineptitude, fiscal profligacy, and moral turpitude. To replace Truman's "negative, futile, and immoral" strategy of containment, Eisenhower pledged to pursue what John Foster Dulles, the prohibitive favorite for secretary of state, labeled a "policy of boldness."[1]

Eisenhower's landslide election confronted him with the task of designing—indeed, defining—this policy. Should the new administration accept an increased risk of general war in order to roll back the Communist tide? If so, how far was it willing to push anxious allies? Perhaps it was preferable to try to negotiate some type of détente with the Soviets, aiming to build up the strength, cohesion, and confidence of the West while inherent divisions and contradictions inexorably crippled the East. But what concessions could the United States afford to make, and could limited accords be reached without settling major issues? Because the Soviets were assumed to be untrustworthy, was it feasible to achieve any agreement on arms reduction or control that did not simply accelerate the erosion of U.S. nuclear superiority? And even if such an

1. Robert Divine, *Foreign Policy and Presidential Elections, 1952–1960* (New York, 1974), 3–85; 1952 Republican Platform, *National Party Platforms, 1840–1956*, comp. Kirk H. Porter and Donald B. Johnson (Urbana, Ill., 1956), 499; John Foster Dulles, "A Policy of Boldness," *Life*, May 19, 1952, pp. 146 +.

agreement were possible, could Allied unity and resolve be sustained over the long haul under conditions of nuclear plenty?

Three competing perspectives produced intense deliberations on these questions. Eisenhower's premise was that although the Kremlin's leaders would continually seek Soviet expansion, they shared with the West a common interest in avoiding war. Hence, as long as the free-world coalition stood together and improved its deterrent capabilities, it could pursue interim settlements, particularly those that mitigated the nuclear predicament. Dulles agreed with the president's main premise but was less inclined to negotiate, for fear of encouraging Allied wishful thinking and neutralism and providing relief for the overextended Soviets. Eisenhower's military advisers, most prominently Joint Chiefs of Staff (JCS) chairman Admiral Arthur Radford, vigorously opposed any negotiations prior to a radical change in Soviet behavior. Instead, in the time that remained before nuclear stalemate, the United States should exploit its superiority to force Moscow to retract its power and influence.

These contrasting points of view framed Eisenhower's foreign and national-security policy making throughout the two and one-half years leading up to the Geneva summit. The debates they generated illuminate why the administration resisted a meeting of the Big Four heads of state, why it ultimately agreed to one, and why, with one notable exception, it was satisfied with the meager results. They also explain why it is misleading to refer in the singular to "American" policy aims at Geneva.

A Chance for Peace?

Eisenhower had barely settled into the Oval Office when the question of summitry arose. On March 5, Joseph Stalin, long perceived as the embodiment of the Soviet state and threat, died. Within a week British prime minister Winston Churchill began to barrage Eisenhower with letters renewing his advocacy of a summit.[2] His urgings intensified after Georgi Maximilianovich Malenkov, now chairman of the Council of Ministers, initiated a "peace offensive" by publicly declaring that negotiations could and should resolve all international disputes. "[W]e ought

2. Churchill had been calling for a summit since 1950. Paul C. Davis, "The New Diplomacy: The 1955 Geneva Summit Meeting," in *Foreign Policy in the Sixties: The Issues and Instruments*, ed. Roger Hilsman and Robert C. Good (Baltimore, 1965), 161.

to lose no chance of finding out how far the Malenkov regime are prepared to go in easing things up all around," Churchill exhorted Eisenhower.[3]

Within days of Churchill's initial letter, Eisenhower's National Security Council (NSC) began debate on Special Assistant to the White House C. D. Jackson's parallel proposal. This is not to say that Jackson's objective was parallel. Rather, the consummate psychological warrior saw Stalin's death as an opportunity to launch an aggressive propaganda campaign to seize the initiative from the Communists. Over a weekend, he and MIT professor Walt Rostow drafted for Eisenhower's use a speech intended to (1) create dissension within the Kremlin by forcing it to make difficult decisions; (2) present a "vision" of U.S. purposes designed to inspire Eastern bloc and neutral peoples to identify their future with America's; (3) foster greater unity throughout the world; and (4) rally Americans behind Eisenhower's programs. Toward these ends, as the "guts" of the speech, the president would invite the Soviets to a four-power conference. Although it would be at the foreign-ministerial, not heads-of-state, level, the United States would nevertheless introduce measures to settle the Korean War, unify Germany, end the occupation of Austria, and promote general arms control and specific security regimes.[4]

Dulles and the State Department immediately objected. Not only would the Soviets demand Communist Chinese participation and thereby complicate negotiations to end the war in Korea, but more fundamentally, to call a meeting without prior Allied accord on the specific agenda and negotiating positions courted disaster. History, Dulles explained to the NSC on March 11, proved that the Soviets "would resort to all their devices for delay and obstruction." They could be counted on to say anything in order to give "new heart" to "neutralists" and di-

3. Churchill to Eisenhower, March 11 and April 5, 1953, in *The Churchill-Eisenhower Correspondence, 1953–1955,* ed. Peter G. Boyle (Chapel Hill, 1990), 31, 36. On Malenkov's speeches and the peace offensive, see James G. Richter, "Perpetuating the Cold War: Domestic Sources of International Patterns of Behavior," *Political Science Quarterly,* CVII (1992), 281–2.

4. "Draft for NSC: Proposed Plan for Psychological Warfare Offensive," March 1953, "*Time,* Inc. File—Stalin's Death: Speech Text and Comments—Full Evolution," C. D. Jackson Papers, DDEL; Jackson to Dulles, March 10, 1953, ibid; "The March 6, 1953, Draft of the Proposed 'Message' and Related Documents," reproduced in Walt Whitman Rostow, *Europe after Stalin: Eisenhower's Three Decisions of March 11, 1953* (Austin, Tex.,1982), 84–90.

vide the West. Dulles was "sure," for example, that they would tie together discussions of German reunification and arms control in an
effort to "ruin every prospect" for achieving ratification of the European
Defence Community (EDC) treaty, drive a deeper wedge between
France and West Germany, and undermine European leaders most
friendly to the administration.[5]

Eisenhower shared Dulles's misgivings. He was also sensitive to the
influence of the Yalta conference on the political consciousness of the
Republican right wing, and he certainly wanted to avoid initiatives that
might make his relations with that faction more difficult than they already were. Nevertheless, if a speech could present "some idea, some
hope, of a better future," the president wanted to give it. Moreover, he
was "ready and willing to meet with anyone anywhere from the Soviet
Union provided the basis for the meeting was honest and practical."[6]

Hence, even as Eisenhower cautioned Churchill that "a formal multilateral meeting would give our opponent the same kind of opportunity
he has so often had to use such a meeting simultaneously to balk every
reasonable effort of ourselves and to make the whole occurrence another propaganda mill for the Soviets," he personally supervised the
drafting of a speech that stipulated what, in his view, could make for an
"honest and practical" basis for a meeting. The president had in mind a
"serious bid for peace" that combined the universal desires for arms
control and improved standards of living. He might propose, for example, that the Americans and Soviets agree to reduce their level of military spending to a percentage of each's gross national product.
Juxtaposed with this proposal could be an "outline" of "the specific
steps . . . necessary to bring about satisfactory relationships with resultant elimination or lowering of tensions throughout the world." These
would include peaceful resolutions to the Indochina and Korean conflicts, free elections to reunify Germany, a treaty ending the occupation
of Austria, and the liberation of Eastern Europe. The United States—and
international opinion—could grade the new Soviet regime according to
this test of the "peace offensive." Eisenhower expected it to fail, and he

5. Walter Bedell Smith, memorandum to George A. Morgan, March 10, 1953, *FRUS,
1952–1954*, VIII, 1111–3; memorandum of NSC discussion, March 11, 1953, ibid.,
1120–1.
6. Gary W. Reichard, *The Reaffirmation of Republicanism: Eisenhower and the Eighty-
third Congress* (Knoxville, Tenn., 1975), 51–68; memorandum of NSC discussion, March
11, 1953, p. 1122.

did not minimize the potential benefits for the West in the psychological battle for the world's hearts and minds. A Soviet response that went beyond propaganda, he nonetheless averred, would indicate that "some kind of *modus vivendi* might at long last prove possible."[7]

Dulles and his advisers remained cool to the idea and ultimately recommended against the president's giving any speech at all. Even if Eisenhower refrained from mentioning a conference, they chorused, just by raising the issues of German reunification and an Austrian treaty he would get "into a corner on this willingness to meet with the Russian leader." At a minimum the Soviets would recycle their neutralization and disarmament schemes. The consequences would derail progress toward free-world unity and collective security, and could prove fatal to the EDC.[8]

Eisenhower recognized these dangers no less than Dulles and his colleagues, but he insisted that they were surmountable "provided we have a plan of action." That plan was for Dulles to follow up Eisenhower's speech with another that left no doubt that "we are going to go RIGHT AHEAD rearming until it's clear we no longer have to." Thus, whereas Eisenhower spoke to the American Society of Newspaper Editors on April 16 of a "Chance for Peace," on April 18 Dulles warned the same audience that the future "must always remain obscure so long as vast power is possessed by men who accept no guidance from the moral law." Belittling Malenkov's peace offensive as a peace *defensive* prompted by the West's successes, he reaffirmed America's commitment to NATO, EDC ratification, and other military measures designed to "deter attack from without." As for negotiations, "we will not play the role of supplicants," Dulles emphasized. A people with "the tradi-

7. Eisenhower to Churchill, April 6 and 11, 1953, in *Churchill-Eisenhower Correspondence*, ed. Boyle, 37–8, 43; Emmet J. Hughes, *The Ordeal of Power: A Political Memoir of the Eisenhower Years* (New York, 1975), 103–5; entries for April 6, 8, and 9, 1953, "Diary Notes 1953," Emmet J. Hughes Papers, Mudd Library, Princeton University, Princeton, N.J. For the argument that Eisenhower sought only a propaganda coup, see Klaus Larres, "Eisenhower and the First Forty Days after Stalin's Death: The Incompatibility of Détente and Political Warfare," *Diplomacy and Statecraft*, VI (1995), 431–69.

8. "Considerations relating to the redraft of March 19, 1953 'Peace Plan Speech,' " and "Suggested specific changes in redraft of March 19, 1953 'Peace Plan Speech,' " attached to Paul H. Nitze memorandum to Dulles, March 20, 1953, "The President's Speech, April 1953," folder 3, Draft Correspondence and Speech series, John Foster Dulles Papers, DDEL; Nitze to Dulles, April 2, 1953, "The President's Speech April 1953 (1)," ibid.; entry for April 11, 1953, "Diary Notes 1953," Hughes Papers.

tion and power of the United States must act boldly and strongly for what they believe to be right."[9]

Apparently Soviet leaders opposed to Malenkov's efforts to forge a dé-tente interpreted Dulles's speech as a truer expression of U.S. goals and intentions than Eisenhower's. From the president's standpoint, how-ever, the two statements were entirely congruent. A secure interna-tional peace required the Soviet Union to reverse, even if only incrementally, the fundamentals of Stalin's policy. Eisenhower's speech focused on how the Kremlin could demonstrate its sincere commit-ment to doing so; Dulles's stressed what the West had to do until it did.[10]

The Soviet official response came on April 25. It placed the "onus" of the cold war squarely on the United States, defended the correctness of past Soviet foreign policy, and proposed no new initiatives. "The state-ment gives no indication that the rulers of the USSR will modify their stand on any of the issues outstanding between East and West" or "that they are prepared to make substantial concessions," a special intelli-gence estimate predictably concluded. Eisenhower's advice to Churchill was equally predictable. "I feel we should not rush things too much," he wrote. "There is some feeling here also for a meeting between the Heads of States and Governments, but I do not think this should be al-lowed to press us into precipitate initiatives. . . . We have so far seen no concrete Soviet actions which would indicate their willingness to per-form in connection with larger issues. In the circumstances, we would risk raising hopes of progress toward an accommodation which would be unjustified."[11]

Alliance Management

Churchill would not be deterred. In a series of letters to Eisenhower, he proposed to visit personally with "Monsieur Malenkov" in Moscow.

9. Entries for March 17, April 6 and 8, 1953, "Diary Notes 1953," Hughes Papers; Ei-senhower, "The Chance for Peace," April 16, 1953, FRUS, 1952–1954, VIII, 1147–55; Dul-les, "The Eisenhower Foreign Policy: A World-Wide Peace Offensive," originally printed April 18, 1953, reproduced in Rostow, Europe after Stalin, 122–31.

10. Vladislav M. Zubok, "Soviet Intelligence and the Cold War: The 'Small' Committee of Information, 1952–1953," Diplomatic History, XIX (1995), 457–61; James G. Richter, "Reexamining Soviet Policy towards Germany during the Beria Interregnum," CWIHP Working Paper no. 3 (1992), 23–6.

11. Charles E. Bohlen to Department of State, April 25, 1953 (two different telegrams), FRUS, 1952–1954, VIII, 1162–66; SE-44, "Soviet Statement of 25 April 1953 in Reply to President Eisenhower's Speech on 16 April 1953," 30 April 1953, ibid., 1168–9; Eisenhower to Churchill, April 25, 1953, Churchill-Eisenhower Correspondence, ed. Boyle, 47.

When Eisenhower protested vehemently, the prime minister upped the ante. A "conference on the highest level should take place between the leading Powers without long delay," he announced to the House of Commons on May 11.[12]

Churchill's seeming obsession with a summit reinforced Dulles's pessimistic diagnosis of the state of the Western alliance. In the midst of the Eisenhower-Churchill exchange of letters, the secretary and president met with several other key security managers in the White House solarium. "It is difficult to conclude that time is working in our favor," Dulles began. Without mentioning Churchill by name, he then described Europe's leaders as "shattered 'old people' " who hoped that the "Soviets, like Ghenghes [sic] Khan, will get on their little Tartar ponies and ride back whence they came." Lacking "the strength, the dynamic" essential to meet a threat more severe than that of Hitler's Germany, they wanted "to spend their remaining days in peace and repose." Consequently, they were "willing and glad to gamble" with the future of the free world.[13]

Eisenhower replied by proposing what became known as Project Solarium as a means to examine the premises and implications of Dulles's presentation.[14] In this way, the issue of a summit contributed directly to a review of national-security policy unprecedented in U.S. history. The core question was not only whether a summit was compatible with free-world security interests; no less important was how the United States could pursue the policies and programs Dulles said that it must in his speech of April 18 without alienating vital allies.

By the end of the year the answers were still ambiguous. NSC 162/2, the statement of basic national-security policy approved in October, made clear that the "various 'peace gestures' so far have cost the Soviets very little" and "there are no convincing signs of [their] readiness to make important concessions." Further, Stalin's death had not impaired the growth of Communist atomic and conventional capabilities, the au-

12. Churchill-Eisenhower exchange between May 4 and May 8, 1953, in *Churchill-Eisenhower Correspondence*, ed. Boyle, 48–55; Churchill, address to the House of Commons, May 11, 1953, in Robert Rhodes James, ed., *Winston Churchill: His Complete Speeches, 1897–1963* (New York, 1974), VIII, 8484.

13. Memorandum of conversation (probably by Cutler), "Solarium Project," May 8, 1953, lot 66D148, SS-NSC files, Record Group 59, National Archives, Washington, D.C.

14. Ibid. On Project Solarium, see Richard H. Immerman, "Confessions of an Eisenhower Revisionist: An Agonizing Reappraisal," *Diplomatic History*, XIV (1990), 335–42; Robert R. Bowie and Immerman, *Waging Peace: How Eisenhower Shaped an Enduring Cold War Strategy* (New York, 1998), 123–38.

thority of the Kremlin, its control over the satellites, or the Sino-Soviet alliance. National security, therefore, required the continued development of credible force levels (proscribing for the present any "major withdrawal of U.S. forces") as well as the atomic capability to inflict "massive retaliatory damage by offensive striking power." But even at "exorbitant cost," the United States could not achieve this "strong military posture" without Allied support. That support "must be rooted in a strong feeling of a community of interest and firm confidence in the steadiness and wisdom of U.S. leadership."[15]

Therein lay the rub. France's resistance to ratifying the EDC treaty not only frustrated military plans, but it also was symptomatic of divisions within the noncommunist community. And Churchill's persistent promotion of a summit was symptomatic of doubts in U.S. leadership. By raising hopes and portraying Washington as an obstacle to easing global tensions, the Soviets were exacerbating these divisions and doubts. So pessimistic had Dulles become by the end of 1953 that he warned that the "NATO concept" was "losing its grip." While the West could still bargain from strength, he mused, as a desperate gamble Eisenhower might try to freeze the status quo on the basis of mutual American and Soviet force reductions and international control of nuclear weapons and missiles. In short, perhaps the "present is a propitious time" to negotiate with the Soviets after all.[16]

Eisenhower challenged Dulles's prognosis. He maintained that it was still possible as well as necessary for the West to pursue programs to build up its strength, which included rearming West Germany within the North Atlantic framework. Yet he wrote that Dulles was right—albeit for the wrong reasons—on one score: "renewed efforts should be made to relax world tensions."[17]

15. NSC 162/2, Statement of Basic National Security Policy, enclosed with James S. Lay to NSC, October 30, 1953, *FRUS, 1952–1954,* II, 577–96.

16. Rolf Steininger, "John Foster Dulles, the European Defense Community, and the German Question," in *John Foster Dulles and the Diplomacy of the Cold War,* ed. Richard H. Immerman (Princeton, 1990), 79–108; Saki Dockrill, "Cooperation and Suspicion: The United States' Alliance Diplomacy for the Security of Western Europe," *Diplomacy and Statecraft* V (1994), 138–82; Stephen E. Ambrose, "The Eisenhower Administration and European Security, 1953–1956," in Bruno Thoss and Hans-Erich Volkmann, eds., *Zwischen Kaltem Krieg und Entspannung: Sicherheits- und Deutschlandpolitik der Bundesrepublik im Mächtesystem der Jahre 1953–1956 (Between Cold War and Détente: Security and German Policy of the Federal Republic in the Power System of 1953–1956)* (Boppard am Rhein, 1988), 25–34; memorandum by Dulles, September 6, 1953, *FRUS, 1952–54,* II, 457. I thank Alexandra Friedrich for providing me with a translation of the Ambrose article.

17. Eisenhower memorandum to Dulles, September 8, 1953, *FRUS, 1952–54,* II, 460–3.

But any such efforts would entail negotiating with the Soviets, and this Eisenhower's military advisers opposed, regardless of the level or agenda. A "basic change in the attitude of the Soviet leaders" combined with "a weakening of the Soviet structure is a probable prerequisite to the achievement of acceptable negotiated settlements," advised the JCS. Thus initiatives intended to relax world tensions, especially those involving arms control, would be "self-defeating" and "directly contrary to the positive, dynamic policy required . . . to bring about a negotiating attitude in the USSR and its resulting accommodation to the security of the United States and that of the free world."[18]

In essence, the service chiefs recommended that the United States forgo all negotiations and pursue a policy of rollback of Soviet influence. But they could not with any specificity explain how the available means could produce this end. In this regard, the JCS's logic apparently caused Dulles to reexamine his own. Because settlements "must be mutually acceptable," he told the NSC, "what was being proposed [by the JCS] appeared to be reversing this Administration's whole policy—a fact that was all the more dangerous in view of the Soviet possession of the H-bomb." What was more, if "you subordinate the achievement of mutually agreeable settlements to improving the power position [i.e., strategic balance] of the United States as against the USSR, you will eliminate all hope of settlements in Korea, Austria, Germany, etc." Echoing Eisenhower's perspective, Dulles now concluded that "if we have a firm foundation in Western Europe," there "may be a fair chance of some settlement with the Russians."[19]

Following Dulles's lead, the NSC agreed that although current signs were "not encouraging," Eisenhower's policy must keep open the possibility of negotiations, "whether limited to individual issues now outstanding or involving a general settlement of major issues, including control of armaments." It also agreed that the prospect of the Soviets' conceding to settlements consistent with U.S. interests depended, above all, on their recognizing the growing strength of the free world and the failure to break its cohesion. As a response to such advances as

18. JCS memorandum for the Secretary of Defense, "Review of Basic National Security Policy (NSC 162)," October 6, 1953, pp. 2–3, and Appendix, 9–10, Records of the Office of the Secretary of Defense, RG 330, NA; JCS draft paragraph, NSC 162, September 30, 1953, *FRUS, 1952–54*, II, 512.

19. Memorandum of NSC discussion, October 7, 1953, *FRUS, 1952–54*, II, 529–30; Dulles to Eisenhower, October 23, 1953, ibid., 1234–5.

the NATO powers' admitting West Germany to the alliance, the "Soviet leadership might find it desirable and even essential to reach agreements acceptable to the United States and its allies, without necessarily abandoning its basic hostility to the non-Soviet world."[20]

Just as the administration was deciding on this policy, Churchill threatened to violate it by reviving his argument that the EDC impasse need not delay a summit. Eisenhower's dissent was unequivocal. But after he and Dulles met with their British and French counterparts in Bermuda to "survey the situation in which we now find ourselves," the president acquiesced to foreign-ministerial talks in early 1954 with an agenda confined to Germany and Austria. At Berlin in February, Dulles supported the "Eden plan": a freely elected national assembly should be entrusted with drafting a constitution for a reunified Germany and negotiating a peace treaty. The Soviets, however, linked German reunification to a comprehensive security pact for Europe. And they insisted that a settlement on Germany was a precondition for withdrawing their troops from Austria. Moscow's intransigence reinforced the position expressed in NSC 162/2 that the new regime would negotiate in good faith only when convinced the alternative was not only futile but hazardous.[21]

But even as EDC ratification remained hostage to the French, Churchill ratcheted up the pressure for a summit. At a White House meeting in June, Eisenhower tried to finesse the problem by telling the prime minister that although he would not rule out such a meeting, he feared giving Malenkov the opportunity to "hit the free world in the face." He suggested that Churchill put a plan down in writing. Instead of writing to Eisenhower, however, Churchill on his return voyage to England wrote Soviet foreign minister Vyacheslav Molotov offering to come to Moscow to explore the possibility of a summit. Eisenhower was livid. It was bad enough that Churchill had taken this initiative on his own. But, making matters worse, its timing could create "the misapprehension that we are in fact party to it, or the equally dangerous

20. NSC 162/2, 584–5, 594.
21. Memorandum of NSC discussion, October 22, 1953, *FRUS, 1952–54*, VII, 718–9; Churchill to Eisenhower and Eisenhower to Churchill, November 5 and 6, 1953, *Churchill-Eisenhower Correspondence*, ed. Boyle, 93–4; paper prepared by Robert Bowie, December 2, 1953, *FRUS, 1952–54*, V, 1731; memorandum of conversation by Dulles, December 4, 1953, ibid., 1739–40; Plan for German Reunification in Freedom, January 29, 1954, *FRUS, 1952–54*, VII, 1177–1180; Anthony Eden, *Full Circle* (Boston, 1960), 75–85. See also Saki Dockrill's essay in this volume, "The Eden Plan and European Security."

misapprehension that your action in this matter reflects a sharp disagreement between our two countries."[22]

Churchill's preemptory strike could have caused a crisis for Washington, particularly after the French National Assembly rejected the EDC the next month. But Soviet unwillingness to accept any overture short of a summit let Eisenhower off the hook. And at London in September, the EDC signatories, along with the United States, Britain, and West Germany, repaired the damage wrought by France. The Federal Republic of Germany (FRG), they agreed, would be invited to join the Western European Union, the renamed executive organ of the revived Brussels Pact. By this mechanism, the FRG would be recognized as sovereign and its forces made available to NATO. When this complex procedure was confirmed in Paris in October, one of the critical U.S. preconditions for useful negotiations had been met.[23]

Eisenhower and Dulles still staunchly opposed a summit. The French must not be given any "pretext" to delay ratifying the Paris accords.[24] Similarly, the Soviets could exploit popular sentiment for reunification to tempt the West Germans to reconsider aligning with the West. Only after the free world signaled that its growing coherence and power were irreversible would the Kremlin leadership face up to this reality and negotiate in earnest. Until then, a summit could be no more than a "social gathering," counterproductively inflating expectations among free people and deflating those of the captives.[25]

But the administration's aim to strengthen the West's hand before sitting down with the Soviets had to be weighed against the equivalent one of managing the alliance. Throughout Europe, as the spring of 1955 progressed, so did the allies' "passionate eagerness" for a summit. In his "Chance for Peace" speech Eisenhower had identified settlement of the wars in Korea and Indochina as two "deeds" that the Soviets must per-

22. Memoranda of meetings between Eisenhower and Churchill, June 25 and 26, 1954, *FRUS, 1952–54*, VI, 1079–80, 1097–9; entry for July 2, 1954, in John Colville, *The Fringes of Power: 10 Downing Street Diaries, 1939–1955* (New York, 1985), 697–8; Eisenhower to Churchill, July 7, 1954, in *Churchill-Eisenhower Correspondence*, ed. Boyle, 153–4.

23. Steininger, "The EDC and the German Question," 103–8.

24. France finally ratified the accords in March 1955.

25. Eisenhower to Churchill, December 14, 1954, in *Churchill-Eisenhower Correspondence*, ed. Boyle, 181–2; Department of State to Embassy in France, January 8, 1955, *FRUS, 1955–57*, V, 119–20; Department of State to the Office of the High Commissioner for Germany, January 19, 1955, ibid., 128.

form. They were now settled, and the Offshore Islands crisis added im-
petus to do more. French prime minister Pierre Mendès-France and his
successor, Edgar Faure, both became champions of a four-power meeting. Konrad Adenauer did as well, after a Soviet invitation for the West
German chancellor to visit Moscow to discuss establishing relations
raised the fear of a unilateral offer to unify Germany that he could not
easily refuse. Even Anthony Eden, "fighting for his political life" after
Churchill's retirement, reversed his position and campaigned that the
"right moment" for a summit had arrived.[26]

Eisenhower and Dulles did what they could to resist the momentum
while maintaining Allied unity. A summit would be reckless, they still
counseled, until the Paris accords were set in stone, and useless until
the Soviets resigned themselves to that reality. It was because of this
latter criterion that the Soviet decision to drop its objections to an
Austrian treaty proved so decisive. That doing so accomplished another
of Eisenhower's deeds—and in CIA director Allen Dulles's opinion
"constituted the first substantial concession to the West in Europe
since the end of the war"—was but part of the reason. More fundamentally, as the administration's ambassador in Moscow, Charles Bohlen,
argued, the Soviets' offer to withdraw from Austria with only the guarantee of Austria's neutrality reflected "their recognition that rearmament of Western Germany cannot be stopped." Hence they sought to
ensure that Austria did not follow the FRG into NATO.[27]

Neither Eisenhower nor Dulles (nor Llewellyn Thompson, High
Commissioner to Austria and Soviet expert) was as sanguine as Bohlen.[28] But after the Senate Foreign Relations Committee's Walter

26. Dulles to Department of State, May 9, 1955, *FRUS, 1955–57*, V, 174–5; Embassy in
France to Department of State, January 16, 1955, *FRUS, 1955–57*, XVII, 126–7; Embassy in
France to Department of State, March 22, 1955, *FRUS, 1955–57*, V, 134–5; memorandum
of conversation, June 13, 1955, ibid., 224; memorandum of conversation, April 1, 1955,
ibid., 137; Eden, *Full Circle*, 320. For further analyses of the Europeans' positions, see the
essays in this volume by Colette Barbier, Eckart Conze, and Antonio Varsori.

27. Office of the High Commissioner for Austria to the Department of State, February
26, 1955, *FRUS, 1955–57*, V, 4; memorandum of NSC meeting of April 21, 1955, "245th
Meeting of the NSC," NSC Series, Ann Whitman File, DDEL; Embassy in the Soviet Union
to the Department of State, March 25, 1955, ibid., 14–6. For a succinct summary of the Soviet initiative in February and the resultant Austrian State Treaty, see John Van Oudenaren,
Detente in Europe: The Soviet Union and the West since 1953 (Durham, 1991), 31–5.

28. Memorandum of conversation, March 25, 1955, *FRUS, 1955–57*, V, 17–8; memorandum of NSC discussion, April 21, 1955, ibid., 53. See also Günter Bischof, "Eisenhower,
the Summit, and the Austrian Treaty, 1953–1955," in *Eisenhower: A Centenary Assessment*, ed. Günter Bischof and Stephen E. Ambrose (Baton Rouge, 1995), 157.

George joined the European chorus, the president, "not wishing to appear senselessly stubborn in my attitude," announced he now favored "exploratory talks." And once Faure pledged to deposit the French instruments for ratifying the Paris accords in early May 1955, Eisenhower agreed to begin joint planning for a meeting with the Soviets. In the interest of Allied unity, moreover, he eventually abandoned efforts to keep the meeting below the heads-of-state level (one suggestion had been that Vice-President Richard Nixon represent the United States). At the Vienna meeting to sign the Austrian State Treaty in mid-May, the United States, Britain, and France invited the Soviets to a summit. Prior to it the foreign ministers would meet to discuss procedures, and they would meet again immediately afterward to develop a process for sustained negotiations. After an exchange of notes, the four powers agreed to convene in Geneva in July.[29]

A Divided Administration

At once the administration began to formulate its strategy and objectives, and at once it became clear that its unity in resisting the summit masked the same acute difference in perspectives and priorities that had driven the fierce debates throughout 1953. All concurred on the need to dampen Western expectations and to limit discussion of Far Eastern problems to the greatest extent possible. But whether the United States should seek to accomplish anything of substance that might reduce cold-war tensions—especially, but not exclusively, because of Allied interest in doing so—became an intensely contested question.

Not all issues evoked much dispute. Indeed, agreement was readily achieved on the central problem of Germany. Had Washington had its druthers, German reunification would have been excluded from the summit's agenda; it would come about inevitably from the situation of strength produced by finally anchoring the FRG to the West. To allow the Soviets to resuscitate neutralization and disarmament schemes

29. *New York Times*, March 21, 1955, p.1; Dwight D. Eisenhower, *Mandate for Change* (Garden City, N.Y., 1963), 506; President's News Conference of March 23, 1955, *Public Papers of the Presidents: Dwight D. Eisenhower, 1955* (Washington, D.C., 1959), 351–5 (hereinafter cited as *PPP*); Dulles to Embassy in France, April 15, 1955, *FRUS, 1955–57*, V, 143–4; Eisenhower to Eden transmitted through Dulles to Makins, May 6, 1955, ibid., 162–3; Dulles to Department of State, May 8, 1955 (Dulte 3 and Dulte 4), ibid., 170–2; Dulles to Department of State, May 9, 1955 (Dulte 12 and 13), ibid., 174–5, 176; editorial note, ibid., 179; Harold MacMillan, *Tides of Fortune, 1945–1955* (New York, 1969), 586–600.

would only muddle the process and risk undermining the fragile harmony produced by the Paris accords to boot.[30]

That harmony would be more gravely and immediately threatened, however, if the United States rejected allied—especially British and West German—appeals to "manifest clearly its intent to continue to work for German unity" by promoting "the process of negotiations toward this end." Therefore the U.S. had to support discussing the "German question" at Geneva. But the discussions should be based on the Eden plan in order to yield the same outcome that had been planned when the issue was addressed at Berlin: a freely elected national assembly to draft a constitution for a unified Germany. The problem was that the British prime minister wanted more. Eden revised his plan according to the proposition that the Soviets could be induced to accept German reunification by linking it to an arms-control regime that enveloped NATO and the Warsaw Pact and a demilitarized zone dividing the forces.[31]

The new Eden plan, Eisenhower and his advisers concurred, required the United States to aim in Geneva at thwarting any Western or Soviet initiatives that projected a mechanism for German reunification beyond free elections. Dulles's suggestion in late 1953 that Eisenhower consider a mutual Soviet-American withdrawal of forces had already generated a consensus on the inherent dangers to free-world security and cohesion of any plan that the Kremlin could manipulate to raise doubts about America's continued military presence in Europe. Back then, moreover, Dulles had been prompted by fears that Allied resolve could not withstand a relative *decrease* in Western strength. He now feared that owing to still insufficient Allied resolve, the West would waste the opportunity to exploit its relative *increase* in strength.[32]

Dulles's primary objective for the summit was to put this increased strength to use. He had long predicted that the burden of trying to match the West's buildup would prove too great for the Soviets. Badly overextended and recognizing that its industrial base was insufficient to

30. Memorandum of conversation in the Department of State, May 20, 1955, *FRUS, 1955–57*, V, 191–2.

31. Ibid.; memorandum of conversation, July 1, 1955, *FRUS, 1955–57*, V, 253–8; paper prepared by the British Foreign Office, n.d., ibid., 261–2; Eden, *Full Circle*, 324–5, 335–6. Later in this volume Saki Dockrill provides the most sophisticated analysis available of the "new" Eden Plan.

32. Memorandum by Douglas MacArthur II, June 2, 1955, *FRUS, 1955–57*, V, 210–2.

"provide both guns and butter," the Kremlin leadership had perforce "cut out the butter." Thus, it was now besieged by demands from domestic and client constituencies. At Geneva, therefore, it hoped to stem the bleeding by negotiating a respite from the cold-war competition. The West's response, Dulles insisted, should be "to press the Soviets hard now" and not "give them the relief that they seek." A "policy of pressures can increase the gap between their requirements and their resources," he was confident, and "lead to [the empire's] disintegration."[33]

Assuming that there would be Soviet proposals cleverly designed to produce an environment of "sweetness and light," how to reject them without the allies breaking ranks was for Dulles the crucial question. His answer was to steer the talks away from substantive issues. For example, optimistic that momentum toward a unified Germany tied to the West was not irreversible, he wanted to defer concrete plans for reunification to subsequent, lower-level meetings. Thus, at the summit the United States would be freed to focus on matters of "principle" which the entire West agreed were nonnegotiable. Specifically, Dulles opined, America's principal aim should be to "raise very affirmatively the issues of freedom for the Soviet satellites and the activities of the international Communist movement." Doing so would fan the flames of discontent throughout the Eastern bloc, perhaps to the extent that the beleaguered regime would be forced to grant its subjects "a status not unlike that of Finland." In sum, Dulles's agenda for the summit was not to settle outstanding problems of war and peace, but to lay the foundation for future progress toward the retraction or rollback of Soviet power. The "big idea," he explained, was "to get the Russians out of the satellite states. . . . Now for the first time this is in the realm of possibility."[34]

Eisenhower did not, of course, object to stressing Soviet suppression of individual and national liberties. He was resolutely committed to liberating captive peoples so long as the risk of general war remained acceptably low. Moreover, he was no more eager than Dulles to address thorny issues such as German reunification while the Soviets still had significant cards to play. Thus, with uncharacteristically brief discus-

33. Memorandum of conversation, February 10, 1955, *FRUS, 1955–57*, II, 253–4, 257–8; memorandum of conversation, June 13, 1955, *FRUS, 1955–57*, V, 226–7.

34. Memorandum of conversation, July 5, 1955, *FRUS, 1955–57*, V, 262–6; Dulles memorandum to Eisenhower, June 18, 1955, ibid., 240; memorandum of conversation, May 20, 1955, ibid., 192; memorandum of NSC discussion, May 19, 1955, ibid., 184–8.

sion, the NSC agreed that at Geneva the United States would "maintain the position that Soviet control of the satellites is one of the principal causes of world tension," would "tax the Soviet leaders for their responsibility for this obstacle to international relaxation," and would "seek every opportunity to weaken or break the Soviet grip on part or all of the satellite area." As for German reunification, the "basic policy on a Germany settlement" would be to support the "essential substance" of the Eden plan as originally proposed at Berlin. Further, "to assure that present arrangements based on the Federal Republic's adherence to NATO and its contribution thereto are not prejudiced by Soviet or other blocking tactics," the United States would agree only that proposals that combined German reunification with European regional security arrangements were appropriate for future "study."[35]

When the administration tried to fashion a position on arms control, however, the president's different priorities resurfaced. In his speech following Stalin's death, Eisenhower's sweeping proposal to limit nuclear weapons had reflected his profound belief that the East and West shared an interest in containing defense spending as well as avoiding a suicidal catastrophe. His belief was unshaken by the Soviets' failure to respond positively to his initiative, and in December 1953 he had delivered another speech, this one titled "Atoms for Peace." Eisenhower had personally conceived its premise: the United States and Soviet Union would contribute to an atomic-energy pool supervised by the United Nations and dedicated to peaceful purposes. My "basic idea," he explained to his brother, was that "possibly a gradual approach would open up new possibilities, new lines of study."[36]

Although this tack had also proved futile, Eisenhower remained convinced that limited measures could open the way for more significant restraints by eroding the Soviet obsession with secrecy. With nothing to show for his initial efforts, he shifted his emphasis to devising methods of verification that the Kremlin might accept. These methods could not be foolproof. But they might be adequate if further progress toward safe-

---

35. NSC 5524/1, Basic U.S. Policy in Relation to Four-Power Negotiations, July 11, 1955, ibid., 292–6; Ronald W. Pruessen, "Beyond the Cold War—Again: 1955 and the 1990s," *Political Science Quarterly*, CVIII (1993), 66–73.

36. Eisenhower address to the UN General Assembly, December 8, 1953, *PPP, Eisenhower, 1953*, 813–22; Robert Cutler memorandum, September 10, 1953, *FRUS, 1952–54*, II, 1213; Eisenhower to Milton Eisenhower, December 11, 1953, "Atoms for Peace," Administrative Series, Whitman File.

guarding the U.S. industrial base and second-strike capability made the risks of their violation less than those of uncontrolled arms racing. Proposals should therefore be evaluated according to this criterion. Eisenhower's bottom line, he made clear at the start of 1954, was that there could be "no final answer to the problem of nuclear warfare if both sides simply went ahead making bigger and better nuclear weapons."[37]

Eisenhower's chief advisers disagreed. Believing that the answer to the problem of nuclear war lay in the collapse of the Communist system, Dulles viewed even limited measures of restraint as counterproductive because they would relieve the pressure on the Soviets to compete economically and militarily with the West. And the JCS viewed them as downright dangerous. On the one hand, the service chiefs continued to maintain, the growth of Soviet nuclear capabilities meant that in "a relatively short span of years" the United States will be placed in "such jeopardy as to render it doubtful that any military establishment which our country could continue to support could be relied upon to defend our territory and our institutions in the years ahead." On the other hand, "Soviet bad faith, evasion, and outright violation would render any disarmament agreement sterile." Thus the JCS reprised its argument that "while it still holds nuclear superiority," the United States's sole objective must be to confront the Kremlin with a choice between unilaterally conceding to Western demands on all "major issues" or facing "grave risks" to its survival.[38]

Throughout 1954 Eisenhower waged his battle against both perspectives. He argued that "we cannot hope to get continued support of public opinion in the free world if we always say 'no' to any suggestions that we negotiate with the Soviets." As for arms control specifically, "It was wrong for the U.S. merely to take a negative view of this terrible problem." Further: "No one in his right mind" could object to the administration's continuing to examine "its position on disarmament and especially to determine whether safeguards could be devised entailing less risk for U.S. security than no limitation of armaments." What was

37. Entry for December 10, 1953, *The Eisenhower Diaries*, ed. Robert H. Ferrell (New York, 1981), 261–2; Eisenhower to Captain E. E. "Swede" Hazlett, December 24, 1953, *FRUS, 1952–54*, II, 1309–10; memorandum of NSC discussion, May 27, 1954, ibid., 1455.

38. Memorandum by the JCS to Secretary of Defense Charles Wilson, June 23, 1954, *FRUS, 1952–54*, II, 680–6; memorandum by Wilson to the executive secretary of the NSC, November 22, 1954, ibid., 785–7; memorandum by the JCS to Wilson, December 17, 1954, ibid., 829.

required was "more imaginative thinking than was going on at present in this government."[39]

Deliberations in early 1955 produced no such thinking. The JCS position remained fixed: it was "not in the security interests of the United States to have any disarmament for the foreseeable future." Dulles was but slightly less categorical. The "greater military potential of the United States," he emphasized, "gives the United States its maximum bargaining power." Personally, he "doubted that the U.S. could work out any disarmament plan with a powerful nation which we did not trust and which we believed had most ambitious goals." The world, however, "would regard such a negative position as indication of U.S. desire to maintain its nuclear superiority or even as indication of U.S. intent to wage aggressive war." Thus for reasons of propaganda and Allied solidarity, Dulles thought it necessary to try to develop some initiative. But America "had to be extremely careful . . . not to walk into a trap."[40]

Dulles—not to mention the JCS—perceived Geneva as the supreme trap. On the day the Kremlin received the invitation to attend a summit, its representative to the Subcommittee of the United Nations Disarmament Commission proposed that negotiations begin on a comprehensive treaty for the "complete prohibition of the use and production of both nuclear and all other weapons of mass destruction," a "major reduction in all armed forces," and the "establishment of a control organ" to guarantee compliance. As a consequence, Dulles announced when the NSC first convened to plan for Geneva, it was certain that "the subject of disarmament would be among the most important matters on which the United States must be prepared for discussions at the conference." Further, because the proposal "had actually gone a long way to meet the British and French position," the discussions would be "hard to handle."[41]

Dulles had little else to contribute—except to stress what a good trap the Soviets had set. In his estimate, the Kremlin's "disarmament propa-

39. Memorandum of NSC discussion, December 21, 1954, *FRUS, 1952–54*, II, 843; memorandum of NSC discussion, May 27, 1954, ibid., 1455; memorandum of NSC discussion, June 24, 1954, ibid., 687–8.

40. Memorandum of conversation, January 4, 1955, *FRUS, 1955–57*, XX, 1–7; draft memorandum by Dulles, "Limitation of Armament," June 29, 1955, ibid., 140–2; memorandum of conversation, February 9, 1955, ibid., 15–20.

41. Editorial note, *FRUS, 1955–57*, XX, 76; memorandum of NSC discussion, May 19, 1955, *FRUS, 1955–57*, V, 183–4.

ganda" had generated popular backing for the Soviet Union's effort "to relieve itself of the economic burden of the present arms race." This was the last thing Dulles wanted. Yet if the United States appeared too inflexible, it risked "forfeiting the good will of our allies and the support of a large part of our own people." As a way to square the circle, Dulles could suggest only that the United States propose "tentative and exploratory" measures designed to divert attention from the Soviets' comprehensive proposals and preempt discussion of any alternative that aimed "quickly or radically to alter the present situation."[42]

The JCS's solution was typically less complicated: "the U.S. approach to the Geneva Conference should be based on the view that the position of the Soviet Union was weakening and that we should accordingly hold its feet to the fire." Hence regardless of Allied opinion, it should propose, support, or agree to nothing whatsoever related to arms control until the Soviets had conceded to the West's demands on political and territorial issues. The JCS's "firm view" remained that without "concrete evidence of a revolutionary change in the ambitions and intentions of the Soviet regime," it would be "better" to continue the "arms race than to enter an agreement with the Soviets."[43]

Eisenhower's patience ran out. How could the JCS "really believe" that a continually "mounting spiral" of arms racing and fear best served American and free-world security interests? he fumed. If this was in fact the case, he "wondered why they did not counsel that we go to war at once with the Soviet Union." He was only slightly more tolerant of Dulles's prescription. To the president there could be no higher priority than mitigating the nuclear predicament. Rather than stonewall, therefore, the United States should be "going to the Geneva Conference hoping to see if we could penetrate the veil of Soviet intentions," Eisenhower insisted. "Trust in the Lord but keep your powder dry" had to be America's motto. But "to find out what these Soviet villains will do [in order for the U.S.] to find out what could be achieved by way of an acceptable inspections system" had to be the chief objective.[44]

42. Dulles memorandum to Eisenhower, June 18, 1955, *FRUS, 1955–57*, V, 239; draft memorandum by Dulles, June 29, 1955, *FRUS, 1955–57*, XX, 140–2.

43. Memorandum of NSC meeting, July 7, 1955, *FRUS, 1955–57*, V, 268–72; memorandum from JCS to Secretary of Defense, June 16, 1955, *FRUS, 1955–57*, XX, 122–5; memorandum of NSC discussion, June 30, 1955, ibid., 145.

44. Memorandum of NSC discussion, June 30, 1955, *FRUS, 1955–57*, XX, 148–52; memorandum of NSC discussion, July 7, 1955, *FRUS, 1955–57*, V, 269–72.

It was for this purpose more than any other that Eisenhower reached out beyond the NSC and appropriated the "Open Skies" plan for a system of reciprocal Soviet and American aerial surveillance. Indeed, over the objections of his primary advisers, the president made the plan the centerpiece of his Geneva strategy. Like Dulles and the JCS, Eisenhower only reluctantly agreed to the 1955 summit and expected not much to come of it. Unlike them, however, he was disappointed that it accomplished so little. As with his "Chance for Peace" and "Atoms for Peace" speeches, Open Skies was not simply another shot in the psychological war but reflected the president's genuine conviction that both because of and despite East-West distrust and hostility, the effort must be made to try to control nuclear weapons. But Open Skies was an effort born of despair and frustration, and Eisenhower received no help from within his own administration, let alone from the Soviets. Therefore his hope that at Geneva he might "open a tiny gate in the disarmament fence" was destined to fail.[45]

45. Eisenhower quoted in Walt W. Rostow, *Open Skies: Eisenhower's Proposal of July 21, 1955* (Austin, 1982), xi–xii. Rostow's "memoir," which highlights Eisenhower's differences with the "Quantico Vulnerabilities Panel" (who formulated the proposal) as well as the NSC, remains the most comprehensive examination of the Open Skies initiative. For a more rigorous analysis, see John Prados's essay in this volume.

Soviet Policy Aims at the Geneva Conference, 1955

VLADISLAV M. ZUBOK

The Geneva Conference of July 1955 marked the first attempt of the Soviet leadership since the beginning of the cold war to develop the new approaches to the West that later became known as "détente." Stalin's death triggered far-reaching changes in Soviet foreign policy that peaked in 1955 and early 1956. Elsewhere I have argued that these changes were not an expression of a new political thinking or strategy on the part of Stalin's successors.[1] The biggest factors in this transformation were the crisis of Stalin's political methods in both the domestic and foreign domains and the power struggle in the Kremlin. The interplay of these two factors gave the transformation a zigzag trajectory. On the one hand, the contenders inside the Kremlin had to respond to the signs of trouble in domestic and foreign policy and vie for better, more effective ways to alleviate the problems. On the other hand, they were constrained by the Stalin cult and official ideology that still remained the sources of legitimacy for themselves and the legions of Soviet elite.

The dilemma that faced the Kremlin rulers after Stalin can be defined very simply: they could not afford to continue the cold war in the same way that Stalin had done, but they did not dream of dismantling the mechanisms and rules he had established. Those few in the Kremlin who were in a position to deal with foreign policy after Stalin's death, even the most dogmatic among them, lacked Stalin's strategic audacity, terrifying will, and authority to continue the game of chicken with the United States. Immediately after Stalin's death, the new leaders agreed with the Chinese and Korean position on the necessity of ending the Korean War as soon as possible. Also, the Soviet Union dropped territorial claims on Turkey and restored diplomatic relations with Israel. The most notable departure from the war scare of Stalin's days was the ap-

1. Vladislav M. Zubok, "Soviet Intelligence and the Cold War: The 'Small' Committee of Information, 1952–1953, "*Diplomatic History,* XIX (1995), 471.

peal for negotiations made by Malenkov on 18 March 1953. He repeated
it on 8 August: "We consider that there is no objective grounds for a col-
lision between the United States and the USSR."[2]

Yet at the same time, Stalin's legacy looked unassailable. The rest of
the leadership still leaned on the established dogmas, regarded Stalin as
an infallible leader, and feared that any distancing from his principles
might lead to collapse or be used by the enemy. Khrushchev, reflecting
this mood, recalled: "In the days leading up to Stalin's death we believed that America would invade the Soviet Union and we would go to
war."[3] Even as the core leadership began to fall apart in the power struggle and some foreign-policy questions became issues of disagreement
and even open dispute, this fear of losing "unity" made all sides cling to
the Marxist-Leninist dogmas as the tool of cohesion.

The restoration of the authority of Vyacheslav Molotov in the shaping of Soviet foreign policy after Beria's arrest contributed to stagnation
of Soviet policy with regard to Germany, Austria, Yugoslavia, and Iran.
A most significant result of the triumph of the orthodox line in the aftermath of the Beria affair was a new determination in the Kremlin to
build a "socialist" German Democratic Republic and to reorient Soviet
foreign policy from the vision (however disingenuous) of a unified, democratic Germany toward attempts to confirm the separate existence of
two German states. Molotov regarded the bipolar division of Europe inherited from the era of Stalin as an immovable status quo. "We cannot
afford to withdraw Soviet troops from Austria," echoed a secret memorandum from senior diplomats in November 1953, "since it would actually mean placing Austria in the hands of the Americans and weakening
our positions in Central and South-Eastern Europe."[4]

The conflict between two trends, toward forced abandonment of Stalin's extremes in foreign policy and toward a search for ideological and
geopolitical cohesion domestically as well as within the Communist
camp, continued into 1954 and was not resolved by the time the Geneva
summit took place.

2. *Izvestiia*, 9 August 1953.
3. Nikita S. Khrushchev, *Khrushchev Remembers: The Glasnost Tapes*, trans. and ed.
Jerrold L. Schechter and Vyacheslav V. Luchkov (Boston, 1990), 100–1.
4. Pushkin, Ilyichev, and Gribanov, top secret draft memorandum to V. M. Molotov, 27
November 1953, Archive of Foreign Policy of the Russian Federation [hereinafter cited as
AVPRF], fond 12a (Molotov's secretariat), papka 46, delo 191, 2–3.

Who Will Talk with the West?

Summits with the leaders of great powers served as an important source of authority and legitimacy for the Soviet leaders from Stalin to Gorbachev. Anyone meeting with Western leaders, in the view of the majority, had to possess special qualities, to be perceptive enough to see through the adversaries' designs. Therefore, the planning for a summit was always intimately related to the domestic power structure and the struggle for preeminence inside the Kremlin. An early summit, as proposed by Winston Churchill in May 1953, would have undermined Molotov's monopoly on the handling of foreign affairs and promoted the authority of Malenkov. At the end of 1954, however, as the prospect of a summit became more likely, Khrushchev began to argue before the other members of the Party Presidium that Malenkov would not be sufficiently tough to succeed in future negotiations with the West. It was an important argument that, among others, led the Presidium and the Central Committee Plenum on 31 January 1955 to dismiss Malenkov as prime minister and replace him with Nikolai Bulganin, a friend and protégé of Khrushchev's. Speaking at the Plenum, Khrushchev recalled sharing with Molotov his fears that "Churchill is overeager to have a summit, and I am afraid, that if he comes [to Moscow] and talks with Malenkov tête-a-tête, then Malenkov would be scared, and give up." In his memoirs Khrushchev repeated this argument: "We had to replace Malenkov. The talks in Geneva required another kind of person."[5]

After 1954, Molotov's dominance in foreign affairs began to fade. Khrushchev quickly found out that Molotov did not tolerate any interference in his conduct of diplomacy, and this intransigence only strengthened Khrushchev's desire to challenge his monopoly. The arena for the struggle for supremacy between the two was the February–April 1955 talks on Austrian neutrality, and the first round ended in a complete political victory for Khrushchev. The documents on this issue stored in the Archive of Foreign Policy of Russian Federation support the Kremlinological intuition of Vojtech Mastny, who argued that the power struggle was the single most crucial factor in formulation of So-

---

5. Plenum of 25–31 January 1955, Protocol no. 7, Storage Center for Contemporary Documentation [hereinafter cited as TsKhSD], fond 2, opis 1, delo 127, p. 45; "Memuari Nikiti Sergeevicha Khrushcheva," *Voprosi istorii*, VIII–IX (1992), 70.

viet foreign policy aims at that time.[6] On several occasions Khrushchev, supported by the majority, prevailed in the Presidium over Molotov's objections and proposed concessions that ensured a bilateral compromise with the Austrians. Finding an opportune moment, Khrushchev instructed the diplomats from the Soviet Ministry of Foreign Affairs that they should not, from then on, regard Molotov as a supreme Soviet statesman but instead take their guidelines from the first secretary of the Party.[7]

Khrushchev's trip to Yugoslavia from 26 May to 2 June 1955 dealt a final blow to the authority of Molotov in foreign affairs. At the Party Plenary meeting of 4–12 July 1955, just on the eve of the trip to Geneva, Khrushchev and his followers passed a resolution "denouncing the politically erroneous position of com. Molotov on the Yugoslav question. . . . The position of com. Molotov led to confirmation of abnormal relations with Yugoslavia and to pushing Yugoslavia further toward the imperialist camp." During the heated debates with Molotov, Khrushchev challenged the overall sanctity of Stalin-Molotov foreign policy (still without blaming Stalin directly). Khrushchev said that "a number of erroneous steps helped mobilize people against us. We started the Korean war. . . . And now we cannot sort it out" even two years after the war was over. "Who needed that war?" Khrushchev visualized Yugoslavia, at the minimum, as a neutral buffer in addition to Austria between the two hostile blocs, and at the maximum, as a future ally. Molotov feared the spread of Titoism over Eastern Europe and insisted on the development of relations with Yugoslavia only as another bourgeois state.[8]

Some political scientists link Khrushchev's ascendancy to the fact that he "could offer much better prospects" than other leaders "for avoiding war and easing tensions without offering concessions that would compromise the Soviet Union's socialist identity or weaken So-

6. Vojtech Mastny, "Kremlin Politics and the Austrian Settlement." *Problems of Communism,* XXXI (1982), 41. See also Günter Bischof, "Eisenhower, the Summit, and the Austrian Treaty, 1953–1955" in Günter Bischof and Stephen E. Ambrose, eds., *Eisenhower: A Centenary Assessment* (Baton Rouge, 1995), 150–8.

7. Vladislav M. Zubok, "Soviet Foreign Policy in Germany and Austria and the Post-Stalin Succession Struggle, 1953–1955," paper prepared for conference "The Soviet Union, Germany, and the Cold War, 1945–1962: New Evidence from Eastern Archives," Essen, Germany, June 28–30, 1994, pp. 21–4.

8. *Istoricheskii arkhiv,* IV (1993), 77; The Plenum of CC CPSU, 4–12 July 1955, Stenographic report of the discussion of Khrushchev's report, July 9, 1955, TsKhSD, fond 2, opis 1, delo 158, 29.

viet military strength."[9] One should not, however, fall into the temptation to see Khrushchev's victory as a result of some deliberate strategy
in international affairs. Rather, the dynamics of the power struggle
pushed Khrushchev to intervene in foreign policy, with dramatic results
that nobody, including himself, expected. Khrushchev, the victor in the
power struggle, was even less receptive than Molotov to complex policy
arguments and information that went beyond what he already knew or
had digested. This may sound paradoxical in light of his innovative role,
but the evidence, particularly oral history interviews, indicates that the
new Soviet leader never quite grasped the strategic and doctrinal intri-
cacies of foreign policy.

Khrushchev's biggest advantage was that past experience did not tie
his hands and clog his mind. It is doubtful that he had ever read Lenin's
works on imperialism that shaped so much the perceptions of Stalin
and Molotov. His crude perceptions and simple, yet persuasive, solutions increased his appeal to the Soviet elites who were completely ig-
norant of the world's realities and the nuances of international
relations. It is no surprise, then, that Khrushchev's set of beliefs, combined with his shrewdness and bold schemes, prevailed over Molotov's
dogmatic "Marxist-Leninist" logic in the Presidium discussions and
eventually made him the most forceful speaker in the Kremlin on the
issues of international affairs.

Perceptions of Confrontation with the West

The Soviet leaders were heirs to the great victory in the Second World
War, and they never wavered in their conviction that all Soviet postwar
aims and conquests had been justified and dictated by purely peaceful,
defensive needs. The strong consensus among them was that the USSR
had been wronged, mistreated by the United States since late 1945, and
that the cold war was a continuation of the policies of isolation, nonrecognition, and intervention that the West had pursued against Soviet
Russia since 1917. Khrushchev, in particular, passionately believed that
Soviet expansion of 1939–1945 into the heart of Europe fulfilled Communist dreams and "saved" the occupied peoples from the "capitalist
yoke."

9. James Richter, *Khrushchev's Double Bind: International Pressures and Domestic
Coalition Politics* (Baltimore, 1994), 68–9.

For all that, Khrushchev and his group were not ideologists: they were mostly state leaders and bureaucrats, economic managers *(khoziaist-venniki)* accustomed to fixing specific problems in specific ways. Sharing an ideologized picture of the world, they nevertheless searched for elements of hope in it, expecting to "fix" the cold war through some kind of settlement with capitalist leaders. Khrushchev seemed to believe that the rigid and belligerent policies of Molotov, Beria, and perhaps Stalin himself played into American hands: "We caught ourselves on the [U.S.] hook." Marshal Georgi Zhukov, Soviet deputy minister of defense and a staunch Khrushchev ally in the rivalry with Molotov and Malenkov, acknowledged in a private talk with Eisenhower at Geneva that both sides had made mistakes in the past, perhaps "because there was wrong information."[10]

The impact of the nuclear revolution on the Soviet perceptions of security and of the cold war is a large topic that I have approached elsewhere.[11] By 1955, nuclear weapons had already begun to change the attitudes of the Kremlin leaders toward the basic question of Soviet security—the probability of war with the United States. The possibility of such a war had been on the minds of the Presidium members. The American rhetoric of rollback, and, later, John Foster Dulles's early-1954 talk of "massive retaliation" created a mood of vigilance and tension in the Kremlin. Khrushchev and Molotov reflected this mood from March 1954–January 1955, when they roundly criticized Malenkov's assertion that the nuclear arms race might lead to a catastrophe for both sides, perhaps to "the end of civilization." Molotov called this idea "theoretically mistaken and politically harmful," and Khrushchev agreed.[12]

There are reasons to think that Khrushchev began to realize quite early that the nuclear revolution made a global war unthinkable. However, the question remained: Did the enemy think so, too? In September 1954, after the Central Committee had received the reports of the mili-

10. *Voprosi istorii,* IX–X (1991), 82, 84, 85; Zapis besedi (memorandum), meeting between G. K. Zhukov and President D. Eisenhower, 20 July 1955, TsKhSD, fond 5, opis 30, delo 116, 122–3. For the U.S. record of this conversation, see *FRUS, 1955–1957,* V, 408–18.
11. See Yuri Smirnov and Vladislav Zubok, "Nuclear Weapons after Stalin's Death: Moscow Enters the H-Bomb Age," *CWIHP Bulletin,* IV (1994), 14–5; also David Holloway, *Stalin and the Bomb: The Soviet Union and Atomic Energy, 1939–1956* (New Haven, 1994), 320–63.
12. Resolution of the Presidium "About com. Malenkov G. M." TsKhSD, fond 2, opis 1, delo 116, 5; Holloway, *Stalin and the Bomb,* 321–2.

tary exercise at Totskoye, where the atomic bomb was used for the first time for training troops, the Secretariat passed a decision to construct underground command posts for executive officials of the defense ministry and the top leadership.[13] For Khrushchev and his colleagues, the foreign policy of Eisenhower-Dulles was based on nuclear blackmail, but neither Khrushchev nor any of his military and political allies could say with certainty how far the Americans were ready to go in the direction of massive retaliation in response to crises or changes that affected their interests and positions in the world. Among the major policy aims of the Soviet delegation at Geneva was to learn more about this and, if possible, to demonstrate to American leaders that the USSR would not be intimidated by nuclear blackmail.

On balance, Khrushchev and the new leaders, for all their attempts at innovation, still acted in the shadow of Stalin and under the burden of a great inferiority complex. Oleg Troyanovsky, later a foreign-policy adviser to Khrushchev, recalled that "Khrushchev constantly feared that the United States would compel the Soviet Union and its allies to retreat in some region of the world." The direst scenario was that of a further NATO advance eastward. These fears colored Khrushchev's perception of the origins of the first post-Stalin summit. Khrushchev later recalled that Churchill's idea of a summit without definite agenda (May 1953) stemmed from the British prime minister's desire to apply pressure on the post-Stalin leaders in order to squeeze some concessions while they were still weak and indecisive.[14] Only by mid-1955 had Khrushchev begun to feel more self-assured. The success of the Austrian treaty was highly important psychologically in that it gave Khrushchev sufficient confidence in his own statesmanship and liberated him from the excesses of spy-mania and xenophobia. A trip to Yugoslavia in May 1955 aimed at reconciliation with Tito was equally important. The rapid progress of Soviet armaments programs, primarily nuclear and missile projects, also contributed to the new Soviet sense of strength.

Before and during the Geneva summit, Khrushchev, Bulganin, and

13. Alexander Volkov and Marina Kolesova, "Soviet Reaction to U.S. Nuclear Policy, 1953–1962," paper presented at the "Conference on New Evidence on the Cold War History," Moscow, January 1993, pp. 6–9.

14. Oleg A. Troyanovsky, "Nikita Khrushchev and the Making of Soviet Foreign Policy," paper presented at the Khrushchev Centenary Conference, Brown University, 1–3 December 1994, p. 38; *Voprosi istorii*, VIII–IX (1992), 69.

Zhukov drummed the theme of unity into the Soviet leadership. During his meeting with Eisenhower, Zhukov recalled Western expectations that the post-Stalin leadership would not survive. He said those expectations had proved to be false, and claimed that the new leadership was more broad-based and efficient than the old. The determination to overcome the inferiority complex and prove to the country, the world, and themselves that they could deal with the Western powers without being intimidated became, in a sense, the most important political goal that the post-Stalin leaders set on the eve of the Geneva summit.[15]

Toward a "New Foreign Policy"

The preoccupation of Khrushchev and his followers with domestic and international prestige overshadowed the tasks of diplomacy in its proper sense—that is, as a technique of dealing with other states' governments, public opinion, and so on. Yet these tasks existed and can be summed up. Troyanovsky even went so far as claim that "the Kremlin was conducting a completely new foreign policy as compared to that pursued in Stalin's later years."[16]

Even before they introduced any changes in the doctrinal foundation of Soviet foreign policy, the new leaders began to look back for guidance to the experience of the Grand Alliance and the still vivid memories of the 1930s, when the Soviet leadership had managed to attract large Western investments and technological assistance, capitalizing on the interest in new and vast Russian markets. Khrushchev and Mikoyan hoped that something similar might happen again once the tension of the cold war began to subside. According to several recollections, the Kremlin leaders naïvely expected that crowds of capitalists would stand in line at the doors of Soviet embassies in Washington, Berlin, and Tokyo. Later Khrushchev himself admitted the mistake: "We then exaggerated a possibility of achieving mutual understanding [with the West]. We considered that after such a bloody war that we had waged together with the Allies against Germany, we could find a reasonable basis for an agreement."[17] What was really exaggerated was the potential of capital-

15. *FRUS, 1955–57*, V, 259, 417–8. James Richter analyzed the same political aim from another angle, see *Khrushchev's Double Bind*, 71.

16. Troyanovsky, "Nikita Khrushchev and the Making of Soviet Foreign Policy," 7.

17. Interviews with Oleg Troyanovsky and Rostislav Sergeev, Moscow, May 1994; *Voprosi istorii*, VIII–IX (1992), 69.

ist rivalry for the new market and of Soviet economic leverage with the West.

More serious, and more exploited, was another approach—the encouragement of Western European neutralism. According to the late Andrei Alexandrov-Agentov, a veteran "Europeanist" in the Ministry of Foreign Affairs, the Khrushchev leadership came to rely on a new approach to European problems. It consisted of "three main elements: to consolidate to the maximum and tie to the Soviet Union the countries of People's Democracy of Eastern and Central Europe; to create, wherever possible, a neutral 'buffer' between the two opposing military-political blocs; and to gradually establish economic and other more or less normal forms of peaceful cooperation with the countries of NATO." The concept of neutralism in this strategy served the purpose of "prevention of further expansion of the zone [of influence] of NATO in Europe."[18]

The Soviet disarmament initiatives in preparation for the Geneva conference were, in part, a spin-off of the army's modernization and introduction of nuclear armaments as integral part of the firepower of the Soviet armed forces. Reduction of the army corresponded to Khrushchev's plans of using the youngest men possible for the tasks of economic construction. In July 1955 the CC Presidium sanctioned a troop reduction of 640,000 men. Earlier, on 10 May 1955, the Soviet Union agreed, to the surprise of many in the West, to lower the ceilings of conventional forces in Europe in the mode proposed in 1954 by Great Britain and France, and to establish a system of inspection at the military "choke-points" (railroads, airports, and the like) to reduce fears of a surprise conventional attack. In the annals of the post–World War II Soviet diplomacy this package became the first serious effort to negotiate the reduction of conventional forces in Europe. The most recent evidence, however, reveals that the Soviet leaders were still more concerned about maximizing the propaganda effect; their initiatives were designed to reduce Western Europeans' fears of a Soviet *Blitzkrieg*. The fact that all reductions were linked to the prohibition of nuclear weapons guaranteed the failure of the plan, a reality the Kremlin leaders knew all too well. Even before the announcement of the initiatives, they confidentially informed their Chinese "friends" that there was no danger that Western controllers would inundate the Soviet secret installations, be-

18. A. M. Alexandrov-Agentov, *Ot Kollontai do Gorbacheva* (Moscow, 1994), 93, 94.

cause the "Anglo-American bloc will not agree to eliminate atomic weapons and to ban the production of these weapons."[19]

In March 1956 Khrushchev, in conversation with Hans-Christian Hansen, prime minister of Denmark, said that after Stalin's death the Soviets "convincingly proved our peace making nature, and we will continue to prove it. Thereby we will shake NATO loose. We will continue to reduce armed forces unilaterally." Then, Khrushchev concluded, "you will find it hard to justify NATO before public opinion."[20] The seeds of this approach can be found in Khrushchev's vigorous diplomacy at the time of the Geneva summit.

Troyanovsky recalled that Khrushchev had always returned to Eisenhower's speech of 16 April 1953, when the U.S. president had addressed Stalin's successors with an appeal to part with Stalin's ways. The Presidium members characterized the speech as an "ultimatum," but Khrushchev remembered "four conditions" set forth by the president— truce in Korea, treaty with Austria, and return of German and Japanese POWs—to be followed by steps to disarmament. By the summer of 1955, from Khrushchev's viewpoint, the Soviet government had met all Eisenhower's conditions and introduced much more far-reaching and constructive disarmament initiatives than Washington. By the summer of 1955 the "new foreign policy" began to change world opinion about the Soviet Union. The Eisenhower administration faced the need to reconsider its long-term policy of resistance to any top-level contacts with the Communist leaders. As John Foster Dulles noted ruefully after the Geneva summit, "we never wanted to go to Geneva, but . . . the pressure of people of the world forced us to do so." There, the Soviet diplomacy shook the American leadership out of its comfortable position of moral superiority and nonrecognition of the Kremlin as a negotiating partner.[21]

19. Richter, *Khrushchev's Double Bind*, 60; Vladislav M. Zubok, "Nebo nad sverkhderzhavami" ("Ski over the superpowers"), *SshA: Ekonomika, politika, ideologiya*, VII (July 1990), 47–55; Zapis besedi N. A. Bulganina s Poslom KNR v SSSR Liu Qiao (memorandum of conversation between Bulganin and the Ambassador of the PRC in the USSR Liu Qiao), 19 March 1955, TsKhSD, fond 5, opis 30, delo 116, 19.

20. Zapis besedi Bulganina, Khrushcheva, Mikoiana I Molotov s premier-ministrom I ministrom inostrannikh del Danii Khansenom (memorandum of conversation of Bulganin, Khrushchev, Mikoyan and Molotov with prime minister and minister of foreign affairs of Denmark Hansen), 5 March 1956, TsKhSD, fond 5, opis 30, delo 163, 33.

21. Troyanovsky, "Nikita Khrushchev and the Making of Soviet Foreign Policy," 5; 256th NSC Meeting, 28 July 1955, *FRUS, 1955–57*, V, 534.

The Division of Germany and the "Chinese Factor"

When it became clear that the Western governments had agreed to meet with the Soviet leaders in Geneva, the top issues on the Soviet foreign-policy agenda were the prospects of security in Europe and the division of Germany. In the long-term perspective, the Kremlin wanted to avoid the combination of U.S. nuclear might (as well as general superiority in military technology) and the rearmed Western Germany as the chief suppliers of the conventional armed power of NATO.

From the Kremlin's perspective, on the political, diplomatic and propaganda fronts the Western powers had been on the offensive since the fall of 1953. Those powers had agreed on the plan of German reunification (the Eden plan) and presented it at the Berlin conference of foreign ministers in January 1954. The plan as it stood was very appealing to the Germans but totally unacceptable to the Soviet side, since it would lead in effect to West Germany's swallowing the GDR. At the same time intelligence reports and foreign-policy analysis since 1953 had persuaded the Kremlin that the Eisenhower-Dulles leadership's whole European strategy was set on the West German integration, and it was only a matter of time before that integration would take place.[22] The firm stance of West German chancellor Konrad Adenauer left no doubts in the Soviet minds that this unified Germany would remain a member of NATO, a new power bent on containing the USSR and even perhaps pushing back, by economic and diplomatic means, its sphere of influence in Eastern Europe.

The Soviet leadership expected that the new diplomacy, particularly the promotion of neutralism and the schemes of disengagements in Central Europe, would diminish the pace of West German integration into NATO. Also, the threat of German militarism, regardless of its negative long-term connotations, proved to be an effective tool in Soviet efforts to consolidate its sphere of influence in Eastern Europe and justify the presence of Soviet troops there through a series of political, and later even politico-legal arrangements (something that Stalin had not bothered too much about). In May 1955, when West Germany finally became a member of NATO, the Khrushchev leadership had created the Warsaw Treaty Organization—a formal political alliance between the USSR and its East European satellites. In the Soviet presentation of the WTO draft, an image of West German "revanchists" had a central

22. See my "Soviet Intelligence and the Cold War," 465–6.

place. They, Premier Bulganin said in Warsaw, "have gained opportunity to set down to an open creation of a cadre army and to supply it with all kinds of modern weapons, including atomic, chemical and bacteriological weapons. . . . German militarism . . . appears again on the European and international arena" and has become "the major hotbed of war danger in Europe." The political platform that the Soviets formulated for their alliance continued to proclaim an alternative of a unified Germany, as a "free, peaceful and democratic state." At the same time, the Paris accords, ratified in May 1955, allowed the Soviets to shirk responsibility for the obvious failure to move toward this goal. Bulganin, in the same speech, stressed that "the restoration of militarism in West Germany renders impossible a restoration of Germany's unity on the peaceful and democratic basis."[23]

Still, the Soviets understood that the discussion of German unity at the summit might turn to their disadvantage. To block a possible Western propaganda campaign on the issue, they were determined to discuss the "German question" only in the broader context of an all-European peace settlement, the dissolution of military blocs, and the creation of some kind of European security system. Such was the origin of the new Soviet position, which culminated in the 1970s in the signing of the Helsinki accords and had a spectacular rebirth in the late 1980s in the idea of the "common European house" promoted by Mikhail Gorbachev. From the viewpoint of Soviet security strategy, this linkage of the German settlement to the broader issue of European security was a considerable achievement: it strengthened the political and propagandist basis of the Soviet European diplomacy.

At the same time, it opened new opportunities for the bilateral Soviet–West German relations. Khrushchev and his closest foreign-policy adviser, Mikoyan, began to push for a rapprochement with those political and economic forces in West Germany that could challenge Adenauer's official course of eventual Anschluss of the GDR and nonrecognition of the new German borders in the East. Many in the Kremlin thought of (and many in the West were afraid of) a "new Rapallo"—a turnabout similar to the one during the Genoa peace conference in 1922. Various emissaries from Moscow met with leading figures from the SED, as well as the business elite, including Erich Ollenhauer and

23. Nikolai Bulganin to the CC CPSU, 7 May 1955; draft of speech of the leader of the Soviet delegation at the meeting in Warsaw, TsKhSD, fond 5, opis 30, delo 126, 50, 54.

the members of the Krupp family.[24] The Kremlin strategists hoped that a combination of pragmatic capitalists and well-intentioned Social Democrats could produce a sufficient deterrent for Adenauer's pro-Western course.

The Soviets realized how much the announcement of the Geneva summit (more than any economic pressure) pushed Adenauer to un-freeze relations between West Germany and the East. The Soviet leaders discussed the draft of a diplomatic note to West Germany twice, at the Party Presidium sessions on 13 and 25 May 1955. They sent an invitation to the West German chancellor in early June: they wanted to meet with Adenauer before the Geneva summit. Even though the chancellor postponed the meeting until September, they were satisfied. The prospect of the normalization of West German–Soviet relations, however vague, made the Soviet negotiating hand in Geneva somewhat stronger.[25]

Since 1950 Soviet foreign policy, like the eagle on the old czarist coat-of-arms, had looked in two directions: to Germany in the West and to China in the East. The relations with the Chinese Communist Party (CCP) changed considerably after Stalin's death. The lack of legitimacy of the new Soviet leadership in the Communist world made it practically impossible for them to continue treating the Chinese leadership as a satellite. That leadership, particularly Mao Zedong, regarded the period of uncertainty and the power struggle after Stalin's death as their chance to revise the equation in Sino-Soviet relations dramatically in their favor. Also, for many reasons, Mao was a bitter opponent to the idea of a summit between the Soviet leaders and the Western leaders—not the least because such a meeting could only enhance the Kremlin's international prestige and make even more painful the international isolation of the PRC. The Chinese leaders also feared that the relaxation of tensions between Moscow and the West would leave their interests aside, particularly the most important point on their domestic-international agenda, the "reunification" of Taiwan, the stronghold of

24. See Vladislav M. Zubok, "Khrushchev and the Issue of Divided Germany, 1953–1964," paper presented at the Khrushchev Centennial Conference, Brown University, 1–3 December 1994, p. 16.

25. *Istoricheskii arkhiv*, 5 (1993), 76. On the timing of the invitation, with regard to the Geneva summit, see *FRUS, 1955–57,* V, 235, and "The Official Outline of Relations between the USSR and the FRG in 1949–1970," report prepared by the Historico-Diplomatic Department of the Ministry of Foreign Affairs of the USSR, TsKhSD, fond 5, opis 64, delo 578, 12. See also Zubok, "Soviet Foreign Policy in Germany and Austria," 25–6.

the Nationalists, with the mainland China. Probably for this reason, in September 1954 Chinese artillery began to shell the offshore islands of Quemoy and Matsu, which were occupied by Nationalist troops. The result was the "first Taiwan crisis," which the Eisenhower administration viewed as one of its most severe challenges since the Korean war.[26]

The struggle for the recognition of the PRC had been one of the fundamental strategic aims of Soviet foreign policy since 1950, but it became a major albatross on the shoulders of the "new foreign policy." The logic of international events forced the Soviets to look over their shoulder and support the anti-American rhetoric of the Chinese leaders. During the Taiwan crisis they had to swallow their concerns and expressed their full solidarity with the PRC, in accordance with the terms of the Sino-Soviet treaty. Bulganin told the Chinese ambassador in March 1955 that "foreign policy of the [PRC as well as the Soviet Union] in the Far East has the character of an offensive, which is exemplified by the common position on the Taiwan issues." According to Bulganin, this policy "has been fully justified" both in the East and in the West.[27]

The "Taiwan crisis" ended abruptly on 23 April 1955, when Chinese Premier Zhou Enlai announced at the Bandung conference the willingness of the PRC to reach a settlement of the two-China issues through negotiations. According to Chinese-American scholars, the Chinese leadership by that time had fulfilled its political task and was looking for a good pretext to end the crisis. But the Soviet factor nevertheless played an important role. The Soviet sources do not corroborate the rumors about Khrushchev-Zhou Enlai meeting, during which Khrushchev allegedly referred to the islands as a local problem and claimed that the continuation of the crisis was inconsistent with the Soviet aim of relaxing tensions with the United States. In a more plausible version, Chinese defense minister Peng Dehuai visited the Soviet Union and Khrushchev told him that at the moment the United States was still very powerful and, therefore, peaceful negotiations should be encouraged to solve international disputes.[28]

The Soviet intervention that helped to end the crisis in the Far East

26. See Qiang Zhai, *The Dragon, the Lion, and the Eagle: Chinese-British-American Relations, 1949–1958* (Kent, Ohio, 1994), 175. On the U.S. strategic view of the crisis, see Gordon H. Chang, *Friends and Enemies: The United States, China, and the Soviet Union, 1948–1972* (Stanford, Calif., 1990), 129–42.

27. Zapis besedi, 19 March 1955, TsKhSD, fond 5, opis 30, delo 116, 19.

28. Chang, *Friends and Enemies*, 137; Qiang Zhai, *Dragon*, 173–4.

was unmistakably linked to the Soviet desire to reduce international tensions in the period leading up to the Geneva summit. This time Chinese leadership preferred to go along with the Soviet analysis of the international trends, and at the Bandung conference Zhou Enlai even attempted to seize the initiative in promoting the principles of "peaceful coexistence." Yet it is clear in retrospect that the Chinese leaders required a price for their compliance, and the Kremlin leaders agreed to pay it. The price was, in part, continuation of the economic assistance to the PRC. Khrushchev's trip to China in October 1954 had been a watershed in Sino-Soviet economic relations in the sense that the Soviet "fraternal" assistance to the PRC became much more generous than under Stalin. In addition, the Soviets pledged to the PRC leadership assistance in the creation of a Chinese atomic program that Mao Zedong had decided to launch sometime in early 1955. On 27 April 1955 the two governments signed an "Agreement on providing assistance of the USSR to the PRC in the matter of development of studies on the physics of atomic nucleus and on the utilization of atomic energy for the needs of people's economy." According to the terms of the agreement, the Soviet side promised to provide nuclear know-how to the Chinese for free.[29] This atomic cooperation contained in itself an implicit admission on the Soviet part that the PRC should not rely solely on the Soviet nuclear umbrella.

Finally, the Soviet leaders promised their Chinese "friends" that the recognition of the PRC would be a *sine qua non* of the normalization of the East-West relations and a lodestar for the Soviet delegation at the Geneva summit. As the meeting itself demonstrated, the Soviets remained faithful to their promise, but also held a rather pragmatic, *realpolitik* view of the Taiwan problem. A momentous exchange took place between Eisenhower and Zhukov on July 20. The latter told the former that the "settlement [of the Chinese problem] was of great importance for the relaxation of tension. There was, first of all, the question of membership in the U.N." On the question of Quemoy and Matsu, Zhukov said he "could not understand why they had not been evacuated. It merely served to inflame Chinese opinion and also that of the United States; that the Chinese regarded this as a matter of their national inter-

29. Documentary collection "The USSR-PRC (1949–1983)," Documents and Materials, Part I, 1949–1963, prepared by the Historical-Diplomatic Division of the Ministry of Foreign Affairs of the USSR, Moscow (1985), 145–6, 147–8. (The *real* transfer of nuclear know-how did not take place, however, until 1958.)

est." The Soviet marshal concluded that the islands "were not major issues in themselves" and that the delay in settling "the question of Taiwan" "was not advantageous even to the United States." Zhukov stopped short of openly nudging the U.S. president to normalization of Sino-American relations.[30]

By early summer 1955 the new Soviet leadership achieved the maximum in probing cracks in the opponent's camp through attempts at rapprochement with West Germany and in cementing the Sino-Soviet alliance, the cornerstone of the "Communist camp." Both developments, dictated by Khrushchev's "new foreign policy," remained implicit policy aims with which the Soviets arrived in Geneva.

Expectations and Lessons

Soviet policy goals at the Geneva Conference revolved around a basic premise: the new Soviet leadership wanted to confront Western leaders, to probe them, and, perhaps to reduce tensions in East-West relations. The very nature of probing and the fear of being ambushed by the much more experienced adversary put a premium on the continuous assessment of Western intentions and plans. For many months before the summit these assessments kept preparing the Kremlin leaders not to expect any substantial results from the meeting and consequently not to fear the conference's ending up with only empty declarations.

The analysis of the time was condensed in one long memorandum prepared for Mikhail Suslov by the Committee of Information at the Ministry of Foreign Affairs on 7 July 1955, "On the possible positions of Western powers on the main international issues at the upcoming meeting of the heads of governments of the four powers." The report stated that the U.S. government "is not interested in the success of the conference of the leaders of governments of the four powers. It only wants that the representatives of the Western powers, having put forth at the conference proposals that would be unacceptable for the USSR but advantageous in propagandist sense, would try to shift to the Soviet Union responsibility for the absence of settlement of the crucial international questions and for the continuation of the 'cold war,' thereby creating more propitious conditions for realization of American military-

30. *FRUS, 1955–57*, V, 416.

political plans, in particular the realization of the Paris Accords."[31] The report predicted no substantive discussions on the issue of disarmament and no progress on the issues of recognition of the PRC and its admission to the United Nations.

At the same time, the report noted that the governments of Great Britain and France feared that a failure of the summit would increase tensions in Europe. The French government in particular, distracted by the colonial war in Algeria, became "seriously interested" in reaching some kind of modus vivendi with the Soviet Union. The analysts predicted that during the conference "representatives of England, and particularly France might try through bilateral relations to probe the possibility of reaching an agreement on this or that question on a basis that would be somewhat different from the one agreed among the Western powers." In one estimate, on 28 June 1955, the analysts of the Foreign Ministry and the Committee of Information did not exclude that the French representatives would approach the Soviet delegation during the conference in order to "discuss the possibility of an assistance on the part of the Soviet Union in settling the North-African question."[32]

On the possible agreed position of the Western powers with regard to the European security issue, the report estimated that the United States would no longer be able to prevent Britain and France from coming up with their own proposals and modifications. Still, the analysts wrote that the Western powers would stick to the "Eden plan" on German reunification, but would modify it to create "an appearance" of the readiness to take the Soviet view into account. "Meanwhile the Western powers and the Adenauer government, as far as official and nonofficial declarations allow to judge," consider that "an escape of a unified Germany out of the bloc of Western powers would be excluded" under any circumstances.[33]

This conclusion was a refrain of many analytical documents sent to the Presidium.[34] Influential Pravda correspondent Pavel Naumov specu-

31. TsKhSD, f. 89, perechen 70, dokument 7, 6.
32. Ibid.; "Aggravation of the situation in French Northern Africa and the influence of this factor on the foreign policy course of France on the eve of the conference of four powers," signed by A. Gromyko, AVPRF, fond 595, opis 6, delo 769, papka 51, 143.
33. AVPRF, fond 595, opis 6, delo 769, papka 51, 12, 18.
34. See, for instance, "On the positions of the governments of the USA, Britain and France on the German question with regard to the upcoming conference of the leaders of governments of the four powers, " a memorandum of the Committee of Information, June

lated in a memorandum to the leadership that "Adenauer understands that on this question [of German unity] his talks in Moscow might fail. Therefore, he is interested in the failure of the discussion on the German Question even before, at the Geneva summit. . . . Bonn's [leaders] feel very comfortable with the intention of the Soviet government to avoid the discussion of the German question at the Geneva summit. . . . Thereby the trip of Adenauer to Moscow and his prestige of a statesman would carry general weight."[35]

Most members of the official delegation on the way to Geneva diligently read these voluminous reports. Another source informs us that the Kremlin leaders were highly concerned about last-minute moves by the other side. According to a veteran of the Committee of Information, Georgi Kornienko, a group of analysts from that committee flew to Geneva with the Soviet delegation and throughout the meeting worked hand in glove with all branches of Soviet intelligence services, supplying the Soviet delegation with fresh intercepts from the other side and helping in their interpretation.[36]

The behavior of the Western leaders at the summit proved to the Soviets that all these assessments and conclusions had been essentially correct. Also, during the summit the Soviet leaders, in their own estimate, achieved their most important goal—they forced the Americans to talk to them as equal partners, without open intimidation or condescension. The American sources, again, prove that this impression was very close to the truth. After Geneva, Dulles regretted the price that the administration, in his mind, had to pay at the summit: "The cost was the breaking down of the blurring of the moral barrier between the Soviet bloc and the free world. As a result we must re-think our basic strategy in order to meet this new situation."[37]

Khrushchev fulfilled his aim of sizing up the American leaders. The

1955, ibid., 29–47, and "The positions of Western powers with regard to creation of a system of collective security in Europe with regard to the upcoming conference of the leaders of governments of the four powers," June 1955, ibid., 29–47, 48–63.

35. Zapiska korrespondenta *Pravdi* v Zapadnoi Germanii Naumova (memorandum of *Pravda* correspondent V. Naumov), 3 July 1955, TsKhSD, fond 5, opis 30, d. 114, 176–7. Dmitri Shepilov, editor-in-chief of *Pravda*, sent the memo to Khrushchev and Bulganin because of its "considerable interest with regard to Geneva summit." The leaders read it on July 20, when the meeting had started.

36. Georgi Kornienko, then a senior analyst of the committee, was in Geneva and participated in this activity. Interview by author, Moscow, April 1990.

37. *FRUS, 1955–57*, V, 534.

Eisenhower-Zhukov informal talks in this regard were of considerable significance: the two military leaders of the Second World War expressed their horror at a possibility of a nuclear exchange. The summit in Geneva, Khrushchev recalled, "convinced us once again, that there was not any sort of pre-war situation in existence at that time, and our enemies were afraid of us in the same way as we were afraid of them." This conclusion, in turn, opened the eyes of the Soviet leadership, at least of Khrushchev, to the bipolar nature of the cold war linked to the development of nuclear bipolarity.[38]

The outcome of the conference, despite its lack of substantive progress, gave a big boost to Soviet diplomacy. The Soviets did not succeed in splitting the Western ranks, but they probed them enough to find room for the development of diplomatic openings to Britain and France in the future. Most importantly, the meeting revealed to them that the Western leaders were not larger than life and were perhaps no more experienced than they. In particular, Khrushchev had gained an impression of Eisenhower as a relaxed, benign, and not particularly impressive leader who delegated all foreign affairs to his secretary of state, John Foster Dulles. Khrushchev was not alone in this belief. Even a young and undogmatic Soviet diplomat Anatoly Dobrynin had the same impression at the time.[39]

A dramatic unveiling of the American "Open Skies" proposal justified Soviet expectations of being ambushed by the Americans. Essentially, this proposal, for all its substantive merits, was a last-minute attempt of the U.S. experts in psychological warfare to top evident Soviet propagandist achievements with one spectacular initiative. Khrushchev quickly reacted to it as a "blatant espionage ploy" and was largely right. The Soviet reaction to Open Skies at the Geneva Conference was of course justified by the existing rules of the cold war: the United States would have gained from aerial intelligence much more than the Soviet Union, and, besides, at that time the effectiveness of the Soviet "deterrent" still relied predominantly on the preservation of uncertainty and ignorance in the United States about the true size of the Soviet strategic arsenal (in reality it was almost nonexistent, with exception of a few "Myasischev" bombers that could make one-way

38. Smirnov and Zubok, "Nuclear Weapons after Stalin's Death," 16; also *FRUS, 1955–57*, V, 413; *Voprosi istorii*, VIII–IX (1992), 76.

39. Anatoly Dobrynin, *In Confidence. Moscow's Ambassador to America's Six Cold War Presidents, 1962–1986* (New York, 1995), 38.

flights to the United States but could not return). The reaction also revealed that bold departures from the past in the Kremlin were still hobbled by the orthodox mood of the majority of the Soviet leadership. In a revealing comment by Anatoly Dobrynin, sometime after the conference in Geneva the Open Skies was discussed at a Presidium session, and Khrushchev insisted that the Eisenhower administration was bluffing and "that no one in the U.S. Congress would agree to allow Soviet planes to fly over, say, the Capitol in Washington." Khrushchev was probably right in his assessments, but the Politburo "would not even hear of letting American planes fly over Soviet territory and rejected Khrushchev's tactic."[40]

In retrospect, the Soviet foreign policy and policy aims in the first half of 1955 look surprisingly cogent and effective, despite everything we now know about the power-driven nature of the Soviet decision making, the lack of experience of the new leadership, and the stifling influence of Stalin's ideological, political, and psychological legacy. A historian who would wonder how it could be so should perhaps look at the nature of the cold-war diplomacy in general, and the U.S. diplomacy in particular. True, the Soviet leaders after Stalin's death did not abandon the basic tenets of ideologized and imperial foreign policy and were far from adopting any "new political thinking" in world affairs. But the American actions and plans at that time were so consistently directed at the encirclement of the USSR, so clearly anti-Soviet and incapable of change, that any chance of transformation of world diplomacy to radically new vistas remained a moot point. In general, the logic of international relations in this period was so rigid and primitive, and so poisoned with nuclear fears, ideological intolerance, and prejudices on all sides that in this atmosphere even a relatively modest and inconsistent shift among Stalin's successors in the direction of flexible *realpolitik* allowed them to gain a high ground with regard to the West and pass before the whole world as successful and innovative statesmen.

40. Ibid., 37–8.

British Policy Aims at Geneva

ANTONIO VARSORI

Introduction

In his study "Détente in Europe," John Van Oudenaren notes that "the origins of the July 1955 Geneva summit usually are traced to Churchill's May 1953 speech in the House of Commons, in which he suggested that 'a conference on the highest level should take place between the leading powers without long delay.' "[1] Van Oudenaren stresses that as early as 1950 the Tory leader had stated his interest in renewing some form of dialogue between the Western world and the Soviet Union. Other scholars have pointed out Churchill's determination to achieve détente with Moscow.[2] Even if Churchill's role in paving the way to the Geneva Conference cannot be denied, the summit was mainly the outcome of Anthony Eden's initiative. During the months preceding the conference, the Eden cabinet tried to work out a clear-cut strategy for the meeting. Britain hoped that the summit might provide the West with an opportunity to formulate a new relationship with the Soviet Union. What were the reasons for such an optimistic view, which sharply contrasted with the pessimism nurtured by U.S. authorities? What were the goals of the British government? Why did Britain's carefully planned strategy meet with outright failure?

1. John Van Oudenaren, *Détente in Europe: The Soviet Union and the West since 1953* (Durham, 1991), 24.
2. See, for example, Martin Gilbert, *"Never Despair": Winston S. Churchill, 1945–1965* (London, 1988); John W. Young, "Cold War and Détente with Moscow," in John W. Young, ed., *The Foreign Policy of Churchill's Peacetime Administration, 1951–1955* (Leicester, 1988), 55–80; John W. Young, "Churchill's Bid for Peace with Moscow, 1954," *History*, LXXIII (1988), 425–48; David Carlton, "Grossbritannien und die Gipfeldiplomatie, 1953–1955," in Bruno Thoss and Hans Erich Volkmann, eds., *Zwischen Kaltem Krieg und Entspannung: Sicherheits- und Deutschlandpolitik der Bundesrepublik im Mächtesystem der Jahre 1953–1956* (Boppard am Rhein, 1988), 51–69; and—most recently—John W. Young, *Winston Churchill's Last Campaign: Britain and the Cold War, 1951–1955* (Oxford, U.K., 1996).

The Roots of British Policy

On returning to Downing Street in autumn 1951, Churchill almost immediately showed his eagerness for a relaxation of tensions between the two blocs. Personal motives and psychological reasons may partially explain the prime minister's cherished goal of renewing dialogue with Stalin. It is obvious that the aging Tory leader regarded himself as the one Western statesman who could restore peace in international relations and put an end to the cold war, which would be the most ambitious and rewarding accomplishment of his long political career. But it is equally impossible to disregard the existence of less personal aims related to Britain's role in the international context. The achievement of détente led by Britain might restore its tarnished image as a great power, and a more peaceful international atmosphere might give London some room for diplomatic maneuver. However, during the early stages of Churchill's second premiership, all of these ambitions proved to be mere wishful thinking.[3]

The Truman administration had no intention whatsoever of softening its attitude toward the Soviet Union—a stance it had assumed during a tough electoral campaign in which the Republican Party had skillfully exploited the Democrats' supposed weakness on the issue of anti-Communism.[4] Furthermore, Western positions in Europe appeared still very weak, while in the Far East the West was being openly challenged from Korea to Indochina. Eden and the foreign office, on the other hand, regarded the West's achievement of a "position of strength" as the main goal, which would result from the rearmament of West Germany, the establishment of an effective defense system in Europe,[5] and the stabilization of the military balance in the Far East. Last but not least, the information that reached London from Moscow and other Communist capitals confirmed the pessimistic view of Soviet intentions nurtured by most Western decision makers.[6]

3. See Gilbert, *"Never Despair,"* and Young, "Churchill's Bid."
4. On the U.S. attitude toward the Soviet Union, see, for example, Peter G. Boyle, *American-Soviet Relations: From the Russian Revolution to the Fall of Communism* (London, 1993), 84–134, and Melvyn P. Leffler, *A Preponderance of Power: National Security, the Truman Administration, and the Cold War* (Stanford, Calif., 1992), 446–95.
5. See Saki Dockrill, *Britain's Policy for West German Rearmament, 1950–1955* (Cambridge, U.K., 1991).
6. See, for example, the opinion expressed in Gascoigne (Moscow) to Hohler (FO), 5 March 1952, secret, FO 371/100830/NS 1026/3, PRO. Transcripts of Crown copyright records in the Public Record Office appear with the permission of the Controller of Her Majesty's Stationery Office.

During the second half of 1952, Churchill hoped that Eisenhower's victory in the presidential election would lead to a change in U.S. policy toward Moscow. However, when the president-elect, in a conversation with the British prime minister, hinted at the possibility of a meeting with Stalin, Churchill suggested a more cautious approach, since he feared that Britain might be excluded from such an American-Soviet meeting. The foreign office was not sure whether the new Republican administration had a common policy for the Soviet Union and suggested to Washington that the Americans should deal with the question with prudence. But Eisenhower was also aware that the American public, those who voted for him, wanted him to pursue a relentless anti-Communist crusade.[7]

Stalin's death in March 1953 and the early symptoms of the "thaw" in Soviet policies led Churchill to believe it was the right time to start a dialogue with Moscow.[8] In fact, however, the reactions on the part of British decision makers to the developments in Moscow were rather pessimistic; while most foreign office officials preferred to wait for some clarification of the Russian scene, the ambassador to Moscow, Sir Alvary Gascoigne, ruled out any Soviet "peace" initiative as a cunning propaganda device designed to sow dissension among the Western powers.[9]

Churchill's attempt to engineer a bold move toward the new Soviet leadership is well known, but the prime minister's optimistic approach met opposition from both the U.S. administration and the British cabinet. While the Eisenhower administration believed that the new Soviet policy was a mere change of tactics, which did not indicate alteration of long-term aims of the Kremlin leaders,[10] Eden and the foreign office re-

7. John Colville, *The Fringes of Power: Downing Street Diaries, II, 1941–April 1955* (London, 1987), 310; minutes by Colville, 8 January 1953, FO 371/106537/NS 1071/29, PRO; Mason (FO) to Steel (Washington), 3 February 1953, top secret, FO 371/106537/NS 1071/30, PRO. On Eisenhower's felt obligation to his voters, see, for example, Jeff Broadwater, *Eisenhower and the Anti-Communist Crusade* (Chapel Hill, N.C., 1992). For a broad assessment of Eisenhower's policies, see Stephen E. Ambrose, *Eisenhower the President*, Vol. II, *1952–1969* (London, 1984) and Günter Bischof and Stephen E. Ambrose, eds., *Eisenhower: A Centenary Assessment* (Baton Rouge, 1995).

8. See Antonio Varsori, "Britain and the Death of Stalin (1953)," in Francesca Gori and Silvio Pons, eds., *The Soviet Union and Europe in the Cold War, 1943–53* (London, 1996), 334–55.

9. Tel. no. 145, Gascoigne (Moscow) to FO, 16 March 1953, priority confidential, FO 371/106524/NS 1021/21, PRO.

10. See, for example, *FRUS, 1952–54*, VIII, 1117–25.

lied on a "wait and see" policy. British foreign-policy makers thought that détente could not be ruled out, but that some preliminary conditions had to be fulfilled. First, the Soviet internal political balance had to be clarified; second, no major international questions could be resolved without the involvement of Britain's allies, including the United States, France, and West Germany; and third, the West's achievement of a "position of strength" was essential before it would enter any serious negotiation with the Russians.[11]

Churchill chose to disregard such sound prerequisites, believing instead in the almost thaumaturgical potential of personal relations and in the positive impact on East-West relations of direct contact with the Russians. However, his speech at the House of Commons in May seemed to be the only alternative left to the prime minister if he wished to pursue his ambition of a summit, since it was clear that neither the U.S. administration nor the British foreign office was willing to negotiate with Moscow at this time. Throughout his May speech it was evident that Churchill knew the die was cast. But additionally, he knew he could rely on the support of Western public opinion, especially in Europe, which was desperately longing for "peace."[12]

If the prime minister was successful in his effort to impose a renewed dialogue with Moscow as the main goal for the West, the achievement of such an objective was postponed for two years. The major Western powers had to first work out a common attitude in their dealing with the Kremlin and also achieve a "position of strength." It was not an easy task to accomplish both prerequisites, whose fulfilment was tied to the solution of two crises that were seriously weakening the Western front: the "querelle de la C.E.D." and the war in Indochina. In both cases the United States, not Britain, appeared to be the key player.

The apparent failure of the U.S. administration between mid-1953 and mid-1954 to play a positive role in both arenas not only offered Britain some room for maneuver, but also prompted a shift in British policy regarding the issue of détente. On one hand, the British authorities began to develop a critical view of U.S. foreign policy as the Eisenhower administration appeared unable to deal with its European partners, especially France; on the other, Eden and the foreign office were increas-

11. For Britain's position see, for example, memorandum C(53)194 "Policy towards the Soviet Union and Germany" by Lord Salisbury, 7 July 1953, top secret, CAB 129/61, PRO.
12. On Churchill's speech, see Gilbert, *"Never Despair,"* 827–45.

ingly concerned about the West's weakness. In Whitehall, both France and West Germany were regarded as unreliable elements, in spite of U.S. efforts to strengthen both countries. Britain also anticipated that in both the Far East and the Middle East, the Soviet Union could exploit growing anti-Western feelings—and Washington did not share London's or Paris's views on how to face such a threat.[13]

These factors led the British authorities, particularly Eden, to assume a more direct role in shaping Western policies. Thus while Churchill remained anxious to attend a high-level conference or to make direct contact with some of the Russian leaders,[14] the foreign secretary and the foreign office took an active part in solving two problems that posed a stumbling block to the achievement of a position of strength. Britain encouraged a negotiated solution to the Indochina question,[15] and Eden's initiatives led to the conclusion of the London and Paris agreements (September–October 1954), thereby overcoming the crisis resulting from the collapse of the EDC scheme.[16]

During both the Geneva conference on the Far East (held in 1954) and the Berlin conference on the future of Germany and Austria, Eden had the opportunity to test Soviet intentions. The foreign secretary thought that on the Asia issue in particular it would be possible to work out some compromise with the Soviets, even if such an attitude was destined to strain Eden's relations with Dulles and the U.S. administration.[17] However, Eden's diplomatic skill was appreciated both in Bonn and in Paris. And at home, his caution won him the confidence of both the foreign office and the cabinet.

In October 1954 the signing of the Paris agreements led to the creation of the Western European Union, to West Germany's admission to NATO, and to a relaxation of tension between Bonn and Paris. Eden's

13. For an overall evaluation of Britain's policy on these issues, see Antonio Varsori, "Britain and Early Détente, 1953–1956," in Gustav Schmidt, ed., Ost-West-Beziehungen: Konfrontation und Détente, 1945–1989 (Bochum, 1993), 175–200. For an analysis of Western policies on the Geneva summit, see Antonio Varsori, "The Western Powers and the Geneva Summit Conference (1955)," in Antonio Varsori, ed., Europe, 1945–1990s: The End of an Era? (London, 1995), 221–48.

14. See the works by Gilbert and Young.

15. See Denise Artaud and Lawrence Kaplan, eds., Dien Bien Phu: L'alliance atlantique et la défense du Sud-Est asiatique (Lyon, 1989), in particular the contribution by G. Warner.

16. Dockrill, Britain's Policy, 133–50.

17. See Anthony Eden, The Memoirs of Sir Anthony Eden: Full Circle (London, 1960), 53–145.

prestige was at its height, and the ratification of the Paris agreements was the last obstacle separating the West from the achievement of its position of strength. The ensuing goal could be some form of dialogue with the Soviet Union.

French and Soviet Initiatives

While the British authorities, mindful of the failure of the EDC treaty to be ratified, preferred to wait for the ratification of the Paris agreements before tackling the issue of a dialogue with Moscow, the French prime minister, Pierre Mendès-France, realized that the French parliament's approval of West Germany's rearmament was closely tied to some type of positive move on the part of the West toward the Soviet Union. Moreover, détente could be advantageous to French international interests. In November 1954, in a speech to the UN Assembly, Mendès-France hinted at a possibility of holding a four-power conference and stated that the future of Austria and disarmament were issues on which the West might successfully negotiate with the Russians.[18]

Washington and London appeared to be worried about Mendès-France's initiative, which in their opinion could threaten the successful ratification of the Paris agreements. On the other hand, the French prime minister's move seemed to be ignored by the Russian leadership. Less than two months later, in early January 1955, Mendès-France sent personal letters to Eisenhower, Dulles, Churchill, and Eden. Once again the Radical-Socialist leader raised the question of a four-power conference and urged them to invite the Kremlin leaders to such a conference as soon as possible. Even though Mendès-France indicated that such a project would facilitate the French parliament's ratification of the Paris agreements, it was obvious that détente was also a goal in itself. In Mendès-France's opinion, the West, and France in particular, would benefit from such a development, since it would deprive Moscow of an effective propaganda instrument. Although both the U.S. and Britain rejected Mendès-France's proposals, London's reaction was rather nuanced. In a conversation with the French ambassador in London, René Massigli, Eden did

18. For Mendès-France's policy toward the Soviet Union, see Georges Henri Soutou, "Pierre Mendès-France et l'URSS, 1954–1955," in *Pierre Mendès-France et le role de la France dans le monde*, ed. René Girault (Grenoble, 1991), 177–206; Antonio Varsori, "Alle origini della prima distensione: la Francia di Pierre Mendès-France e la ripresa del dialogo con Mosca (1954–1955)," *Storia delle relazioni internazionali*, VIII (1991), 63–98.

not rule out the need "to find some other method" of convincing the Kremlin of the West's peaceful intentions. Churchill, in a personal letter to Mendès-France, stressed that "a Top Level Meeting might be productive of real advantages if the time and circumstances were well chosen."[19] Churchill and Eden were not hostile to détente, but they regarded Mendès-France's proposal as premature.

In any case, Mendès-France was not deterred from pursuing his policy. In mid-January he raised the question of a four-power conference with Adenauer at a meeting in Baden Baden. The German chancellor showed some interest in Mendès-France's plans and both leaders agreed on the need to set up a Western working group whose main goal would be the study of some form of dialogue with the Soviet Union.[20] As a consequence of the Baden Baden conversations, American and British diplomats were approached by French and German colleagues, who advocated the creation of such a body. Both Paris and Bonn confirmed their optimism about the ratification of the Paris agreements.

In London, fears and doubts about West Germany's and France's internal balance were growing. Britain did not doubt Adenauer's faithfulness to Bonn's "Western" choice nor his determination to have the Paris agreements ratified, but feared that after Adenauer's disappearance, Bonn could be tempted by neutralism as a way to achieve reunification; the Rapallo syndrome was still alive.[21] Postwar France had always been perceived in London as one of the weak links in the Western chain, and in early February 1955 this perception appeared to be confirmed by Mendès-France's resignation from office, since the Radical-Socialist leader had been regarded by Britain as the only French politician who could save the discredited Fourth Republic.[22] It is not surprising that the creation of a Western working group began to be taken seriously in London, while Britain was also encouraged by the positive American attitude toward this issue.[23]

19. Pierre Mendès-France, Oeuvres complètes, III, Gouverner c'est choisir, 1954–1955 (Paris, 1986), 652–63; tel. no. 34, Eden (FO) to Jebb (Paris), 12 January 1955, secret, FO 371/118196/WG 1071/31, PRO; Churchill to Mendès-France, 13 January 1955, top secret, FO 800/791, PRO.

20. DDF, 1955, I, Annexes, 225–36.

21. See, for example, tel. no. 52 Saving, Hoyer Millar (Bonn) to FO, 27 January 1955, priority confidential, FO 371/118199/WG 1071/134, PRO.

22. For an example of British views on the French political situation on the eve of Mendès-France's resignation, see tel. no. 38 Saving, Jebb (Paris) to FO, 26 January 1955, confidential, FO 371/118108/WF 1015/11, PRO.

23. Memorandum "East/West relations. Dr. Adenauer's proposal for a study group" by Hancock, 31 January 1955, FO 371/118199/WG 1071/144, PRO.

In February 1955 Western attention focused on the sudden events that took place in Moscow: Malenkov was forced to resign from office, while Khrushchev's star appeared to be steadily rising. In Washington these developments confirmed the pessimistic view that the U.S. administration had nurtured about the relationship between the West and the Soviet Union,[24] but London was more concerned about the international consequences of the struggle for power in Moscow. William Hayter, who had replaced Gascoigne, wrote to the foreign office that although Khrushchev "was not the mad dictator type," but "fundamentally a sane and perhaps even good-natured character, a kind of un-neurotic Goering," "we are not yet back in the Stalin era; but we have moved nearer to it."[25]

In spite of these evaluations Whitehall believed that the new Soviet leadership had to be judged on the basis of their future policies. Furthermore, on 9 February the British ambassador in Bonn, Sir Frederick Hoyer Millar, reported that in Adenauer's opinion Khrushchev "was a more practical and down to earth sort of person and might have a greater sense of reality, and therefore be more satisfactory to deal with than some of the other Russian leaders."[26] If internal developments in the Soviet Union appeared to slow the pace of British policy development regarding the issue of détente, France's unstable political balance prompted a new shift in Western attitudes.

In late February, the radical Edgar Faure was appointed French prime minister, while the moderate Antoine Pinay became foreign minister. The Paris agreements, which had been approved by the Assemblée Nationale, had still to be ratified by the Conseil de la République. In Washington it was suggested that Eisenhower should pay an official visit to Paris. Such a visit would stress U.S. friendship toward France and might ease the Paris agreements' ratification by the French senate. In reporting to London about this plan, the British ambassador in Washington, Sir Roger Makins, added that Eisenhower could profit from his visit to "lay

24. See *FRUS, 1955–57*, XXIV, 22–4.
25. Despatch no. 23S, Hayter (Moscow) to Eden (FO), 10 February 1955, confidential, FO 371/116637/NS 1017/29, PRO.
26. Minute by Ward, 9 February 1955, FO 371/116631/NS 1015/14 and minute, Ward to Kirkpatrick, 12 February 1955, FO 371/NS 10345/18, PRO; tel. no. 83, Hoyer Millar (Bonn) to FO, 9 February 1955, confidential, FO 371/116637/NS 1017/10, PRO.

plans for a meeting with the Soviets in a sustained effort to reduce tensions and the risks of war."[27]

This vague hint renewed Churchill's hope for a top-level conference, but Eden poured cold water on the prime minister's dream. The question was debated in the cabinet, but the reactions to Churchill's proposal for a summit conference was lukewarm at best. The foreign secretary was not hostile to some form of détente, which was advocated also by large sectors of the British public, but he feared that the prime minister's hope for a high-level four-power conference could lead Churchill to forsake his decision to resign from office, a decision which would further postpone Eden's premiership. In a few days, however, Churchill's hopes suffered a shattering blow when Makins informed London that the plan for the president's visit to France had been ruled out and Eisenhower had no intention whatsoever of meeting the Russian leaders.[28] This disillusionment appeared to exert a deep influence on the prime minister's final decision to leave office, and on 5 April Churchill resigned.

It is ironic that almost contemporaneously with Churchill's decision to resign his office, the French authorities, prompted in part by the British prime minister's renewed interest in détente, worked out a proposal calling for an early meeting of the Western working group; the creation of such a body was advocated by Faure in a personal letter to Eisenhower and Churchill. As usual, both U.S. and British reactions were cautious, but a sudden Soviet move led to a dramatic change in Britain's attitude.[29]

On 25 March the Russian authorities publicly stated their intention of solving the Austrian question, and to that end they invited Austrian chancellor Julius Raab to visit Moscow. The move caused deep concern in the major Western capitals, especially London. Britain feared that Moscow's goodwill toward Vienna was mainly designed to influence West German public opinion before the Paris agreements could be fully

27. Quoted in Gilbert, "Never Despair," 1103.
28. Minute no. PM/55/21, Eden to Churchill, top secret, FO 800/763, PRO; 23rd Conclusions, 14 March 1955, secret, CAB 128, PRO. On the episode regarding Eisenhower's canceled visit, see Gilbert, "Never Despair," 1105–11.
29. DDF, 1955, I, doc. 113, 285; ibid., doc. 133, 320–1; ibid., doc. 139, 331–22. For an example of the U.S.-British reaction, see tel. no. 647, Makins (Washington) to FO, 24 March 1955, immediate secret, FO 371/118204/WG 1071/278, PRO.

implemented. Furthermore, Britain believed that the Kremlin's decision demonstrated the skill of the new leadership, thereby stealing the
diplomatic initiative from the West.[30] Consequently, Britain decided to
take the lead in calling for a summit conference.

Britain Takes the Lead

In late March the foreign office thoroughly reassessed Western policy
toward Moscow in a memorandum entitled "Talks with the Soviet
Union." It stated that as a result of the Paris agreements, the West had
now achieved a position of strength and that it could therefore begin negotiations with the Soviet Union about outstanding issues. The foreign
office, however, realized that the West's favorable negotiating position
could be short-lived: progress in thermonuclear weapons might encourage a revival of isolationist feelings in the U.S.; the "Germans are always awkward allies and are likely to be more awkward after Dr.
Adenauer has left the scene; and the French cannot yet be relied on to
maintain a consistent policy."[31] Furthermore, Moscow could hope to
strengthen its influence in the Far East and "so long as Germany is divided the attachment of West Germany to the Western Group will be
precarious." This evaluation underscored the need for serious negotiations with the Soviet Union at the earliest feasible date. The British document tried also to single out the international issues that would be
easiest to negotiate with Moscow. Accordingly, Far Eastern questions
were ruled out, as Britain did not wish to encourage the Soviet Union to
invite Communist China to the forthcoming conference. London anticipated that Washington would not accept China's participation. Thus
"European problems [which included Austria, Germany, and the creation of a European security system] seem to offer the only possibility
of fruitful discussion this year."

30. For examples of Britain's concern, see tel. no. 412, FO to Vienna, 26 March 1955,
immediate confidential, FO 371/117787/R 1071/61, PRO; tel. no. 1312, FO to Washington,
29 March 1955, FO 371/117787/R 1071/69, PRO; Eden's minute to tel. no. 66, Wallinger
(Vienna) to FO, 29 March 1955, immediate secret, FO 371/117787/R 1071/84, PRO. For a
broad analysis, see Günter Bischof, "The Anglo-American Powers and Austrian Neutrality,
1953–1955," in *Mitteilungen des Osterreichischen Staatsarchivs*, XLII (1992), 368–93, and
"Eisenhower, the Summit, and the Austrian Treaty, 1953–1955," in Bischof and Ambrose,
eds., *Eisenhower*, 136–61.

31. Memorandum C(55)83 "Talks with the Soviet Union," 26 March 1955, secret,
PREM 11/893, PRO.

British plans remained broad, except a statement they issued suggesting that the Western powers offer the Soviet leaders "a declaration stating that they had no intention of altering frontiers or using force to alter them and giving the Soviet Union a guarantee of assistance if force was used against her or her satellites."[32] And finally, the foreign office document confirmed Western interest in a reunified Germany tied to the West.

The memorandum was a landmark in British policy toward Moscow, and London appeared determined to play a leading role in shaping relations between East and West. Significantly, this document advocating a policy of détente was examined by the cabinet on 19 April, after Churchill's official resignation and Eden's appointment, yet no objections were raised by the ministers who had previously criticized Churchill's peace overtures.[33] As early as late March, the foreign office had already assented to the French proposal for creating a tripartite working group, which could be followed by tripartite conversations at the foreign ministers' level, perhaps joined by West Germany.[34] The United States, on the other hand, believed in the working group meeting only after the successful ratification of the Paris agreements. The French government, of course, welcomed the British project, but it objected to any direct participation by West Germany, while Adenauer stressed Bonn's desire to be included in the early tripartite discussions. In spite of these contrasting opinions, London was determined to prompt a four-power conference, which Britain thought justifiable on account of the progress being made in the negotiations between the Soviet Union and Austria. On 12 April the Austrian delegation, led by Raab, left for Moscow. Two weeks later, the tripartite working group met for the first time in London, to prepare for possible four-power talks with the Russians.[35]

In the meantime, the newly appointed prime minister resolved to call a general election in order to strengthen his leadership. Its outcome was

32. Ibid.
33. C.M. (55) 4th Conclusions, 19 April 1955, secret, CAB 128/29, PRO.
34. See, for example, tel. no. 1294, FO to Washington, 28 March 1955, immediate secret, FO 371/118204/WG 1071/285, PRO.
35. *FRUS, 1955–57*, V, 136–8; tel. no. 128, Jebb (Paris) to FO, 5 April 1955, priority confidential, FO 371/118205/WG 1071/340, PRO; tel. no. 134, Jebb (Paris) to FO, 7 May 1955, immediate secret, FO 371/118206/WG 1071/356, PRO. On this topic see, for example, Rolf Steininger, "1955: The Austrian State Treaty and the German Question," *Diplomacy and Statecraft*, 3 (1992), 494–522; as well as G. Bischof's studies.

uncertain, meaning that a resounding diplomatic initiative on the part of Britain in the context of East-West relations would constitute a much-needed boost to the Conservative Party's fortunes. Furthermore, during the electoral campaign the Tory leadership had skillfully exploited Eden's image as both a successful mediator able to resolve difficult international crises and a man "working for peace."[36] This elevation rendered the creation of the tripartite working group only a minor sop to British public opinion; similarly, a four-power conference at the foreign ministers' level would also be regarded as a less outstanding achievement. The prospect of a summit conference, however, might enhance the Tories' chances in the forthcoming general election in late May.

It is not surprising that at a meeting of the tripartite working group, the British delegation insisted that an "approach to Soviet Government for meeting four heads of government should be held to discuss all outstanding points of difference between Russia and the Western allies." Geoffrey Harrison, the head of the British delegation, further explained that such a move would strengthen Eden's position on the eve of the general election.[37] In spite of such a plea, the U.S. delegation, which acted on Dulles's instructions,[38] was unable to go further than studying the broad possibility of a four-power conference. The final report drafted by the tripartite working group supported a four-power conference, but this would then have to be examined by the three foreign ministers in early May in Paris.[39]

On 6 May, the eve of the meeting in the French capital, Eden sent Eisenhower a personal letter in which he strongly advocated the plan for a summit conference. The prime minister stressed that "much in our country depends upon it; this is not a party question here, but responds to a deep desire of our whole people." Neither Eisenhower nor Dulles

36. On these aspects see, for example, David Carlton, *Anthony Eden: A Biography* (London, 1981), 373, and Richard Lamb, *The Failure of the Eden Government* (London, 1987), 4, 10.

37. *FRUS, 1955–57*, V, 153–4, and "Official Working Party to Prepare Four Power Conference: Record of Second Plenary Meeting," 27 April 1955, secret, FO 371/119209/WG 1071/479, PRO. The British delegates suggested Geneva as the venue of the conference, but such an idea was regarded as "psychologically unwise" by U.S. delegates.

38. *FRUS, 1955–57*, V, 158–60. On Dulles's position, see Richard Immerman, ed., *John Foster Dulles and the Diplomacy of the Cold War* (Princeton, 1990); see also Ronald Preussen, "Beyond the Cold War—Again," *Political Science Quarterly*, CVIII (1993), 59–84.

39. The text of this report is in *DDF*, 1955, I, Annexes.

was satisfied with the prime minister's proposal, but they believed it impossible to reject a request put forward by their nation's major ally. Furthermore, Eden's proposal enjoyed the support of the French government. In any case, the U.S. administration stressed that the Western powers needed to work out their strategy carefully and did not conceal their skepticism about the possibility of a top-level conference leading to concrete results. In a subsequent message to Eisenhower, Eden, however, stressed how "your understanding help is so valuable to me."[40]

Even if we cannot discard the roles played by internal policies or personal ambitions, both of which helped shape Eden's position, Britain's plea for a summit conference was also affected by its foreign-policy considerations. The West's weaknesses that had been sketched out in the foreign office memorandum of 26 March appeared to be confirmed by subsequent events. France was a minor factor in British eyes, and in late April, for example, the British Embassy in Paris stressed the inconsistencies of French foreign policy.[41] The Eisenhower administration, on the other hand, seemed unable to work out any effective policy toward the Soviet Union as U.S. decision makers remained suspicious of Russian intentions.

British decision makers felt that something was happening in both Bonn and Moscow. The British ambassador to the Federal Republic of Germany, in a message sent to the foreign office on 25 April, argued that Adenauer's position was weakening and that the "Germans are expecting the Allied Governments to make a genuine and constructive attempt at secure reunification and they will not be content with a repetition" of the Berlin conference.[42]

Doubting that the Kremlin was willing to be persuaded by the West to agree to the reunification of Germany on Western terms, the Federal Republic put forward its own proposal in the hope that it might be used if the summit conference took place. Herbert Blankenhorn, Adenauer's close adviser, told Ivone Kirkpatrick that in order to achieve reunification the Federal Republic could accept some limitation to its rearma-

40. Tel. no. 2139, FO to Washington (Eden to Eisenhower), 6 May 1955, immediate top secret, PREM 11/883, PRO; *DDF*, 1955, I, doc. 250, 580; *FRUS*, *1955–57*, V, 165–7; ibid., 166, footnote 3.

41. Note by Reilly, 28 April 1955, confidential, FO 371/118110/WF 1015/63, PRO. In Reilly's opinion such inconsistencies were the consequences of contrasts between Faure and Pinay.

42. Tel. no. 239, Hoyer Millar (Bonn) to FO, 25 April 1955, confidential, FO 371/118209/WG 1071/457, PRO.

ment program. Blankenhorn also suggested that "Germany should volunteer to maintain a neutral strip (say, the whole of the Russian Zone) which might form a part of a neutral strip running from the Baltic to the Adriatic—a corner of Czechoslovakia, a corner of Austria, and perhaps a corner of Yugoslavia." During a meeting of the tripartite working party, Blankenhorn added that the creation of a European security system was another topic that might be discussed with the Kremlin leaders.[43] Such suggestions would not have been unheeded in London.

As far as the Soviet attitude was concerned, British decision makers were impressed by the Russian move regarding Austria. In a telegram to the foreign office, William Hayter explained that the Kremlin's initiative served many purposes: the likely settlement of the Austrian question through neutrality could avoid Vienna's involvement in the Western defense system, could offer the Germans "a useful pattern to follow," and could "demonstrate Soviet willingness to settle outstanding questions as a preliminary to wider Great Power negotiations." The foreign office stated that the Western powers "must be prepared to try to make the best of the apparently forthcoming Soviet attitude," and a few days later, in a memorandum to the cabinet, Foreign Secretary Harold Macmillan stressed that while Moscow's goodwill over Austria was aimed at influencing West German public opinion, such an initiative could also be regarded as a first step toward "wider Great Power negotiations."[44] If the Soviet Union appeared ready to start some form of dialogue with the West, it was up to the Western powers, Britain in particular, to take the initiative (i.e., to invite the Russian leaders to a summit conference) and to work out a clear-cut strategy.

In this connection, British decision makers thought it useful to take into careful consideration West Germany's opinions. In late April, the head of the U.S. delegation to the tripartite working group reported back to the State Department Kirkpatrick's opinion about the topics for fu-

43. Minute "Germany and Four Power Talks" by Kirkpatrick, 28 April 1955, FO 371/118209/WG 1071/477, PRO; "Official Working Party to prepare for Four Power Talks—Record of Third Plenary Meeting," 28 April 1955, secret, FO 371/118209/WG 1071/480, PRO. On West Germany's position, see Eckart Conze's essay in this volume.

44. Tel. no. 358, Hayter to FO, 15 April 1955, immediate confidential, FO 371/117789/RR 1071/134, PRO; tel. no. 1795, FO to Washington, 15 April 1955, immediate confidential, FO 371/117789/RR 1071/129, PRO; memorandum C.P.(55)12 "Austria" by Macmillan, 26 April 1955, secret, CAB 129/75, PRO. See also Günter Bischof's essay in the present volume.

ture negotiations with the Soviet leaders. The foreign office senior official thought the "Soviets might be attracted by a 'neutralized' zone
extending from Eastern Germany through a part of Czechoslovakia,
through Austria and making use of Yugoslavia middle position." Kirkpatrick also hinted at a "united Germany in NATO, although Eastern
portion would be demilitarized."[45] But further information and suggestions came from Adenauer, who in early May had a conversation with
Sir Christopher Steel, the British representative at NATO. The chancellor stated his conviction of Moscow's weak position, which, according
to the information that had reached Bonn, was the consequence of both
economic and political difficulties. On this occasion Adenauer "agreed
that the time had come when we ought to try to profit from these weaknesses in the Soviet position and open negotiations with them" and
stressed that the "establishment of some kind of demilitarised zone in
Eastern Europe" could be a bargaining chip.[46]

Before shaping a definite policy toward the Soviet Union, the British
authorities had to convince their U.S. and French partners of the useful-
ness of a four-power summit conference. Such was the objective of conversations between Macmillan, Dulles, and Pinay in Paris in early May.
In spite of Dulles's doubts and fears, the three foreign ministers, who
were also in contact with Adenauer, complied with Britain's proposal,
drafting an official note to Moscow. The note not only put forward the
proposal for a summit conference but also listed, if in vague terms, possible topics for discussion, including the German question, nuclear
weapons, disarmament, European security, the situation in the satellite
countries in Eastern Europe, and the Far East. The summit proposal was
discussed by the three Western foreign ministers and Molotov when
they met in Vienna for the signing of the Austrian State Treaty. The Soviet reply was a positive one, and it was further agreed that details concerning the future conference would have to be examined at the foreign
ministers' level in June when the four ministers were scheduled to meet
in the United States to celebrate the tenth anniversary of the UN's organization.[47]

45. *FRUS, 1955–57*, V, 160–2.
46. Tel. no. 76, Steel (NATO-Paris) to FO, 8 May 1955, confidential, PREM 11/893,
PRO. On these aspects, see Saki Dockrill's essay in the present volume.
47. Documents about the Paris and Vienna meetings and conversations are to be found
not only in PRO but also in *FRUS, 1955–57*, V, and *DDF, 1955*, Annexes.

Britain's Strategy

Once the Soviet leaders had agreed to the proposal for a top-level conference, the main aim of the three Western powers was to work out a coherent common policy. To that end, several working groups were set up,
while both formal and informal meetings were held among U.S., British,
and French decision makers. West German representatives were also invited to the discussions dealing with the German question. Opinions
and interests in the Western front were far from unanimous. The U.S.
administration, which had accepted the idea of a top-level conference
only because of pressure from the European partners, was unlikely to
develop an effective policy before the eve of the summit. The French authorities focused their attention on disarmament and would similarly
work out a plan only at the last minute. Moreover, neither Washington
nor London was willing to conceal their disagreement with the French
project. The British intended to play a leading role and would sketch out
a coherent strategy; Eden's policy would be based on a plan for the solution of the German question and the creation of a European security
system.[48]

Between late May and early June there appeared to be a brief lull in
Britain's decision-making process, which was perhaps the consequence
of the general election. In contrast, Soviet authorities were very active
in the international field during this period. Moscow formed the Warsaw Pact. Khrushchev and Bulganin paid a much-publicized visit to Yugoslavia in order to mend fences with Tito. Finally and more
significantly, the Kremlin leaders invited Adenauer to pay an official
visit to Moscow, a preliminary step toward Moscow's diplomatic recognition of West Germany. These episodes were carefully examined in
London. The creation of an Eastern counterpart to NATO was regarded
by the foreign office as an obvious consequence of Bonn's involvement
in the Atlantic alliance, as well as evidence of the Russian leadership's
determination to strengthen its control over Eastern Europe.[49]

The foreign office was divided in its view of the Soviet visit to Yugoslavia.[50] Adenauer's invitation to Moscow caused some concern in

48. These issues are thoroughly examined in Dockrill's essay.
49. Memorandum "Assessment of Soviet Policy and the Internal Situation in the Soviet
Union," 11 June 1955, secret, FO 371/116633/NS 1015/40, PRO.
50. See the contrasting views expressed by Sir F. Roberts and Sir W. Hayter: tel. no. 416,
Roberts (Belgrade) to FO, 3 June 1955, confidential, FO 371/118027/RY 10338/91, PRO;
despatch no. 86, Hayter (Moscow) to Macmillan (FO), 10 June 1955, confidential, FO 371/
116252/NS 1021/40, PRO.

Whitehall; such a move was interpreted as a further device to sow dissension between Bonn and the Western powers, since the Soviet authorities could try "to deal directly with the West Germans and bring them to sit down with the East Germans to work out a common destiny." In spite of this apprehension, British decision makers believed that the Kremlin was ready to leave some "room to manoeuver over German reunification." From a broader perspective, it became obvious that the Russian leaders were mainly interested in negotiating with the Western powers about the issues of Europe's military balance and Germany's future. If this opportunity were missed, a foreign office memorandum stated, "the initiative will have passed to the Soviet Union." To this end, the British authorities devoted their energies to the formulation of plans dealing with the issues on which Moscow seemed to be focusing its attention (i.e., Germany and European security).[51]

Britain was also aware that any proposal had to be agreed upon by Washington and Paris. In mid-June tripartite meetings at the foreign ministers' level were held in New York. A general agreement was reached that Geneva was the best venue for the summit and that the four powers would have to deal with a broad range of topics. On the occasion of a private conversation with Dulles, the British foreign secretary tackled some questions of substance; he mentioned that London was considering "the possibility of a demilitarised strip in Eastern Europe between the two opposite sets of forces." Dulles, for his part, hinted at "German reunification within the framework of an agreement about levels of forces in Europe"[52] and such a vague statement led Macmillan to speak about a combination of both possibilities.

On 17 June the three Western foreign ministers were joined by Adenauer. Macmillan, in an optimistic mood, informed Eden that "a definite picture is beginning to evolve . . . in line with what I think is your idea . . . of a package deal." In fact, in a private conversation the chancellor had with Macmillan that afternoon, the German leader outlined the plan for a demilitarized zone, which would have included "the whole East German Zone and part of Poland and Czechoslovakia, as well as the whole of Austria." In this area "no military forces would be allowed to be stationed permanently or temporarily"; "no military installations

51. Memorandum "Assessment," FO 371/116633/NS 1015/40, PRO; memorandum "Germany," 11 June 1955, top secret, FO 371/118222/WG 1071/771, PRO.
52. Tel. no. 473, Dixon (UK Del UNO) to FO, 16 June 1955, immediate top secret, PREM 11/894, PRO.

or depots would be permitted; . . . no fortifications, training areas or air-fields etc. would be allowed; . . . all armament industry should be abolished; . . . [and] military flights over the area would be forbidden." Furthermore, "on the East as well as on the West side of this demilita-rized area, there would be zones in which conventional forces would be permitted provided that they were of the same character and of equal numbers. Only tactical forces would be permitted and no emplace-ments for rockets and guided missiles. . . . To the East as well as the West of these zones there should be two further zones in which should be no restrictions." In Adenauer's opinion such a plan should be dis-closed not at Geneva but at an ensuing foreign ministers' conference; the German chancellor added that he had informed the U.S. administra-tion about his plan, but he thought it was better to leave the French au-thorities in the dark since the "French system . . . was so happy-go-lucky." It is interesting to note that if Adenauer did indeed mention his plan to Dulles, U.S. papers did not record that the secretary of state had shown much interest in it.[53]

On his way back to Europe, the West German leader stopped in Brit-ain and met Eden at Chequers. On this occasion Adenauer stressed "the greater effectiveness of Russian propaganda" and reminded the prime minister that "reunification was Russia's best bait to get Germany out of N.A.T.O. and the Western Alliance"; furthermore, he mentioned the project he had spoken about with Macmillan. Eden replied that the "free countries must maintain the initiative" and that "it was not a matter merely of modernising the so-called 'Eden Plan.' " In the prime minister's opinion, the Western powers had to develop "ideas of our own designed to make unification of Germany possible for the Russians at a reasonable price which we could afford to offer them." In this con-nection, the West "could work out what had been described as a package proposal."[54]

While Eden was thus determined to pursue his policy, contrasting sig-nals came from the Russian authorities. In the latter half of June, the

53. Tel. no. 498, Dixon (UK Del UNO) to FO, 18 June 1955, immediate top secret, FO 371/118219/WG 1071/735, PRO; tel. no. 499, Dixon (UK Del UNO) to FO, 18 June 1955, immediate top secret, FO 371/118219/WG 1071/736, PRO; tel. no. 500, Dixon (UK Del UNO) to FO, 18 June 1955, immediate top secret, FO 371/118219/WG 1071/736, PRO; *FRUS, 1955–57,* V, 299. On Adenauer's position, see Conze's essay.

54. "Record of a Discussion with Dr. Adenauer at Chequers on June 19," PREM 11/894, PRO. For the details of the Eden plan, see Dockrill's essay.

three Western foreign ministers met Molotov in San Francisco for the purpose of working out practical details in connection with the Geneva summit. The Russian foreign minister had a friendly conversation with Macmillan and almost immediately agreed with the proposal for a four-foreign-minister conference to be held after the summit meeting. However, a meeting between him and Pinay gave the French foreign minister the impression that "the Russians at Geneva would not be prepared to proceed on the basis of a discussion of German unification."[55]

In the meantime in Washington, British diplomats discussed with U.S. colleagues Adenauer's idea for a demilitarized area in Central Europe. American officials doubted the feasibility of such a plan, saying they were not prepared "to offer any substantial views, save to express certain doubts about its appeal to the Russians, who would have to make almost all the concessions." Six days later, at another Anglo-American meeting in Washington, U.S. diplomats had still not formed any definite opinion about such projects. In spite of these negative signals, British decision makers went on working out a clear-cut strategy, which had as its pillars definite proposals for the issues of European security and German reunification. Eden's "package deal" was approved by the cabinet on 14 July.[56]

On the eve of the Geneva summit, Macmillan had further meetings in Paris with Dulles and Pinay. In reporting to London of a conversation with his U.S. colleague, the foreign secretary wrote that "on the vital issue of European security and German reunification the Americans were very obstinate." Little progress was made in further conversations, even though Macmillan perhaps appeared to be less pessimistic. On 16 July the four delegations at last reached Geneva, where the summit was scheduled to open on Monday the eighteenth. Eden still hoped his plan could be successful, but in a few days it became evident that Britain's ambitions were doomed to failure.[57]

55. Tels. Nos. 32 and 33, Macmillan (San Francisco) to FO, 22 June 1955., immediate top secret, FO 371/118221/WG 1071/766, PRO; tel. no. 58 UK Del (San Francisco) to FO, immediate secret, PREM 11/894, PRO. Eden minuted, "We must have our plan ready."

56. Tel. no. 1529 Makins to FO, 2 July 1955, immediate top secret, FO 371/118224/WG 1071/823, PRO. See also tel. no. 1530, Makins (Washington) to FO, 2 July 1955, immediate top secret; CM(55)23rd Conclusions, 14 July 1955, top secret, PREM 11/895, PRO.

57. Tel. no. 256, Jebb (Paris) to FO, 15 July 1955, immediate secret, PREM 11/895, PRO; tel. no. 260 Jebb (Paris) to FO, 15 July 1955, immediate secret and tel. no. 261 Jebb (Paris) to FO, 16 July 1955, immediate secret, FO 800/673, PRO. For a thorough analysis of the conference, see the essays by Prados and Immerman. See also Varsori, "The Western Powers," 235–41.

Conclusions

Détente with Moscow had been a major goal for Churchill once he had come back to office in late 1951. The relaxation of tensions in East-West relations and the attainment of an atmosphere of mutual understanding were not only important aims in themselves, but they were also intended to meet the expectations of Western European public opinions. Such a development might also help Britain to recover a relevant and fully independent role in international affairs. However, a number of obstacles prevented Churchill from achieving his goal, particularly that until March 1953 most Western decision makers believed it impossible to develop any dialogue with Stalin. Furthermore, the Eisenhower administration did not show much sympathy toward Churchill's ambitions. Although Eisenhower was less a cold warrior than has previously been suggested, the president knew his victory in November 1952 resulted in part from the American public's weariness of Truman's alleged softness toward Communism. The timing also coincided with the height of McCarthyism. And finally, it was difficult to envisage any dialogue with Moscow if the West felt that their positions were threatened by the East in Europe as well as in the Far East.

The death of Stalin and the appearance of a new Soviet leadership marked a turning point in East-West relations, and détente suddenly seemed a feasible goal. In spite of U.S. opposition and foreign office caution, Churchill succeeded in imposing some form of dialogue with Moscow as a Western aim. But such an objective could be pursued only on the condition that the West achieve its "position of strength." In this regard Eden's diplomatic skill was of some relevance. The 1954 Geneva conference on Indochina and especially the Paris agreements offered the West the long-awaited position of strength, but Eden and the foreign office preferred to wait for the final ratification of the Paris agreements before starting any initiative aiming at détente. Thus London rejected Mendès-France's proposal for an early move toward the Soviet Union.

It was not until the spring of 1955 that the Soviet move regarding Austria and the growing fears about France's reliability and West Germany's future led the foreign office to reassess its policy toward détente: a dialogue with Moscow had to be started as soon as possible. Such an aim was based on several assumptions: (a) the "position of strength" achieved through the Paris agreements was a temporary factor and time was not on the Western side; (b) the question of German unification was still unsolved and the uncertainty about Germany's fate could be exploited by Moscow; (c) the Soviet leaders appeared ready to enter serious negotiations with the West, or at least it would be useful to probe Moscow's peaceful intentions; (d) British public opinion and Western European public opinion in general supported some dialogue with the Soviet Union.

Personal ambitions and party interests influenced Britain's positions. Eden, who became prime minister in early April, was determined to take the initiative in holding a top-level conference with Moscow. This would also help the Conservatives in the May general elections. In any case, London's decision to take the lead regarding détente implied Britain's determination to maintain its global leadership. Once Washington had agreed to the idea of a summit, Whitehall focused its attention on the issues of Germany's unification and European security. In the opinion of British decision makers such a choice appeared to be the best option: Germany was still regarded in London as a weak link in the Western chain, the Soviet Union seemed to be interested in working out some lasting European settlement, and the West German authorities skillfully played Britain's card in order to achieve their own goals.

Eden's strategy was doomed to failure, however, because some of its assumptions were wrong. U.S. decision makers, especially Eisenhower, were interested in détente, but they also recognized that relations with Moscow were "too serious a business" to be left to their European allies.[58] On the other hand, détente was viewed as one of the new Soviet "tactics," which had to be faced through new instruments, in particular through skillful propaganda moves. Nothing substantial could be achieved at Geneva, but the summit could create the image of a peace-loving U.S. administration, and the "Open Skies" plan served just that purpose. Moreover, only a few weeks earlier, in June 1955, the outcome of the Messina conference had indicated that Bonn was going to further strengthen its ties with Western Europe. In the eyes of U.S. decision makers, the European scene had been satisfactorily stabilized; competition with Moscow was continuing, but it was likely to move to other geographical areas such as the Middle East and the Far East, where Washington would be operating alone.

58. See, for example, Richard A. Melanson and David Mayers, eds., *Reevaluating Eisenhower: American Foreign Policy in the Fifties* (Urbana, Ill., 1987) and Bischof and Ambrose, eds., *Eisenhower.*

Another erroneous assumption that negatively influenced British decision makers was their interpretation of Soviet aims. Actually, Moscow had no intention whatsoever of starting serious negotiations about Germany's unification, and the Kremlin leaders appeared to be satisfied with the European status quo founded on the division of Germany. Thus it was likely that Russia's main goal at Geneva was the recognition by the West of Communist leaders as decent and reasonable statesmen with whom it was possible to develop normal relations.[59] As for the relationship with the Western world, Eden hoped for some time that, even if Britain's strategy had failed at Geneva, the summit could offer London as a "bridge" between the Soviet Union and the United States. This proved to be merely wishful thinking.[60] Britain could be a useful instrument in Russian foreign policy, but the United States was perceived by the Kremlin leaders as the real and main enemy, as well as the real and main Western actor. As for the U.S. authorities, they would go on to confirm, first in the Far East and later at Suez, their belief in a bipolar world. After the Geneva summit, only Washington and Moscow had the capacity to create some form of détente.

59. See Stephen R. Ashton, *In Search of Détente: The Politics of East-West Relations since 1945* (London, 1989), 73–8; Caroline Kennedy-Pipe, *Stalin's Cold War: Soviet Strategies in Europe, 1943 to 1956* (Manchester, 1995), 171–87.

60. Antonio Varsori, "Le gouvernement Eden et l'Union Soviétique (1955–1956): De l'espoir à la désillusion," *Relations Internationales,* LXXI (1992), 273–98.

French Policy Aims at Geneva

COLETTE BARBIER

In July 1955, in Geneva, the heads of state of the United Kingdom, the United States, France, and the Soviet Union met for the first time since the end of the WWII. After having been excluded from the Yalta and Potsdam conferences, France was invited to participate in the Geneva summit.

Since 1945, the international power structure as well as the diplomatic and strategic context had changed considerably: both the United States and the USSR were now nuclear powers, while Great Britain possessed the A-bomb. The USSR had increased its nuclear capacity considerably and was on the way to closing the gap between itself and the United States. Two superpowers and two blocs were thus face to face. Many nations feared conflict between NATO and the Soviet bloc and the accompanying specter of nuclear warfare.

After Stalin's death in March 1953, the next two years seemed a turning point in history, with the end of the Korean War, the establishment of new collegial leadership in Moscow, the building of a European Community, and the prospect of German rearmament. The culmination came with the 1955 summit, which gave rise to a relaxed international atmosphere filled with what was known as the "spirit of Geneva."

The summit meeting was convened largely at Western instigation. President Eisenhower's appeal to the USSR on April 16, 1953, was fully supported by British prime minister Winston Churchill, who delivered a memorable speech of his own on May 11, 1953, opening up the possibility of "some accommodation with Russia, which made a dramatic impact on World opinion." The idea of a summit to ease international tensions was a popular one, viewed by the public as the first real diplomatic move toward peace, but it would take two more years before Western and Eastern powers finally agreed to meet "to adjust by discussion and negotiation their conflicts of national interest and ideological difference which have divided and distressed the world during the last decade."[1]

In 1955 France was the weakest member of the Western alliance. It was not a nuclear power and therefore did not belong to the exclusive "Nuclear Club," which consisted of the United States, Great Britain, and the USSR. France's chronic political instability, its defeat in the Indochina war followed by the rejection of the European Defence Community (EDC) treaty by the French National Assembly (on August 30, 1954), and the outbreak of the North African rebellion had ruined the nation's prestige and diplomatic influence not only in Europe but throughout the world. France felt isolated, and its influence in NATO was declining.

During the Fourth Republic, France's priorities were those of rank and status; it wanted to be recognized as a major power and treated as an equal. Since the end of WWII, it had consistently feared and opposed German rearmament. The French feared a remilitarized Germany and greater German influence within NATO and in Europe. In spite of its obvious weakness, however, France attended the Geneva Conference as one of the great powers. This was significant because it resulted in part from the personal obstinacy, the stubborn efforts, and the initiatives of two successive prime ministers, Pierre Mendès-France and Edgar Faure.

What were French policy aims at Geneva and French perspectives on the main issues, including the German question, disarmament, and the cold war? What role did the French play? All official documents, statements, proposals, and directives have been published and, for the most part, translated. Everything seems to have been said and done on the matter.[2] However, biographies, memoirs written by the actors themselves, and recent research on the history of the Fourth Republic give us some additional insights.[3] To understand France's policy aims, it will be

1. President Eisenhower's Address to the Annual Conference of the American Society of Newspaper Editors, in *Keesing's Contemporary Archives*, vol. IX (London, 1952–1954), 12885; Harold Macmillan, *Tides of Fortune, 1945–1955* (London, 1969), 478; Lester B. Pearson, "After Geneva: A Greater Task for NATO," *Foreign Affairs*, XXXIV (October, 1955), 14. Churchill's immediate response to Eisenhower's April initiative to the USSR was "We give him our resolute and wholehearted support" (Glasgow, April 17, 1953). *Keesing's*, IX, 12886.

2. For some examples, see *DDF*, 1954, 1955, Annexes I (January–June) and II (July–December); *FRUS, 1955–1957*, V, 119–528; *Keesing's*, vols. IX and X; *L'Année Politique*, 1954 (Paris, 1955).

3. For some examples, see Jacques Bloch-Morhange, *La grenouille et le scorpion* (Paris, 1982); D. Colard, *Edgar Faure* (Paris, 1975); Anthony Eden, *Memoirs, Full Circle, 1951–1957* (London, 1960); Georgette Elgey, *Histoire de la IV République*, vol. III: *La république*

necessary to examine the French approach to the summit conference, an intense period of major diplomatic initiatives.

The French Approach to the Summit Conference

The two prime ministers, Mendès-France (from June 1954 to February 1955), then Faure (from February 1955), were both eager to hold a top-level conference with the Russians. The French National Assembly rejected the EDC treaty on August 30, 1954, mainly because of its supranational character and "the provisions regulating the whole question of atomic weapons."[4] Mendès-France then signed the London (September 1954) and Paris agreements (October 23, 1954). Those agreements allowed the restoration of sovereignty to the Federal Republic of Germany (FRG) with the termination of the Occupation Regime, permitted the entry of the FRG and Italy into an expanded Brussels Treaty Organization, now named the Western Europe Union (WEU). The WEU was a substitute for the EDC, without supranationality. Another important factor was the admission of West Germany to the North Atlantic Treaty Organization. Chancellor Konrad Adenauer made a declaration whereby his nation vowed not to manufacture atomic, biological, or chemical weapons, while Sir Anthony Eden promised that Britain would maintain military forces in Europe.

These agreements had to be ratified by the signatories, including France. The crucial issue at stake in the French parliament's ratification was the acceptance of German rearmament, and this vote was essential to the outcome of the diplomatic initiatives. Conflicting pressures were put on France by the United States and the USSR. The U.S. made ratifi-

des tourmentes, 1954–1959 (Paris, 1992); Edgar Faure, Mémoires, 2 vols. (Paris, 1982–84); André Fontaine, Histoire de la guerre froide, vol. II, De la guerre corée à la crise des alliances, 1950–1963 (Paris, 1967); Alfred Grosser, La IV République et sa politique extérieure (Paris, 1961); Sylvie Guillaume, Antoine Pinay ou la confiance en politique (Paris, 1984); René Massigli, Une comédie des erreurs, 1943–1956 (Paris, 1978); Pierre Mendès-France, Gouverner c'est choisir, vol. II: Juin 1954–Février 1955 (Paris, 1974); François Bédarida and Jean-Pierre Rioux, eds., Pierre Mendès-France et le Mendésisme: L'expérience gouvernementale (1954–1955) et sa postérité (Paris, 1985); J. Nantet, Pierre Mendès-France (Paris, 1967); Jules Moch, Une si longue vie (Paris, 1976); and Christiane Rimbaud, Pinay (Paris, 1990). Also see Renata Fritsch-Bournazel, "Frankreichs Ost- und Deutschlandpolitik im Zeichen der Genfer Gipfelkonferenz von 1955," in Bruno Thoss and Hans-Erich Volkmann, eds., Zwischen Kaltem Krieg und Entspannung: Sicherheits- und Deutschlandpolitik der Bundesrepublik im Mächtesystem der Jahre 1953–1956 (Boppard am Rhein, 1988), 71–92.
  4. Wilfrid L. Kohl, French Nuclear Diplomacy (Princeton, 1971), 21.

cation a precondition for the holding of a summit. Washington tried to prevent any French delay or rejection of the agreements, as had been the case with the EDC. Conversely, the USSR wanted a summit conference to be held first, with one objective being to prevent the rearmament of the Federal Republic and her admission into NATO.

Against this background, as soon as the London and Paris agreements were signed, Moscow hurriedly sent two series of notes. The first, on October 23, 1954, was addressed to the ambassadors of the United States, Britain, and France in Moscow. The Soviet government proposed that the foreign ministers of those three Western countries meet with Soviet representatives in November to examine several issues, among them the convening of a general conference to discuss the establishment of a system of collective security in Europe. This was followed by a second Soviet proposal on November 13, 1954. The second note, which was sent to the United States and all European countries with which the USSR maintained diplomatic relations, proposed to convene a conference on collective security in Europe, in either Paris or Moscow on November 29, 1954.[5]

Pierre Mendès-France strongly believed that a dialogue with the USSR was not only possible but essential. Talks at the highest level between the great four would, he hoped, alter the adverse spirit that had characterized international relations over the past ten years. But the prime minister was not prepared to meet at any price. He had already approached Molotov on July 10, 1954, during the Geneva conference on Indochina, with the request that the USSR make a move on such important issues as Austria, disarmament, and Germany, with a view to resuming dialogue and permitting East-West negotiations.[6] But the USSR did not move. Therefore he seized the opportunity of the signing of the London and Paris agreements to make new overtures to the USSR, even though he believed that such a step might not be acceptable to either Washington or London. Thus, during his visit to New York, Mendès-France made a speech at the United Nations General Assembly on November 22, 1954. While stressing the importance of the ratification of the Paris agreements by all powers concerned, he dismissed the Soviet proposal calling for a top-level conference at the end of November as neither realistic nor reasonable. He suggested, however, the holding of a four-power conference in May 1955. He continued:

5. *Keesing's*, IX, 1952–54, pp. 13876, 13904.
6. Nantet, *Mendès-France*, 195.

The French Government hereby affirms that its will to take action for peace has not faltered. . . . The door to negotiations is not closed, quite to the contrary. It may be expected that the signatories of the Paris agreements will have completed the ratification procedures by the beginning of next spring. That will certainly be true of France. . . . Why then should we not decide that a Four-Power Conference should be held, for instance, in May? The French government is prepared to organize such a conference in Paris, if convenient to the other three participants.[7]

Then, expressing his view on disarmament, he declared:

The London and Paris Agreements organize . . . a system of regulation, limitation, control and publication of armaments. Later, exchanges of information and mutual assurances could take place between the two systems. Perhaps, even the limitations or controls might take on a contractual form. A flexible regional plan would thus gradually be set up, with the field of application of limitations, reductions and control increasing progressively.[8] He also appealed to the USSR to sign the Austrian State Treaty.

Mendès-France's dramatic proposal, appeal to world opinion, and gesture of independence were new and were met with great enthusiasm in New York as well as in France. Philip Williams wrote, "Pierre Mendès-France's aims and methods were not to everyone's taste; but he did bring about a new style of action, a new approach to problems."[9] However, the United States was reluctant to respond too readily to such an overture of dialogue and laid down a number of prerequisites for any four-power conference.

Both domestic and foreign-policy considerations underlay Mendès-France's address. The London and Paris agreements had to be ratified by the French Parliament, but the prime minister knew he would not obtain the vote of the Parliament unless the fear of German rearmament was addressed. Therefore, he used his support of the four-power conference as one of his strongest arguments in favor of ratification.[10] He felt the two were linked closely enough so that this would work.

Intervening in the debate at the French National Assembly on December 28, 1954, Mendès-France emphasized: "There would be no ques-

7. *Le Monde*, November 23–4, 1954; *Keesing's*, IX, 1952–54, p. 13911.
8. *Keesing's*, IX, 1952–54, p. 13911.
9. Philip M. Williams, *Politics in Post-war France: Parties and the Constitution in the Fourth Republic* (2nd ed., London, 1958).
10. *New York Times*, January 3, 1955.

tion of any four-power negotiations" if the Assembly rejected the Paris agreements; in that case, he went on, "there might at a later date be a two-power or three-power meeting." In such an eventuality, France would no doubt remain in the Atlantic Alliance, but would no longer have any influence in that organization. If, on the other hand, the agreements were ratified, France would have an important role to play both in NATO and in any future four-power negotiations. Mendès-France wanted to restore France's status and rank among the great powers. He was intent on ensuring that France continued to play a leading role in world affairs. After the rejection of the EDC treaty, rejection of the Paris agreements would mean isolating France even more. What he feared was the formation of a Bonn/London/Washington axis from which France would have been excluded. In his mind Western cohesion was at stake. The USSR might be encouraged to hope for further division among the Western allies. On December 30, 1954, at the end of a long debate, the French National Assembly ratified the Paris agreements and also the Franco-German agreement on the Saar (by 287 votes to 256 with 70 abstentions).[11]

It is crucial to note that the French premier, returning from the United States, had come to the conclusion that France should possess the A-bomb if it wanted to play an important part in international negotiations. Moreover, now that France had accepted German rearmament, possession of the A-bomb would set it above Germany, which had renounced all ABC armaments as part of the Paris agreements. France would regain leadership by virtue of being the sole nuclear power in continental Western Europe. Therefore, at an important interministerial meeting convened on December 28, 1954, by Mendès-France, "though no formal agreement was reached on the question of a French bomb, it was decided to undertake the construction of a nuclear powered submarine and to develop a nuclear energy infrastructure." A new military unit was established within the CEA (Atomic Energy Agency): the General Studies Bureau. Four years later, this bureau became the powerful Military Applications Directorate (DAM). There was no written report of the interministerial meeting, though the conclusions reached are mentioned in a memorandum of March 21, 1955, prepared for the National Defense Committee. According to Dominique Mongin,

11. *Le Monde*, December 23, 25, 28, 29, 1954; *Keesing's*, X, 1955–56, p. 13965.

Pierre Mendès-France was the first prime minister of the Fourth Republic to set his country decisively on the path toward military applications of nuclear energy.[12]

With the National Assembly's ratification of the Paris agreements, the prime minister was only halfway to his objective; he still had to obtain the vote of the Council of the Republic. This second chamber of parliament particularly disliked the prospect of a remilitarized Federal Republic of Germany. So the French premier had to do something before the debate. Looking for British support, he sent a letter to Churchill on January 5, 1955, accompanied by a memorandum that he sent to Eisenhower, Eden, and John Foster Dulles. In the memo, Mendès-France suggested two possible procedures for inviting the USSR to join in a four-power meeting. The first option was a unilateral French *démarche*; the second, favored by the French premier, a joint invitation from the three Western allies. In his reply, on January 12, 1955, Churchill flatly rejected the French proposal on the grounds that there would be neither negotiations nor a meeting by foreign ministers or heads of state until the London and Paris agreements were ratified by all signatories. The British prime minister also expressed a clear warning to France against "leaving an empty chair at international conferences lest it be occupied by some other nations." Eisenhower, Dulles, and Eden all made the same point: no talks nor any invitation prior to the ratification of the agreements. The American view had always been that "increased strength and unity of Europe resulting therefrom [i.e., from ratification] would put the West in better position to negotiate with Soviets on German reunification, etc."[13]

Eden suggested "the possibility of a tripartite working group in Paris whose work would be secret but whose existence would be known,"[14] seemingly with a view toward reassuring the French parliament regarding eventual East/West talks. Washington, or rather Dulles, disliked the idea and was strongly opposed to such a working group.

12. Georges-Henri Soutou, "The French Military Program for Nuclear Energy, 1945–1981," Occasional Paper 3, Nuclear History Program, Center for International Security Studies, Maryland School of Public Affairs, University of Maryland, 1989, 1–14; Dominique Mongin, "La genèse de l'armement nucléaire français, 1945–1958" (Ph.D. dissertation, University of Paris I, 1991), 360.

13. *DDF*, 1955, Annexes, I, 213–5; *Keesing's*, X, 14227–8; Dulles to Achilles, January 8, 1955, *FRUS, 1955–1957*, V, 119–21; Dulles to Achilles, January 15, 1955, ibid., 124f., Achilles to Dulles, January 16, 1955, ibid., 126–9; Dulles to Conant, January 19, 1955, ibid., 128f.

14. Achilles to Dulles, January 16, 1955, *FRUS, 1955–1957*, V, 126–8.

Mendès-France was ousted from office on February 4, 1955, over a dispute about North African policy, thus instigating a lengthy political crisis. On February 23, 1955, Edgar Faure formed a new government and was given a vote of investiture (369 votes to 210). Faure, who was a lawyer, a right-wing radical, a member of the French prosecution team at the Nuremberg trials, and one of the most brilliant and talented statesmen France had ever produced, had previously served as prime minister for a short time in 1952. More recently he had been finance minister under both Laniel and Mendès-France, and, since January 20, 1955, foreign minister. He had not always been on speaking terms with Mendès-France, but he endorsed the foreign-policy objectives and choices of his predecessor, thus ensuring continuity of French objectives. His main priorities were to reduce French isolation and to revive the dialogue with the USSR, which he hoped to accomplish by obtaining the Council of the Republic's ratification of the London and Paris agreements and making progress toward the convening of a four-power summit meeting.

Presenting his cabinet to the National Assembly and outlining his government's foreign-policy objectives, Faure stated that "the Government would complete the ratification of the London and Paris agreements in the shortest possible time. The government would at the same time seek every opportunity for East-West peace by negotiations. 'As soon as the agreements are ratified,' Faure went on, 'I shall propose that a study be undertaken, together with our allies, of the conditions for negotiations both in Europe and Asia. The two bases of the government's foreign policy—an assiduous search for peace through every opportunity for negotiation, and the organization of Western security in irrevocable fidelity to the Atlantic alliance'—could, it was hoped, lead to a general and controlled reduction of armaments."[15]

In spite of his continued affirmation of Atlantic solidarity, Edgar Faure was less an "atlanticist" than Mendès-France. He wanted to take fresh initiatives of his own in a renewed effort to bring about negotiations with the Soviet leaders. He saw the USSR not only as a Communist regime but also as the old, eternal Russia, and he strongly believed in the power of the ancient links between the Gauls and the Slavs to

15. *Le Monde,* 24 February 1955; M. Faure's declaration of February 24, in *Keesing's,* X, 14071.

contain German expansionism.[16] However, he had to overcome American opposition to such a policy.

This opposition was expressed by the State Department in a "guidance cable" sent on March 15 to American ambassadors in Europe.

> The Department is advised that the French Government desires a meeting of the three Western powers immediately after ratification of the Paris agreement. As reported by the Embassy in Paris, it is the intention of the French Government to discuss at this conference the policy of the Western powers in implementing these treaties with a particular view to using the intervening time for a renewed effort to negotiate with Soviet Russia. It can be assumed that these efforts of the French Government are in fulfillment of certain pledges by the former Prime Minister Mendès-France. . . . The Department would be more favorably disposed to a conference including the Federal Republic as this would be a sound counter-agent against any delaying treaties. . . . In case of continuing French insistence, it might prove necessary to notify other W.E.U. informally to solicit their support against this plan or, if advantageous, to turn it into a W.E.U. conference with the U.S. included.[17]

Edgar Faure did not agree with the proposal to include the FRG, at least not initially. Two or three days prior to the debate at the Council of the Republic, Gaston Palewski, attaché to the *président du conseil* in charge of atomic matters, invited to an informal, private lunch at his home Sergei A. Vinogradov, the Soviet ambassador to Paris, and Premier Faure. Faure, who spoke Russian, took this opportunity to speak freely with the Russian ambassador. The premier told Vinogradov that he strongly believed in an East-West rapprochement to put an end to the cold war and that prospect of ratification of the London and Paris agreements by the Council of the Republic was beyond question. Faure renewed his pledge that a top-level conference would be convened after the ratification. The message was relayed to Moscow. In his *Mémoires*, Faure writes that he accepted the invitation to that lunch for reasons of domestic policy. He had to deal very tactfully with Palewski, a founding member of the Gaullist party and one of the figures closest to General de Gaulle. Palewski had voted against the London and Paris agreements at the National Assembly. He had even said that "a straight ratification

16. Elgey, *La république des tourmentes*, 544.
17. *DDF*, 1955, I, no. 145, 23 March 1955, p. 342.

... would constitute an immense national defeat by setting German re-armament automatically in motion without proper safeguards." Knowing that Palewski might have an adverse influence on some senators regarding the vote at the Council of the Republic, Faure preferred to have him on his side. The same day, immediately after this lunch, Faure wrote to Churchill and Eisenhower on his own initiative, "reiterating that he would obtain an unconditional and undelayed approval by the Senate, but that in process, he and Pinay had taken moral commitment to do everything possible to bring about early talks with the Russians."[18] Such prompt and direct diplomatic action and firmness of attitude were, following Mendès-France's lead, innovative.

The Council of the Republic opened its debate on the Paris agreements on March 23. During the debate, Faure stated that the time had come for France to make a decision and put an end to the constant hesitations and tergiversations of French policy. He went on: "If France now changes her mind, it will not be I who will tell the Americans." Then, he "expressed his profound conviction that French policy must be clear, straightforward and unequivocal." The premier recalled that France had never supported the American doctrine of "rollback," nor had she been attracted to "containment." He expressed his determination to pursue efforts for a four-power conference, but at the same time insisted on the part France could play immediately after ratification. Being a member of the Western camp, France could not assume the role of mediator, but could recommend and instigate the negotiations. On March 28, the London and Paris agreements were ratified unconditionally by the Council of the Republic. The protocol on the amendments to the Brussels Treaty and the setting up of the Western European Union, involving the rearmament of FRG and its entry into WEU, passed by 184 votes to 110, and the protocol on the admission of FRG to NATO by 200 to 114. Those agreements were signed by President Coty on April 3, promulgated on April 8, and the instruments of ratification deposited on May 5. The implementation of the Paris agreements consolidated the Western alliance and gave the West a position of strength with respect to the Soviet Union. On March 29, in a memorandum sent to Washington and Paris, Great Britain expressed its desire to renew dialogue with the USSR. On April 5, France sent its aide-mémoire to London and Wash-

18. Faure, *Mémoires*, II, 134–41; *Keesing's*, X, 13967; *DDF*, 1955, I, no. 139, March 22, 1955, 331; Achilles to Dulles, March 22, 1955, *FRUS, 1955–1957*, V, 134f.

ington, calling for the immediate establishment of a Franco-Anglo-American working group in order to prepare for talks with the Soviet Union. In that aide-mémoire, France agreed with the British proposals regarding the main issues to be studied by the tripartite group: "Austria, Germany and European security [and] ways and means of dealing with all other issues outstanding between East and West." It was agreed that Austrian and German representatives would be invited to participate in the sessions relating to their countries.[19]

On April 25, plans for a Western overture to the Soviet Union regarding the four-power conference were announced in a joint statement in London, Washington, and Paris. The president of the United States had finally agreed to a meeting of heads of government, although Secretary of State Dulles and the State Department did not understand such an "eagerness of Great Britain and France for the four-power talks at Heads of State level without, apparently, any substantive objectives, and especially their theory that a miracle can be brought about without concrete ideas of how it can be done." Edgar Faure now turned his attention toward ensuring that the initiative of such a conference did not fall into the hands of the USSR. A lengthy period of diplomatic exchanges and multilateral discussions followed. Different working groups were established and met to study procedures and examine the issues to be discussed. On May 10, the ambassadors of the three powers in Moscow presented identical notes inviting the USSR to a "two-stage" conference of heads of government and foreign ministers. In the meantime, the Soviets made a series of spectacular moves in the international arena. They concluded the Austrian treaty; Khrushchev and Bulganin visited Yugoslavia; they invited Chancellor Adenauer to come to Moscow; they formed the Warsaw Pact; and new Soviet proposals on reduction of armaments were introduced on May 10. All of this radically altered the context for the prospective summit, for which they accepted the invitation on May 26. As Georgette Elgey writes: "Moscow was no longer Moscow."[20]

19. *Journal officiel de la république français*, no. 28, compte rendu, March 25, 1955, pp. 997–9; ibid., no. 30, March 27, 1955, p. 1104; *Keesing's*, X, 1955–56, p. 14229; *DDF*, 1955, I, no. 157, March 29, 1955, pp. 362–4, and no. 172, April 5, 1955, pp. 401–2; Dulles to London, March 28, 1955, *FRUS*, 1955–1957, V, 135f.

20. *Keesing's*, X, 14191; Hoover to Dulles, May 8, 1955, *FRUS*, 1955–1957, V, 177f.; *DDF*, 1955, Annexes, I, 1125; *Department of State Bulletin*, May 23, 1955, pp. 832–3; Elgey, *La république des tourmentes*, 550f.

During the months of March and May 1955, crucial decisions were made and steps taken for the full development of French military applications of atomic energy. Dominique Mongin has argued: "The policies of the successive cabinets . . . after that of Mendès-France, show the subtle differences between what was officially said and what was really done." This is illustrated by the fluctuating attitudes of Edgar Faure and of his successor, Guy Mollet, on the atomic military issue; they vacillated between a declared opposition and a decisive but covert support. On March 16, Faure stated at a press conference that France should consider building a nuclear weapon. He went on to say: "It seems clear that there will soon be two classes of nations, 'strong and aristocratic' nations possessing thermo-nuclear weapons, and 'inferior' nations—not from the moral but from the material point of view—who do not possess them. . . . France cannot remain a 'diminished great power' in face of this new criterion." But on April 13, Faure announced that atomic research in France would be devoted solely to peaceful purposes and that the French government would not manufacture either A- or H-bombs. No further explanation was given on this ostensible change of attitude by the French premier. But it should be noted that the Socialist Party took an official position on the nuclear weapons issue at the March 12 meeting. Atomic weapons were condemned because they were immoral. The entire French nuclear program was blasted. A few weeks later, this condemnation was reaffirmed. Faure needed Socialist "support for his domestic as well as his foreign policy." Yet on May 20, "a secret protocol was signed which recorded agreement between the CEA and the Ministry of Defense on a joint program for the 1955–1957 period, carried out by the CEA, to extend basic nuclear infrastructure and conduct technical research. . . . Thus, a coordinated military atomic program was being launched at the same time that the government declared itself officially opposed to such a development."[21]

French Policy Aims and Views at the Summit

The West had assigned only limited objectives to the conference. The purpose of the meeting was to measure the political atmosphere in the

21. Mongin, "La genèse," 390; Dominique Mongin, "The Genesis of French Nuclear Forces, 1945–1948," paper presented at the Nuclear History Program, Stiftung Wissenschaft und Politik, Ebenhausen, Germany, June 1991, p. 7; Keesing's, X, 14362f.; Philip Engamarre, "Les partis politiques et l'opinion face à la bombe atomique français" (M.A. thesis, University of Paris, 1985); Kohl, French Nuclear Diplomacy, 24.

cold war and test the real intentions of the new Soviet leaders. President Eisenhower told the State Department that "the purpose of the meeting was to be exploratory only, and no substantive problems or decisions should be considered. It would locate areas of tension and disagreement, and assign them to working groups or to organizations such as the UN." On May 24, the American ambassador to Paris, in conveying a message to Foreign Secretary Pinay, reaffirmed the limited purpose of the meeting: "The purpose of the meeting is not to engage in any substantive discussion of issues but simply to formulate the issues to be worked on and to agree on methods to be followed for their solution."[22] What did France expect from the Geneva Conference, what was the French position on various issues?

With the joint tripartite invitation to the USSR and the planning of the four-power conference, France's principal policy goal was already attained: France was one of the three inviting nations, equal to the great powers in rank and status as one of the World War II Allies. In contrast to the situation of the Federal Republic of Germany, French great-power status was recognized:

> Agreement among the United States, England and France on the necessity for these talks has made the French feel for the first time in years that they are in step with American foreign policy and furthermore they are now importantly right in the second row, instead of angrily straggling somewhere far behind and as likely as not heading in the opposite direction. Sir Winston Churchill put England in the front row early with his demand for a new talk with the Russians; Pierre Mendès-France moved France into the second row when he spoke out boldly for his country which had long so passionately wished for such a denouement. Only Washington, the French have noted, is distinctly in the third row having so lately come to the point of talking.

From the telegrams exchanged and records of the preparatory discussions and meetings, it is obvious, however, that France was still isolated. Franco-American relations were bad at the time. The two countries differed sharply on Indochina. Neither the Americans nor the Germans had confidence in France. Faure was considered "brilliant but unreliable." What the Americans distrusted most was the French policy of negotiations with Soviet Russia. Washington feared that the French

---

22. Hoover to Dulles, May 15, 1955, *FRUS, 1955–1957*, V, 179f.; *DDF*, 1955, 1, no. 296, Paris, May 25, 1955, 682.

"might even agree to make a deal with the Russians in order to keep the Germans down" and "were so uncertain, so unhappy, and in such a mess all over everywhere" that they might "fall for some Soviet trick which would give France the illusion of being protected against a re-armed Germany."[23]

Washington and Bonn also distrusted the French because they had no-ticed a rivalry between Faure and Pinay: "There is considerable jealousy between Faure and Pinay. Faure wants a meeting at the Heads of Gov-ernment level, and Pinay wants it at the foreign ministers' level. Inci-dentally," Dulles went on, "Adenauer privately whispered to me that he felt that it would be wise to avoid bringing Faure into the discussions with the Soviets. He does not seem to feel that he is very 'solid.' " In-deed, some discrepancies existed between the prime minister and his foreign minister, or at least that was what Adenauer intimated. "The Chancellor . . . was concerned over France. He said that Faure had told him of his intention to shift Pinay to the Ministry of Defense and take over the Quai d'Orsay himself." Further disagreements existed between Pinay and Palewski and between the foreign minister and his officials in the Quai d'Orsay, which might explain a certain lack of coordination in policy. "The Chancellor trusts Pinay and has had good talks with him, but in some countries, power is divided between the Minister and the Ministry."[24]

The American delegation to the London working group did not think much of the French either: "French in working group were extremely inquisitive and volubly uncertain. They wish as approach to Soviets stress improvement has already occurred and that further détente should be pursued. They have raised question whether security guaran-tees with Soviet Russia could not be based upon acceptance split-Germany and indirectly broached this suggestion to Germans in ple-nary meeting who gave flat rejection. Quite probably they will adopt strong co-existence line. [sic]"[25]

France, then, was not exactly in line with American foreign-policy

23. Letter from Paris, *New Yorker*, June 4, 1955; Merchant to Dulles (private conversa-tion with Adenauer), June 15, 1955, *FRUS, 1955–1957*, V, 228f.; memorandum of discussion at the 254th Meeting of the National Security Council, July 7, 1955, ibid., 268–84; C. D. Jackson log entry, July 11, 1955, ibid., 301–5.

24. Dulles to Department of State (for Eisenhower), May 9, 1955, *FRUS, 1955–1957*, V, 174f.; Merchant to Dulles, June 15, 1955, ibid., 228–30; memorandum of conversation, May 7, 1955, ibid., 167–70.

25. Beam to Department of State, April 30, 1955, ibid., 160–2.

objectives. The French premier did not conform to the American recommendation that no concrete plans or proposals be presented at the Geneva meeting. Faure attended the conference and chaired sessions and made constructive proposals. Speaking in the name of France, he expressed French views on the outstanding East-West issues, although he remained in the second row, as did British prime minister Eden; the leading figure at the conference was President Eisenhower.

The principal French policy objective at the summit was to prevent the Soviet leaders from taking the initiative on constructive proposals at the conference. Faure envisaged East-West relations from a completely new perspective. That is why he made the following suggestions to the three chiefs of government, just before the meeting: 1) We will need to look to the future and not to the past; hunting for principles of agreement for future action. 2) Since it is a conference at the "highest level," we should examine problems from the same viewpoint. 3) We should try to see the other's viewpoint.[26]

Since the end of the war, France's policy toward Germany had been one of "give and hold back." After having accepted German rearmament, Faure made a positive, courageous, and impressive statement, "doubly so coming from a Frenchman in his opening address at the Geneva Conference." He declared persuasively that German reunification should remain an essential goal, but that this reunification raised a problem of security. He went on to explain that he was strongly opposed to any neutralization of Germany for the following reasons: 1) In international law, there could be no discrimination against a sovereign country; 2) neutralization would mean putting responsibility on the German people and not on the Nazi state; 3) no similar neutralization measures had been applied to other belligerents; 4) neutralization would provoke a desire for revenge among Germans; 5) technical measures for controlling neutralization would be impossible to implement "materially and morally"; 6) neutralization, while suitable perhaps for a small nation, was impossible for a nation with a population and geographical position like that of Germany. He added: "For my part, I believe that a reunified Germany should live in the Western and European Atlantic Pact system. This seems to me best both in law and in fact." This announcement had been made for propaganda reasons, for the purpose of

26. *New York Herald Tribune* (Paris edition), July 14, 1955.

preventing France from being ostracized in the eyes of the German public, and also to reassure the United States.[27]

Since German unification and European security were intertwined, the nations needed to examine the possibility of meeting the Soviet demands for security. Toward this objective, the French prime minister put forward the following proposals: 1) A unified Germany should accept arms and armament limitations as contained in the Western European Union Treaty; 2) the Western Powers should extend to the Soviet Union the guarantees embodied in the Paris agreements and the Federal Republic of Germany should also extend to the Soviet Union an undertaking (under the Paris agreements) that it would not use force to obtain reunification or the modification of Germany's present borders; 3) a unified Germany should be included in a general security system, which could be extended to all European States wishing to join. Faure had in mind the creation of an all-inclusive European Organization in addition to the two existing organizations, the Western European Union and the Warsaw Pact. In an earlier (July 16) meeting in Paris with high Western officials, Faure had stated, "It would even be in the interest of the West to have some such overall organization as it would provide the mechanism for controlling German arms and armament in case, considered to be theoretical, Germany should choose to remain neutral and not join the West or the East."[28]

Faure preferred a system of collective security containing reciprocal agreements providing for limitations of armament. The French idea was to better control a reunited Germany by containing it in regional and/or international organizations. France's reconciliation with the Federal Republic of Germany did not take place until three years later (March 1958), when Konrad Adenauer visited General de Gaulle at Colombey-les-deux Eglises. In 1955, Faure gave higher priority to stabilization of the present situation in Europe than to German reunification.

Another French policy aim was a psychological one. Faure wanted to appeal to world opinion and demonstrate that France, in spite of defeat in Indochina and difficulties in North Africa, was taking into account

27. Grosser, *La IV République et sa politique extérieure,* 400; Delegation Record of the First Plenary Session of the Geneva Conference, July 18, 1955, *FRUS, 1955–1957,* V, 364–6; *DDF,* 1955, Annexes, II, 19–27; *Keesing's,* X, 14325;

28. Note from the Europe Directorate of the Quai d'Orsay, *DDF,* 1955, Annexes, II, no. 7, Paris, July 4, 1955, p. 10f.; delegation at the tripartite foreign ministers' meeting (Paris) to the Department of State, July 16, 1955, *FRUS, 1955–1957,* V, 333–5.

the resolutions of the Bandung Conference of April 1955. In hopes of using the Geneva Conference to achieve such psychological and propaganda advantages, the prime minister laid emphasis on what he considered a new approach, disarmament and transfer of resources for peaceful purposes to underdeveloped nations. A broad outline of this plan for economic and budgetary controls was revealed on July 13, during a press conference held by Faure in Paris. He presented it again in his opening statement at Geneva, and once more on July 21 as an elaborate plan in his "Memorandum on Disarmament."[29]

The French disarmament plan rested on two basic ideas: that the first condition for a lasting peace was progress toward disarmament, and that civilized nations should provide assistance to the peoples of underdeveloped countries.

> The French Government believes that these two forms of activity should be carried out side by side and that the possibility of establishing an organic link between them should be investigated. . . . The French Government proposes that the four powers should agree to a reduction in their military expenditures, and that the financial resources thus made available should be allocated, either in whole or in part, to international expenditures on equipment and mutual aid. . . . These proposals . . . will make possible the transfer of military to productive expenditure at the international level.[30]

Yet this French initiative turned out a complete flop. "Neither the Americans nor the British seemed very keen about it," writes Harold Macmillan in his *Memoirs*. He continues: "Fortunately we had no Treasury representatives with us; so we gave a polite if insincere assent to these ideas." The Americans found the idea completely unsound, even though it was not new. Eisenhower had made a similar suggestion in his speech of April 16, 1953, "on the connection between the reduction of armaments and economic and social questions,"[31] and in his opening statement at Geneva: "All recognize that present levels of armaments are a heavy burden on the various nations and should be reduced, not

29. Delegation Record of the First Plenary Session of the Geneva Conference, July 18, 1955, *FRUS, 1955–1957*, V, 364–6; proposal of the French delegation, July 21, 1955, ibid., 521–4; *DDF*, 1955, Annexes, II, 163–5; *Keesing's*, X, 14325.

30. *DDF*, 1955, Annexes, II, 163–5; Proposal of the French Delegation, July 21, 1955, *FRUS, 1955–1957*, V, 521–4; *Keesing's*, 14328–9.

31. Macmillan, *Tides of Fortune*, 616; *New York Herald Tribune*, July 14, 1955; memorandum of conversation at the tripartite luncheon, President's Villa, Geneva, July 17, 1955, *FRUS, 1955–1957*, V, 343–54.

merely as a measure of economy but because armaments designed for security may in fact lead to war."[32]

Faure had developed his plan in consultation with Senegalese leader Leopold Sedar Senghor, members of the French parliament, the secretary of state (who was attached to the *président du conseil*), and Valéry Giscard d'Estaing, a young finance expert, deputy director of the prime minister's cabinet. Both Faure and Pinay had previously been finance ministers. For domestic political reasons, Faure felt compelled to propose the initiative. He had to report to Parliament upon his return, and he was constrained to take into account the conclusion of the French Socialist Party Congress of July 3 that disarmament was the only way to put an end to the progressive increase in inequality between industrial and underdeveloped countries. France's troubles in North Africa mandated that Faure take into account the emergence of the third world, as revealed by the Bandung conference. But among all plans presented at Geneva, Eisenhower's "Open Skies" proposal, making use as it did of new technical control capabilities, most captured world opinion and imagination.[33]

Another French policy aim at Geneva was a very ambitious one: the progressive reestablishment of European unity. Faure wanted to create on both sides of the iron curtain closer relationships between the peoples, easier contact between individuals, and wider exchanges between their economic systems. He wanted to promote the improvement of East-West relations in order to reduce ideological conflict, thereby ensuring a lasting peace. He envisaged a Europe from "the Atlantic to the Ural." The French premier was ahead of his time. He put forward nine proposals: facilitation of the free movement of men, ideas, and goods, as instruments of peace; permission for travel by individual tourists; exchange of professional groups and delegations, and of students and lecturers; exchange of books, newspapers, scientific reviews, and documentary films; free access to sources of information; exchange of all types of statistics; development of international trade relations; association between the countries of Eastern and Western Europe in common organizations, particularly in the fields of transport and electrical power; and the creation of a common investment fund in Europe for the

32. Opening statements, Delegation Record of the First Plenary Session, July 18, 1955.
33. *DDF*, 1955, Annexes, II, 174; proposal of the French delegation, Geneva, July 22, 1955, *FRUS, 1955–1957*, V, 526.

institution of public works of general value, from which the different countries could benefit commonly.[34]

The final aim was one to improve social contacts between world leaders. Faure did not want to leave the USSR isolated. He wanted to create an atmosphere of relaxation and confidence through the establishment of personal and social contacts. To this end, the French premier was the first to invite the Soviet leaders to a private dinner at his villa in Geneva on Sunday, July 17. He gave another lavish reception on July 22, in a relaxed and happy atmosphere. Behind the scenes, in private conversations, the discussions dealt mostly with the situation in the Far East (Indochina, Formosa, and the Quemoy and Matsu Islands crisis).

France played an important role at the Geneva summit, although the USSR and the United States did not need the participation of either Great Britain or France. The two superpowers were able to enter a dialogue between themselves. The true revelation of the conference was this new bilateral structure of power, with the superpowers in control of international affairs.

Conclusion

The conference was neither a success nor a complete failure. The Big Four did not arrive at far-reaching decisions. They "failed to get anywhere with any of the three substantive problems on the Agenda: Germany, European security and disarmament." There was a détente but not an entente. "Geneva was an exercise in procrastination." As to the French, they "seem to have been turning some invisible psychological corner and to have rediscovered themselves." The conference was designed to be the beginning of a series of high-level meetings. Perhaps the most significant move of all was the decision to hold the conference—a decision which was obtained above all by France's determination to make possible a summit meeting with the Russians and by Britain's support of France's position.[35]

But what was the impact of the Geneva Conference on French public opinion? After his return, the premier emphasized at a press conference (on Saturday, July 23) how important and moving an experience it had been to participate in the summit. He paid tribute to the president of

34. See the Prados essay in this volume.
35. *New Yorker*, July 30, August 6, 1955.

the United States, who with his proposal had set the emotional high point of the meeting. With regard to the results, Faure was neither optimistic nor pessimistic. He said only that this had been a first step. Reporting before the Council of Ministers and the Foreign Affairs Commission, Faure pointed out the part played by the French Delegation, although he recognized that the Geneva summit had been primarily an American-Soviet dialogue. He observed that his plan for the transfer of military expenditures to the benefit of underdeveloped countries had been well received in several countries of Asia and Africa. What seemed to him the most important thing was the assertion that the reunification of Germany was the common responsibility of the Big Four. He concluded by saying that if the conference had not been a success, it had not been a failure either. A greater success would have been difficult to imagine, for it would have implied the defeat of one of the major players or the sacrifice of Germany.

The French press pointed out that for the first time in the cold war, direct communications had been established between the heads of state and, beyond them, between the peoples. But the French public took little notice. As famed commentator André Fontaine wrote in *Le Monde* on August 4, 1955, they were much more preoccupied by the Moroccan question and by their summer vacations than by the Geneva Conference. He noted that without the support of the nation, the head of the French government was in a weaker position to play a leading role. Faure would have liked to be the intermediary between the superpowers, but, as Fontaine put it, the two did not need an intermediary. The Western powers realized that the USSR was not, for the present time, interested in the reunification of Germany, because it wanted, first of all, to keep Germany under its influence. According to Fontaine, the Paris agreements, which confirmed the division of Germany and Europe, confirmed the maintenance of East Germany, its uranium, its industrial potentialities, and its revolutionary cell within the Communist world. About this there seems to be no doubt. At Geneva, the cold war did not end, it had just been temporarily suspended.

The Making of the Austrian Treaty and the Road to Geneva

GÜNTER BISCHOF

Introduction

The Austrian State Treaty, next to the German question, was one of the principal issues on the East-West negotiating agenda in what has been called the "first" cold war in Europe.[1] Coming out of the unresolved World War II "peace agenda," Austria remained a subissue of the German problem until the new Soviet leadership in the Kremlin under Nikita Khrushchev decided to break that linkage early in 1955, after the final division of Germany with the military and political integration of the Federal Republic into the West. The Kremlin dreaded the prospect that the Western powers' secret rearmament of their occupation zones in Austria was directed at integrating the Western Austrian bridge as well into the Western defense system. The increasingly loud Soviet campaign in late 1954 and early 1955 for Austrian "guarantees" against a "new Anschluss" referred to such an "annexation" to Western Europe. The decisive 1955 breakthrough in the Austrian treaty negotiations and the neutralization of Austria came only after West German rearmament had become irreversible. The Kremlin concessions ensured that Austria

I would like to thank Saki Dockrill for her invaluable suggestions for improving this essay.

1. Gerald Stourzh, *Geschichte des Staatsvertrages 1945–1955: Österreichs Weg zur Neutralität*, 3rd ed. (Graz, 1985); Kurt Steiner, "Negotiations for an Austrian Treaty," in *U.S.-Soviet Security Cooperation: Achievements, Failures, Lessons*, ed. Alexander George, Philip J. Farley, and Alexander Dallin (New York, 1988), 46–82; Audrey Kurth Cronin, *Great Power Politics and the Struggle over Austria, 1945–1955* (Ithaca, N.Y., 1986); Günter Bischof, "Between Responsibility and Rehabilitation: Austria in International Politics, 1940–1950," 2 vols. (Ph.D. dissertation, Harvard University, 1989). See also Robert H. Keyserlingk, *Austria in World War II: An Anglo-American Dilemma* (Kingston, Canada, 1988). Fred Halliday characterizes the period 1946–1953 as the "First Cold War" (*The Making of the Second Cold War*, 2nd ed. [London, 1986], 3). Given the dogged U.S. resistance to Soviet offers of "peaceful coexistence," I would extend the period to 1955; the finalization of the division of Germany with the ratification of the Paris agreements, the signing of the Austrian treaty, the beginning of arms limitations negotiations, and the Geneva summit ended the most confrontational age of the cold war.

would not follow West Germany into NATO. They also indicated a new departure for the new, more accommodating post-Stalin Soviet foreign policy under Nikita Khrushchev, which went beyond mere tactical maneuvering.[2]

Ever since the crises of 1948–49 and the outbreak of the Korean War in 1950, both superpowers were mainly interested not in good-faith diplomacy but in seizing the initiative in the escalating bad-faith cold-war propaganda battles.[3] The Austrian treaty negotiations, which had almost been successful in the fall of 1949, became one of the principal victims of this superpower descent into psychological warfare in lieu of diplomatic negotiations, turning Austria into a hostage of the militarization of the cold war during the Korean War. Ever since the Communist coup in Prague in February 1948, the Pentagon had urged the

2. See the sources mentioned in the previous note, as well as Robert Graham Knight, "British Policy towards Austria, 1945–1950" (Ph.D. dissertation, University of London, 1988) and Manfried Rauchensteiner, *Der Sonderfall: Die Besatzungspolitik in Österreich 1945 bis 1955* (Graz, 1979). On the Moscow CFM, see also my introduction and Charles P. Kindleberger, *The German Economy, 1945–1947: Charles P. Kindleberger's Letters from the Field* (Westport, Conn., 1989); on 1948 progress, see Günter Bischof, " 'Prag liegt westlich von Wien': Internationale Krisen im Jahre 1948 und ihr Einfluss auf Österreich," in *Die bevormundete Nation: Österreich und die Alliierten 1945–1949*, ed. Günter Bischof und Josef Leidenfrost (Innsbruck, 1988), 315–45.

The clearest statement of "lost momentum" and "seizing the initiative" was expressed by Secretary of State Dean Acheson; see memorandum of conversation, March 7, 1959, folder "March 1950," Box 65, Acheson Papers, Harry S. Truman Library, Independence, Mo. The best description of the context is Melvyn S. Leffler's essay "Wresting the Initiative," in his *Preponderance of Power: National Security, the Truman Administration, and the Cold War* (Stanford, Calif.,1992); see also Ernest R. May, ed., *American Cold War Strategy: Interpreting NSC 68* (Boston, 1993). On the "militarization" of the cold war, see Vojtech Mastny, "Stalin and the Militarization of the Cold War," *International Security*, IX (1984–85), 109–29, and Thomas J. McCormick, *America's Half Century: United States Foreign Policy in the Cold War* (Baltimore, 1989), 92–108.

3. NSC 38 "The Austrian Treaty in the CFM," December 8, 1948, in *FRUS, 1948*, II, 1510–35 (quotation, 1513). On the discussions of the Austrian problem in the National Security Council, see Oliver Rathkolb, "Von der Besatzungsmacht zur Neutralität: Österreich in den aussenpolitischen Strategien des nationalen Sicherheitsrates unter Truman und Eisenhower," in *Die Bevormundete Nation*, 371–405; for an extensive discussion of these national-security-related American concerns based on formerly unused or recently opened American documents, see Günter Bischof, "Österreich—ein 'geheimer Verbündeter' des Westens? Wirtschafts—und sicherheitspolitische Fragen der Integration aus Sicht der USA," in *Österreich und die europäische Integration 1945–1993*, ed. Michael Gehler and Rolf Steininger (Vienna, 1993), 425–50, and " 'Austria Looks to the West': Kommunistische Putschgefahr, geheime Wiederbewaffnung und Westorientierung am Anfang der fünfziger Jahre," in *Österreich in den Fünfzigern*, ed. Thomas Albrich et al. (Innsbruck, 1995), 183–209.

Truman administration not to sign an Austrian treaty, which would create a strategic vacuum in the center of Europe before the nucleus of an Austrian army was completed. The new basic policy directive National Security Council document NSC 38, dominated by the thinking of the American high commissioner in Austria, General Geoffrey Keyes, and the Pentagon, stated that "the occupation forces should not be withdrawn until such time that the Austrians have organized equipped and trained a security force reasonably adequate to perform [the] tasks envisaged in the treaty." American military leaders intended a "retardation mission" for the nucleus of a future Austrian army that they secretly armed and equipped during the Korean War: "The strategic objective for Austrian defense forces will be maintenance of internal security and a limited capability of delaying Soviet Bloc attack toward key passes into Italy and Western Europe." During the Korean War, the Pentagon advanced the rearmament of Western Austria ahead of its efforts to rearm the Federal Republic of Germany, turning Austria into a quasi-"secret ally" of the West.[4] From the Pentagon's perspective, as long as there was no serious East-West diplomatic contact, no Austrian treaty would be signed and Austria would not become a strategic vacuum on the highly contested Central European front line.

At the time of Stalin's death, Austrian treaty negotiations had reached their lowest point in the almost eight years that the East and West had been trying to reach an agreement regarding Austria. All avenues of diplomacy had broken down as a consequence of the superpower standoff: the leaders had not met in a summit since Potsdam in 1945; the foreign ministers had failed to sit down since Paris in 1949; and even the foreign ministers' special deputies, who had performed the lion's share of negotiating the Austrian treaty in 260 special sessions, were no longer meeting with the intention of finishing the treaty during the Korean War. The *idée fixe* in Washington was that the West had to rearm first and that one could only negotiate from a position of strength with the Communists.

4. Quotation, Admiral Radford (Chairman of the JCS) to Secretary of Defense, September 11, 1956, 763.5–MSP/10–1056, RG 59, NA. For the "Keyes Plan," see Keyes to Department of the Army, February 1, 1950, *FRUS, 1950,* IV, 476–8; for further background on the remilitarization of Austria, see Bischof, "Geheimer Verbündeter des Westens?" 441–9, and "Austria looks to the West," 191–200; for the "secret ally" thesis, see Gerald Stourzh, "The Origins of Austrian Neutrality," in *Neutrality: Changing Concepts and Practices,* ed. Alan T. Leonhard (Lanham, Md., 1988), 35–57.

On the insistence of the Pentagon, rearmament took priority even in Austria over finishing the treaty. Meanwhile, the U.S. pretended to the desperate Austrian population that it still maintained an interest in concluding the treaty. The "abbreviated treaty" draft, presented in March 1952, was supposed to seize the initiative for the West. It was clear to all informed observers that the Soviets would find this short treaty unacceptable. In drafting it, the U.S. State Department was answering Soviet obstructionism on the Austrian issue with a propaganda initiative of its own that pleased no one. It was obvious from the very beginning that the abbreviated treaty would accomplish nothing substantial; as an American official on the State Department's Austrian desk observed disarmingly, "Its advantage to us is purely propaganda."[5]

From the Kremlin's perspective, such American moves to strong-arm Austria into a separate agreement with the West looked sinister and could only lead to "a formal integration of Austria into the aggressive bloc [NATO] with its territory becoming an American military foothold in the center of Europe."[6]

While the Japanese got their "separate" treaty in 1951, and the Western powers initiated "separate" negotiations with the West German

---

5. On the initial four-power declaration, see NSC 38/5, April 27, 1950, in *FRUS, 1950*, IV, 389. The text of the abbreviated treaty can be found in the *Department of State Bulletin*, March 13, 1952, 448–50, and in Stourzh, *Geschichte der Staatsvertrages*, 220–2. The most extensive treatment of the origins and diplomacy of the abbreviated-treaty proposal is my own unpublished paper "Lost Momentum: The Militarization of the Cold War and the Demise of Austrian Treaty Negotiations, 1950–1952." For the Stalin notes in Germany, see Rolf Steininger, *The German Question: The Stalin Notes of 1952 and the Problem of Reunification* (New York, 1990); on the basis of American and British sources, I first noted the diplomatic interaction between the Stalin notes and the abbreviated-treaty proposal in my "Karl Gruber und die Anfänge des 'Neuen Kurses' in der österreichischen Aussenpolitik 1952–53," in *Für Österreichs Freiheit: Karl Gruber—Landeshauptmann und Aussenminister 1945–1953*, ed. Lothar Höbelt and Othmar Huber (Innsbruck, 1991), 144–51. This diplomatic interlude is now treated more extensively, on the basis of Austrian and French sources, by Michael Gehler, "Kurzvertrag für Österreich? Die westliche Staatsvertrags-Diplomatie und die Stalin-Noten von 1952," *Vierteljahrshefte für Zeitgeschichte*, XLII (1994), 243–78. The leading critic of rigid four-power Austrian diplomacy was Austria's foreign minister Karl Gruber; see his *Gruber: Reden und Dokumente*, ed. Michael Gehler (Vienna, 1994), 286, 292, 334, 336, 407, 413. For the "propaganda" citation, see the memorandum "New Approaches to an Austrian Settlement," Rutter to Allen, June 29, 1951, 663.001/6–2951, Box 2968, RG 59, NA.

6. See Vladislav Zubok, "Soviet Intelligence and the Cold War: The 'Small' Committee of Information, 1952–53," *Diplomatic History*, XIX (1995), 458. This quotation in Zubok's fascinating essay is based on a Committee of Information report to Stalin, dated August 23, 1952, and located in the Foreign Ministry files.

government of Konrad Adenauer for limited sovereignty and the inclusion of German units in the European Defence Community, the "separate" treaty initiative on Austria got nowhere. The Austrian issue was bogged down more deeply than ever in the morass of East-West tensions and the unwillingness of the superpowers to make any meaningful concessions in either Germany or Austria, let alone sit down and negotiate face to face. George Kennan was accurate in his observation that "the Soviets would like to reserve their position on Austria until they know roughly what shape the German settlement is going to take. Their position in Austria represents a card in their hands which they might wish to play in the final phases of the German settlement."[7]

Western Response to the New Looks in the Kremlin and the Ballhausplatz (1953–1954)

All of this changed dramatically after Stalin's death (March 5, 1953), when the international climate at last appeared to be warming in Austria's favor. A new collective leadership quickly emerged in the Kremlin—with Georgi Malenkov operating as *primus inter pares* in a *troika* with Nikita Khrushchev and Lavrenti Beria. Their policy departure toward peaceful coexistence with the West seemed to indicate previously unheard-of opportunities to reduce cold-war tensions. But was this a genuine policy reversal or merely a new propaganda offensive? Policy makers then and scholars today still cannot agree.[8]

The Kremlin's offensive for peaceful coexistence underwent a dynamic process from being primarily a propaganda initiative in 1953 to becoming a full-fledged and sincere policy departure by 1955. Recent evidence from Soviet archives suggests that the Soviet peace offensive in the spring of 1953 was a product of Soviet domestic politics and Kremlin political infighting rather than a genuine reversal that truly moved away from hardline Stalinist foreign policy. When Molotov regained control of Soviet foreign policy, he concentrated on blocking West German rearmament by hook or by crook. But when Molotov's intransigent

7. Kennan to Department of State, July 18, 1952, *FRUS, 1952–1954*, II, 1770f. I have corrected the garble in the cable by filling in the abbreviations and correcting the grammar in this quotation.

8. For new studies debating this issue, see Vladislav Zubok and Constantine Pleshakov, *Inside the Kremlin's Cold War: From Stalin to Khrushchev* (Cambridge, Mass., 1996); John Lewis Gaddis, *We Now Know: Rethinking Cold War History* (Oxford, U.K., 1997); see also the Immerman and Zubok essays in the present volume.

European policy lay irreversibly stymied by the Paris agreements, Khrushchev's ascendancy took some of the propaganda wedge out of "peaceful coexistence." The diplomacy of 1955 represented the triumph of Khrushchev's more moderate and realistic policy over Molotov's old-line Stalinist principle of not giving up an inch of territory conquered by the Red Army in World War II.[9]

This seemingly more flexible policy of guarded cooperation with the West was designed to ease the new Kremlin leaders' fear of instability in the Soviet Union after Stalin's death and the perceived threat that the new Eisenhower administration would take advantage of such instability. The internal power struggle among the collective Kremlin leadership most clearly came to light in the experimental and ultimately contradictory "New Policy" toward the Soviet puppet regime in East Germany. In late May and early June 1953, Beria pushed for a departure from the strict support of the Ulbricht regime and initiated a policy of neutralizing and unifying Germany. But after the East German riots of June 17, which were in part precipitated by this policy departure, Molotov insisted that Beria's policy be reversed and, in a return to Stalinism, Ulbricht's regime be salvaged. Beria paid for the failed experiment with his life. The new evidence suggests that Western rearmament of West Germany remained a top worry of the new Kremlin leadership, who planned new propaganda to counter the Western moves. As James Rich-

9. As early as 1982, on the basis of his usual brilliance in sleuthing through the available public records, Vojtech Mastny identified the outcome of the power struggle in the Kremlin and Khrushchev's ascendancy as the principal reason for the 1955 Austrian treaty breakthrough; see his "Kremlin Politics and the Austrian Settlement," *Problems in Communism*, XXXI (1982), 37–51. More recently, on the basis of new Soviet archival evidence, Vladislav Zubok arrived at similar conclusions in his paper "Soviet Foreign Policy in Germany and Austria and the Post-Stalin Struggle, 1953–1955," presented at the 1994 International Cold War Project conference "The Soviet Union, Germany, and the Cold War, 1945–1962: New Evidence from Eastern Archives," in Essen, Germany. On political infighting, see also Zukov, "Soviet Intelligence and the Cold War," 471, as well as his essay in the present volume; Amy Knight, *Beria: Stalin's First Lieutenant* (Princeton, N.J., 1993), 176–99; and James Richter, "Re-examining Soviet Policy towards Germany in 1953," *Europe-Asia Studies*, XLV (1993), 671–91. For further background on the domestic context of Soviet foreign policy vis-à-vis Germany, see Olga Ivanova, "Stalin's German Policy and the 'Missed Opportunities' of 1952," M.A. thesis, University of New Orleans, 1993.

Molotov's excessive unreconstructed Stalinism emerges in Albert Resis, ed., *Molotov Remembers: Inside Kremlin Politics—Conversations with Felix Chuev* (Chicago, 1993). For a succinct portrait of Molotov as foreign minister, see Steven Merritt Miner, "His Master's Voice: Viacheslav Mikhailovich Molotov As Stalin's Foreign Commissar," in *The Diplomats, 1939–1979*, ed. Gordon A. Craig and Francis L. Loewenheim (Princeton, 1994), 65–100.

ter argues, "the rhetoric of unification served as propaganda to excite opposition in the West against the militarization of West Germany."[10]

One of the great missed opportunities in post-Stalin Soviet foreign policy seems to have been Molotov's failure to pursue Austrian neutrality as early as 1953, in order to derail West German rearmament. Vladislav Zubok has shown that both Vladimir Semyonov in a 1959 analysis and the prominent Soviet diplomat and German expert Valentin Falin wondered why Kremlin diplomacy did not pursue Austrian neutrality more actively early on in order to "throw a monkeywrench" into plans for West German rearmament.[11] The answer appears to be twofold: first, given the Western determination to rearm the Federal Republic, Soviet efforts would not have mattered, and second, they did in fact make such efforts, although not on the top diplomatic level, where the hardliner Molotov refused to make concessions. On a lower working level, Soviet and Austrian diplomats and journalists in Washington, Bern, and Vienna started to gingerly test, behind the scenes, the neutral option and Austria's staying out of the Western alliance system as a means of concluding a treaty and breaking the diplomatic impasse.[12] The new scholarship, based on recently opened Soviet archives, has failed to see that in Vienna and the Soviet zone of occupation, "peaceful coexistence" was more than mere rhetoric; in Austria, the Kremlin's new look induced a remarkable easing of restrictions in the Soviet occupation regime.[13]

Even if the Kremlin's 1953 "new policy" was largely a defensive propaganda maneuver, a profound policy shift occurred in the Vienna Ballhausplatz, one that had major repercussions on Austrian treaty

10. Richter, "Re-examining Soviet Policy," 671–91 (citation 681); Knight, *Beria*, 191–7; Zubok, "Soviet Intelligence in the Cold War," 460–72. For Molotov's views on the power struggle over German policy, see *Molotov Remembers*, ed. Resis, 333–7.

11. Falin's memoirs, published in German, *Politische Erinnerungen*, 324, cited by Zubok, "Soviet Foreign Policy," 19; Zubok, "Soviet Intelligence and the Cold War," 462. The latter claim is based on an analysis by Vladimir Semyonov of October 17, 1959.

12. Such low-level behind-the-scenes contacts on neutrality can best be retraced in Alfons Schilcher's selection of Austrian diplomatic documents, *Österreich und die Grossmächte: Dokumente zur österreichischen Aussenpolitik 1945–1949* (Vienna, 1980), 154–79. See also Stourzh, *Geschichte der Staatsvertrages*, 86–9; Ludwig Steiner, "Die Aussenpolitik Raabs als Bundeskanzler," in *Julius Raab: Eine Biographie in Einzeldarstellungen*, ed. Alois Brusatti and Gottfried Heindl (Linz, 1986), 217; and Bischof, "Gruber und die Anfänge des 'Neuen Kurses,' " 154ff.

13. These concessions are most succinctly described in Rauchensteiner, *Der Sonderfall*, 316–8.

diplomacy. The assumption of power by the conservative no-nonsense realpolitiker Julius Raab as chancellor, along with the brilliant young Socialist Bruno Kreisky as state secretary in the foreign ministry, represented a new look in the Ballhausplatz, which turned out to be particularly fortunate for Austria. In a remarkable bipartisan consensus, the Raab-Kreisky duo reversed foreign minister Karl Gruber's excessively pro-Western policy, which had isolated Austrian treaty diplomacy.[14] Raab had evoked much criticism both at home and abroad by publicly welcoming the conciliatory Soviet gestures, including the easing of their occupation regime—but by the summer of 1953 the chancellor had no choice but to accept the fact that under Molotov's new ascendancy in Kremlin politics, intransigence and propaganda had come to prevail once again. In late June, the Ballhausplatz stepped up its testing of Soviet intentions and began to show a more even-handed approach toward the USSR. The Raab government asked the neutral Indians to feel out with Molotov the question whether it would be "useful if Austria were to give an undertaking of neutrality." Molotov dryly replied that it would be "useful but not enough." Today we know that Molotov—against the advice of some of the best intelligence available to the Kremlin—was firmly committed against Austrian neutrality. He feared that the Americans, with or without a treaty, would "pocket" Austria for the Western defense alliance.[15] One may divine that the Kremlin's answer to the Austrian initiative might have been quite different only a few weeks earlier, at the height of Beria's campaign for German neutralization and unification.

The cautious Austrian bilateral diplomatic initiatives toward the new Kremlin leadership over neutrality and *Blockfreiheit* scared and even

14. Gruber's domineering role in Austrian foreign policy and his extreme pro-Western position is stressed in Günter Bischof, "The Making of a Cold Warrior: Karl Gruber and Austrian Foreign Policy, 1945–1953," *Austrian History Yearbook*, XXVI (1995), 99–127. For a spirited defense of Gruber's role as shrewd *realpolitiker*, see the introduction in Gehler, *Gruber: Reden und Dokumente*, 11–34, and Gehler, " 'Die Besatzungmächte sollen schnellstmöglich nach Hause gehen': Zur Interessenpolitik des Aussenministers Karl Gruber 1945–1953 und zu weiterführenden Fragen eines kontroversiellen Forschungsprojekts," *Christliche Demokratie* XI (1995), 27–78.

15. Bischoff to Foreign Ministry, July 1, 1953, in *Österreich und die Grossmächte*, ed. Schilcher, 176f.; Rauchensteiner, *Sonderfall*, 201–3; Stourzh, *Geschichte der Staatsvertrages*, 81–9; Steiner, "Aussenpolitik Raabs," 212–4; Günter Bischof, "The Anglo-American Powers and Austrian Neutrality, 1953–1955," *Mitteilungen des Österreichischen Staatsarchivs*, XLII (1992), 374f. On Molotov's firm stance against Austrian neutrality, see Zubok, "Soviet Intelligence and the Cold War," 462.

upset most decision makers in the West. With their one-track minds set on West German rearmament, they feared above all the spillover effects on Germany. Austria's bilateral diplomacy, outside of the American-controlled East-West context in which a strict "no negotiations" policy prevailed, threatened to provide an alternate model for the West Germans in their dealings with the Kremlin. Specifically, it threatened to throw the veritable Anglo-American obsession to complete West German rearmament (which would result in the preservation of Germany's division) off track. Walter Lippman was surely correct in observing that "the Western diplomatic structure was fragile and highly vulnerable to a serious Soviet peace offensive"—the survival of the EDC was at stake. The Office of Intelligence Research of the Department of State concluded as early as the end of August 1953 that Vienna's "new approach" reflected Austrian confidence that they could handle their own relations with the Soviets: "In pursuing their Eastern policy, the Austrians have deliberately proceeded without consulting the Western powers." This emancipation of Austrian foreign policy increasingly worried Western diplomats and statesmen in the years 1953 to 1955.[16]

The old German linkage continued to prevail on the mental map of most Western statesmen, who viewed the possibility of Austrian neutrality strictly from the perspective of its possible repercussions on German rearmament and Western integration. In May 1953 Frank Roberts, the brilliant head of the foreign office's German desk, argued—as had his old Moscow friend George Kennan a year earlier—that the Soviets wanted to hold the Austrian and German zones as cards "until they can bargain them against western concessions over Germany."[17]

Eisenhower continued Truman's uncompromising containment strategy, which gave high priority to psychological warfare vis-à-vis the Kremlin and put a low premium on East-West diplomacy.[18] If Molotov

16. Lippmann's column in *New York Herald Tribune*, April 7, 1953, quoted in Larres, "Eisenhower after Stalin's Death," 449; Report no. 6403, August 31, 1953, cited in Jürg Martin Gabriel, *The American Conception of Neutrality after 1941* (New York, 1988), 181.

17. See Hancock, Allen, and Roberts minutes of May 13, May 22, May 24, 1953, FO 371/103762/CA 1071/CA 1071/123 and 137, PRO; for more detail, see Bischof, "Anglo-American Powers," 377–81.

18. For insightful discussions of Eisenhower as cold warrior and his fascination with psychological warfare, see Henry W. Brands, *Cold Warriors: Eisenhower's Generation and American Foreign Policy* (New York, 1988), especially the essay on C. D. Jackson, 117–37. See also Brands, "The Age of Vulnerability: Eisenhower and the National Insecurity State," *American Historical Review,* XCIV (1989), 963–89, and Blanche W. Cook, *The Declassified Eisenhower: A Divided Legacy of Peace and Political Warfare* (New York, 1981), 175–80.

missed opportunities, so did Eisenhower. The new evidence suggests that the two were mirror images of unbending cold warriors. Eisenhower refused to negotiate with the new Kremlin leadership, let alone meet them on the summit level to test the sincerity of their peace offensive. Although Soviet leaders may well have feared that the Eisenhower administration would take advantage of instability in the Kremlin in the wake of Stalin's death, they would have been flabbergasted to have learned how unprepared the USA actually was for such a contingency.[19]

To make matters worse, Western misperceptions of Soviet intentions were compounded by the fact that the U.S. did not even have an ambassador in Moscow at the time. George F. Kennan, who had been declared persona non grata in 1952, had not yet been replaced by Eisenhower's new appointee Chip Bohlen, whose Senate confirmation was held up by McCarthyites precisely at the time of Stalin's death. The extreme anti-Communist Republican right wing had purposely held up Bohlen's appointment because he had translated for Roosevelt at the infamous Yalta summit and thus was guilty by association of the "sellout of Eastern Europe." The McCarthyite assault on Bohlen put the Eisenhower administration on notice that any kind of summitry with the Communists remained anathema. During the 1952 Republican campaign, party

---

On Eisenhower's defense strategy (with an excellent overview of the literature), see Saki Dockrill, "Cooperation and Suspicion: The United States' Alliance Diplomacy for the Security of Western Europe, 1953–54," *Diplomacy and Statecraft*, V (1994), 138–82. For readings of the Eisenhower-Dulles diplomacy more in the realpolitik vein, which give less weight to psychological warfare and more to subtlety and pragmatism, see Richard H. Immerman, ed., *John Foster Dulles and the Diplomacy of the Cold War* (Princeton, 1990), and Saki Dockrill, *Eisenhower's New-Look National Security Policy, 1953–61* (New York, 1996).

19. March 6, 1953, "Diary Notes of Meetings, Oct. 1951–1953," box 1, in Emmet John Hughes Papers, Mudd Library, Princeton University; almost identical quote in Emmet J. Hughes, *The Ordeal of Power: A Political Memoir of the Eisenhower Years* (New York, 1963), 101. For more detail, see Günter Bischof, "Eisenhower, the Summit, and the Austrian Treaty, 1953–1955," in: *Eisenhower: A Centenary Assessment*, ed. Günter Bischof and Stephen E. Ambrose (Baton Rouge, La., 1995), 140–2; for even greater detail on the Eisenhower administration's infighting over how to respond to Stalin's death and the subsequent peace offensive by the new men in the Kremlin, see Klaus Larres, "Eisenhower and the First Forty Days after Stalin's Death: The Incompatibility of *Détente* and Political Warfare," *Diplomacy and Statecraft*, VI (1995), 431–69, as well as Steven Fish, "After Stalin's Death: The Anglo-American Debate over a New Cold War," *Diplomatic History*, X (1986), 334–6. Indeed, many in the Kremlin feared that "weakness and indecisiveness at the moment of Stalin's death might encourage Western powers to press the Soviet Union into unilateral concessions, especially on a German settlement" (Zubok, "Soviet Intelligence and the Cold War," 460).

extremists had roped Eisenhower into supporting a Republican platform that denounced Yalta and demanded "liberation" of the Eastern European "captive nations"; with the Kersten Amendment they even set aside funds for a Volunteer Freedom Corps of Eastern European refugees to be trained for rollback and liberation. Once Eisenhower was in office and even before Stalin died, the Republican extremists had kept the pressure on the president by stepping up their campaign against Yalta— the symbol for the secret diplomacy of the Roosevelt Democrats, the outcome of which could only be making concessions to the Communists on the negotiating table. Even though various Senate resolutions to repudiate Yalta had failed, along with Senator Bricker's proposed constitutional amendment to curtail unchecked executive authority in the foreign-policy arena in order to prevent future Yaltas, by the time of Stalin's death the Republican extremists had made clear to the Eisenhower administration just how they felt about summitry. Isaac Deutscher summed up the climate in Washington in the spring of 1953 quite accurately: "Large sections of American opinion are clamouring for a crusade [of liberation]; and official Washington at times behaves as if it were anxious to yield to the clamour."[20]

Unquestionably, the Republican extremists breathing down Eisenhower's neck and crying "no more Yaltas" at the height of their anti-Communist crusade effectively nipped in the bud any chance for a positive response to the Soviet peace campaign. Never displaying the courage of his convictions, Eisenhower failed to publicly distance himself from McCarthy's crusade. While he privately detested the uncouth senator from Wisconsin, he agreed with much of the conservative Republican anti-Communist message.[21] Eisenhower's personal ideology

20. Isaac Deutscher, *Russia after Stalin* (London, 1953), 156. Deutscher's contemporary analysis is remarkably insightful about post-Stalin Kremlin politics. On the Bohlen fight before the Senate Foreign Relations Committee, see Günter Bischof, "Before the Break: The Relationship between Eisenhower and McCarthy, 1952–1953" (M.A. thesis, University of New Orleans, 1980), 107–24. On the 1952 campaign promises, the Senate Yalta resolutions, and the Bricker Amendment, see Athan G. Theoharis, *The Yalta Myths: An Issue in U.S. Politics, 1945–1955* (Columbia, Mo., 1970), 130–94; on the Kersten Amendment, see Bennett Kovrig, *Of Walls and Bridges: The United States and Eastern Europe* (New York, 1991), 45–9.

21. Bischof, "Before the Break: Eisenhower and McCarthy"; Günter Bischof, "The Politics of Anti-Communism in the Executive Branch during the Early Cold War: Truman, Eisenhower, and McCarthy(ism)," in *Anti-Communism and McCarthyism in the United States (1946–1954): Essays on the Politics and Culture of the Cold War*, ed. André Kaenel (Paris, 1995), 53–78 (includes extensive discussion of the historiography); Jeff Broadwater, *Eisenhower and the Anti-Communist Crusade* (Chapel Hill, 1992).

and these domestic strictures coming from his own party have not been sufficiently stressed by historians in analyzing the president's failure to respond to the Soviet peace initiative.

In spite of such an ugly domestic climate, Eisenhower nevertheless did his best to react in a statesmanlike manner, especially since his old friend Winston Churchill pressed him to meet Malenkov for a summit.[22] In Washington, next to the psychological warriors C.D. Jackson and Walt W. Rostow, Secretary of State Dulles turned out to be the principal roadblock to either a four-power meeting on any level or any sort of response to the Soviet peace offensive; Dulles felt that this offensive was based on the Kremlin's weakness and was most reluctant to entertain the possibility of responding positively to it.[23] Four weeks of intensive speech writing produced Eisenhower's April 16 "Chances for Peace" address to the American Society of Newspaper Editors. In that speech, the president threw the ball back into the Soviet court by urging the Kremlin leaders to back up their talk of peace with actual deeds. Ending the hostilities in Korea, reducing armaments, ending the division of Germany and Europe, and signing the Austrian treaty represented some specific actions whereby the Kremlin could demonstrate that their initiative was more than propaganda. Dulles quickly qualified Eisenhower's offer by noting that the Kremlin was trying to "gain a respite." He insisted that a "settlement based on the status quo" would be nothing more than an "illusion of peace." He thought it essential that the United States make "clear to the captive people that we do not accept their captivity as a permanent fact of history." With his unspo-

22. The best treatment of Churchill's determined effort to test the new Kremlin leadership in a summit is Peter G. Boyle, ed., *The Churchill-Eisenhower Correspondence, 1953–1955* (Chapel Hill, 1995); see also Josef Foschepoth, "Churchill, Adenauer und die Neutralisierung Deutschlands," *Deutschland Archiv*, XVII (1984), 1286–1301; Steininger, *The German Question* (1990), 100–12; Larres, "Eisenhower after Stalin's Death," 435–8. David Carlton believes Churchill's push for the summit had largely domestic political roots—to stay in 10 Downing Street and keep Anthony Eden out of it; see "Grossbritannien und die Gipfeldiplomatie," in *Zwischen Kaltem Krieg und Entspannung: Sicherheits- und Deutschlandpolitik der Bundesrepublik im Mächtesystem der Jahre 1953–1955*, ed. Bruno Thoss and Hans-Erich Volkmann (Boppard am Rhein, 1988), 51–70.
23. Recent scholarship has seen Dulles in a more positive light. See Immerman, ed., *John Foster Dulles and the Diplomacy of the Cold War*; for a hagiographic view, see Frederick W. Marks III, *Power and Peace: The Diplomacy of John Foster Dulles* (Westport, Conn., 1993). For a remarkably balanced portrait, see Richard D. Challener, "Dulles: Moralist As Pragmatist," in *Diplomats, 1939–1979*, ed. Craig and Loewenheim, 135–66.

ken allusions to "liberation of the captive peoples," Dulles obviously wanted to allay the fears of those who demanded "no more Yaltas."[24]

With the "Chances for Peace" speech, Eisenhower tried to regain the initiative in the battle for world public opinion. On the one hand, Klaus Larres's interpretation of the address stresses that the president was "divided against himself" but in essence more interested in psychological warfare than in "friendly gestures"; Larres concludes, "His genuine bid for peace was an equally genuine manoeuver in the Cold War." Kremlin intelligence took a similar view, as Vladislav Zubok has noted: the "small" Committee of Information reported to the foreign ministry that "Eisenhower had begun a propaganda counterattack in order to neutralize the Soviet peace offensive."[25] On the other hand, Saki Dockrill has shown that the "realist" Eisenhower's cautious approach to the Soviet peace offensive had the full backing of his principal NATO allies and the British foreign office, if not of Churchill himself.[26]

If Eisenhower's speech was supposed to calm world public opinion regarding American diplomatic intransigence, it failed. Both Eisenhower's ineffective behind-the-scenes approach to McCarthy and his failure to respond to the Soviet peace offensive gave rise to a declining confidence in American leadership and a growing resentment of American policies abroad. An inquiry into U.S. embassies around the world on the state of American prestige abroad produced disquieting results. A summary of the European survey noted that what tarnished Eisenhower's image above all else was his failure to confront McCarthy and Americans' col-

24. March 16, 1953, Diary, box 1, Hughes Papers, Princeton. The text of the speech is in *FRUS, 1952–1954,* VII, 1147–55. After C. D. Jackson and Walt W. Rostow, whose input was essential, Hughes as speech writer was the principal source for the "Chances for Peace" address, rising to the challenge of incorporating the conflicting interests of the Eisenhower administration; see Hughes, *Ordeal of Power,* 98–115. Rostow and Jackson were the principal forces behind the psychological warfare edge of the speech; see Walt Rostow, *After Stalin: Eisenhower's Three Decisions of March 11, 1953* (Austin, Tex., 1982). The best discussion of the White House infighting, which is based largely on the Rostow record, is Larres, "Eisenhower after Stalin's Death," 438–58; another view of the speech's complicated genesis, one based on the Hughes drafts, is Deborah Welch Larson, "Crisis Prevention and the Austrian Treaty," *International Organization,* XLI (1987), 35–9. See also Bischof, "Eisenhower and the Austrian Treaty," 140–5.

25. Larres, "Eisenhower and the First Forty Days after Stalin's Death," 434; Zubok, "Soviet Intelligence and the Cold War," 461. My own interpretation does not put as much weight on propaganda warfare as Larres's; see "Eisenhower and the Austrian Treaty," 140–7. For a more positive reading of the Eisenhower-Dulles speeches, see the Immerman essay in this volume.

26. Dockrill, *Eisenhower's New-Look National Security Policy,* 28f.

lective hysterical anti-Communism. In European minds, " 'McCarthy-ism' has become synonymous with neo-fascism." The survey also noted that the "fear is growing that United States policies will not be suffi-ciently flexible to put Soviet peace moves to a fair test." Europeans were particularly worried that an American policy departure toward "rolling back the iron curtain" would mean "substantially increased risks for European security and eventual war." American policies toward Eastern Europe also "will indefinitely prevent the United States from finding a basis for a negotiated settlement of differences with the Soviet Union."[27]

Top U.S. and Soviet leaders had not met for a summit since Potsdam in 1945, and Eisenhower made sure they would not meet before West German rearmament was a fait accompli. The foreign ministers had not gathered since Paris in June 1949. A Soviet offensive to resume talks on this level failed over negotiating an agenda (with the German question as top priority) at the 1951 Palais Marbre Rose talks in Paris. The West-ern powers blocked the Soviet diplomatic offensive with the battle over the "Stalin notes." The Soviets blocked the American "abbreviated" treaty offensive to sign a separate agreement with the Austrians, effec-tively ending the negotiations on the Austrian deputies' level, which had constituted one of the most productive diplomatic arenas in the first cold war. The Soviets increased the pressure on Eisenhower to re-sume negotiations further by putting him into a quandary with their unanticipated agreement to a Korean armistice. Here was one of the deeds Eisenhower had precisely stipulated in his April 16 speech. In Au-gust, the Kremlin resumed its diplomatic offensive by calling for a four-power meeting at the foreign ministers' level. When the Austrians and the reluctant Americans finally officially withdrew the abbreviated Austrian treaty in the late summer of 1953 to resume negotiations on the "long" draft of 1949, Western diplomacy finally started to gear up for a four-power meeting by carefully narrowing down the agenda to

27. Fred Greenstein, *The Hidden-Hand Presidency: Eisenhower As Leader* (New York, 1982); Livingston Merchant memorandum on "European Attitudes toward the United States," August 24, 1953, *FRUS, 1952–1954,* I, pt. 2, pp. 1470–2; "Reported Decline in U.S. Prestige Abroad," Special Report Prepared by the Psychological Strategy Board, September 11, 1953, ibid., 1486; memorandum of discussion at the 164th Meeting of the National Se-curity Council, October 1, 1953, ibid., 1546–8. On the "prestige project," see also Bischof, "The Politics of Anti-Communism in the Executive Branch," 68–71.

Germany and Austria. In late November 1953 the Soviets unexpectedly agreed to a meeting with an exclusively German and Austrian agenda, dropping their earlier demands to also talk about European security, China, and global disarmament.[28]

In the summer of 1953 the Eisenhower administration had concentrated on formulating its basic national-security strategy, the "new look." Resumption of East-West negotiations was not high on the agenda. The revised basic national-security memorandum NSC 162/2 argued that a "general settlement" with the Soviets was considered highly unlikely: "There is no evidence that the Soviet leadership is prepared to modify its basic attitudes and accept any permanent settlement with the United States, although it may be prepared for a *modus vivendi* in *certain issues*" (emphasis mine). Eisenhower undoubtedly had Austria in mind as such an issue.[29]

As a way to deflect Churchill's insistence on summitry with the Soviets, Eisenhower agreed to hold a three-power summit of Western leaders. Churchill's illness led to postponement of this summit until early December 1953 in Bermuda. After its discussions on Eisenhower's "Atoms for Peace" speech and its giving the go-ahead to the foreign ministers to meet in Berlin, the Bermuda summit is memorable for the American president's spilling his guts on what he really thought of the Soviets: "[Eisenhower] said that as regards the P.M.'s [Churchill's] belief that there was New Look in Soviet Policy, Russia was a woman of the streets and whether her dress was new, or just the old one patched up, it was certainly the same whore underneath. America intended to drive her off her present 'beat' into the back streets." Half a year later and in more guarded language, Eisenhower confided in the prime minister his

28. Even though the work is mainly concerned with Germany, the most lucid discussion of the various levels of East-West diplomacy at this time can be found in Hermann-Josef Rupieper, *Der besetzte Verbündete: Die amerikanische Deutschlandpolitik, 1949–1955* (Opladen, 1991), 228–375; see also his "Die Berliner Aussenministerkonferenz von 1954: Ein Höhepunkt der Ost-West-Propaganda oder die letzte Möglichkeit zur Schaffung der deutschen Einheit?" *Vierteljahrshefte für Zeitgeschichte*, XXXIV (1986), 427–30. On Austria, see Stourzh, *Geschichte der Staatsvertrages*, 88–90; 111–6, and Bischof, "Gruber und die Anfänge des 'Neuen Kurses,' " 159–70.

29. See the National Security memorandum NSC 162/2 "Basic National Security Policy," which replaced Truman's NSC 68, October 30, 1953, *FRUS, 1952–1954*, II, pt. 1, pp. 577–96; for more detail about NSC debates on the desirability of negotiations with the Soviets, see the Immerman essay in this volume.

"utter lack of confidence in the reliability and integrity of the men in the Kremlin."[30]

Only John Foster Dulles surpassed Eisenhower in his suspicions of Communists and his reluctance to sit at the conference table with the likes of Molotov. However, the Berlin Council of Foreign Ministers of February 1954 offered good propaganda opportunities with respect to both the German and the Austrian issues. As in the previous four-power foreign-minister meetings, negotiations quickly deadlocked and kept the Austrian issue hostage to the powers' intransigence on German issues.[31]

With the offer of armed neutrality and refusal to join military blocs, Berlin was supposed to bring the breakthrough on the Austrian treaty front. In a crucial NSC meeting in October 1953, the Pentagon leaders came out strongly against a neutralization of Austria, fearing the repercussions of such a development on German rearmament and on their strategic planning. But Dulles convinced the NSC that if the Austrians wanted to be neutral, the U.S. could not stop them. Harold Stassen had already suggested armed neutrality as the deus ex machina for the Austrian solution when he noted in this NSC discussion that "the status of neutrality did not necessarily imply disarmament."[32] This is the compromise formula on which Eisenhower focused when he discussed the Austrian issue with Dulles before the secretary of state left for Berlin. Eisenhower "could see no objection to the neutralization of Austria if this did not carry with it the demilitarization. If Austria could achieve a status somewhat comparable to Switzerland, this would be quite satisfactory from a military standpoint."[33] This is the position that Dulles

30. John Colville, The Fringes of Power: 10 Downing Street Diaries, 1939–1955 (New York, 1985), 683; Eisenhower to Churchill, July 22, 1954, in Churchill-Eisenhower Correspondence, ed. Boyle, 163.

31. Berlin is the insufficiently studied CFM. On Dulles's reluctance, see Richard Immerman, "The United States and the Geneva Conference of 1954: A New Look," Diplomatic History, XIV (1990), 47–8. Rupieper believes the Soviets were more moderate and inclined to compromise in Berlin than historians have given them credit for; see his "Berliner Aussenministerkonferenz," 427–53.

32. Memorandum of discussion at the 166th meeting of the National Security Council, October 13, 1953; this discussion centered on the Eisenhower administration's revised paper on Austria NSC 164/1, October 14, 1953 (FRUS, 1952–1954, VII, pt. 2, pp. 1909–22).

33. Memorandum of breakfast conference with the president, January 20, 1954, folder "Meetings with the President 1954 (2)," box 1, Memoranda Series, John Foster Dulles Papers, Mudd Library, Princeton University. On the NSC discussions in October 1953 and the "compromise formula" for neutrality, see also Gabriel, The American Conception of Neutrality, 175f.

presented during the Berlin CFM meeting: "A neutral status is an honorable status if it is voluntarily chosen by a nation. Switzerland has chosen to be neutral, and as a neutral she has achieved an honorable place in the family of nations. Under the Austrian State Treaty as heretofore drafted, Austria would be free to choose for itself to be a neutral like Switzerland. Certainly the United States would fully respect its choice in this respect, as it fully respects its choice in the respect of the Swiss nation." But in Berlin, Molotov was not yet prepared to evacuate Austria for the price of a neutral Austria. He kept insisting on the old linkage with Germany when he tied a final pullout of occupation troops from Austria with the conclusion of a German peace treaty.[34] Austria still might come in handy as a bargaining chip with the West to derail West German rearmament.

The Berlin CFM affirmed Eisenhower's belief that the Kremlin leadership was not prepared to make major diplomatic concessions in the international arena in general and on the Austrian treaty in particular. Soviet intransigence in Berlin convinced Eisenhower more than ever that the Soviets were not prepared to compromise. Nevertheless, Churchill's dogged insistence on meeting the Soviets for a summit continued to grow. In late June Churchill personally traveled to Washington to plead with the president for signing an Austrian treaty at a summit. But Eisenhower was convinced that a summit would "serve no useful purpose" and on the Austrian issue, the Soviets had demonstrated in Berlin their unwillingness to give an inch.[35]

Given the adverse international climate, there was absolutely no movement on the Austrian treaty in 1954, in spite of Raab's effort to keep the diplomatic channels open. The chancellor told the Soviets that neutrality for his country was still on the table and that his government was "ready to negotiate what, when and where it might be possible." The Soviets kept parroting their propaganda line, warning about the dangers of a "new Anschluss." In Kurt Steiner's analysis, Soviet warnings about a "new Anschluss" were merely "a short hand term at the time for the suspected Western objective of integrating Austria into the emerging Western security system." Raab counseled patience, realizing

---

34. Dulles in 18th meeting, February 12, 1954 and Dulles in 19th plenary session, February 19, 1954, *FRUS, 1952–1954*, VII, pt. 1, pp. 1061–5, 1088–9. See also Stourzh, *Geschichte der Staatsvertrages*, 116–25. On the Americans, Dulles, and neutrality, see also Gabriel, *The American Conception of Neutrality after 1941*, 166ff.

35. This paragraph is based on Bischof, "Eisenhower and the Austrian Treaty," 151–3.

that prospects for a neutralization of Austria could only benefit from a strong Western security system that included the Federal Republic.[36]

Ultimately, only the dramatic international developments of fall 1954 made the Austrian solution of 1955 possible. France's voting down of the EDC in late August and Britain's engineering of the Paris agreements with the direct integration of the Federal Republic into the Western defense system left Molotov's hardline European policies in a shambles. John Van Oudenaren is persuasive in his view that in the spring of 1955 Soviet motivation to block ratification of the Paris treaties and West German rearmament diminished: "Resigned to West Germany's becoming a part of NATO, *they saw the treaty as guarantee against a new Anschluss, as well as the price that needed to be paid to achieve a broad East-West relaxation of tensions in the absence of a German settlement*" (emphasis mine).[37]

Toward the Austro-Soviet Moscow Summit of April 1955: Preventing a 'New Anschluss' and the Breakthrough in Bilateral Austrian Treaty Diplomacy

The key to breaking the Austrian treaty standoff rested in Kremlin politics. The emergence of Khrushchev as the invisible architect of a new post-Stalin foreign policy and his increasing circumvention of Molotov broke the deadlock in the Kremlin over making concessions on Austria.[38] When the Paris agreements were signed and West Germany was

36. Steiner, "Negotiating for an Austrian Treaty," 126–9; Bischof, "Eisenhower and the Austrian Treaty," 154f. The lack of treaty progress in 1954 is discussed in Sven Allard, *Russia and the Austrian State Treaty: A Case Study of Soviet Policy in Europe* (University Park, Pa., 1970), 120–30, and Bruno Thoss, "Modellfall Österreich? Der österreichische Staatsvertrag und die deutsche Frage 1954–55," in *Zwischen Kaltem Krieg und Entspannung,* ed. Thoss and Volkmann, 94–107.

37. John Van Oudenaren, *Détente in Europe: The Soviet Union and the West since 1953* (Durham, N.C., 1991), 32. On the British role in engineering the Paris agreements, see Saki Dockrill, "Britain and the Settlement of the West German Rearmament Question in 1954," in *British Foreign Policy, 1945–56,* ed. Michael Dockrill and John W. Young (London, 1989), 149–72, and Rolf Steininger, "Das Scheitern der EVG und der Beitritt der Bundesrepublik zur NATO," *Aus Politik und Zeitgeschichte,* B 17/85 (27 April 1985), 3–18; see also James G. Hershberg, " 'Explosion in the Offing': German Rearmament and American Diplomacy, 1953–1955," *Diplomatic History,* XVI (1992), 511–49. For the highly biased view that Dulles engineered Germany's integration into NATO, see Marks, *Power and Peace,* 58–69.

38. Until the end of his days, Molotov never forgave Khrushchev for his "deceptive" new policy and maligned him as a "Bukharinite," an unprincipled "rightist," and a "pacifist"; Molotov denounced "Khrushchevism" as "the bourgeois spirit" and "playing up to public opinion" and dismissed "peaceful coexistence" as a "slogan" and a "slippery expression." See Resis, *Molotov Remembers,* 354–65, 388–91, and *passim.*

rearmed and integrated into the Western defense system, Khrushchev insisted on undoing Molotov's Berlin CFM linkage of tying the presence of Soviet troops in Austria to the conclusion of a German peace treaty. Khrushchev was also prepared to make economic concessions with regard to Austria and to accept less stringent guarantees against a future "Anschluss." The failure of Molotov's hardline Stalinist policy to resolve the German problem in a manner acceptable to the Soviet Union (i.e., a manner other than the division of Germany), unquestionably led to his declining influence in the Kremlin and facilitated the Austrian breakthrough. Khrushchev personally insisted to Molotov that it was high time to end the "abnormal situation" in Austria and pull the troops out; in his memoirs he added that "we had to settle the [Austrian] issue against the wishes of the minister of foreign affairs." Khrushchev later told Raab that he wanted to give the West a clear indication that the Soviet Union was prepared to withdraw troops from territory captured by the Red Army in World War II "to make the new course credible in the West." Along with the demotion of Malenkov also came the end of Molotov's nonconcessionary iron rule over Soviet foreign affairs. In his lengthy keynote address to the Supreme Soviet on February 8, 1955, Molotov publicly announced what had already been determined by the party hierarchy earlier, namely the end of his iron-clad linkage of the Austrian and the German issues. In a policy reversal engineered behind the scenes by the ascendant Khrushchev, Molotov announced that he saw no reason "for any further delay in concluding a state treaty with Austria," if she undertook "not to join any coalitions or military alliances."[39] Khrushchev thus initiated the end to what Isaac Deutscher called "the bizarre unreality and rigidity in Stalinist diplomacy."[40]

39. Khrushchev characterized Molotov's Stalinist foreign policy in the following manner: "Stalin was gone but Molotov was still around, and he had put together that policy along with Stalin. Therefore, the views of Stalin were really the views of Molotov and Stalin. Which one of them played the first violin? No doubt Stalin. But Molotov had played his own violin as loud as possible." On Khrushchev's personal initiative for ending "unfinished business" in the Austrian question, see Nikita S. Khrushchev, *Khrushchev Remembers: The Glasnost Tapes*, trans. and ed. Jerrod L. Schecter and Vyacheslav V. Luchkov (Boston, 1990), 72–80 (citations 74–6). Bruno Kreisky cites Khrushchev's reasoning to Raab in 1958 in his first volume of memoirs, *Zwischen den Zeiten: Erinnerungen aus fünf Jahrzehnten* (Vienna, 1986), 472. In his highly perceptive "Kremlin Politics and the Austrian settlement," 41ff., Vojtech Mastny largely divined the repercussions in the Kremlin power struggle on the Austrian treaty; now, Vladislav Zubok is able to firm up the crucial departure in Khrushchev's new Soviet foreign policy with much fresh evidence from Soviet archives. See his essay in this volume.

40. Deutscher, *Russia after Stalin*, 141.

With Khrushchev breathing down his neck to conclude the Austrian treaty as soon as possible, Molotov, who wanted a high-level four-power conference, lured the Austrians toward serious bilateral negotiations by telling the Ballhausplatz that "it would depend mainly on Austria" if they wanted to conclude the treaty. If the Austrians and the Soviets could reach a bilateral agreement, argued Molotov, "the others would find it difficult to say no"—exactly what Dulles had predicted in the NSC in the fall of 1953. Over the next six weeks, Norbert Bischoff, the extremely confident and savvy Austrian ambassador in Moscow who had been serving there since 1946, busily probed the exact meaning of Molotov's words. The Western powers watched this intense round of Austro-Soviet bilateral diplomacy more or less from the sidelines, in total disbelief.[41]

Austro-Soviet bilateral diplomacy culminated on 24 March in the Kremlin's invitation to Chancellor Raab for a state visit to Moscow. The Soviets charged ahead with this bilateral diplomacy and no longer demanded a high-level four-power meeting, which the West would never have accepted before the ratification of the Paris agreements was complete. Raab received with the invitation a Soviet memorandum laying out the diplomatic agenda for such a meeting. Neutralization along the lines of the "Swiss model" had been specified by Soviet and Austrian diplomats and politicians in private behind-the-scenes meetings in Vienna in mid-March, and now Molotov wanted to have "anti-Anschluss safeguards and guarantees" discussed, in an effort to salvage Soviet security interests in Central Europe after the ratification of the Paris agreements. West German rearmament looked irreversible and the Kremlin had to adapt to it as a fait accompli. It is doubtful that even Molotov thought that the completion of West Germany's Western integration could be stopped at this late point, particularly after the French Council of the Republic ratified the Paris agreements on March 28 (the German *Bundestag* had done so already on February 27). It was high time to clarify the "anti-Anschluss guarantee" to make sure that Austria would not be integrated into Western defense plans along the lines of the West German model.[42]

41. Allard, *Russia and the Austrian State Treaty*, 154–91; Stourzh, *Geschichte der Staatsvertrages*, 132–8; Thoss, "Modellfall Österreich?" 107–23; Schilcher, ed., *Österreich und die Grossmächte*, 236ff.; Mastny, "Kremlin Politics," 41ff.; Zubok, "Soviet Foreign Policy in Germany and Austria."

42. Bohlen to Dulles, March 25, 1955, *FRUS, 1955–1957*, V, 14–6. For a copy of the Soviet foreign ministry's March 24 note, see FO 371/117787/RR 1071/62, PRO. See also Stourzh, *Geschichte der Staatsvertrages*, 136–40; Allard, *Russia and the Austrian State*

It was clear immediately in the Western capitals that the Austrians found themselves in a quite difficult dilemma. Given the expectations of the Austrian population to see an end to the occupation, Raab could not reject the Kremlin's invitation. Western crisis management therefore found itself on the sidelines, observing a vigorous bilateral Austro-Soviet treaty diplomacy and reduced to the unsavory task of trying to preserve the Vienna Ballhausplatz's diplomatic room to maneuver. Most observers felt that the inexperienced Raab was operating from a dangerously weak base. Dulles warned Gruber, the former foreign minister turned Austrian ambassador to Washington, that Moscow was "a dangerous place to go alone"; Raab should not assume that he could speak for the West. Dulles raised the specter of Molotov trying to design "anti-Anschluss" guarantees that ultimately would lead to "Communist domination" of Austria and categorically rejected the idea of a four-power conference on Austria at the foreign ministers' level before the completion of German rearmament, since the Soviets would inevitably bring up the German question during such a meeting in order to "break up the position of the West." For Dulles the Soviet motive could only be to use "the present approach on Austria as a back door to the German problem."[43]

British worries about gauche Austrian diplomacy were similarly intense. The foreign office felt that Raab was inept in diplomacy and out of his depth attempting to negotiate with the Kremlin. Minister of State Anthony Nutting informed the Austrian ambassador, Felix Schwarzenberg, that there would be no four-power discussions with the Soviets prior to ratification of Paris agreements. "Even if there were to be a conference merely to discuss Austria," he warned, "this would not deter Mr. Molotov from talking about other subjects, Germany in particular, with consequent unfortunate effects elsewhere." Geoffrey Harrison, the experienced chief of the Austrian desk, felt that neutralization might be "followed by isolation and then a process of communist infiltration

Treaty, 171–84; and Thoss, "Modellfall Österreich?" 118–23. For Molotov's motives, based on new Soviet foreign ministry archival evidence, see Manfried Rauchensteiner, "Es war einmal ein prächtiger Frühlingtstag," Die Presse, May 11–2, 1991, "Spectrum" weekend section, 1–2.

43. Memorandum of conversation, March 25, 1995, FRUS, 1955–1957, V, 16–9. Recalled by Raab for an ambassadors' conference in Vienna on March 28, Gruber strongly voiced Dulles's warnings; for a summary, see Schilcher, ed., Österreich und die Grossmäche, 254–67. Robert Bowie, Dulles's head of the State Department Policy Planning Staff, analyzed the situation in the same vein; see personal oral history of Robert Bowie, June 15, 1986, Washington, D.C.

from the East." Anthony Eden added: "I am sorry that Austrians were not more firmly warned against Moscow's wiles. I hope I shall not wake up some morning soon & find Raab in Moscow." Harrison concluded: "The Austrians seem intent, like the Gadarene swine, on rushing over the precipice to their own doom."[44]

In spite of an obviously large Kremlin foreign-policy reversal after the ratification of the Paris agreements went through the French parliament, there was almost unanimous agreement among Western observers that the Soviets had made only tactical shifts and hoped to utilize the Austrian card as a last-minute trump to block German rearmament.[45] Llewellyn Thompson, the gifted Soviet expert and American ambassador in Vienna, played Cassandra vis-à-vis the Austrians. He warned Kreisky, who he felt was the "most intelligent member" of the Austrian government, that the Soviet motive in reopening the Austrian question was "not with Austrian objectives in mind but rather German problems."[46] Thompson was certain that the Soviets were not prepared to forego their Berlin positions on the Austrian treaty but rather intended to shatter Western unity in German rearmament with their Austrian card. Their hope may well have been that by "quick conclusion of an Austrian Treaty, followed by generous use of carrot and stick in Germany, they can prevent German rearmament by influencing the Germans themselves." After the Austrian delegation's successful trip to Moscow, President Eisenhower argued along the same lines, declaring that "the Soviet gambit on Austria was definitely made with Germany in mind as the real target."[47]

44. Harrison minute, March 22, 1955, FO 371/117786/RR 1071/45, PRO; Sykes minute of Nutting-Schwarzenberg conversation, March 16, 1955, FO 371/117786/RR 1071/43, PRO; Harrison "Record of Conversation with the Austrian Ambassador," March 25, 1955, with handwritten Eden minute, March 25, 1955, FO 371/117787/RR 1071/74, PRO.

45. In fact, Soviet diplomats in Vienna fretted over the fact that the Western powers dismissed the Soviet foreign policy departure in February–March 1955 as merely tactical: "And in spite of all these concessions we have not been able to convince any of the Western powers that our foreign policy has undergone not just tactical but a real and sweeping change." The extremely well-informed Swedish ambassador Sven Allard records this conversation in *Russia and the Austrian State Treaty*, 144.

46. In his memoirs Kreisky returned the favor by praising Thompson as "the best negotiator with Moscow that the West ever had" and "the most important American diplomat that I had the pleasure to meet." See Bruno Kreisky, *Im Strom der Politik: Der Memoiren zweiter Teil* (Vienna, 1988), 72.

47. Thompson to Dulles, March 30, 1955, *FRUS, 1955–1957*, V, 22–4; and Thompson to Dulles, April 4, 1955, NA, RG 59, Box 2662, 663.001/4–55; 245th NSC meeting, April 21, 1955, *FRUS, 1955–1957*, V, 53.

In the British foreign office, Geoffrey Harrison urged extreme caution in the issues of neutralization and guarantees for Austria, since the West had "so often been led up the garden path, from one concession to another." It was very likely that the Kremlin "was only using Austria as a card of re-entry into talks about Germany." He added, "There had throughout the recent exchanges been in the background the *motif* that, while the Austrian question might be discussed separately, it could not be entirely dissociated from the German question." Harrison feared that the Austrian negotiating in Moscow would "slip from one concession to another . . . without any *quid pro quo*" (emphasis in original). Harrison instructed Schwarzenberg that Raab should remember when he went to Moscow that "one never earned any gratitude by making unrequited concessions to the Russians; they merely pocketed the concessions and asked for more."[48]

Chip Bohlen, the American ambassador in Moscow and an experienced longtime Kremlinologist, turned out to be one of the few major Western voices who disagreed with the almost unanimous trend in Western analyses of Soviet motives in reopening the Austrian question. Undoubtedly, Bohlen agreed, it was a response to German rearmament. But the Kremlin was acting "defensively and as a result in response to recent developments in Western Europe, particularly adoption of Paris agreements." Bohlen insisted that the "chief immediate motivation of Soviets in reopening Austrian question is to endeavor to insure neutralization of Austria in order *to prevent military integration three western zones of Austria into NATO set-up* or, in the event Soviet demands in this respect are rejected by the three Western powers and the Austrian government to prepare a way for safeguarding Soviet military position in eastern Austria" (emphasis mine). On balance the Soviets preferred "complete neutralization of Austria as a whole to the alternative of mere retention of the Soviet military position in eastern Austria with the three Western zones moving toward military incorporation in the Western defense organization."[49]

Bohlen and Bischoff argued then—with the concurrence of keen contemporary observers such as the well-informed Swedish diplomat Sven Allard and Austrian leader Bruno Kreisky as well as later scholars Kurt

48. Geoffrey Harrison, "Record of Conversation with Austrian Ambassador," March 25, 1955, FO 371/117787/RR 1071/74, PRO.

49. Bohlen to Dulles, April 8, 1955, NA, RG 59, Box 2662, 663.001/4–855; Bohlen to Dulles, March 31, 1955, *FRUS, 1955–1957*, V, 26–8.

Steiner and Bruno Thoss—that Austrian neutralization and the anti-Anschluss guarantees the Soviets were asking for were directed against Western Austria's military integration into the Western defense system rather than to a future Anschluss with Germany, which had already been taken care of by Article 4 in the treaty draft.[50] Indeed, the Pentagon-inspired secret rearmament of Western Austria had been steadily progressing since 1951. The question was whether the Western powers in general and the American military defense establishment in particular could live with this, as Harrison clearly recognized: "In the past, the Americans have favored a 'forward strategy' in Austria. They would have liked Austria, after the Treaty, to join the western military club."[51] It should not come as a surprise that the Pentagon resisted the rapid progress on the Austrian treaty question in general and the neutralization of Austria in particular. With the successful bilateral Austro-Soviet diplomacy, the Austrian question had become a "crash area," and the State Department insisted in the National Security Council recommendations that Dulles be given full authority for the final negotiating rounds on the Austrian treaty in spite of the Pentagon's security concerns.[52] Ultimately, the Pentagon agreed to neutralizing Austria only because it would be "armed neutrality." The American defense establishment had vigorously pushed Austria's secret rearmament, and now wanted to make sure that post-treaty Austria would not be a military

50. Bischoff also thought that Soviet "anti-Anschluss" moves were designed to prevent a partition of Austria (as was the case with Germany) and terminate the American presence in Western Austria, which was leading to an ever tightening Austrian military integration into the West. See his telegram to the foreign office, February 27, 1955, in Schilcher, ed., *Österreich und die Grossmächte*, 242–5. Allard explains that ever since late in 1954, Soviet propaganda had made Austrian "rearmament" and integration into Western defense the major theme of their campaign against the Paris agreements and the repercussions of those agreements on Austrian treaty negotiations (*Russia and the Austrian State Treaty*, 131–54, especially 150). According to Kreisky, Molotov told Raab in 1958 that the Kremlin decided to conclude a treaty in 1955 because "it was the time of the genesis of NATO and many strategists expected Western Austria to become a bridge in the Western alliance" (*Zwischen den Zeiten*, 472). Steiner writes, "As far as Austria was concerned, the USSR feared an extension of NATO to include at least western Austria, and a neutral Austria must have seemed preferable to such a prospect" ("Negotiations for an Austrian State Treaty," 62, 70). Thoss's contribution is found in "Modellfall Österreich?" 199–201.
51. See the Harrison minute "Austria," March 23, 1955, FO 371/117787/RR 1071/72, PRO. Kurt Steiner has concluded in a similar vein, "The volumes on *Foreign Relations of the United States* and other sources reveal a good deal of evidence that Austria's integration into the Western orbit was the goal of American policymakers at various levels" ("Negotiations for an Austrian State Treaty," 69).
52. 245th NSC meeting, April 21, 1955, *FRUS, 1955–1957*, V, 52f.

vacuum. Some seven to ten thousand trained were available as the core for a future Austrian Army and American arms stockpiles stored in Germany and Italy would be handed over to Austria to equip another twenty thousand or so.[53]

From the advantageous position of historical hindsight it is usually forgotten that the alternative outcome of a partition of Austria still frightened not only Bohlen in Moscow but many contemporary Vienna observers on the eve of the Moscow trip. Each superpower suspected that the other wanted to divide Austria; the Soviets feared an integration of Western Austria into NATO while the West was wary of an absorption of Eastern Austria into the Soviet empire. Llewellyn Thompson counseled the State Department "to make a determined effort to achieve an Austrian treaty now," for if the Moscow meeting failed to produce a breakthrough, "the Soviets may begin a 'creeping paralysis' of Eastern Austria with a view to eventual partition." He added: "Soviets have given many indications they have this in mind, although these may have had the purpose of softening up Austrian for negotiations. Such measures would be extremely difficult to counter and could probably be stopped only by threat of war."[54]

Indeed, background interviews with U.S. Embassy staff members (and it may be assumed that as thorough a professional as Thompson was he read these memoranda of conversation) indicate that leading Austrian Socialist politicians raised the specter of the alternative outcome of partition if Raab's gamble to go to Moscow failed. Bruno Pitterman, the Socialist leader in parliament, mentioned this possibility, as did Oskar Helmer, the outspokenly anti-Communist interior minister. Both con-

53. As soon as the Austrian treaty was signed, preparations for building and expanding a future Austrian army moved to the center of Austro-American diplomacy. Exact figures on the size of the trained Austrian police force that would form the nucleus of the future Austrian army differ; for a good summary, see the NSC's Operations Coordinating Board "Progress Report on United States Policy toward Austria (NSC 164/1)," October 14, 1955, in: *FRUS, 1955–1957*, XXVI, 23–8. On Austrian rearmament, see also Bischof, "Österreich—ein 'geheimer Verbündeter' des Westens?" 447–50; and Oliver Rathkolb, "Historische Bewährungsproben des Neutralitätsgesetzes 1955 am Beispiel der US-amerikanischen Österreich-Politik 1955 bis 1959," in *Verfassung. Juristisch-politische und sozialwissenschaftliche Beiträge anlässlich des 70-Jahr-Jubiläums des Bundesverfassungsgesetztes*, ed. Nikolaus Dimmel and Alfred-Johannes Noll (Vienna, 1990); Rathkolb, "The Foreign Relations between the USA and Austria in the Later 1950s," in Günter Bischof, Anton Pelinka, and Rolf Steininger, eds., *Austria in the Nineteen Fifties* (New Brunswick, N.J., 1995), 24–38; and, in greater detail, Rathkolb, *Washington Ruft Wien: U.S.-Grossmachtpolitik und Österreich 1953–1963* (Vienna, 1997).

54. Thompson to Dulles, April 6, 1955, NA, RG 59, Box 2662, 663.001/4–655.

sidered it "less likely," yet still worried that "the Soviets might be planning to partition Austria in the event that their current diplomatic maneuvering in Austria fails to bring the results that they expect." The Socialist vice chancellor Adolf Schärf, a member of the Moscow delegation, also feared that partition might be the alternate outcome of no breakthrough in Moscow; in fact, Schärf had always suspected that some conservative ÖVP politicians had not completely rejected the idea of partition along the Enns river. Gruber's warnings were more oblique, as when he made it clear to Dulles that a conclusion of the Austrian treaty after the Moscow meeting represented "Austria's last chance for independence."[55] Clearly the specter of partition was on the minds of the Austrian leaders and spurred them toward a compromising mind-set as they traveled on their historic mission to Moscow.

The decisive round of bilateral Austro-Soviet diplomacy peaked at the highly successful Austro-Soviet summit meeting in Moscow, the culmination of the "new look" diplomacy in both Moscow and Vienna. The Western powers tried to severely limit the negotiating space for the Austrian delegation by issuing a tripartite note on April 5, reminding the Austrians that their visit was only a "fact-finding mission" and they should "not get down to drafting formulae."[56]

Raab and his delegation ignored these strictures and engaged in extensive redrafting of treaty provisions, thus demonstrating the growing emancipation of Austrian diplomacy that had started in 1953.[57] From April 11 through 15, 1955, in heady negotiations with the entire Kremlin leadership, a high-level bipartisan Austrian delegation led by Chan-

55. Memoranda of conversation by Alexander Johnpoll based on confidential interviews with Pitterman, March 25, 1955, and Helmer, April 8, 1955, NA, RG 59, Lot 58 D 72, Box 7; Department of State to Thompson, April 19, 1995, *FRUS, 1955–1957,* V, 49f. On Schärf, see Karl R. Stadler, *Adolf Schärf: Mensch—Politiker—Staatsmann* (Vienna, 1982), 419; Schärf's suspicion of ÖVP leaders is cited in Allard, *Russia and the Austrian State Treaty,* 140.

56. Instructions to the Ambassador, Foreign Office to Vienna, April 2, 1955, and Tripartite Statement, Foreign Office to Vienna, April 4, 1955, FO 371/117788/RR 1071/95 and 99, PRO.

57. Wallinger had seen it coming when he observed the composition of the Austrian delegation: "The strength of the delegation will certainly lead the public to anticipate 'decisions.' From our standpoint the worst feature may be the inclusion of Doctor Verosta, legal adviser of the Ministry of Foreign Affairs. He is personally sound, and Political Director wanted his presence to provide himself with additional professional ballast; but his presence must make if difficult to avoid getting down to details." Wallinger to Foreign Office, March 29, 1955, FO 371/117787/RR 1071/84, PRO.

cellor Raab accomplished the decisive breakthrough.[58] The Soviets demanded Austrian neutrality to block Austrian integration ("Anschluss") into either Germany or the Western defense system. But the Kremlin agreed that along the lines of the Swiss model, Austrian neutrality could be armed (armed neutrality had been the Eisenhower administration's condition since the fall of 1953 and would ultimately defeat Pentagon resistance to neutralization). Moreover, the Soviets did not stipulate that Austrian neutrality had to be written into the treaty (which would have made the Western powers guarantors—a treaty provision that most likely never would have passed the scrutiny of the U.S. Senate). The Soviets also made decisive concessions in the unagreed-upon economic clauses of the treaty, agreeing to a staggered payment schedule of the $150 million lump sum for buying back the "German assets" in Eastern Austria, which could be paid in kind rather than in cash. The details of these bilateral agreements were written down in a memorandum of understanding. On the successful delegation's return to Vienna, the Austrian people cheered and lionized the team. In early May, a five-power ambassadors' conference (including Austria) met in Vienna to put the finishing touches on the treaty. On May 15, only a month after the bold Austro-Soviet Moscow summit, the foreign ministers met in Vienna to sign the Austrian State Treaty. After ratification, the occupation forces started to withdraw. On October 26, the occupation of Austria officially ended, the last soldiers having left and the Austrian Parliament passing its constitutional law of permanent neutrality.[59]

58. Intense partisan disagreements over the question of neutrality afflicted the Austrian delegation before and during the negotiations in Moscow, yet they were ultimately overcome. The disagreements are explicitly voiced in the Johnpoll interviews with Helmer and Pitterman, especially in the April 8, 1955, discussion with Helmer. Ferdinand Graf of Raab's conservative party, state secretary in the interior ministry, argued that Raab suffered from a "messianic complex," such that when it came to neutrality it was quite impossible to argue with him on the subject. See Johnpoll interviews in NA, RG 59, Lot 58 D 72, Box 7. These partisan disagreements remain part of the historiography of the Moscow trip, especially among party historians. For the Socialist perspective, see Stadler, *Adolf Schärf*, 409–31; for the People's Party perspective, see the essays and sources in Alois Mock, Ludwig Steiner, Andreas Khol, eds., *Neue Fakten zu Staatsvertrag and Neutralität* (Vienna, 1980).

59. This diplomacy can now be traced in considerable detail in *FRUS, 1955*, V, 1–117. The dramatic events of Austria's annus mirabilis are admirably analyzed in Stourzh, *Geschichte der Staatsvertrages*, 131–72; see also Günter Bischof, "Österreichische Neutralität, die deutsche Frage und europäische Sicherheit 1953–1955," in *Die doppelte Eindämmung: Europäische Sicherheit und die deutsche Frage in den Fünfzigern*, ed. Rolf

International Repercussions of the Austrian Treaty Breakthrough

The unanticipated rapid conclusion of the Austrian treaty in May 1955 had three important repercussions on international diplomacy: first, the fear that the Soviets intended it as a model for Germany, voiced most prominently by the West German Adenauer government; second, the Soviet "deed" that capped Eisenhower's April 16, 1953, demands, which forced the U.S. at last to agree to a summit meeting; and third, the expectation that Austrian neutrality might serve as a model (or "Trojan horse") for rolling back Communism in Eastern Europe.

As soon as the neutralization of Austria and the dramatic diplomatic breakthrough became public after the Moscow meeting, the West German Adenauer government was forced to engage in massive damage control by denying and denouncing the utility of the "Austrian solution" as a model for the disposition of Germany.[60] Raab was the first voice to calm the waters by reassuring Adenauer that only the Paris agreements and German rearmament had made the Austrian solution possible; moreover, the relative international importance of the two countries was so different that the Austrian model could never be applied to solve the German problem. Raab also confidentially let the Germans know that "one major premise for their willingness agree to neutralization of Austria is that the Federal Republic is firmly integrated with the West; moreover that if Germany were to be neutralized Austria's situation would be hopeless."[61]

Steininger et al. (Munich, 1993), 154–66, and Van Oudenaren, *Détente in Europe,* 30–5. Kreisky gives an engaging personal account of the Moscow visit in *Zwischen den Zeiten,* 467–76.

60. There is a vigorous debate over whether the Soviets intended the "Austrian model" as a bait for the neutralization of a unified Germany. Oliver Rathkolb and Bruno Thoss do not believe that the Kremlin intended Austria to be a model for Germany; see Rathkolb's "Deutsches Unbehagen an der Neutralität Österreichs 1955 und 1990. Ein 'unhistorischer' Vergleich mit verblüffenden Parallelen," in *Österreich und Deutschlands Grösse: Ein schlampiges Verhältnis,* ed. Oliver Rathkolb, Georg Schmid, and Gernot Heiss (Salzburg, 1990), 85–93, and Thoss's "Modellfall Österreich?" What could be called the Innsbruck school, with its anti-Adenauer animus, thinks that the Kremlin intended Austria to be a model for Germany; see Rolf Steininger, "1955: The Austrian State Treaty and the German Question," *Diplomacy and Statecraft,* III (1992), 494–522, and Michael Gehler, "State Treaty and Neutrality: The Austrian Solution in 1955 as a 'Model' for Germany?" See also Bischof, Palinka, and Steininger, eds., *Austria in the Nineteen Fifties,* 39–78.

61. West Germany's representative Müller-Graaf in Vienna to Foreign Office (Bonn), April 23, 1955, Political Archives of the Foreign Ministry (PA-AA), Bonn, 312, vol. 40, 210–01/94.19; Conant to Dulles, April 28, 1955, NA, RG 59, Box 2662, 663.00/4–2855.

Raab's perspective ran counter to the generally held assumption in the Western diplomatic community that "the creation of a neutral belt of neutral states consisting of Sweden, Germany, Austria and Yugoslavia" was the basic Soviet objective, as the British ambassador in Vienna Geoffrey Wallinger put it. Sir Geoffrey added: "In view of the apparent recent trend in Yugoslavia towards neutralism, creation of situation in which Germany would be only missing link in this chain must have great attraction for the Soviets."[62]

But the pressure on Adenauer to seize the Austrian model for a German solution came mainly from the Socialist opposition in his own country. Ever since the Stalin notes of 1952, Socialist pressure to test bilateral negotiations with Moscow had threatened Adenauer's unrelenting policy of Western integration and activated what his biographer Hans-Peter Schwarz calls Adenauer's "neutralization trauma." The Christian Social deputy leader Wilhelm Krone warned the West that an Austrian solution "would tend to create impression here that the SPD program calling for alliance free status for Germany had been correct and that the Government had been *deluded by Western tactics designed to get German soldiers*" (emphasis in original).[63]

After the Moscow meeting finalized the neutralization of Austria, the pressure on Adenauer to be more open to negotiations with Moscow mushroomed even further. A vigorous campaign was started to dismiss the utility of the "Austrian model" for Germany. As early as April 19, Heinz Krekeler, the West German ambassador in Washington, reminded the State Department that the Austrian and German cases were very

---

German scholar Thoss has argued persuasively that the Adenauer administration was right—Austria was not a model for Germany ("Modellfall Österreich?" 123–36).

62. Wallinger to Foreign Office, March 23, 1955, FO 371/117786/RR 1071/53, PRO. Bischoff in Moscow also thought the creation of a neutral Swiss-Austrian-Yugoslav zone in Central Europe might be the Soviet motive; see his telegram to Foreign Office of February 27, 1955, and his presentation at the top ambassadors' meeting in Vienna, March 28, 1955, in Schilcher, ed., *Österreich und die Grossmächte*, 242–5, 254–6.

63. Conant to Dulles, April 14, 1955, NA, RG 59, Box 2662, 663.001/4–1455; Hans-Peter Schwarz, *Adenauer—Der Staatsmann: 1952–1967* (Stuttgart, 1988), 184. Adenauer relentlessly drove home a message to the Germans that neutralization of Germany would mean the end of NATO and a free Europe; see his speech in Hamm, February 9, 1955, Adenauer Foundation, folder "Reden—Interviews—Aufsätze 1955," Rhöndorf. On the German Social Democratic Party's policy toward Soviet "peaceful coexistence" and its repercussions regarding German reunification, see Hans-Erich Volkmann, "Die sozialdemokratische innerparteiliche Diskussion über Sicherheit, Entspannung und deutsche Einheit (1953–1955)," in *Zwischen Kaltem Krieg und Entspannung*, ed. Thoss and Volkmann, 153–78.

different, because Austria featured no puppet government that needed to be discredited in order to reach a solution; moreover there were no frontier problems. On April 20, the German foreign ministry in Bonn advised its embassies worldwide how to respond to the "Austrian model" theory. Austria was not a model for solving the German question because Germany and Austria were very different in terms of their respective geographic size and geostrategic importance in the world. Adenauer vigorously rejected the Austrian model for a neutralization of a unified Germany since it would lead to Soviet control not only of Germany but of all of Western Europe.[64]

During the preparatory Western diplomatic meetings for the Geneva summit Adenauer missed no opportunity to stress that the Federal Republic's Western integration carried for him much higher priority than unification.[65] Gordon Craig has observed how "Adenauer had an obsessive suspicion of new approaches to the Soviet Union."[66] Adenauer violently resisted any idea of neutralization because he was determined "to avoid at all costs giving any impression that the Federal Republic would waver in its allegiance to WEU and NATO." Therefore he reiterated his strong resistance to any Austrian treaty solutions for Germany because of the obvious abundant dissimilarities of the two cases.[67] At times Adenauer, who personally disliked Austrians, could become gravely agitated about the Austrian model of self-chosen neutrality—"this entirely disgusting Austrian mess" (*"die ganze Österreichische Schweinerei"*). He suspected a conspiracy of Austrian Socialists with State Department officials designed to keep neutrality schemes alive and even feared Ei-

64. Lyon, "memorandum of conversation" with Krekeler, April 19, 1955, NA, RG 59, Box 2662, 663.001/14–1955; Walter Hallstein, "Informationserlass zur Regelung der Sprache" April 20, 1955, PA-AA, 312, vol. 49, 304.512–03/94.19/537/55, Bonn; Adenauer Speech in Goslar, April 22, 1955, Adenauer Foundation, folder "Reden-Interviews-Aufsätze, 1955," Rhöndorf.

65. Klaus Gotto, "Die Sicherheits- und Deutschlandfrage in Adenauer's Politik 1954–55," in *Zwischen Kaltem Krieg und Entspannung*, ed. Thoss and Volkmann, 137–52. For a critical view, see Rolf Steininger, *Deutsche Geschichte seit 1945*, vol. 2: *1948–1955* (Frankfurt, 1996), 321–33; for an admirably succinct and balanced introduction to Adenauer's diplomacy, see Gordon A. Craig, "Adenauer and His Diplomats," in *Diplomats, 1939–1979*, ed. Craig and Loewenheim, 201–27.

66. Craig, "Adenauer and His Diplomats," 213.

67. Reporting discussions with Adenauer's closest foreign policy confidant, Herbert Blankenhorn, London Working Group to Department of State, April 28, 1955, *FRUS, 1955–1957*, V, 153f.

senhower was turning toward Swiss-style armed neutrality.[68] Dulles consistently supported his friend Adenauer by publicly reiterating that a small country of seven million people could be neutralized, but a policy of neutrality "had no application" to seventy million Germans. Austrian neutrality backed by an Austrian army was acceptable; an independent Germany "with an unlimited army" was not acceptable. Behind the scenes Dulles was more candid about his motives vis-à-vis German neutralization and reunification; in a conversation with Charles de Gaulle in 1958, he claimed that "a disengaged Germany would constitute an element between the two blocs that would use bargaining and blackmail for its own ends, which could very well lead to another war." A divided Germany and the integration of the Federal Republic into the West was the best containment of the German power potential.[69]

The second international repercussion of Austrian treaty breakthrough was its demonstration that one could do business with the Soviets, thus removing the final roadblock to East-West summitry. In his lengthy final analysis of the importance of Austrian treaty diplomacy for East-West relations, Geoffrey Wallinger argues that "the speed with which the Austrian settlement was concluded was required as an object-lesson to Germany, and perhaps to others as well, on the desirability and utility of direct negotiations with Moscow. It was certainly striking that, as soon as the Austro-Soviet agreement had been made, the Moscow press began to hold it up as a model for other possible settlements."[70]

---

68. Schwarz, *Adenauer—Der Staatsmann*, 184. Little did Adenauer know that the Austrian Socialists deceived even the German Socialists on the issue of the "model case." The Austrian Socialists were supposed to test for their German comrades Soviet ideas about German unification and neutralization in Moscow. But after the Kremlin had at last separated the two issues, Schärf and Kreisky muffled German expectations because they did not want to raise the slightest expectations on resumption of four-power talks where the Soviets might once again discuss the German problem and ignore the Austrian issue. See Gehler, "State Treaty and Neutrality," 56–9. On Adenauer's *"Abneigung gegen Österreicher,"* see the candid analysis by Kreisky, *Zwischen den Zeiten*, 448–53.

69. Background news conference, May 24, 1955, Dulles Papers, folder "Germany, 1955," Box 82, Mudd Library, Princeton University; Dulles to de Gaulle, quoted in Challener, "Dulles: Moralist As Pragmatist," in *Diplomats, 1939–1979*, ed. Craig and Loewenheim, 156. On Dulles's close relationship with Adenauer, see Detlef Felken, *Dulles und Deutschland: Die amerikanische Deutschlandpolitik 1953–1959* (Bonn, 1993).

70. Wallinger to Macmillan, May 24, 1955, FO 371/117801/RR 1071/450, PRO.

Direct negotiations with Moscow on any level were precisely what the Eisenhower administration had resisted so vigorously ever since Stalin's death. The White House never gave up its basic perception that along with domestic preoccupations and fear of war, the Kremlin's new "soft line" represented a tactical maneuver to divide the West. Basic national security memorandum NSC 5501 noted in early 1955: "The Soviet leaders have almost certainly regarded their 'peace offensive' as their most effective present tactic for dividing the free world and isolating the U.S. from its allies."[71]

In May 1955 the pressure from these very allies at last forced Washington to agree to a summit. The spring of 1955 saw some of the most dramatic weeks in East-West diplomacy in the entire cold war. Even Dulles was overwhelmed in the course of his historic visit to Europe with the deposit of the ratification instruments of the Paris agreements on May 5, the formal acceptance of West German integration into NATO, and the signing of the Austrian State Treaty on May 15 in Vienna. As a backdrop to Austro-Soviet negotiations and particularly after the ratification struggle in the French National Assembly, the French governments of Pierre Mendès-France and his successor Edgar Faure had increased their pressure in late 1954 and early 1955 for a four-power meeting to test the sincerity of the Kremlin's new policy. This had led to the setting up of a tripartite working group in London to develop a Western agenda for a future summit meeting.[72]

With the successful completion of West German integration into the West and the conclusion of the Austrian treaty only a matter of final details, British prime minister Anthony Eden, who had just succeeded

71. NSC 5501 "Basic National Security Policy," January 7, 1955, *FRUS, 1955–1957*, XIX, 24–38 (citation 29).

72. This can be traced down to the final report of the London working group in *FRUS, 1955–1957*, V, 119–64. Based on exclusively British documents, the most competent summary of these tripartite diplomatic activities can be found in Rolf Steininger, "Zwischen Pariser Verrägen und Genfer Gipfelkonfernz: Grossbritannien und die Deutsche Frage 1955," in Steiniger et al., eds., *Die doppelte Eindämmung*, 177–211. A particularly useful summary of French efforts toward a summit with the Soviets is Renata Fritsch-Bournazel, "Frankreichs Ost- und Deutschlandpolitik im Zeichen der Genfer Gipfelkonferenz von 1955," in *Zwischen Kaltem Krieg und Entspannung*, ed. Thoss and Volkmann, 71–92; on Mendès-France and four-power talks, see Jean Lacouture, *Pierre Mendès-France*, trans. George Holoch (New York, 1993), 312–27, and Rene Girault, "La France dans les rapports est-ouest au temps de la présidence de Pierre Mendès-France," in *Pierre Mendès-France et le Mendésisme: L'expérience gouvernementale (1954–1955) et sa postérité*, ed. François Bédarida et Jean-Pierre Rioux (Paris, 1985), 251–60.

Churchill at 10 Downing Street and needed some international expo-
sure to win an upcoming election campaign, put additional pressure on
Eisenhower to give in and meet for a summit with the new Kremlin
leaders. Eden appealed to the American president's emotions by noting
that a summit would stir "the imagination of all the peoples of the
world" and by arguing that " 'top level' talks between heads of government could play a useful part in the reduction of world tension." Eisenhower and Dulles finally relented, but cautioned Eden that the West
would have to carefully prepare a limited agenda for such a summit
meeting. The upcoming foreign ministers' meeting in Vienna should be
utilized to talk about such a summit.[73]

As Richard D. Challener has observed, Dulles had displayed "a continuing resistance to summit conferences" ever since 1953 and was still
reluctant to accept the need for such a meeting in 1955. He felt that
summits raised in the public mind undue expectations that could not
be achieved and might also result "in a letdown in the will and determination of the American people." Dulles continued to believe this in
spite of the spectacular show of Soviet good will in finishing the Austrian treaty. After the new British foreign secretary, Harold Macmillan,
insisted on a high-level four-power meeting, Dulles aired his displea-
sure in a cable to Eisenhower:

> I am somewhat concerned over the passionate eagerness here in Europe for
> a meeting of the Big Four, particularly at the Head-of-Government level on
> the theory that this will produce some kind of miracle. No one seems inter-
> ested in trying to think up how there can be any discussion which will in
> fact be fruitful. The mere fact of meeting seems of itself to be enough. The
> Macmillan proposal is at least an effort to grapple with the realities of the
> fact that it is hopeless to believe, and wrong to bring the public to believe,
> that in three or four days you and Bulganin could settle such problems as
> the unification of Germany, the elimination of atomic weapons and general
> disarmament.[74]

73. Eden to Eisenhower, May 6, 1955, and Dulles to Makins (British ambassador in
Washington) with letter from Eisenhower to Eden, May 6, 1955, FRUS, 1955–1957, V,
164–7. Eden gives a rather bland description of his motives in The Memoirs of Anthony
Eden: Full Circle (London, 1960), 290f. On Eden's partisan political motives for summitry,
see also Carlton, "Grossbritannien und die Gipfeldiplomatie 1953–1955," in Zwischen
Kaltem Krieg und Entspannung, ed. Thoss and Volkmann, 51–69. A good survey of preparations for the Geneva summit can be found in Van Oudenaren, Détente in Europe, 35–8.
74. Challener, "Dulles: Moralist As Pragmatist," 159; Dulles to Department of State for
President, May 9, 1955, FRUS, 1955–1957, V, 174f.

But given overwhelming world public opinion, the die was cast for a summit. During their meetings in Vienna, Dulles seized the opportunity to discuss with Molotov and the French and British foreign ministers the forthcoming four-power meeting. Dulles had to make it clear that under no circumstances would the summit be a "five-power meeting" (with Communist China) and that Vienna could never be the venue as Molotov had suggested. Why not? Because "it would have a very disastrous effect upon Germany if Vienna, as a reward for becoming neutral, should instantly be made the center of European activity, including discussion of the future of Germany." He strongly urged the group to meet in Switzerland. In his talks with Adenauer in Paris, the German chancellor confirmed Dulles's suspicions of the supposedly "new" course the Kremlin was taking. Adenauer viewed "the recent Soviet moves re Austrian treaty etc. as not being fundamental changes in Communist motives or objectives, but rather represented shift in tactics." Dulles never changed his view on a summit with the Soviets, since he reported to the National Security Council after the conference that "we never wanted to go to Geneva, but the pressure of people of the world forced us to do [so]."[75]

The third effect of the neutralization of Austria that paved the way for summitry was the possibility that it suggested a model for the neighboring Eastern European satellites to shake off the Soviet presence and the Kremlin's iron rule. Austrian politicians such as the SPÖ leader Pitterman hoped that Austrian neutrality might act as a Trojan horse for the West to gain a foothold in Eastern Europe and presumably to temper Soviet control.[76] Even before the conclusion of the Austrian treaty, Eden had hinted as much to Eisenhower when he explained his motive for a top-level four-power meeting: "The hopes of so many people, on both sides of the Iron Curtain, have been raised and kind of mystique surrounds the idea."[77] Indeed, as the conclusion of the Austrian treaty was

75. Dulles to Department of State for President, May 15, 1955, *FRUS, 1955–1957*, V, 180–2; Dulles to Department of State, May 8, 1955, *FRUS, 1955–1957*, V, 172f.; 256th NSC discussion, July 28, 1955, *FRUS, 1955–1957*, V, 535. See also memorandum of conversation with Macmillan and Pinay, May 15, 1955, Dulles Papers, Box 95, Mudd Library, Princeton University. After American refusal to meet in Vienna and Soviet refusal to meet in Lausanne, Geneva was selected as the compromise site of the summit. See draft letter Hoover to Pinay, May 31, 1955, Dulles-Herter Series, Box 4, folder "May 1955," Ann Whitman Files, DDEL.

76. These thoughts from the Ballhausplatz were reported by the French ambassador to the Quai d'Orsay and are quoted in Gehler, "State Treaty and Neutrality," 54.

77. Eden to Eisenhower, May 6, 1995, *FRUS, 1955–1957*, V, 164.

the final Soviet "deed" to break the White House's resistance to a summit—a deed that Dulles himself had stipulated after Stalin's death—Dulles added a new spin on the importance of the treaty.[78] After his return to Washington, Dulles gave a memorable report to the American people on national television on May 17. Introduced by Eisenhower and speaking from the president's office in the White House, Dulles termed the German and Austrian breakthroughs "historic." Ad-libbing, he praised the Austrian people for "keeping their nerve" during the endless negotiations for the treaty. Not wanting to share the limelight with Ballhausplatz diplomats, he suggested obliquely that this was a great accomplishment of Western diplomacy: "It is just one of these breaks that come, if you keep on steadily, steadily, keeping the pressure on." Then he added his hope that the Austrian outcome would create a mounting desire among her neighbors behind the iron curtain "to get the same freedom from that type of occupation that the Austrians had got." *Time* magazine dubbed Dulles's exercise in public relations as "Foster's Hour."[79]

Without in-depth investigations of Czech and Hungarian responses, it is hard to gauge how much the satellite neighbors were impressed by German rearmament and Western integration, Khrushchev's visit to Tito, and the "Austrian model" and the Geneva summit, or how much

78. In a memorandum to Emmet Hughes, the president's principal writer for the April 16 speech, Dulles had specifically asked to list Austria as one of the issues where breakthrough was possible: "Austria, which is, I believe, next to Korea the clearest test of Soviet intentions which we should welcome." See Dulles memorandum for Hughes, April 10, 1953, John Foster Dulles Papers, Draft Presidential Correspondence and Speech Series, Box 1, folder "President's Speech 1953 (1)," DDEL.

79. For Dulles's speech, see "An Historic Week," *Department of State Bulletin*, May 30, 1955, 871–6; *Time*, May 30, 1955, 10f. Eden similarly neglected the accomplishments of Austrian diplomacy when he stressed "our Austrian success"; see *Full Circle*, 291. Based on the new documentation available from Western archives, I have consistently stressed Western resistance to Austro-Soviet bilateral treaty diplomacy in March–April 1955, examining the issue in great detail in a number of essays; see my "Anglo-American Powers and Austrian Neutrality," 368–93; "Gruber und die Anfänge des 'Neuen Kurses,' " 161–70; "Österreichische Neutralität, deutsche Frage, und europäische Sicherheit," 146–66; "Eisenhower and the Austrian Treaty," 156–61. This view has hitherto been ignored by Anglo-American scholarship. Traditional American cold-war scholarship has given no credit to "third actors," such as Austria, vis-à-vis the superpowers. Ignoring Austrian scholarship written in German, American authors have interpreted the Austrian breakthrough as originating with the Kremlin to test American resolve, or as a great triumph of American diplomacy (Dulles's "negotiating from strength"). Representative of the former is Larson, "Crisis Prevention and the Austrian Treaty"; of the latter, Marks III's fawning heroization of Dulles and his "Art of Negotiation," in *Power and Peace*, 47–69.

they were incited by Dulles's rhetoric about "liberation" and "roll-back." Clearly it had an effect on Hungary, where reformers proclaimed Hungarian armed neutrality at the height of their revolution in early November 1956. In May 1955, however, Hungary had undergone a re-Stalinization and American diplomats recognized no immediate impact on public opinion. The U.S. embassy in Prague vaguely reported that these events "had some effect." The Poles felt that the "West, particularly US, has lost diplomatic offensive to USSR during period starting with Soviet visit Belgrade." Polish sources felt that the Soviet moves resulted from German rearmament and were "carefully calculated, calmly executed maneuvers." U. Alexis Johnson, the outgoing American ambassador to Czechoslovakia, told Eisenhower in a personal meeting of the "extravagant hopes of the people for some miracle to arise out of the recent Geneva Conference which would bring about their liberation from Communist rule."[80]

The opening of the American records made clear that its loud propaganda about "rollback" to the contrary, behind the scenes the Eisenhower administration was extremely cautious and never pursued an active policy of "liberation." As early as December 1953, the administration states in its basic national security document on the satellites that liberation should be pursued mainly by means of psychological warfare. In order to eventually eliminate Soviet influence, Eisenhower supported Titoism and "national communism" in the satellites. He also encouraged exploiting future disturbances along the lines of the East German riots but stressed the importance of avoiding "incitement to premature revolt." Hence the ultimate conclusion of NSC 174: "A deliberate policy of attempting to liberate the satellite peoples by military force, which would probably mean war with the USSR and most probably would be unacceptable to the American people and condemned by world opinion, cannot be given serious consideration." This policy was not substantially changed in 1955 updates of NSC 174 nor in the basic NSC memorandum NSC 5501: "The stability of the USSR and its hold over European satellites are unlikely to be seriously shaken over the next few years, despite measures which the U.S. may find it feasible to take to weaken Soviet control."[81]

80. Downs (Budapest) to Department of State, May 11, 1955; Johnson (Prague) to Department of State, June 14, 1955; Jacobs (Warsaw) to Department of State, June 20, 1955; memorandum of conversation, July 29, 1955, *FRUS, 1955–1957*, XXV, 25–41, 51.
81. See the "top secret" NSC 174 "Statement of Policy Proposed by the National Security Council on United States Policy toward the Soviet Satellites in Eastern Europe," De-

In spite of heavy pressure from conservative Republicans, Eisenhower never gave the go-ahead to establishing and training a "Volunteer Freedom Corps" of Eastern European refugees in West Germany as a vanguard for rolling back Communism in the satellites. Given the heavy-handed Soviet occupation and the experience of the Hungarian uprising in 1956, surely such a refugee guerilla force would hardly have fared better than the Cubans in the Bay of Pigs.[82] Viewed from this vantage point, Eisenhower's extreme caution in actively engaging in "liberation" seems wise. Under his administration the prospect of revising the division of Europe "flickered briefly, then died out," Bennett Kovrig has concluded, adding: "This was a dismal outcome for an administration whose election campaign had been marked by sonorous promises to restore freedom to the oppressed."[83]

Not that Eisenhower had not tried to raise the issue of oppression in the Eastern European satellites at Geneva. But the Soviets strictly declined to discuss that sphere. Before an evening dinner during the summit, Eisenhower tried to engage Premier Nikolai Bulganin in a discussion about the satellites, noting that "there were millions of American whose origins were in Central and Eastern Europe" and that "they had very strong feelings over the captivity of the Eastern European countries." Bulganin, however, refused to pursue the subject at Geneva, impressing on the president that "if he did anything about it at this conference he would not be allowed to return to the Soviet Union." But Eisenhower himself was not interested in returning home with any

cember 11, 1953, in *FRUS, 1952–1954*, VIII, 110–27. For NSC 5501 "Basic National Security Policy," January 7, 1955, see *FRUS, 1955–1957*, XIX, 27. NSC 5501 reflected "a somewhat subtler strategy" than NSC 174; see NSC 5505/1, Rockefeller to Hoover, September 30, 1955, *FRUS, 1955–1957*, XXV, 84f. The best discussions of Eisenhower's policy toward Eastern Europe are Kovrig, *Of Walls and Bridges: The United States and Eastern Europe*, 50–102, and László Borhi, "Rollback, Liberation, Containment, or Inaction: U.S. Policy and Eastern Europe in the 1950s," *Journal of Cold War Studies*, I (1999), 67–110.

82. On the "Volunteer Freedom Corps," see NSC 143/2, May 20, 1953, *FRUS, 1952–1954*, VIII, 213–8, and the Progress Report on NSC 143/2, August 3, 1954, *FRUS, 1955–1957*, XXV, 53–64; see also Kovrig, *Of Walls and Bridges*, 65f. For an outstanding treatment of Congressman Charles Kersten's 1953–54 labors to establish and finance such a Volunteer Freedom Corps, and Eisenhower's sympathy for it, see Charles Byler, "Trouble for Joe Stalin in His Own Backyard: The Kersten Amendment and the Debate over American Policy in Eastern Europe," paper delivered at the annual SHAFR meeting in Annapolis, Md., June 1995. I am grateful to Professor Byler for sharing with me with a copy of his unpublished paper.

83. Kovrig, *Of Walls and Bridges*, 50; Gabriel is similarly critical of Eisenhower's vague approach to neutrality vis-à-vis Eastern Europe, where the policy had promise (*The American Conception of Neutrality after 1941*, 185).

agreements from Geneva. After his return, the president briefed the congressional leaders, telling them that "we had tried to initiate a discussion of the satellite states and International Communism but they had declined." Eisenhower opened the briefing session by categorically assuring the suspicious congressional leaders (among them stalwart Republican senators Styles Bridges and William Knowland) that "there were no secret agreements made, nothing initialed, nothing signed."[84] There would not be any Yaltas under Eisenhower.

In the spring of 1955, the conclusion of the Austrian treaty removed a major obstacle on the twisted path to Geneva. The Eisenhower administration had only reluctantly accepted the conclusion of the treaty because it had not been able to stop the dramatic progress in bilateral Austro-Soviet diplomacy. With the Austrian success story accomplished, Eisenhower no longer could resist the pressure from his principal Western allies to finally meet with and test the new Kremlin leadership in a summit. Eisenhower and Dulles never expected "spectacular results" from the Big Four conference; rather, Eisenhower told his friend 'Swede' Hazlett: "Nevertheless, I should think that Foster and I should be able to detect whether the Soviets really intend to introduce a tactical change that could mean, for the next few years at least, some real easing of tensions." The Austrian diplomatic breakthrough indicated that the changes in Kremlin foreign policy represented much more than tactical maneuvers, a fact the Eisenhower administration never fully acknowledged. The neutralization of Austria was the Kremlin's response to German rearmament. It prevented a "new Anschluss"—the dreaded integration of Western Austria into the Western defense system. The new Soviet diplomacy was prepared to make more than tactical concessions and utilized the Austrian treaty as the "test case for détente."[85]

84. For the Geneva discussion with Bulganin, see "Memorandum for the Record of the President's Dinner," July 18, 1955, *FRUS, 1955–1957*, V, 372f.; for the Bipartisan Legislative Meeting, July 25, 1955, see Legislative Meetings Series, Box 2, folder "July–August 1955 (4)," Ann Whitman Files, DDEL. The U.S. had stressed in the Western tripartite working group meeting in Paris preceding the summit that "continuing pressure" must be put on the Soviets over their control of the satellites and that the Western powers should emphasize the "Soviet need to solve satellite problem before a real reduction of tension could be achieved in Europe." See U.S. Delegation to Department of State, July 9, 1996, *FRUS, 1955–1957*, 312f.

85. Eisenhower to Hazlett, June 4, 1955, in Robert Griffith, ed., *Ike's Letter to a Friend 1941–1958* (Lawrence, Kans., 1984),146; Thoss, "Modellfall Österreich?" 136.

Left to right: John Foster Dulles, Anthony Eden, Leopold Figl, and an unidentified diplomat meet during the Berlin Council of Foreign Ministers in 1954. *Dulles Papers, Princeton University Library*

The Kremlin leaders welcome the Austrian delegation in Moscow, 11 April 1955. Front row left to right: Deputy Chairman of the Soviet Council of Ministers Anastas Mikoyan, Foreign Minister V. M. Molotov, Chancellor Julius Raab, and Ambassador Norbert Bischoff. *Julius-Raab-Archiv, Vogelsang Institut, Vienna*

After signing the State Treaty, Chancellor Raab toured the Austrian oil fields still under Soviet control. Part of the "German external assets" in Austria seized by the Soviet Union after the war, these valuable installations were the sticking point in Austrian treaty negotiations and were returned to Austria with the treaty. *Julius-Raab-Archiv, Vogelsang Institut, Vienna*

President Dwight D. Eisenhower and Secretary of State John Foster Dulles at work in the White House preparing for the Geneva Summit. *Dwight D. Eisenhower Library, Abilene, Kansas*

Eisenhower, Ambassador to Bonn James B. Conant, John Foster Dulles, and Chancellor Konrad Adenauer during Adenauer's visit to Washington in preparation for the Geneva Summit. *Dwight D. Eisenhower Library*

Eisenhower and Churchill during Churchill's last visit to the U.S., in May 1959. Hoping to ease tensions, particularly at a time when the production of hydrogen bombs made the nuclear age even more dangerous, Churchill had been urging a summit with the new leadership in the Kremlin ever since Stalin's death in 1953. *Dwight D. Eisenhower Library*

Eisenhower and Khrushchev during Khrushchev's visit to the U.S. in September 1959. At the time of the Geneva Summit, Khrushchev emerged as Stalin's successor in the Kremlin; more than anyone he was responsible for the signing of the Austrian treaty and giving "peaceful coexistence" a chance. *Dwight D. Eisenhower Library*

Dulles and Eisenhower at the Geneva Summit in July 1955. U.S. ambassador to Moscow Charles E. Bohlen leans in to give advice. On Bohlen's right is the U.S. ambassador to Vienna, Llewellyn E. Thompson, one of the architects of the Austrian treaty and one of the State Department's premier Soviet experts; Douglas MacArthur II, the State Department counselor, sits at Eisenhower's left. *Associated Press*

Left to right: Harold Macmillan (Great Britain), John Foster Dulles, Antoine Pinay (France), and V. M. Molotov (Soviet Union) during the Geneva Council of Foreign Ministers in November 1955, as portrayed by the Swiss cartoonist André Neiger ("Derso"). *Dulles Papers, Princeton University Library*

The Eden Plan and European Security

SAKI DOCKRILL

At the summit conference in Geneva in July 1955, British prime minister Anthony Eden was determined to draw the Russians into a discussion about German unity and European security. The West's attempts to negotiate with the Russians over the German question were not new. The most recent occasion had been on 11 May 1953, when then prime minister Winston Churchill appealed to the Kremlin leaders to agree to hold high-level talks. Churchill's initiative raised hopes in the West, albeit temporarily, that a settlement of the cold war in general, and of the German problem in particular, was possible. Consequently, the three Western foreign ministers met the Soviet foreign minister in Berlin from 25 January to 18 February 1954. At that conference, Eden, then foreign secretary, presented the West's plan for the reunification of Germany, calling for free elections throughout Germany and the formation of an all-German government to take place before the negotiation of a peace treaty with the four occupying powers. The united Germany would then be free to "assume or reject" alignment with either the East or the West.[1]

Although the Berlin conference of foreign ministers failed to reach any agreement on the German question, the "Eden plan" remained the basis of the West's approach to the issue of German reunification. However, the "so-called Eden plan," as Eden himself customarily referred to it, was not of Eden's own devising. As U.S. secretary of state John Foster Dulles reminded C. D. Jackson (Eisenhower's special assistant until

I am grateful to both the British Academy and the Department of War Studies for travel grants that funded archival research in Germany, the USA, and Britain. Copyright material from the Public Record Office, Kew, appears by permission of Her Majesty's Stationery Office.

1. Eden (Berlin) to Churchill, tel.83, 4 February 1954, PREM 11/909, PRO; Anthony Eden, *The Memoirs of Sir Anthony Eden: Full Circle* (London, 1960), 66–70. For the Eden plan presented at the Berlin Conference, see command paper, Cmd. 9080, Annex A ("Plan for German Reunification in Freedom") 120–2, and *FRUS*, VII, 1177–80.

1954) on 11 July 1955, "it was an accident of the seating arrangement that made our agreed-upon proposal for the unification of Germany be spoken by Eden, at which time it became labeled as 'Eden plan.' " As it turned out, the Eden plan for the reunification of Germany did not become central to Britain's preparatory work for the Geneva summit and played only a small part in the discussions at that meeting. Unlike at Berlin, the Eden plan was not an agreed-upon Western proposal for Geneva, and its details were never fully discussed by the Western powers prior to the summit. Furthermore, while the Eden plan was fully documented and published in the records of the Berlin conference, at Geneva it was never introduced as a clear-cut proposal. Instead, the prime minister outlined only the essential features of the British plan for German reunification and European security.[2]

Finally, while the Eden plan at Berlin concentrated on how to proceed with the reunification of Germany, the Eden plan for the Geneva summit placed the German question in the wider context of European security. The gist of what became known as another Eden plan at Geneva was summarized by the prime minister before the cabinet on 14 July 1955:

> The so-called Eden Plan would not alone suffice. We should have to show, in addition, that safeguards could be devised to ensure that a united and independent Germany need not represent an increased military threat to Russia. These safeguards might have to include some limitation on the strength and location of forces in Germany and in countries neighbouring Germany, and possibly some arrangements for the demilitarisation of a part of Germany, so as to separate the Forces of the East and West. These provisions might be accompanied by some sort of security pact which would not involve guarantees of frontiers.[3]

The creation of a demilitarized area in Central Europe, an agreement on the limitation of armaments within specified areas of Central Europe, and the conclusion of a European security pact were all part of a package proposal Eden had in mind before the opening of the Geneva summit.

That the Eden package for Geneva was not adopted is well known.[4]

2. *FRUS, 1955–1957*, V, 301.
3. Cabinet 23rd meeting, 14 July 1955, CAB 128/29, PRO.
4. For recent studies on the Geneva Conference, see Bruno Thoss and Hans-Erich Volkmann, eds., *Zwischen Kaltem Krieg und Entspannung: Sicherheits-und Deutschlandpolitik der Bundesrepublik im Mächtesystem der Jahre 1953–1956* (Boppard am Rhein, 1988);

Perhaps a more intriguing set of questions is why Eden was so keen to resolve the German question and its related European security problems at Geneva, how serious he was in believing that this could be done, and why his plan was never implemented.

Origins of the Eden Package Proposal

When Eden became foreign secretary in the Conservative government formed by Churchill in the autumn of 1951, the former did not display much enthusiasm toward, or understanding of, the integration of Western Europe and the role in which an independent and rearmed West Germany might play in the proposed European Defence Community (EDC). By the spring of 1955, however, Eden had become one of the most successful foreign ministers in Europe, having so transformed his earlier image of being hostile to European unity that by September 1954 he had skillfully negotiated a resolution of the question of West German rearmament, then at the top of NATO's agenda.[5] Not only was he confident, by that time he was also, given his extensive experience with European affairs, one of the best-qualified politicians to deal with Europe. Eden benefitted from the advice of a number of experts on Europe in the foreign office, who in the early 1950s had dealt with Britain's difficulties with Europeans, Americans, and Russians over the German question and European security. For instance, Sir Ivone Kirkpatrick, Lord Hood, Sir Geoffrey H. Harrison, Sir Frank Roberts, and Patrick Hancock were all active in the foreign office when Eden took over the premiership from Churchill in April 1955.[6]

Two days after Eden entered 10 Downing Street on 7 April, the foreign office requested the chiefs of staff to make recommendations about Britain's policy toward German unification and European security for a pos-

---

Rolf Steininger, "Zwischen Pariser Verträgen und Genfer Gipfelkonferenz: Grossbritannien und die Deutsche Frage 1955" in *Die doppelte Eindämmung: Europäische Sicherheit und die deutsche Frage in den Fünfzigern*, ed. Steininger et al. (Munich, 1993), 177–211; Antonio Varsori, "Le gouvernement Eden et l'Union soviétique (1955–56): de l'espoir à la désillusion" *Relations Internationales* 71 (1992), 273–98.

5. On Eden's role in the question of West German rearmament, see Saki Dockrill, *Britain's Policy for West German Rearmament, 1951–1955* (Cambridge, U.K., 1991), 80–150.

6. Sir Ivone Kirkpatrick was permanent undersecretary of state for foreign affairs, following his service as British High Commissioner to Germany between 1950 and 1953. Lord Hood was head of the Western Organisations Department and Sir Geoffrey H. Harrison the assistant undersecretary after 1951. Sir Frank Roberts was ambassador to Belgrade after 1954, and Patrick Hancock was head of the Central (Europe) Department after 1953.

sible meeting with the Soviet Union. So far, the Soviets had insisted on the withdrawal of all foreign troops upon the conclusion of a peace treaty with a united Germany. Nor would the Russians be at all likely to accept a reunified Germany tied closely to the Western bloc without receiving a substantial quid pro quo from the West.

The foreign office considered four different possible cases for the reunification of Germany. The first was that upon the creation of a unified Germany, all troops would withdraw, and the reunified Germany would be given the freedom to choose between the East and the West—and would, in NATO's view, choose association with the West. Germany would then raise twelve divisions under NATO, and the Supreme Commander for Allied Powers in Europe (SACEUR) would reserve the right to station other Western troops in Germany. This was almost identical to the Western approach at Berlin and the foreign office was by no means optimistic about its acceptability to the Russians. The second case also assumed that a reunified Germany would choose NATO, but with the condition that the Russians should withdraw their troops to the east of the Oder, while the Western forces withdrew to the west of the Rhine. The third scenario again assumed that a reunified Germany would remain in NATO, but with a more extensive agreement on troop withdrawal, namely that no foreign troops would be stationed in Germany. Case four proposed that a reunified Germany would remain neutral and that no foreign troops or bases would remain on German soil. There would also be an agreement on the maximum level of military strength the new Germany would be allowed. This final plan came the closest to the Russian requirements.[7]

In response to the foreign-office proposals, the joint planners of the chiefs of staff argued that case 1 would be totally unacceptable to the Russians, while case 4 would be most undesirable for the West. Cases 2 and 3, which entailed a partial or total evacuation of foreign troops of both blocs from Germany, would certainly weaken the military position of NATO. Nevertheless, the planners concluded that they were "militarily acceptable if this is the only means of securing a satisfactory political settlement" of the German question. In both cases, they suggested that it would be desirable to increase the level of German troops now planned under NATO, presumably in order to compensate for the evacuation of non-German NATO troops stationed in Germany.[8]

7. COS(55)74, 7 April 1955, DEFE 5/57, PRO.
8. JP(55)30 (Final), 20 April 1955, DEFE6/29, PRO.

The exchange of these initial views between the foreign office and the chiefs of staff was based on similar studies in the autumn of 1953 in response to Churchill's call for a top-level meeting with the Soviets in May of that year. In a speech on this subject, the then prime minister put forward the rather broad and vague idea of applying the "Locarno" principle to the problem of a reunited Germany and to future Soviet relations with it as a possible means of securing a peace settlement for Germany. In Churchill's view, the West would have to offer some quid pro quo in return for obtaining Soviet agreement to a plan for Germany that was acceptable to the West. During the latter part of 1953, a number of plans were drafted in Europe, such as the Adenauer plan and the Van Zeeland plan, which were centered on either the formation of demilitarized zones or the limitation of forces in Central Europe.[9]

However, the prospect for the ratification of the EDC treaty was hanging in the balance, and West Germany's future position in the West remained uncertain. West German chancellor Konrad Adenauer had told American high commissioner James Conant on 31 August 1953 that his country's government was uneasy about the West taking any further steps beyond insisting that reunification be based on freedom.[10] Consequently, Churchill's initial idea of proposing some quid pro quo for the Westernization of the whole of Germany was pigeonholed in the West until spring 1955, when four-power talks once again became a possibility.

It was obvious that the rehash of the Berlin conference's Eden plan for all-German free elections would not be sufficiently appealing to the Russians; something would have to be added to make the plan more attractive to Moscow if the West wanted the Soviet Union to be drawn into discussions on Germany. Thus the new British prime minister was now keen to discuss not only German reunification but also European security. Eden was by no means optimistic about the Russian response, but he was anxious to make them agree to "step back a little if given positive assurance." In his view, the prospect of reaching any accommodation with the Russians over disarmament or the nuclear-weapons

9. Dockrill, *West German Rearmament*, 124–32. Two more recent studies on Churchill's summit diplomacy and the German question are Klaus Larres, *Politik der Illusionen: Churchill, Eisenhower und die deutsche Frage, 1945–1955* (Göttingen, 1995) and John W. Young, *Winston Churchill's Last Campaign: Britain and the Cold War, 1951–5* (Oxford, U.K., 1996).

10. Conant (Bad Godesberg) to Dulles, 31 August 1995, *FRUS, 1952–54*, VII, 629.

issue was too "remote" to be worthy of urgent discussion. Alternatively, if the West agreed to discuss subjects of an "all embracing character," the Russians might insist on bringing the Chinese into the discussions with the result that the Americans would probably refuse to attend the talks. This was typical of Eden's approach; he preferred to concentrate on a relatively narrow agenda where he could display his knowledge and his negotiating skills rather than attempt talks of a wide-ranging nature, which had been Churchill's style.[11]

In early May, the U.S. State Department and the Pentagon agreed on the need to explore a new European security system which would include a reunified Germany. However, they were also interested in other issues, such as disarmament and the problems of the Soviet satellites. By mid-May, Washington was persuaded by the "tremendous demand in U.K. and France" to agree to a summit conference rather than a meeting of the four foreign ministers, but Dulles took the line that the heads of the governments should leave discussions of any substance, such as the German question, to the subsequent meeting of the four foreign ministers in the autumn.[12]

Nor was Adenauer initially pleased with the idea of putting forward a new proposal for German reunification, which might involve more concessions to the Soviet Union by the West. He continued to believe that the reunification of Germany would be difficult while Europe remained divided. As was the case with Churchill's call for a top-level conference in May 1953, it was ironic that the incentive to talk about German reunification with the Russians in 1955 did not come from the Germans themselves. Once the prospect of four-power talks became certain, however, German press, party leaders, and its public naturally took a keen interest in the subject, and the government of the Federal Republic began to encourage the three Western leaders to take the initiative in the discussions with the Russians on German reunification. However, Bonn was not prepared to accept any new security agreements which might prejudice the Paris agreement and Germany's integration into the

11. Eden, *Full Circle* 292; Eden minute, C(55)83, 26 March 1955, CAB129/74, PRO.

12. National Security Council (NSC) 249th meeting, 19 May 1955, *FRUS, 1955–57*, V, 182–9; Hermann-Josef Rupieper, "Deutsche Frage und europäische Sicherheit: Politisch-strategische Überlegungen, 1953–1955" in *Zwischen Kaltem Krieg und Entspannung*, ed. Thoss and Volkmann, 195–7; Roger Makins, Washington to Foreign Office (FO) tel.1064, 5 May 1955, FO371/118210, PRO; record of meeting, U.S. embassy in Vienna, 14 May 1955, PREM11/893, PRO; State Department meeting, 23 April 1955, *FRUS, 1955–57*, V, 145–6, 191–2.

West. The French were also strongly opposed to any idea of reunification through neutralization, while the Germans agreed that they did not want an "Austrian" solution either. The French, the Germans, and the Americans also realized that the Russians might decide that it was safer to "leave Germany divided."[13]

Since the Soviet Union had failed to prevent the West from including West Germany in NATO and in the Western European Union, Moscow could, in retaliation, still refuse to allow any progress toward the reunification of Germany. William Hayter, the British ambassador to Moscow, thought that the Soviets would remain reluctant to discuss German unification "as long as we continue the present policy." Similarly, Frank Roberts, the British ambassador to Belgrade, surmised on 27 April that the Russians might "wait for the Austrian settlement to exercise a disintegrating effect on German public opinion." Nevertheless, foreign office officials were by no means wholly pessimistic about the Soviet attitude toward German reunification, nor were they as hostile to Eden's determination to discuss the subject as they had been when Churchill unexpectedly called for a meeting with the Russians in May 1953. Geoffrey Harrison, the superintending undersecretary of the Western Department in the foreign office, minuted on 9 May 1955 that the West might work out "something attractive [to the Russians] and harmless [to the West]" in order to keep West Germany or a reunified Germany in the West. Harold Macmillan, the foreign secretary, was well aware that Eden, because of domestic political calculations, wanted the summit rather than the four-power foreign-minister talks, but he also agreed with Dulles that the four heads of government should not try to negotiate substantial issues with the USSR.[14]

13. Hans-Peter Schwarz, *Adenauer: Der Staatsmann, 1952–1967* (Stuttgart, 1991) 178–9, 184; Rupieper, "Deutsche Frage" 199; Conant to Merchant, 25 April 1955, *FRUS, 1955–57,* V, 147–51; G. Steel to FO, tel.76 re Macmillan-Adenauer meeting, 8 May 1955, PREM11/893, PRO; Beam to State Department, tels.4785, 4812, and 4818, 27–9 April 1955, *FRUS, 1955–57,* V, 151–8; Jebb to FO, tel.180, 2 May 1955, FO371/118176, PRO; Dulles-Eisenhower conversation, 20 May 1955, Ann Whitman File Diary, May 1955(2), Box 5, Ann Whitman Diary Series, Dwight D. Eisenhower Papers as President (Ann Whitman File), DDEL. For Adenauer's initial conditions for German reunification, see Schwarz, *Adenauer,* 183; see also Beam (of the American delegation at the London working group) to State Department, 28 April 1955, *FRUS, 1955–57,* V, 153–4; Harrison minute, 23 April 1955, and Hoyer Millar to FO, 29 April 1955, both in FO371/118210, PRO.
14. Hayter minute to Harrison, 27 April 1955, FO71/118210, PRO; Frank Roberts to Hancock, 27 April 1955, FO371/118210, PRO; record of London meeting of tripartite study group (Hancock, Beam, and Seydoux), 29 April 1955, FO371/118210, PRO; Harold Macmil-

The Canute Operation: The Making of the Eden Package Proposal

With the summit talks now definitely arranged, Sir Norman Brook, the head of the cabinet secretariat, recommended to Eden on 2 June the setting up of a small group of top cabinet members and officials, including the prime minister, the lord president of the council, the chancellor of the exchequer, the foreign secretary, and the minister of defense, to discuss Britain's strategy and tactics for the Geneva summit. Eden approved the proposal, and the exercise was called "Canute." Canute was also extended to bilateral meetings in Washington between Roger Makins, the British ambassador, and the State Department. The idea of excluding the French from such discussions came from Dulles in his meeting with Macmillan on 12 May in Paris; the secretary of state was afraid that the French might leak the information to the Russians, and the British foreign secretary readily accepted the request to exclude them.[15]

In cooperation with the foreign office, the chiefs of staff were continuing to work on the European security arrangements which might be adopted after a reunified Germany joined NATO. As mentioned earlier, neither the foreign office nor the chiefs were discounting the possibility that NATO troops might have to withdraw from Germany once it was united but remained in NATO, thus leaving only German effectives stationed there. However, during a meeting with Eden at Chequers on 19 June, Adenauer made it clear that any plan involving a massive withdrawal of Anglo-American troops currently stationed in West Germany would be totally unacceptable to the Germans.[16] This was also a precondition for the Heusinger plan, named after General Adolf Heusinger, Adenauer's trusted defense adviser. Submitted to the chancellor on 11 June, it proposed the maintenance of the existing NATO troops and the prospective twelve German divisions in West Germany, while the bulk

---

lan, *Tides of Fortune* (London, 1969), 584–7; Macmillan to Reilly, Paris, tel.277 (re Macmillan's meeting with French ambassador), 5 May 1955, FO800/672, PRO; Macmillan's meeting with Dulles, Paris, 7 May 1995, *FRUS, 1955–57,* V, 170 n. 4.

15. Norman Brook to Eden, 2 June 1955, PREM 11/895, PRO; conversation between Dulles and Macmillan, Paris, 12 May 1955, FO 800/689, PRO.

16. Kirkpatrick minute to P. H. Dean, 20 June 1955, FO371/118222, PRO; Adenauer-Eden meeting, 19 June 1955, CAN/5/55 (Canute document), PREM11/894, PRO; Kirkpatrick to Makins, Washington, tel.2910, 21 June 1955, FO371/118222, PRO. General Heusinger strongly supported the continued presence of Anglo-American troops on German soil; see Schwarz, *Adenauer,* 181.

of East Germany was to be included in the demilitarized zone. Adenauer outlined the Heusinger plan to Dulles in Washington on the thirteenth, to Macmillan in New York on the seventeenth, and to Eden during the Chequers meeting on the nineteenth. Adenauer admitted that the plan was only a broad outline at the moment, but said he approved it "on political grounds."[17]

Consequently, it was necessary that the security arrangements offered by Britain to the Russians not undermine the Paris agreements nor alter radically the deployment of existing NATO troops in West Germany. The chiefs of staff were asked to draft a plan on the basis of the information Adenauer had given the British ministers about the Heusinger plan. The plan they developed called for the division of Europe into three zones, each with a different degree of demilitarization and limitation of forces. Zone A, in the most central part of Europe, included the whole of East Germany, part of Poland, part of Czechoslovakia, and part of Austria, and was to be completely demilitarized. On one side of Zone A, Zone B, of about equal depth, would include the whole of West Germany, in which only conventional forces of about thirty divisions and tactical air forces would be allowed to stay. On the other side of Zone B, Zone C, also of equal depth, would cover France, the Netherlands, Belgium, Luxembourg, and Italy (but would exclude Spain and Britain), in which no restrictions would apply except that the East and West would maintain forces of the "same character and equal strength." This plan amounted to the demilitarization of Eastern Germany and of part of Eastern Europe, thereby involving the Russians in a massive redeployment of their forces in return for the nonnuclearization of West Germany and the inclusion of the whole of Germany in NATO. Under the plan, West Germany could still raise its proposed twelve divisions, while NATO would keep its existing eighteen divisions in Zone B. This British zonal plan, which took account of what was believed to be the basic features of the Heusinger plan, differed significantly from that plan in the area of the proposed demilitarized zone.

17. Rupieper, "Deutsche Frage," 201–2; Schwarz, *Adenauer*, 186–8; Merchant minute, 15 June 1995, *FRUS, 1955–57*, V, 228–30; Macmillan, *Tides*, 607; Adenauer-Eden meeting, 19 June, PREM 11/894, PRO; Dixon (Macmillan) to Eden, tel.499, 18 June 1955, AP 20/22/40, personal papers of Anthony Eden, 1st Earl of Avon, Special Collection Department, University Library, The University of Birmingham; Dulles-Adenauer meeting, 13 June 1995, *FRUS, 1955–57*, V, 229.

For example, the British were prepared to include part of southern West Germany in Zone A.[18]

Eden was critical of the British zonal plan modeled on the Heusinger plan, which he thought would have little appeal to Moscow. In their revised paper dated 5 July, the chiefs of staff attempted to make the zonal plan more attractive to the Soviets, such as by reducing the eastern part of Zone A and allowing existing armament industries to remain there or by lifting the restrictions on force levels in Zone B.[19]

Apart from the zonal plan, the chiefs of staff on 6 July prepared another plan for the creation of a demilitarized strip in Germany between River Oder and River Rhine, with the western boundary running from Wismar, Halle on the River Saale, to Nürnberg. The demilitarization of the bulk of East Germany was to be offset by the demilitarization of the area south of the Thuringian mountains, a part of southwestern Germany where American forces were currently stationed under NATO. However, NATO could move its defense line further East, beyond the boundary of East Germany. The foreign office and the Canute committee thought the demilitarized-strip plan would be both simpler and more attractive to the Russians than the zonal plan, i.e., the Heusinger plan. Macmillan wrote to Makins on 29 June that the Heusinger plan was of a rather "complicated and even ambitious character," a verdict with which the Americans soon came to agree. Thus these two powers regarded the German plan as a nonstarter, but they decided not to "say anything yet" to Adenauer about their negative reaction.[20]

However, these two plans, a demilitarized strip in Germany and the creation of three zones in Europe (demilitarized, controlled, and nonrestricted areas), were not as separate as they appeared to be. Britain was also exploring the possibility of some arms-control measures in Central

18. Kirkpatrick to Makins, Washington, tel.2910, 21 June 1955, FO371/118222, PRO; Macmillan to Makins, Washington, tel.3035, 29 June 1955, PREM11/894, PRO; COS(55)143, 28 June 1955, PREM11/894, PRO. See also JP(55) 56(F), 23 June 1955, DEFE6/30, PRO.

19. COS(52)152, 6 July 1955, PREM 11/895, PRO; COS(55)143, 28 June 1955, PREM 8/894, PRO.

20. COS(55)151, 6 July 1955, PREM 11/895, PRO; see also JP(55)59(F), 1 July 1955, DEFE6/30, PRO; Macmillan to Makins, Washington, tel.3035, PREM 11/894, PRO; Makins, Washington to FO, tels.1530 & 3182, 1 & 8 July 1955, PREM11/894, PRO; Macmillan (drafted by Kirkpatrick) to Makins, Washington, tel.3182, 8 July 1955, FO371/118227, PRO; Makins to FO, tel.1602, PREM 11/895, PRO.

Europe, and the idea of creating an arms-control area in Central Europe under the Heusinger plan was similar to British thinking. Nor was the concept of a demilitarized strip really "our first thought," in Macmillan's words, because a similar idea had also been mentioned by Herbert Blankenhorn, Adenauer's close adviser and the German representative on NATO, earlier in April during a conversation with Kirkpatrick. As will be discussed later, it was not surprising that the Canute committee soon combined these two ideas into one formula: a security pact, controlled armaments, and a demilitarized strip.[21]

Parallel with studies on security arrangements, Canute was also considering the possibility of offering the Russians a five-power security pact. According to a minute by Macmillan, he first mentioned this possibility at a Canute meeting on 13 June, and it was again put forward at another Canute meeting on 29 June, when Eden proposed that the West should offer the Soviets a "further safeguard against an additional threat to their security arising from German reunification." The security treaty draft was prepared by the foreign office with the help of its legal adviser and submitted to Eden in early July. The treaty assumed that Germany had been reunified and that an all-German government would be a signatory, together with the United States, the Soviet Union, France, and Britain. The treaty, comprising seven articles, was modeled on the collective defense arrangements under the United Nations Charter. Thus, as in article 5 of the NATO treaty, all contracting parties would regard "an armed attack in Europe by any one of them against any other Party or Parties" as "an attack against all the other Parties." Consequently, the parties would take the necessary action under article 51 of the UN charter. Britain was prepared to go further than this, proposing an automatic guarantee, similar to that which had been incorporated into the Brussels Treaty. However, London realized that the United States constitution would not allow it to go beyond the terms of NATO's article 5. Overall, the five-power security pact was designed to provide the Soviet Union with a security guarantee by France, Britain, and the USA against a reunified Germany—an idea similar to one that

21. Macmillan to Makins, Washington, tel.3035, 29 June 1955, PREM11/894, PRO; permanent undersecretary, FO, to Eden (re Britain's policy for disarmament), CAN/8/55, 29 June 1955, PREM 11/894, PRO; Kirkpatrick minute, 28 April 1955, FO371/118209, PRO; Steininger, "Genfer Gipfelkonferenz" 201–2.

had been examined by the foreign office in September 1953. Eden approved it on 4 July 1955.[22]

American Responses to the Eden Package Proposal

In mid-June, through the Canute channel, the British were encouraged to discover that the American Joint Chiefs of Staff were also considering the military implications of the redeployment of NATO forces, including naval and air elements, in Germany. The JCS seemed to think it possible to undertake such a redeployment despite the attendant political and financial difficulties.[23]

At the same time, the Canute Anglo-American talks reexamined the so-called Eden plan for reunification. The British did not think it necessary to make any major alterations to the original Eden reunification plan per se, since it had undergone months of discussion and preparation before being introduced at Berlin in January 1954. The State Department, however, wanted to modify it so as to minimize the risk of a reunified Germany deciding not to join NATO. Patrick Hancock, the head of the Western Department in the foreign office, disagreed with the Americans. He wrote to Makins in Washington on 15 June that "we cannot now alter our stand on the question of principle," since this would not only upset the Germans but also confuse the French. In the end, the Western four-power study group on the Eden plan, which met in Bonn between 24 June and 5 July, confined its task to updating the reunification plan with a few technical changes, thus meeting the British desiderata.[24]

Between 1 and 5 July, on Eden's instructions, the foreign office sent

22. Milford to Eden, 4 July 1955, PREM 11/895, PRO; Hood minute, 29 June 1955, FO371/118227, PRO; Burroughs, PUSD, 5 July 1955, FO 371/118227, PRO; Millard to Pallister, 5 July 1955, PREM11/895, PRO; Harrison and Kirkpatrick minutes, 1 and 2 July 1955, FO371/118227, PRO.

23. MacArthur minute to Dulles, 3 June 1955, *FRUS, 1955–57*, V, 209–13; Record 224 of Anglo-American Canute talks, CAN/4/55, 14 June 1955, PREM11/894, PRO; Dixon (Macmillan) to FO, tel.473, 16 June 1955, PREM 11/894, PRO; Dean minute to Kirkpatrick, 18 June 1955, FO371/118222, PRO.

24. Makins on the Anglo-American Canute talks, CAN/4/55, n.d. (possibly 14 June), PREM 11/894, PRO; Hancock minute, 15 and 16 June 1955, FO371/118217, PRO; Hoyer Millar, tel.364. 23 June 1955, FO371/118222, PRO; Conant to State Dept., tel.37, *FRUS, 1955–57*, V, 266–8; Macmillan to Eden (minute containing a copy of the revised Eden plan), PM/55/83, 4 July 1955, FO 800/673, PRO.

the State Department, via Makins, a series of British draft plans including a two-page official position paper (the so-called formula) outlining
the British approach to the Geneva summit, two kinds of military plans
(a zonal plan for Europe modeled on the Heusinger plan and a plan for a
demilitarized strip in Germany), and a copy of the five-power security
pact. The American response to the Eden package was anything but enthusiastic. The State Department believed that neither the zonal plan
nor the demilitarized strip would be attractive to Moscow. While the
zonal plan proposed a nuclear-free area in Zone B, the Americans felt
that it would be extremely difficult to draw a clear line between conventional and atomic weapons, since some weapons had dual capabilities.[25]

The British two-page formula outlined the essence of the Eden package proposal: the creation of a demilitarized strip, the signing of a security pact, and agreement on a ceiling for military forces in countries
bordering Germany. Dulles did not like the idea of mentioning these
proposals, even in general terms, at Geneva.[26] However, what the State
Department and Dulles disliked most was the proposed British security
pact. Makins was warned on 8 July by State Department counselor
Douglas MacArthur II that "such a treaty did not stand 'a Chinaman's
chance' of being accepted by the Senate." The Americans were aware
that the Eden reunification plan would "no longer suffice," but they admitted that they did not have any definite ideas about how to modify
the plan without undermining the "existing Western position." The
United States placed little faith in the possibility that the Soviets might
be induced to compromise with the West over the German question.
This lack of trust meant that there was no question of the United States
entering into a security pact with Moscow. During a meeting with Makins on 9 July, Dulles was more diplomatic, assuring Makins that he was
not "opposed to throwing these ideas into the hopper, or to dangling
such bait before the Russians," although he warned the ambassador that

    25. Canute meeting, Washington, 1 July 1955, *FRUS, 1955–57*, V, 252–8; Makins to FO,
tels.1529 & 1530, 1 July 1955, PREM 11/894, PRO.
    26. For the formula, see Macmillan minute to Eden, PM/55/79, 30 June 1995, PREM 11/
894, PRO, and Macmillan to Makins, tel.3084, 2 July 1955, FO371/118225, PRO. The second draft of the formula (n.d.) can be found in *FRUS, 1955–57*, V, 261–2; Macmillan to Kirkpatrick (minute) 1 July 1955, PREM 11/894, PRO; and Makins to FO, tel.1534, 2 July 1955,
FO371/118225, PRO. For Dulles's response, see Makins to FO, tels.1581 & 1582, 8 July
1955, FO371/118227, PRO.

"the Russians were so adept at propaganda . . . [and] the West could not counter in kind."[27]

The Joint Chiefs of Staff were equally grudging. Hitherto, Britain had had little information about JCS thinking on the Eden package proposal, and it was not until 14 July, four days before the start of the summit, that the British Joint Services Mission (BJSM) in Washington met with Admiral Arthur Radford, chairman of the JCS. The State Department, apparently at Makins's request, had asked the JCS to make comments on the British plans at short notice. Radford complained that the State Department had provided the JCS with only a brief record of their conversation with Makins and that as a result, they had had "little time for reflection." However, he made it clear that the JCS were opposed to the concept of the demilitarized strip, which was too "narrow to be of appreciable value." In their view, the British plan, if implemented, would increase tensions in Central Europe.[28]

Macmillan was critical of Dulles's unwillingness to reduce the Russian fear of a reunified and rearmed Germany in the West, and he wrote to Makins on 8 July that "if the Russians are so adept at propaganda, . . . we must this time be ahead of them by doing something more than just hint at our plan." In his response on 9 July, Makins reminded the foreign secretary that, while the stereotyped European image of Americans was that they "jump to conclusions, take snap decisions, work fast and are go-getters," in fact American policy makers "move very slowly and take months to mature their decisions, which, once taken, are correspondingly hard to alter." The ambassador also believed that the Americans were "afraid of being trapped by the Russians, or of being led down the garden path by their allies, or both." Makins suggested that it would not be sensible to "press the Americans too hard to commit themselves to specific plans . . . especially if these have not been fully elaborated" by the British. He continued that "their hesitation and slowness stem not from ill-will or myopia but from their temperament and their political

27. Makins to FO, tel.1583, 8 July 1955, PREM11/895, PRO; Makins to FO re Canute meeting, tel.1570, 8 July 1955, FO371/118227, PRO; Makins to FO, tel.1600, 9 July 1955, PREM11/895, PRO; Dulles to Beam (delegation at the Paris Working Group), tel.95, 9 July 1955, *FRUS, 1955–57*, V, 313–4.

28. Makins to FO, tel.1615, PREM 11/895, PRO; Ministry of Defence, London, to BJSM, Washington, tel.OZ4884, 14 July 1955, FO371/118228, PRO; BJSM, Washington to Ministry of Defence, tel. JW148, 14 July 1955, FO371/118228,PRO.

system." Kirkpatrick could not agree more, and he suggested that "we should leave him [Dulles] alone now."[29]

At a State Department meeting on 5 July, Dulles mentioned that Eden was insisting on "putting forward some new version of the Eden plan," while the Russians "would be anxious to deal with matters of substance."[30] From then on, Dulles became even more determined to prevent the British and French from engaging in substantive discussion at Geneva.

Eden's Opening Statement

Britain and France had long appreciated America's unwillingness to introduce concrete proposals at the forthcoming Geneva summit. Thus Western preparatory meetings, which took place in Washington, San Francisco, and New York during June, focused mainly on broad strategy and procedural matters. Macmillan and the foreign office were willing to support the American approach and Eden was not prepared to fight against it. However, what Eden wanted to do at Geneva was display "boldness and imagination," in order to appeal to world public opinion and to set the direction for the subsequent foreign ministers' meeting on the subject of German unity and European security. It was therefore essential for him to deliver an impressive opening speech on the subject at Geneva.[31]

However, the tripartite working group that met in Washington between 8 and 14 June suggested that, to avoid unnecessary overlap, each head of government concentrate on certain specific subjects in his opening speech. According to the proposed division of labor, the British prime minister was expected to deal with the cold war, the East-West military balance, and general disarmament, while the French prime minister would talk about Germany and European security, and the American president, international Communism and the Soviet satellites. In a minute to Eden on 14 June, Macmillan wrote that "the division proposed seems to be sensible. . . . There cannot be anything very

29. Macmillan to Makins, tel.3183, 8 July 1955, FO371/118227, PRO; Macmillan to Makins, tel.3189, 8 July 1955, PREM 11/895, PRO; Makins to Macmillan, 9 July 1955, FO371/114364, PRO.

30. State Department meeting, 5 July 1955, FRUS, 1955–57, V, 262.

31. Macmillan to Makins, tel.3183. 8 July 1955 FO371/118227, PRO.

new to say about Germany and European security, which is to go to M. Faure. It seems to me that you will have the best of it." Macmillan was a member of the Canute committee and it is difficult to believe that he was unaware of Eden's eagerness to talk about Germany and European security. But Macmillan's statement confirms that he was more skeptical than Eden about the progress that could be made on Germany at the Geneva summit. Other top officials in the foreign office responded rather more sympathetically to Eden's wishes. Hancock, for example, minuted that the choice of France to speak on the subject of German unity and European security was not "altogether a happy one." Eden was, of course, annoyed by the arrangement, and he insisted that he "must reserve the right to handle his opening speech at the meeting in the manner which seems fit to him."[32]

The question of the opening speeches was left to the final preparatory meetings in Paris from 8 through 14 July. The three foreign ministers also met on 15 July. On the eve of Macmillan's visit to Paris on 13 July, the Canute ministers approved the final draft of the military plan for European security, which combined the previous ideas of the demilitarized strip and the zonal plan. In this final plan, the western boundary of the demilitarized zone was along the line Wismar, River Saale through Regensburg to Austria, thereby reducing the size of the area where the American troops were currently stationed. This was to make the plan more palatable to the USA. The plan abolished Zone C in the previous zonal plan, but retained Zone B—the restricted zone—where troops and armaments would be "limited in kind and possibly in number." The previous plan for the demilitarized strip had proposed that that strip would lie in exclusively German territory and that it would end on the Oder/Neisse line, then the eastern border of East Germany. However, in view of German sensibilities, the final plan placed the restricted zone next to the demilitarized zone, in hopes of reducing the danger of "prejudging the Oder/Neisse line" as Germany's eastern frontier and avoiding the impression that only German territory would be subject to controlled demilitarization. Macmillan presented the final plan to Dulles at Paris, but, as it turned out, this final plan did not have any more

32. Lord Hood to Caccia, FO, 10 June 1955, FO371/118217, PRO; Makins to FO, tel.1370, 11 June 1955, FO371/118217, PRO; Macmillan minute to Eden, PM/55/68, 14 June 1955, FO371/118217, PRO; Hancock minute, 13 June 1955, FO 371/118217, PRO; Graham to Rumbold, 16 June 1955, FO371/118217, PRO.

favorable impact than had the previous one on the American secretary of state.[33]

By that time, Eden had made up his mind: in defiance of American pressure to avoid serious discussions with the Russians, and also in opposition to Macmillan's advice to accept the proposed contents of his opening speech suggested by the Washington working group, the prime minister told the Canute meeting on 13 July 1955 that he was going to draw the Russians into substantial discussion about German reunification at Geneva. Eden's opening speech was then completely rewritten in accordance with his wishes and was presented to him on 14 July. The prime minister was planning to spend the following two days in giving "some thought," with Kirkpatrick's assistance, to the redrafting of the opening speech.[34]

During the Canute meeting, Macmillan also promised that in the forthcoming Paris meeting he would try to persuade Dulles to accept that the West should put forward a unified proposal outlined in the British two-page formula. The foreign secretary, prior to the 13 July Canute meeting, met Jean Chauvel, the French ambassador to London, and presented him with the outline of Britain's approach to the Geneva Conference. The record of the discussion was sent to Antoine Pinay, the French foreign minister, on the same day.[35]

With the summit only a few days away, Macmillan became more supportive of Eden's approach, and did his best to prepare the ground for the prime minister to launch his new proposal at Geneva. During the Paris tripartite meeting[36] of foreign ministers, Pinay expressed concern about the British concept of the demilitarized zone to be created in East Germany. He believed that such a proposal might lead the Soviet Union to ask the West to do the same in West Germany, which might result in the "ultimate neutralisation of Germany." Dulles echoed the French concern and also pointed out that the concept of a demilitarized zone

33. CAN 4th meeting, 13 July 1955, PREM11/895, PRO. For the final plan, see COS(55)158, CAN/15/55, 12 July 1955, PREM 11/895, PRO; see also JP(55)64(F), 11 July 1955, DEFE6/30, PRO, and Hancock minute, 7 July 1955, FO800/672, PRO.

34. Draft program for the Geneva Conference dated 13 July 1955, PREM 11/895, PRO; initial draft opening statement by the prime minister dated 13 July 1955, PREM 11/895, PRO; Rumbrow to Pitblado (minute plus the revised opening statement),14 July 1955, PREM 11/895, PRO.

35. CAN 4th meeting, 13 July 1955, PREM 11/895, PRO; *DDF*, 1955, II, 72–3.

36. Record of the Paris meeting, *FRUS, 1955–57*, V, 309–35; see also FO 371/118232 and PREM 11/895, PRO.

did not take into account Germany's "own internal security."[37] However, Pinay later confessed to Macmillan during a lunch that the French
were not opposed so much to the concept of a demilitarized zone as to
the timing of introducing such a concept at the Geneva summit. A similar reservation was also voiced by Blankenhorn, who participated in
some of the Paris preparatory meetings concerning Germany.[38]

During the discussion of tactics, Dulles made a renewed effort to persuade the French and the British not to introduce any specific ideas at
Geneva. In response, Pinay told Dulles that the French prime minister
would like to be "as positive as possible in his opening statement" on
German reunification, European security, and disarmament. Macmillan
also stated that Eden "wanted to go further" at Geneva than Dulles desired. No agreement was reached in Paris on the question of how far the
Western leaders should go in the their respective opening statements;
this was left for the three heads of Government to decide in Geneva before the opening of the summit conference.[39]

However, the Paris working group did produce a lengthy report,
which was approved by the three foreign ministers. The section on Germany and European security was written in consultation with Blankenhorn. This section was not intended to be a detailed proposal, but it
contained two new interrelated ideas. First, the West now formally
agreed to link the reunification of a free Germany to "European security," whereas the three Western powers had simply pursued the reunification of Germany in isolation at the Berlin conference. This linkage
was important if the West wanted to safeguard the existing West German position in the Western bloc. The West was not therefore prepared
to agree to any new European security agreement with the Russians unless such an agreement entailed Russian acceptance of a reunified Germany staying within NATO. Second, the West now accepted the
proposition that "security in Europe is unattainable as long as Germany
remains divided." The unspoken Western assumption so far had been

37. Record of tripartite meeting of foreign ministers, 15 July 1955 (10.30 A.M.), FO371/
118232, PRO; Jebb (Macmillan) to Eden, tel.259, 15 July 1955, PREM11/895, PRO. See also
FRUS, 1955–57, V, 323–5.
38. Jebb (Macmillan) to FO (Eden), tel.260, 15 July 1955, PREM11/895, PRO; U.S. delegation at the Paris working group, tel.125, 9 July 1955, FRUS, 1955–57, V, 310.
39. Record of Paris meeting of foreign ministers, 15 July 1955, FO371/118232, PRO;
Dulles-Macmillan meeting, 14 July 1955, FRUS, 1955–57, V, 321.

that "the reunification of Germany is unattainable as long as Europe remains divided."[40]

The Eden package proposal was based on these two new propositions, and the fact that the West agreed to them, at least on paper, was helpful to the prime minister as he finalized his forthcoming opening statement. Moreover, during the Paris meeting Blankenhorn warned his colleagues that the West must be prepared to "advance concrete ideas" on German unity and European security, because of the "public opinion factor" in West Germany. France, too, wanted to maximize the Geneva summit by presenting France's ideas and proposals. While the Eden package proposal never acquired the full support of the three Western powers and West Germany, the climate before the summit was not too discouraging for the British prime minister.[41]

The Geneva Conference

Eden, Eisenhower, and Faure met twice at Geneva on 17 July, one day before the opening of the summit. Eisenhower repeated a Dulles plea that no "plans or proposals were to be presented" at Geneva, and indeed there existed "no specific agreed tripartite substantive proposals" for the conference. Eden took advantage of these preliminary meetings to accomplish two things. First, he stressed that "by far the most important issue at this conference was the question of German unity" and Faure immediately agreed with this.[42] Eisenhower by that time had decided to present some ideas about mutual aerial inspection in the field of disarmament, and he did not raise any objections to Eden's stress on the importance of German reunification.[43] Second, because of the suspicions of the other allies about the "demilitarized zone," Eden promised not to indicate which area was to be demilitarized. The prime minister

40. The report of the Paris working group, July 8–14, can be found in PREM 11/895, PRO.
41. American delegation to the Paris working group, tel.125 & 11, 9 & 15 July 1955, *FRUS, 1955–57*, V, 309, 322; Stark minute to Pitblado, 15 July 1955, PREM 11/895, PRO.
42. Tripartite meeting of heads of government, 17 July 1955, *FRUS, 1955–57*, V, 341–2; record of tripartite meeting, 17 July 1955, FO371/118233, PRO. Harrison emphasized a similar point during a meeting with Blankenhorn on 17 July 1955; see NL 351/49b, Blankenhorn papers, Bundesarchiv, Koblenz.
43. For Eisenhower's Open Skies proposal, see Saki Dockrill, *Eisenhower's New-Look National Security Policy, 1953–1961* (New York, 1996), 139–48.

had also been reminded by Macmillan a few days earlier that the Heu-singer plan envisaged a demilitarized zone to be created on both sides of the Oder/Neisse line, whereas the same line, in the British plan, was intended to be the zone's eastern boundary. Eden's proposed opening statement was approved by the tripartite working group on the afternoon of 17 July, by which time it was clear that the division of topics for the opening speeches had fallen into abeyance.[44]

The Geneva summit opened on 18 July. The agreed-upon procedures were that the conference would begin with four opening statements by each of the heads of government, followed by an exchange of views on the outstanding topics (the agenda was to be prepared by the four foreign ministers during the morning prior to the discussions by the heads of government). At the end, the four heads of government were to agree on the content of the directives, which were to be discussed at the subsequent foreign ministers' meetings in the autumn.[45]

Eden's opening speech, in which he outlined the essence of the package proposal, lasted about ten minutes. He suggested that the West was prepared to offer a security pact with the Soviet Union, to agree on a level of forces and armaments in and around Germany, and possibly to agree to the creation of a demilitarized zone "between East and West," but without specifying the exact area Britain had in mind. A member of the U.S. delegation, Livingston Merchant, assistant secretary of state for European affairs, recorded: "We had moved a great distance from the Berlin Conference where the central Western proposal was the 'Eden plan' for free elections. Eden went to the heart of our new offer."[46]

The French prime minister spoke three times longer than Eisenhower (the first speaker) or Eden. Two-thirds of Edgar Faure's speech was devoted to the question of Germany and European security. France was also prepared, in order to encourage the USSR to accept a reunified Ger-

44. Jebb (Macmillan) to Eden, tel.261, 15 July 1955, PREM 11/895, PRO.

45. The record of the Geneva summit can be found in *DDF*, 1955, Annexes, II, 15–178; this publication contains verbatim records of all formal meetings of heads of government and foreign ministers. A similar record can also be found in *FRUS, 1955–57*, V, 361–512, which includes minutes and records of some informal meetings that also took place in Geneva. The opening statements and the closing remarks by the four heads of government as well as the directives can be found in Command Papers, no. 9543 (London, 1955). For verbatim records of formal meetings, telegrams, minutes at the Geneva summit, see Foreign Office files FO371/118232–118245 & PREM 11/895 and CAB 129 series, PRO. There are also numerous reports and telegrams written by Herbert Blankenhorn, the German observer at the summit, in the Blankenhorn papers, Bundesarchiv.

46. See American delegation record, *FRUS 1955–57*, V, 368.

many staying in NATO, to offer security arrangements to the Russians, such as the creation of a "general security organisation" to include all the European states wishing to join, by "superimposing it on the existing [defense] organisations" in the East and the West. The Americans especially disliked this idea of fusion, since it implied that the Warsaw pact was "comparable" with NATO; Dulles had raised the point during the tripartite meetings in Paris and Geneva but to no avail.[47]

The British opening statement was followed by a speech by Nikolai Bulganin, the chairman of the Soviet council of ministers. Bulganin's statement contained nothing new; he repeated previous Soviet statements to the effect that the Paris agreements (under which West Germany was now formally admitted to the Western European Union and to NATO) constituted the "main obstacles" to Germany's reunification. Bulganin also stated that European security was the "important issue," while "any unity for Germany was a matter for the more distant future." There was thus no indication that the Russians had changed their position on Germany.[48]

However, as Eden hoped, the question of Germany was fully discussed during the first day of the Geneva Conference. On the following morning, the nineteenth, the four foreign ministers were surprisingly quick (even to Blankenhorn, the German observer) to agree to Macmillan's proposed agenda for the afternoon's meeting of the four heads of government: in ascending order, "German reunification," "European security," "Disarmament," and "Development of East-West contacts."[49]

On the second day of the summit, the British prime minister emphasized the urgency of settling the German question, thereby disagreeing vehemently with Bulganin's argument that a new European security system should be set up by liquidating existing defense organizations in Europe (along lines similar to those suggested by Molotov at the Berlin conference) before Germany could be reunited. Eden also pointed out that the proposed British five-power treaty would be much simpler and

47. For America's concern about the French proposal, see Jebb, Paris to FO, tel.259, 15 July 1955, PREM11/895, PRO; tripartite meeting, Geneva, 17 July 1955, *FRUS, 1955–57*, V, 349; Macmillan to FO, tel.20, 18 July 1955, FO 371/118232, PRO.
48. *FRUS, 1955–57*, V, 368–70; Macmillan to FO, tel.20, 18 July 1955, FO 371/118232, PRO.
49. *FRUS, 1955–57*, V, 383–4; Macmillan to FO, tel.33, 19 July 1955, FO371/118233, PRO; Blankenhorn to Auswärtiges Amt, Bonn, tel.215, 20 July 1955, NL 351/49b, Blankenhorn papers, Bundesarchiv.

would offer a similar security guarantee, enabling German reunification to be accomplished more quickly than might otherwise be the case. Eisenhower concentrated on explaining the defensive nature of NATO, which made it comparable to the proposed Soviet security system, and he and Faure joined Eden in emphasizing the danger of delay in reunifying Germany if the Soviet proposal were adopted.[50]

The Russians were on the defensive, since the three Western powers had put them into the embarrassing position of having to explain why they did not wish to reunify Germany as quickly as the West hoped. However, the Russians also put the West in a difficult situation by asking "what would be [the] attitude of Western powers if Soviets were to make unification of Germany dependent upon united Germany participating in Warsaw Treaty?" At the end of this session of the heads of government there was no agreement on Germany, but at Eden's request the group made plans to return to the subject if it so wished.[51]

During an Anglo-Russian dinner on the night of 19 July, the Russians stressed their lingering fears of the Germans, but Eden countered that in this nuclear age it was inconceivable that the Russians could perceive a German threat to their security. The prime minister pressed the Russians further on the impracticability of the proposed Soviet all-European pact, asking whether "Tito and Franco could be accommodated together." Bulganin laughed and admitted that "maybe the Soviets cast their nets too wide." By the end of the dinner, however, it had become crystal clear that the Russians did not intend to negotiate with the West over German reunification.[52]

The negative attitude of the Russians on the German question hardly surprised the West German leaders. The account by the head of the German observer team, Blankenhorn, of the 19 July meeting stressed that the Russians obviously sought the reduction of tensions and the maintenance of stability on the basis of the status quo, and they did not show even the slightest inclination toward any revision of the territory they controlled. During an informal meeting with Blankenhorn on 21 July, Dulles was sympathetic to the West German case. He told Blankenhorn that the entire battle so far was about the question of reunification and

50. Macmillan to Foreign Office, tel.35, 19 July 1955, FO 371/118233, PRO; *FRUS, 1955–57*, V, 388–97; *DDF*, Annexes, II, 47–61.

51. *FRUS, 1955–57*, V, 390.

52. Eden minute, 19 July 1955, PREM11/895, PRO; Eden-Eisenhower breakfast meeting, 20 July 1955, *FRUS, 1955–57*, V, 399.

that it would be tragic for the West to give way to the Soviet position on such crucial questions as Germany and Europe. Of course, Dulles was well aware that there was little chance of a breakthrough over Germany at Geneva. In an informal conversation with the American secretary of state on 19 July, Molotov stated that he wished the "Conference will drop entirely the matter of German unification." Eden had suspected all along that the Russians might be inflexible about German unity. He had told Faure and Eisenhower at a preliminary meeting prior to the summit that the Russians would probably not want to discuss the subject and that it was in the "Russian interest to delay a settlement on Germany." Therefore, it was even more important for Eden to seize the initiative by presenting new ideas about Germany which the Russians would find difficult to reject, in order to keep the discussion alive during the summit.[53]

The third day (20 July) began with an inconclusive foreign ministers' meeting in the morning. A new Russian tactic was to suggest that, since the conference had fully discussed the German question, it should move on to the second topic, i.e., European security. The Western foreign ministers insisted that these two subjects were inseparable, but they eventually agreed with Russia that the heads of government would discuss European security that afternoon. When the four chiefs met at four o'clock, it soon became clear that the Soviets wanted to press their grandiose idea of a pact for all Europe in an effort to divert attention from the question of German reunification. Faure, Eisenhower, and Eden were all united in the view that the questions of German unity and European security were closely linked. The discussion became bogged down and the four heads of government asked the foreign ministers to draw up a directive to guide further discussion on the two topics by the foreign ministers in the autumn.[54]

The issue now returned to the foreign ministers on the morning of 21

53. Blankenhorn to Adenauer and Auswärtiges Amt, Bonn, 19 July 1955, and Blankenhorn minute (for minister for German question), 20 July 1955, both in NL 351/49b, Blankenhorn papers; Blankenhorn to Auswärtiges Amt, Bonn, tel.18, 21 July 1955, NLS351/49b, Blankenhorn papers; Dulles-Molotov meeting, 19 July 1955, *FRUS, 1955–57*, V, 397–8; Dulles to State Department, tel.24, 20 July 1955, ibid., 403; three-power meeting, 17 July 1955 (11:00 A.M.), FO 371/118233, PRO (see also *FRUS, 1955–57*, V, 341–2).

54. Four foreign ministers' meeting, 20 July 1955 (11:00 A.M.), *FRUS, 1955–57*, V, 405–7; see also Dulles-Molotov meeting, 20 July 1955 (1:15 P.M.), ibid., 419–20. For the fourth meeting of heads of government, 20 July 1955 (4:00 P.M.), see 421–4; the British record is in FO 371/118245, PRO, and the French in *DDF*, Annexes, II, 74–83.

July. Molotov adamantly refused to accept the close link between the two subjects and the meeting continued into the afternoon. Meanwhile, the heads of government convened in the afternoon to discuss the issue of disarmament. The American president then captivated the audience by presenting the "Open Skies" proposal.

On 22 July, the Russian foreign minister still disagreed on the order of directives about German reunification and European security, so that when the heads of government finally resumed their sixth plenary meeting at five in the afternoon, they found the issue of the directives still unresolved. Moreover, the question had become further complicated by Molotov's insistence on inserting into the directives a provision that representatives from West Germany and East Germany might be included in the forthcoming four-power foreign ministers' meetings.[55] This was a sore point for West Germany, since Adenauer had made it clear prior to the opening of the summit that West Germany should not participate in the discussion formally, because this would only prompt the Russians to invite the East German delegation to the conference, thereby giving implicit recognition to the existence of two Germanies. The three foreign ministers were not therefore prepared to agree to Molotov's new suggestion in toto.[56]

There were two more foreign ministers' meetings during the evening of 22 July, but not much progress was made, and it was not until the afternoon of 23 July, the final day of the summit, that the four powers were able to agree on the contents of the directives. The bone of contention had hitherto remained the order in which the directives should be taken: in ascending order, the Russians insisted on "European security," "disarmament" and "the German problem," while the three Western powers insisted on "German reunification," "European security," and "disarmament." Eden suggested a parallel study of European security and German reunification, an idea Dulles had introduced at a meeting of foreign ministers that had convened at 10:30 the previous night. The American president joined Eden in arguing that neither question could be solved without the other. Toward the end of the meeting, the Russians gave way slightly to the Western position by reordering the place of "Germany" before "disarmament" and after "European security,"

55. Macmillan to FO, tels.79 and 84, 22 and 23 July 1955, FO 371/118235, PRO; see also *FRUS, 1955–57,* V, 436–8, 468–71, 472–4.

56. Adenauer-Eden meeting, CAN/5/55, 19 June 1955, PREM 11/894, PRO; Dulles to State Department., tel.31, 23 July 1955, *FRUS, 1955–57,* V, 484.

and Faure, in the chair, described this as "a new proposal." The differences were now minimized between East and West but had not disappeared completely.[57]

During the 23 July afternoon meeting of the heads of government, Faure, in the chair, stated that it would be natural to stick to the order of business employed at the Geneva summit in the forthcoming foreign ministers' meeting, that is, German reunification, European security, and disarmament. Bulganin objected that the order of the agenda was "a question of substance, not merely one of procedure." Eisenhower then proposed "making the two subjects of equal priority rather than putting them into a serial relationship," and Bulganin gave way.[58]

The last hurdle was now how to find a compromise between the phrases "the German problem" and "German reunification." The Soviets persisted with the use of "the German problem," which in their view included the questions of German unification, West German rearmament, and West Germany's participation in NATO.[59] The three Western powers and the West German government were united in the view that the Paris agreements must not be affected by any new security arrangements for Europe. Thus, the West took the position that the German question was now resolved except for the issue of reunification. Once again, the American president broke new ground by proposing the combined title, "European security and *Germany*" (emphasis added) which became the final language in the directive. The Geneva summit then adjourned.[60]

Conclusion

From the very beginning of Britain's preparations for Geneva, Eden became almost obsessed with the question of German reunification and European security. Even after he was made aware of American opposition to the British approach, he continued to maneuver himself into a position whereby he could initiate the discussion on Germany and Eu-

57. *DDF*, Annexes, II, 141; *FRUS, 1955–57*, V, 486; record of the seventh session of the Geneva Conference, 23 July 1955, *FRUS, 1955–57*, V, 493–501.

58. Record of the second part of the seventh session of the Geneva Conference, *FRUS, 1955–57*, V, 505, 508.

59. For instance, see the third meeting of heads of government, 19 July 1955, ibid., 390, and seventh session, ibid., 506.

60. Ibid., 508–10. For the final directives, see *DDF*, Annexes, II, 177–8 and Cmd. 9543, 29–30.

ropean security once the summit was underway. Once it had actually begun, the three Western powers displayed unity in claiming that German reunification was an urgent issue which must be resolved by the four powers and without which there could be no security in Europe. Despite the fact that Eisenhower's Open Skies proposal garnered the greatest publicity during the summit, the conference records reveal the bulk of the discussions to have dealt with German reunification and European security. If Eden aimed at creating the impression at Geneva that it was the Russians who were hindering the reunification of Germany, he succeeded.

There are a number of features that characterized the Eden package proposal. First, strictly speaking, it was not authored by Eden. The idea of offering the Soviet Union some quid pro quo, in the form of a security pact or other concession, came mostly from Churchill. Whether the package proposal would include the demilitarized strip and/or armaments-controlled areas in Europe was also strongly influenced by West German planning, and the idea of combining these two ideas was apparently proposed by Macmillan in mid-June. There was also some overlap between the ideas behind the package proposal and British policy for disarmament in Europe. All this contributed to making the Eden package proposal appear more complicated than his clear-cut approach to the settlement of West German rearmament in 1954 or Eisenhower's Open Skies proposal.[61]

Second, while the Russians finally acceded to the Western view that "European security" and "Germany" (but not the other way around) were closely linked, they rejected another Western proposal, namely that the Russians and the Western powers should then work together on a new European security arrangement to embrace a reunified Germany. This meant that security arrangements containing various kinds of permutations that Britain, France, Germany, and the USA had been considering before the summit would have no chance of being accepted by the Russians at a later conference of foreign ministers.

The Eden package was thus doomed even before the details had been discussed with the Russians. However, even among the Western powers alone it would have taken months of negotiations to reach agreement on the details of the armaments-controlled zone or the creation of a demilitarized zone. For instance, Eden referred briefly to the need for su-

61. Dixon (Macmillan) to FO, tel.473, 16 June 1955, PREM11/894, PRO.

pervising these zones "effectively" in his opening speech, and during the discussion of disarmament on 21 July he proposed (this time not directly connected with his package proposal) a scheme for setting up joint inspection forces to be established in Europe around areas of "fixed depth on either side of [the] line dividing East and West Europe." The scheme was discussed with Eisenhower and Alfred Gruenther, SACEUR, prior to Eden's presentation, but it would have been difficult if not impossible to establish an inspection system that both the West and the Russians could accept and which would not make the Germans feel supervised by the four powers.[62] After all, under the Eden package proposal, German territory was subject to either demilitarized or controlled armament zones.

Finally, the Eden package proposal looked toward creating a new balance of power in Europe with a new reunified Germany. As John Young argues in this volume, Britain and France tended to deal with the opponent by presenting attractive proposals, whereas the Americans were preoccupied by their suspicions of Soviet intentions. The Eden package proposal suggested that eventually détente might be established on the basis of a reunified Germany, a first step toward the end of the cold war in Europe. Britain, now a medium-sized power, could perhaps lead a regional, if not a global, détente. Alternatively, Eden thought that as a result of informal contacts with the Russians during the Geneva summit, Britain might be able to act as a mediator between the two superpowers. However, as Antonio Varsori also concludes in this volume, this was merely wishful thinking on Eden's part.[63]

The year 1955 was not yet ripe for creating an independent European détente in the way Eden wanted. American nuclear weapons were becoming integrated into NATO forces and the security of Western Europe still depended upon American nuclear deterrence and the American military presence there. Also, the timing was not suitable for the Russians: Nikita Khrushchev was trying to achieve a Soviet status coequal to that of the United States. The global dominance of the superpowers was demonstrated by the Camp David talks in September 1959.[64] The

62. See Eden's opening statement, Cmd. 9543, 18; *FRUS, 1955–57,* V, 455; Eden-Dulles-Eisenhower breakfast meeting, 21 July 1955, PREM11/895, PRO and *FRUS, 1955–57,*V, 401; Gruenther-Eden lunch meeting, 21 July 1955, FO 371/118239, PRO. On German anxiety over this, see Millar to FO, tel.411, 22 July 1955, FO 371/118235, PRO.

63. See Eden minute, 19 July 1955, PREM 11/895, PRO.

64. For the Camp David talks, see Dockrill, *Eisenhower's New-Look National Security Policy,* 251–6.

Russians were certainly uninterested in making a deal with the Western Europeans for the sake of détente in Europe at the cost of East Germany, and the Geneva summit confirmed how deep was the gulf between East and West over Germany. In this respect, Eden's assessment of the Russian attitude was unconvincing. He stated at the cabinet meeting before he left for Geneva and also during the informal three-heads-of-government meetings at Geneva that "the pressure for an Austrian settlement which the Western Powers had brought to bear on the Russians at the Berlin Conference had in the end borne fruit. It was not impossible that similar pressure now might have the same result in respect of Germany." Frank Roberts and the majority of the foreign-office officials offered a more persuasive explanation for this. In their view, the Russians linked the settlement of Austria to the question of West German rearmament. When the latter had been finalized, there was no further motive for the Russians to keep the Austrian question as a bargaining chip. Hence Moscow agreed to conclude the Austrian State Treaty in May.[65]

When the Geneva Conference ended, the British prime minister admitted that the Western powers had failed to change Russia's views about Germany. He somewhat oddly attributed Russian inflexibility to their "genuine fear" of German revanchism. He seems to have held this opinion mainly because the success of the Eden package proposal depended on the Russians' willingness to admit the need for security arising from a reunified Germany staying within NATO. The more plausible possibility was that the Russians would refuse to accept German reunification within the Western bloc under any circumstances.[66]

The outcome of the Geneva summit was clear in that it failed to achieve any agreement about Germany. One could, of course, argue about the possible negative consequences if the West had agreed not to engage in any discussion over Germany at Geneva. This might have created the impression that the Western powers had given up the hope of German reunification as unattainable. But Eden seemed to have gone too far: from the beginning, he was determined to take the initiative over Germany, to deliver his speech on the package proposal no matter what the circumstances, and to keep the subject alive at any cost. All

65. Meeting of three western heads, 17 July 1955, FO 371/118233,PRO; Cabinet 23rd meeting, 14 July 1955, CAB 128/29, PRO; Eden, *Full Circle*, 290–2; Roberts to Hancock, 27 April 1955, FO 371/118210, PRO.
66. Cabinet 26th meeting, 26 July 1955, CAB 128/29, PRO.

this contributed to creating unnecessary publicity for the Eden package proposal prior to the summit, thus raising false hopes in Europe and especially in Germany. Adenauer accepted the news calmly, but, as Blankenhorn admitted to Dulles privately on 21 July 1955, the summit seemed to have led to exaggerated hopes in Germany about the possibility of friendship with the Russians.[67] For these reasons, the foreign office, like the United States, was never keen on a top-level conference as "an instrument of diplomacy."[68] Macmillan, after listening to the discussions between Bulganin and the Western leaders over Germany, felt that the conference was a "great waste of time."[69]

Eden could console himself with the thought that he had taken every opportunity to expose the Russians to the difficulty of agreeing to an early unification of Germany at Geneva, but his efforts also demonstrated that the Western inability to unify Germany depended entirely upon the Russian inability to do so.

67. Blankenhorn to Auswärtiges Amt, Bonn, tel.18, 21 July 1955, NL 351/49b, Blankenhorn papers; Schwarz, *Adenauer*, 204–6; Millar, Bonn to FO, tel.411, 22 July 1955, FO 371/118235, PRO.

68. See Sean A. Faughnan, "The Politics of Influence: Churchill, Eden and Soviet Communism" (Ph.D. thesis, Cambridge University, 1993); Macmillan, *Tides*, 584–5.

69. Macmillan, *Tides*, 618.

No Way Back to Potsdam

The Adenauer Government and the Geneva Summit

ECKART CONZE

On October 23, 1954, one day before the Paris treaties sealed West Germany's admission to NATO, Chancellor Konrad Adenauer faced an international press conference. Proudly and self-confidently, he announced: "We are now part of the biggest and most powerful military alliance in history. . . . From now on, the whole Atlantic community will powerfully support our objective, German reunification; and very soon this reunification will be achieved in peace and freedom."[1] The German chancellor had no choice but to spread this kind of optimism. For years—at home and abroad—he had declared that West Germany's firm integration into the West was the decisive precondition for the nation's reunification. With this argument he had effectively foiled every attempt to explore other options to solve the national question, as for example Stalin's 1952 note on German unity. The relationship between integration in the West and reunification had taken shape long before West Germany joined NATO; the years 1950–55 had made it only too clear that progress toward one of the two objectives could only be achieved at the cost of the other. But time and again Adenauer answered his critics, both in the opposition and within his own party, who attacked him for abandoning reunification: "We do not have a single objective, we have two aims which are, however, shaped by the common purpose of creating a reunified Germany in peace and freedom."[2]

1. Henning Köhler, *Adenauer. Eine politische Biographie* (Frankfurt/Berlin, 1994), 852; cf. Rudolf Morsey, *Die Deutschlandpolitik Adenauers. Alte Thesen und neue Fakten* (Opladen, 1991), 50–4.

2. Quoted in Klaus Gotto, "Die Sicherheits- und Deutschlandfrage in Adenauers Politik 1954–55," in *Zwischen Kaltem Krieg und Entspannung: Sicherheits- und Deutschlandpolitik der Bundesrepublik im Mächtesystem der Jahre 1953–1956*, ed. Bruno Thoss and Hans-Erich Volkmann (Boppard am Rhein, 1988), 145–6.

However, the end of the postwar years and the hardening of the blocs, to which Germany's admission to NATO had contributed substantially, created less rather than more scope for action in Germany's Deutschlandpolitik. In its rhetoric Bonn stood by its aim of reunification, but even Adenauer's closest collaborators could not see a realistic concept for an active reunification as part and parcel of an operative Deutschlandpolitik.[3] Within the larger framework of East-West relations, the end of the bloc formation phase in 1954–55 marked the beginning of a period of détente. This détente, however, was based on the division of Germany and Europe and therefore could not contribute to the overcoming of those divisions. Instead, the divisions of both Germany and Europe, born of mutual misperceptions between East and West and of an unintended escalation of conflicts, was explicitly confirmed in 1954–55.[4] The Geneva summit was basically no longer looking for ways to undermine the status quo but for ways to render it less dangerous and explosive. The Adenauer government was confronted with a dilemma: After the ratification of the Paris treaties, the general public in Germany was now expecting concrete steps toward reunification. But the overall efforts of the four powers—particularly the United States and the Soviet Union—were not at all conducive to bringing about Germany's reunification. Had the EDC treaty, or the Paris agreements that replaced it, actually forestalled reunification, as even West German government circles had always feared?[5] The position of the West German government toward the Geneva summit was determined by these contradictions and open questions. The meeting of the four heads of state confronted the Adenauer government with impossible requirements: on the one hand, Bonn had to demonstrate alliance solidarity by supporting the Western détente efforts, while on the other it had to avoid sacrificing the German right to reunification on the altar of détente.

3. On April 5, 1955, Heinrich Krone noted in his diary: "Do we have a concept for reunification? Not that I know of. Are we well prepared for the forthcoming talks?" Heinrich Krone, "Aufzeichnungen zur Deutschland- und Ostpolitik, 1954–1959," in Konrad-Adenauer-Studien III (Mainz, 1974), 136–7. A complete edition of Heinrich Krone's diaries from 1945 to 1961 has recently been published in Germany: Heinrich Krone, Tagebücher. Erster Band: 1945–1961 (Düsseldorf, 1995).

4. Cf. Wilfried Loth, "Blockbildung und Entspannung: Strukturen des Ost-West-Konflikts, 1953–1956," in Zwischen Kaltem Krieg und Entspannung, ed. Thoss and Volkmann, 19.

5. Wilhelm G. Grewe, statement, in Entspannung und Wiedervereinigung. Deutschlandpolitische Vorstellungen Konrad Adenauers, 1955–1958 (Stuttgart/Zurich 1979), 41.

Adenauer's single most important political aim at the turn of 1954–55 was the ratification of the Paris treaties, which ensured not only West German sovereignty but also comprehensive security guarantees, full German participation in the process of Western European integration, and a firm commitment of the Allies to German reunification.[6] According to the concept of a policy of strength (Politik der Stärke), which meant more than simply military strength, Germany's integration into the West was, for Adenauer, a precondition for East-West détente and thereby a solution of the German question: "Only the firmness and solidarity of our European unity, the alliance between a free Europe and the Atlantic world could offer the preconditions to start without fear the political and diplomatic action which would lead to the détente of East-West conflict. Only the realization of the treaties could bring about the preconditions for successful negotiations with the Soviet Union. Only from a position of Western unity could these problems be discussed with the Soviet Union openly and seriously."[7]

It was the chancellor's *ceterum censeo* that Germany's national objectives could only be achieved together with the Western allies. While neutralization, for example, would certainly bring about reunification, a neutral Germany would sooner or later fall into the Soviet orbit with dire consequences for the remaining Western European states. Additionally, neutralization would not extend Germany's political scope of action. On the contrary, "In the best case, we would have the pleasure of sitting between the chairs on the bare floor, and the others would clean their shoes on us. But we wanted to sit *on* the chairs, and we wanted to cooperate equally with the other nations for world peace."[8] In the months between the signing of the Paris treaties and their ratification, the Adenauer government faced mounting pressure from the social-democratic opposition, and a number of extraparliamentarian movements sought, in a last attempt to achieve reunification, to renounce NATO membership. SPD (Sozialdemokratische Partei Deutschlands, the Social Democratic Party) chairman Ollenhauer urged Adenauer in January 1955 to argue for negotiations with Moscow on the basis of the Soviet note of January 15, 1955. The chancellor's answer was as clear as

6. Cf. Gotto, "Sicherheits- und Deutschlandfrage," 137, 143.
7. Konrad Adenauer, *Erinnerungen, 1953–1955* (Stuttgart, 1966), 434.
8. Ibid., 416; cf. Adenauer, "Wir haben wirklich etwas geschaffen" (5.2.1955) in *Die Protokolle des CDU-Bundesvorstandes, 1953–1957*, ed. Günter Buchstab (Düsseldorf, 1990), 374.

it was, at least in his view, logical: "If we now ask the three Western powers to approach the Soviet Union, they will refuse to do so by pointing at their unanswered note of November 11th 1954. We would then run the risk of failing to ratify the Paris Treaties, of endangering the obligation of the three Western powers to pursue together with us a reunification in peace and freedom, while not getting such a commitment from the Soviet Union. In short, we would run the risk that Germany, as so many times over the last decades would—without friends—fall between two stools. We would remain in a state without freedom until the Four Powers come to an agreement."[9]

In February 1955, the German Bundestag ratified the Paris treaties by a clear majority; only the Saar Statute squeaked through narrowly. On March 27, the French Conseil de la République approved the treaties. In the East-West context the main question was now whether East-West relations would deteriorate substantially, as the Soviet Union had frequently threatened. Would there be a new ice age? The contrary turned out to be the case; on several occasions Moscow demonstrated its willingness to ease East-West tensions: by giving way on the Austrian question, by reconciling with Tito's Yugoslavia, by accepting an East-West summit, and by proposing to Bonn that the two countries establish diplomatic relations. On one level, Bonn did not hesitate to interpret these moves as the result of the FRG government's purposeful, unwavering, uncompromising policy. But the moves toward détente did not create the kind of radical break Bonn had expected. The danger of East-West arrangements was by no means banned.

Bonn, however, could not afford to slow down the process of détente. Especially with a view to its own population, the Adenauer government now had to try to turn the Soviet interest in détente into a German success regarding reunification. From January 1955 Chancellor Adenauer had demanded a Western working group with the task of developing proposals for reunification. He knew how important it was to secure ratification of the Paris treaties by creating the impression that after ratification the international community would immediately turn to the problem of German reunification. As long as the Paris treaties were not yet in force, Adenauer had opposed four-power negotiations, and the three Western powers had supported this course of action. But now that West Germany was a sovereign state and a member of NATO, the chan-

9. Adenauer, *Erinnerungen, 1953–1955*, 414.

cellor had to agree, at least in principle, to a four-power conference. He owed this to his own party, to his coalition, to the opposition, to the broad German public, and also to the Western allies. According to Adenauer, it now should be the task of German policy to make clear to the Western allies that a solution to the German problem had to be an integral part of any détente. The chancellor was well aware, however, of the fact that détente was conceivable—at least from the point of view of the three Western powers—even without solving the German question, i.e., with Germany remaining divided. To the executive committee of his CDU party Adenauer declared, "That is thinkable, but it is not desirable."[10] It was in this situation that his advisers in the chancellory developed the German objectives for a forthcoming conference with the Soviet Union. Herbert Blankenhorn, the chancellor's closest foreign-policy adviser, informed the Western high commissioners of four basic German positions: the Austrian solution was not acceptable for Germany; the territories east of Oder and Neisse were not to be given up; the Eden Plan for free all-German elections must be tightened; and the German Bundestag resolution of June 10, 1953, must be the basis of a reunified Germany's future status.[11]

Bonn could not and would not prevent a four-power summit. The German public had pinned big hopes on such a meeting; with the Paris agreements in force, the West was, in Adenauer's view, strong and united as never before, while the Soviet Union showed an interest in détente out of a position of weakness. However, the nearer the date of the summit drew, the stronger became the chancellor's skepticism, his mistrust, his never-waning pessimism. While the French government of Edgar Faure and British prime minister Anthony Eden enthusiastically welcomed the Soviet détente signals, Adenauer was much more cautious in his judgment of the Soviet motives and aims. Between Washington and Bonn the degree of agreement was higher. But when it came to evaluating the Soviet moves and analyzing their underlying motives, Adenauer's opinion diverged even from that of John Foster Dulles.

10. Adenauer, "Wir haben wirklich etwas geschaffen" (3.6.1955), 504 (3.6.1955), 529.
11. Cf. Hermann-Josef Rupieper, *Der besetzte Verbündete: Die amerikanische Deutschlandpolitik, 1949–1955* (Opladen, 1991), 408; cf. also Adenauer's preliminary views concerning the conference with the Soviets on German unity, March 3, 1955, Decimal File 762A.00/3-8-55, RG 59, NA.

Washington and especially the State Department interpreted the Soviet behavior as a clear change of course and even saw realistic possibilities for a policy of rollback—which had until then been merely part of American political rhetoric. To the National Security Council, Dulles declared that "we were now confronting a real opportunity in the present situation for a rollback of Soviet power. Such a rollback might leave the present satellite states in a status not unlike that of Finland."[12] After the Austrian State Treaty, Dulles saw a realistic opportunity for German reunification: "I feel more confident than ever before that the present trend of events is going to bring about a reunification of Germany. I can't document that or prove it, but I feel that that kind of thing is in the air; that what has happened here has loosened forces which I think the Soviet Union will have to respect." Dulles and Adenauer agreed in their judgment that the change in Moscow's behavior was the result of Western strength and unity. But while Dulles obviously believed in a real change of tide, the German chancellor remained skeptical. In his view, the Soviets were thinking "in long periods of time. . . . And in these long periods Communist ideology allowed breathing spaces, breaks that were necessary to consolidate the achieved gains. The West should be very careful not to construe such a breathing space as a real change of Soviet ideology and therefore reduce its caution."[13] As early as 1952 the chancellor had expressed his conviction that, in view of growing Western strength, Russia would soon have to turn to its own domestic problems. Very soon the Soviet Union would no longer be able to ignore its huge problems and it would face them even more readily if Western strength had convinced them that a conquest of Europe was no longer possible. This would then be the moment to start negotiations with the Soviet Union. In the early summer of 1955, however, this real change in Moscow had in Adenauer's view not yet begun. Hence the time had not yet come for German reunification to have a real chance. All the greater was for him the risk that British, French and American détente euphoria—together with the German interest in re-

---

12. Adenauer, *Erinnerungen, 1953–1955*, 451; Detlef Felken, *Dulles und Deutschland. Die amerikanische Deutschlandpolitik 1953–1959* (Bonn/Berlin, 1993), 287.

13. Adenauer, *Erinnerungen, 1953–1955*, 438; cf. Herbert Blankenhorn, *Verständnis und Verständigung. Blätter eines politischen Tagebuchs 1949 bis 1979* (Frankfurt/Berlin/Vienna, 1980), 216–7.

unification, which not only the SPD advocated—would open the door to highly dangerous ideas of neutralization.[14]

Specifically, Adenauer believed that the American interest in liberating the satellite states and the Soviet objective to neutralize Germany could eventually meet, thus confronting the Federal Republic or a united Germany with the threat of nonalignment, which was Adenauer's nightmare.[15] It was this concern, the fear of neutralization, that made the chancellor more and more skeptical the closer the summit came. For Adenauer it was obvious that the Soviet compromise on the Austrian question had less to do with Austria itself than with the effects of the Austrian solution on Germany and the Germans. He therefore never tired of stressing that the German and Austrian situations were absolutely dissimilar. Bruno Kreisky's reports on his talks with Soviet deputy prime minister Anastas Mikoyan only strengthened the chancellor's views on this. Austria's neutralization, however, provided arguments not only for Adenauer's domestic critics but also even, at least in May 1955, for Washington. At a press conference on May 18, 1955, President Eisenhower himself presented the idea of a neutral belt in central Europe: "There seems to be developing the thought that there might be built up a series of neutralized states from north to south through Europe." Adenauer was shocked. As much as he advocated German reunification, it was unthinkable for him under such conditions. It had taken him five years to push through, against powerful opposition at home and abroad, the Federal Republic's integration into the West,

14. Hans-Peter Schwarz, "Die deutschlandpolitischen Vorstellungen Konrad Adenauers," in Entspannung und Wiedervereinigung, 17; Schwarz, "Die deutschlandpolitischen Vorstellungen," 24. It is a question of considerable interest how Adenauer's view of the Soviet Union was shaped. Apart from generational experiences and his day-by-day information, he relied heavily on the judgment of former prisoners of war in the Soviet Union. In 1955 he was strongly influenced by a book written by Wilhelm Starlinger, who had spent many years in Soviet prisons and camps, on the limits of Soviet power. The similarity of argumentation is astonishing. Cf. Wilhelm Starlinger, Grenzen der Sowjetmacht [Würzburg, 1955). Starlinger later summarized his theses again in another volume, which also became part of Adenauer's reading: Wilhelm Starlinger, Hinter Russland China [Würzburg, 1957). Then in 1959–60 a popular analysis of the Soviet Union (Dieter Friede, Das russische Perpetuum mobile [Würzburg, 1959]) confirmed the chancellor's judgment and dominated his explanation of Moscow's behavior. Adenauer quoted from this book at almost every press conference he gave during these years.

15. Cf. Mechthild Lindemann, "Die Deutschlandfrage auf der Gipfelkonferenz und der Aussenministerkonferenz von Genf 1955," in Die Deutschlandfrage vom 17. Juni 1953 bis zu den Genfer Viermächtekonferenzen von 1955, ed. Dieter Blumenwitz (Berlin, 1990), 181.

and this was meant to be binding also for a reunified Germany. West Germany's firm alliance with the West should not be sacrificed to achieve short-lived successes regarding détente. Such a prospect was anathema to Adenauer. He would never approve of a renewed German *Schaukelpolitik* between East and West, to which a neutralized Germany would almost automatically lead. Only the firm integration into the Western community could, in the long run, protect the European states against the Germans and protect the Germans against themselves.[16]

Additionally, Adenauer regarded Moscow's plans to neutralize Germany as merely a tactical method of achieving their own long-term objectives toward Germany, and believed that the plans for neutralization should not be taken as indicators of Soviet weakness or readiness to compromise in a broader East-West context. A neutralized Germany would be an invitation for Moscow to extend its power all over Western Europe. What would be left of Europe once a neutral belt became a reality? Only Italy, France, and Spain. In Adenauer's own words, "England cannot be counted as European. What would have been achieved: Our European policy would be completely eradicated." The neutralized states of central Europe would without a doubt be sucked into the Russian orbit, and the Soviet Union would have realized its objective: the removal of the U.S. from Europe and the domination of Western Europe's economic and armament potential. The chancellor did not tire of warning. "I repeat, the idea is not yet dead. It will come up again in the course of the conferences lying before us. It will be presented by the Soviet Union or by somebody else. . . . For us Germans this idea poses a very great, indeed deadly danger." Even Federal president Theodor Heuss received a written analysis by the chancellor which culminated with the remark: "The signing of the treaties has suddenly produced a very dangerous situation for German foreign policy."[17]

Adenauer had identified the dangers. But how did he react? First, in a dramatic gesture, he ordered the German ambassadors in Washington,

16. Adenauer, *Erinnerungen, 1953–1955*, 441; Krone, *Aufzeichnungen*, 137; *FRUS, 1955–1957*, IV, 9; quoted in Felken, *Dulles*, 290.
17. Adenauer, *Erinnerungen, 1953–1955*, 445; Adenauer, "Wir haben wirklich etwas geschaffen," 500–1; Adenauer to Theodor Heuss, May 5, 1955, in Hans Peter Mensing, ed., *Heuss-Adenauer. Unserem Vaterland Zugute. Der Briefwechsel, 1948–1963* (Berlin, 1989), 182.

London, and Paris back to Bonn for consultations. Ambassador Krekeler in Washington did not leave the U.S. without first informing the secretary of state about the chancellor's irritation. And Adenauer's friend Dulles proved reliable as always. A few days after Eisenhower's public statement the secretary declared: "It is the view of the United States that a policy of neutrality has no application to a country of the character of Germany." For the time being Bonn was reassured, but the chancellor's mistrust together with his fear of German neutralization remained basically unchanged. In this situation Adenauer's trip to the United States to receive an honorary degree from Harvard University became all the more important. In Washington he had the opportunity to once again present the German position to President Eisenhower and Secretary of State Dulles—always being basically convinced that the U.S. would serve as the best advocate of German interests during the forthcoming summit.[18]

Even if after Adenauer's visit to Washington the danger of neutralization as such seemed to have been dismissed, it still was probable that the participants at the summit would discuss ways and means to enhance security in Europe, thereby bringing back the concept of neutralization through the back door or—even worse—leading to a recognition of the status quo of German division. This could indeed happen very easily if, for example, the border between the two German states were to be used as a demarcation line for an East-West arms-control or inspection zone. In Bonn's eyes this would mean international recognition of the GDR, which the Federal Republic could not accept. In such a case Adenauer's opponents would be confirmed in their argument that the treaties with the West would directly lead to a deepening of Germany's division. Détente, yes, but not at the price of deepening German partition. Adenauer's advisers tried concertedly to develop a German proposal for the Geneva talks. For Adenauer himself "the best way to counter Western ideas of neutralization was . . . to develop a plan which, on the one hand, would respect Soviet security needs but not, on the other, make impossible the deployment of American and other Western troops on the territory of the Federal Republic."[19] If Bonn had to bow to the inevitable, i.e., to accept arms-control or inspection zones, it would do so only under the condition that such plans did not impede Germa-

18. Quoted in Felken, *Dulles*, 290.
19. Adenauer, *Erinnerungen, 1953–1955*, 446.

ny's alignment with the West, with continued European integration as its most important goal; only under the condition that the plans would not discriminate against the Federal Republic politically; only under the condition that they would not make militarily worthless the deployment of American forces in Western Europe; and only under the condition that they avoided the danger of recognizing the status quo.[20]

The so-called Heusinger Plan, which was developed in Bonn under strictest secrecy, took all these conditions into account. In June 1955 Adenauer presented this plan in Washington. It envisaged the creation of a troop-free space on both sides of a line through Stettin to Prague to Vienna to Trieste. The Western half of this space covered large parts of GDR territory, and its Western border did not coincide with the border between the GDR and the Federal Republic. To the east and west of the core space, zones with reduced armament were to follow, approximately to the Rhine in the west and to a line between Riga and Brest in the east. The cornerstone of this plan was Germany's reunification and the continued existence of NATO. The Heusinger Plan, however, provided no information about concrete steps toward reunification. As Helga Haftendorn argues: "Basically, Heusinger's proposals would have meant a demilitarization of the GDR and a reduction of the dominance of Eastern conventional forces in Europe, while, at the same time, NATO defence planning would not be restricted. . . . The demarcation lines of the various zones were drawn according to military criteria; at the same time, it was avoided that they would coincide with political borders, thus prejudging a border settlement in a peace treaty with Germany."[21]

Whatever plan the West should finally decide to present at Geneva, in Adenauer's view it had to reaffirm the pledge of the West German government and the three Western powers to German unity. The chancellor was only too aware of what he had promised his own party, his governing coalition, his opposition, and the German people: The Geneva summit had to be about German reunification, otherwise the federal chancellor would completely lose his credibility. If reunification were

---

20. Cf. Helga Haftendorn, *Sicherheit und Entspannung. Zur Aussenpolitik der Bundesrepublik Deutschland, 1955–1982* (Baden-Baden, 1986), 80.

21. Haftendorn, *Sicherheit und Entspannung*, 82; cf. Hermann-Josef Rupieper, "Deutsche Frage und europäische Sicherheit: Politisch-strategische Überlegungen, 1953–1955" in *Zwischen Kaltem Krieg und Entspannung*, ed. Thoss and Volkmann, 199–204 (with detailed maps).

not to be, the politics of Western integration up to 1955 would prove to be frustrating rather than facilitating that goal. The chancellor had made this point sufficiently clear in Paris in early May, when the Western powers were discussing their inviting of the Soviet Union to a summit meeting. While the three Western powers, especially Britain and France, showed no interest in fixing a concrete summit agenda in the invitation, Adenauer argued strongly for such an agenda, with the German question on top of it: "I declared in Paris that we had pushed through the Bundestag the ratification of the Paris Treaties with the argument that these treaties would end uncertainty and that the road to talks about German reunification would then be free. Not to mention the German question in the invitation addressed to Moscow would disappoint me strongly."[22]

But why should London and Paris consider German reunification to be in their national interest? Was it not much more in the British and French interest to reduce tensions in Europe through arms-control agreements, even if these eventually perpetuated the status quo of the division of Germany? What use was there in a policy that blocked all progress toward détente by insisting that German unity be the highest priority? Adenauer knew only too well what Paris and London were thinking. While in Washington, he once again voiced his conviction that solving the security and disarmament problems was not possible as long as Germany's division continued. Without reunification, so the chancellor's argument went, Europe would never find stability, order, and peace, because Germany's partition would always upset the balance of power.[23] Adenauer was convinced that reunification could be achieved as an integral part of a general process of détente, possibly through an East-West negotiating marathon stretching over several years, but he saw no use at all in the short-term successes of a détente policy of the kind London, Paris, and some American politicians seemed to prefer.[24] That kind of détente would always run the risk of implicitly recognizing and consolidating the status quo. Time and again the chancellor stressed the connection, as it had been declared in 1954, between European security in general and German reunification, and he warned Western politicians not to untie this package just to obtain

22. Adenauer, *Erinnerungen, 1953–1955,* 440.
23. Ibid., 454.
24. Cf. Adenauer, "Wir haben wirklich etwas geschaffen" (May 2, 1955), 432.

short-lived successes for their détente policies. For the Adenauer government it was vitally important to prevent, on the one hand, an agreement based on the status quo with implicit recognition of the GDR and the Oder-Neisse line, and, on the other, an agreement that would endanger the Paris treaties.[25]

For Adenauer, endangering the Paris treaties meant jeopardizing German rearmament. And such was an inherent danger in security and disarmament measures ventilated in early 1955, especially on the banks of the Thames and the Seine. In 1955 the Federal Republic did not yet have a single Bundeswehr battalion, which was what made German territory so attractive for all kinds of arms-control proposals. Through the Paris treaties the Federal Republic had formally become a sovereign state, but Adenauer was aiming at real equality within the West, for which rearmament was an essential precondition. The chancellor liked to quote John Foster Dulles: "A state without armed forces—and this is also valid for the idea of neutralization—is a protectorate in the best case, but not a state."[26] This fundamental conviction helps explain Adenauer's objective of a long-term East-West negotiating process as well as the motive behind his repeatedly presented concept of universal, controlled disarmament ("allgemeine kontrollierte Abrüstung") as a precondition for real détente that would automatically lead to reunification.[27]

Almost simultaneously with the Western summit initiative, Chancellor Adenauer tried to speed up the formation of the first Bundeswehr units; the Blank office, in charge of defense affairs, was instructed to speed up preparations for the volunteer levy, and Adenauer informed the federal president that he had the firm intention of pushing this law through parliament before the summer recess: "Especially with respect to certain trends in the American public . . . we will have to build up our first volunteer units as soon as possible. Despite my recent experiences with the Blank office, I hope that it will be possible to have the laws passed prior to the Bundestag's summer recess." Appearing before the CDU executive committee, party chairman Adenauer stressed his urgency to implement "the possibilities which the Paris Treaties gave

25. Cf. Lindemann, "Deutschlandfrage," 180.

26. Schwarz, "Die deutschlandpolitischen Vorstellungen," 23–4.

27. Cf. Gregor Schöllgen, " 'Kontrollierte Abrüstung.' Konrad Adenauer, der Kalte Krieg und die Entspannungspolitik," in Gregor Schöllgen, Die Macht in der Mitte Europas: Stationen deutscher Aussenpolitik von Friedrich dem Grossen bis zur Gegenwart (Munich, 1992), 125–47.

us, and to fulfill the obligations arising from these treaties." He continued: "We have to use these chances and obligations, otherwise we will
lose our reputation as a state. If we do not succeed in passing the volunteer law before the parliamentary summer recess at the end of July—the
conference will probably start at the end of June—the Russians will be
given a great opportunity, and the West's confidence in our will will be
sapped."[28]

The Washington talks seem to have reassured the chancellor in this regard. German rearmament would not be negotiated in Geneva, Dulles
declared, and an NSC memorandum on demilitarized zones in central
Europe explicitly stated: "The U.S. could accept the concept that a demilitarized zone be established as part of the settlement establishing
German unity, providing the Western military position in Europe is not
thereby jeopardized and Germany is not precluded from effectively rearming."[29] This NSC guideline has to be judged as much a success of
Adenauer's policy as the fact that the issue of German reunification was
put on top of the summit agenda. Even before the summit began, it
seemed condemned to failure because it was highly doubtful whether
the Soviet Union, which on May 14, 1955, had made the GDR a signatory power of the Warsaw Pact, would still be committed to discussing
the establishment of an all-German state. It seemed much more likely
that Moscow, after May 1955, had finally come to terms with the long-
term existence of two German states. For this reason, Moscow would
no longer propagate concepts for reunification—which had always been
detrimental to the East German government—but instead would come
out for international recognition of the GDR and thus its internal stabilization. In any case, Moscow's two-state theory ("Zwei-Staaten-
Theorie") was born long before the Geneva summit, even if it was only
officially announced in East Berlin by Khrushchev and Bulganin on July
24, 1955, on their way back from the conference. Further proof of the
fact that Moscow had abandoned its reunification and neutralization
policy prior to Geneva was the invitation extended to Adenauer at the
beginning of June 1955 to visit Moscow and to establish diplomatic rela-

28. Adenauer to Heuss, May 22, 1955, in *Heuss-Adenauer*, ed. Mensing, 180; Adenauer,
"Wir haben wirklich etwas geschaffen" (June 3,1955), 511.
29. Memorandum NSC 5524/1, Basic U.S. Policy in Relation to Four-Power Negotiations, July 11, 1955, Decimal File, Folder Europe, Box 64, Lot 66 D 70, RG 59, NA. Cf. Felken, *Dulles*, 298–9.

tions between West Germany and the Soviet Union, thereby gaining at least de facto confirmation of the existence of two German states. Given the general mood of the German public, especially in connection with the question of the German prisoners of war, Adenauer could not afford to refuse the Soviet offer, even if this meant compromising West Germany's claim to be the sole legitimate German state ("Alleinvertretungsanspruch") and exposing the hollowness of his own claims to be seeking to restore the unity of the country.[30]

A second argument against Adenauer's accepting the Soviet overture of diplomacy was equally important. Would not a visit by the West German chancellor to Moscow, i.e., a bilateral Soviet-German meeting, lead to strong suspicions in Washington, London, and Paris? Beyond doubt, in the summer of 1955 the specter of Rapallo was haunting the international community almost more clearly than ever before. Was it not probable that the Russians and Germans would reach a deal in Moscow? A German-Soviet agreement would offer gains for both sides: a solution of their national question for the Germans, and, for the Soviets, a massive weakening of the West. But Adenauer was eager to reassure the Western powers "that we shall stand by our treaty commitments and that direct negotiations with Moscow, which I consider inevitable in view of German public opinion, will not change our basic positions." From the very beginning Adenauer was apparently successful in dispelling all thoughts of a secret policy behind the back of the Western allies, especially of the United States. The same was the case with the informal contacts in the summer of 1955 between Adenauer's finance minister Schäffer (CSU) and the East German Police General Vinzenz Müller.[31]

There was no doubt that the chancellor would accept Moscow's invitation. Adenauer was well aware that this invitation was a Soviet attempt to drive a wedge between West Germany and its allies just before the summit and that the Soviets intended to exclude the German question from the summit agenda, thereby circumventing the Western pack-

30. Cf. Loth, "Blockbildung," 19–20.
31. Adenauer, *Erinnerungen, 1953–1955,* 449; Department of State, secretary's memorandum of conversation with Ambassador Krekeler of Germany, June 4, 1955, Dulles Papers, General Correspondence & Memoirs Series, Box 1, folder "Memos of Conversations—General—J through K" (2), DDEL. Cf. Hanns Jürgen Küsters, "Wiedervereinigung durch Konföderation? Die informellen Unterredungen zwischen Bundesminister Fritz Schäffer, NVA-General Vinzenz Müller und Sowjetbotschafter Georgij Maksimowitsch Puschkin 1955–56," in *Vierteljahrshefte für Zeitgeschichte,* XL (1992), 107–53.

age of reunification and security. But he was also aware of the invitation's domestic value. Moscow, by inviting Adenauer, had refuted not only its own threats but also the criticisms and dire prognoses of the SPD with regard to an ice age after the signing of the Paris treaties. Furthermore, the trauma of Rapallo could contribute substantially to giving West Germany's position more weight in Western circles. If Bonn saw its aims and objectives adequately represented by its Western partners, there would be no need for separate agreements with Moscow. Seen in this perspective, the Rapallo trauma was a political trump card for the Federal Republic, even if it was partly relativized by Bonn's fear of neutralization schemes. Between 1949 and 1955, the Rapallo trauma and the fear of neutralization therefore had a stabilizing effect not only in an East-West context, but also on relations between the Western powers. While Rapallo increased the status of the Federal Republic, particularly in American calculations, the central importance of the USA for Bonn's foreign policy increased continuously, especially in the light of French and British attitudes. But before Bonn could start its preparations for the delicate visit to Moscow, it had to await the results of the Geneva summit. Not without profound worries did Konrad Adenauer wait for the Geneva meeting and not without deep skepticism did he watch and comment on the events in Geneva from his Swiss holiday resort in Mürren.[32]

After all the agitations and irritations of the weeks leading up to the summit, the conference itself—even for the chancellor—passed in a strange atmosphere, tense yet calm. Since the old man himself did not want to be in Geneva as an observer, he was kept supplied with information by his key foreign-policy advisers, Foreign Minister von Brentano, Undersecretary of State Hallstein, Assistant Secretary of State (Ministerialdirektor) Grewe, ambassador to NATO Blankenhorn, and ambassador to the United Nations von Eckardt, Adenauer's former press secretary who had been temporarily ordered to Geneva from his new post in New York. These advisers kept the chancellor in contact with the Western delegations in Geneva, above all the American one. Briefing the chancellor, who resided at almost two thousand meters altitude in the Swiss Alps, was a laborious task since Adenauer's chalet in

32. Adenauer, *Erinnerungen, 1953–1955*, 448–9; Hans-Jürgen Schröder, "Kanzler der Alliierten? Die Bedeutung der USA für die Aussenpolitik Adenauers," in *Adenauer und die Deutsche Frage. Zwölf Beiträge*, ed. Josef Foschepoth (Göttingen, 1988), 140.

Mürren was inaccessible by car. Instead, the advisers had to use a mountain cable car, the last leg of the ascent to Adenauer's domicile being a
narrow mountain path accessible only on foot. Heavily burdened with
folders and files, Adenauer's advisers more than once had occasion to
curse their (in a double sense) Sherpa's job. Sporadically, but then all the
stronger, the chancellor's mistrust flickered up, first when French
prime minister Faure in his opening speech on July 18 hinted at the possibility of dissolving the two pact systems and extending certain armament restrictions, so far only in force for West Germany, to a reunited
Germany. The latter proposal was the maximum concession the Germans were willing to make, should it become absolutely necessary in
the course of the negotiations.[33] Adenauer's mistrust flared up again
when President Eisenhower reportedly declared that the cause of peace
in Europe should "not be made dependent on anything else."[34] In both
cases, Secretary of State Dulles calmed the chancellor down by making
explanatory press statements or by telegraphically confirming the continued linkage of reunification and European security. In Adenauer's
view, the most dangerous proposal for the West was the disarmament
initiative launched on July 21 by Britain's prime minister Eden. Eden
had rightly based his proposal on the conviction that the only results
the conference could achieve were in the field of disarmament. To make
such results possible he untied the knot linking the reunification, security, and disarmament questions and separately proposed a central
European armament-inspection zone.[35] This zone was to have the intra-
German border as its demarcation line, and it would eventually be established even without progress in the matter of German reunification.
The German observers in Geneva were insufficiently informed about
the British initiative.[36] Despite the fact that Eden's proposal was not officially negotiated in the final phase of the conference, it remained on
hold in the Western capitals until the foreign ministers' meeting of October 1955, causing considerable irritation and a severe crisis in Anglo-

33. Cf. Daniel Kosthorst, *Brentano und die deutsche Einheit. Die Deutschland- und
Ostpolitik des Aussenministers im Kabinett Adenauer, 1955–1961* (Düsseldorf, 1993), 47.
34. Kosthorst, *Brentano*, 47–8; Adenauer: *Erinnerungen, 1953–1955*, 471.
35. For Eden's initiative see "Memorandum der britischen Delegation zur Abrüstungs-
frage," July 21, 1955, in *Dokumente zur Deutschlandpolitik, III. Reihe/Bd. 1, 5. Mai bis
31. Dezember 1955* (Frankfurt/Berlin, 1961), 199.
36. Cf. Wilhelm G. Grewe, *Rückblenden 1976–1951: Aufzeichnungen eines Augenzeugen deutscher Aussenpolitik von Adenauer bis Schmidt* (Frankfurt/Berlin/Vienna,
1979), 227.

German relations. Adenauer's evaluation of the situation was as sober as it was realistic: "During the Geneva negotiations I gained the impression that the Western position was no more as firm. . . . There was indeed the danger that the Western arms control initiative could be taken as a security plan. This arms control initiative, however, was based on a still divided Germany. I had strongest reservations."[37]

Ultimately, the Soviet Union turned out to be the chancellor's best ally; by obstructing every concrete move in the question of German reunification and trying to push through disarmament and security measures based on the status quo, Moscow indirectly strengthened the position of the federal chancellor, who once again was able to blame the Soviets for the lack of progress in the question of reunification. Even on the domestic German scene this was not without relevance. While on the one hand Adenauer could always reproach advocates of a German neutralization for finally doing business with Moscow, on the other hand he could tell those, even in his own party, who were desperately waiting for Germany's reunification that Moscow was obstructing a solution of the national question. From this perspective the continued call for reunification was also an integral part of Adenauer's anti-Communist strategy to protect the concept of Western integration.[38]

Adenauer approved the summit's directive for the planned foreign ministers' conference later in 1955 because it did not touch the linkage of German reunification and European security. However, Khrushchev's and Bulganin's stop in East Berlin on their way back from Geneva on July 24 made clear the pointlessness of maintaining the linkage and the extent to which it was based on mere illusions. After Geneva, the period of Soviet initiatives for German reunification—under whatever auspices—was definitely over. From then on, Moscow's German policy was guided by the premise of the "two-states theory" ("Zwei-Staaten-Theorie").

In Bonn and Mürren the first—or rather, the first public—reaction to the summit and its results, few though those were, was rather positive. The chancellor publicly expressed his satisfaction, especially with the fact that the West had been able to maintain the crucial linkage. Adenauer,

---

37. Adenauer, *Erinnerungen, 1953–1955,* 470; cf. Adenauer, *Erinnerungen, 1955–1959* (Stuttgart, 1967), 31–3.

38. Josef Foschepoth, "Westintegration statt Wiedervereinigung: Adenauers Deutschlandpolitik 1949–1955," in *Adenauer und die Deutsche Frage,* 56.

of course, had very good reasons not to overemphasize possible German reservations. "For psychological reasons," he told journalists informally, "it would be a mistake to stress too much the negative aspects of the conference. The international community might then get the impression that Germany was interested in a continuation of the tensions."[39] Internally, Adenauer's judgment of the summit was much more ambivalent. In a letter to FRG president Heuss, for example, he wrote: "We can be content with the course of the conference, because it has served its purpose and because the foreign ministers' conference due in October may bring about real progress. I am, however, worried about the effects of Soviet behavior on public opinion, especially in the United States, in London and in Germany."[40]

The gradual shift in Adenauer's judgment is best expressed in his correspondence with Secretary of State Dulles. While the first letters, written almost immediately after the summit, were characterized by Adenauer's relief that the summit had produced so few results, this relief gave way very soon to the chancellor's usual skepticism and deep-rooted pessimism. It was true, he wrote to Dulles on July 25, that the Western powers in Geneva had reached their objectives. But the end of the conference for him marked the beginning of a new phase of East-West relations which would by no means be less dangerous than the last one. Soviet détente maneuvers would from now on be the main danger, détente initiatives aimed at winning over public opinion and obscuring the real Soviet intentions.[41] When in Washington even Dulles himself joined the chorus of détente euphoria and publicly declared German reunification to be in the air,[42] the last glimmer of a positive judgment disappeared: "My fear about the psychological effects of the Geneva conference became stronger from day to day."[43] Almost with a wagging finger, the chancellor stated that the conference had been "a complete success for the Russians who had reached their aim to render forgotten through cheap gestures everything written in their ledger. Moscow had not given up the hope to prise the Federal Republic out of the Western

---

39. Quoted in Kosthorst, *Brentano*, 50; cf. memorandum of the German foreign office, in Lindemann, "Deutschlandfrage," 196.
40. Adenauer to Heuss, July 30, 1955, in *Heuss—Adenauer*, 192.
41. Adenauer, *Erinnerungen, 1953–1955*, 472.
42. Cf. Felken, *Dulles*, 314.
43. Adenauer, *Erinnerungen, 1953–1955*, 477.

alliance by postponing reunification indefinitely."⁴⁴ Dulles's answer was open and clear: "Your letter is one interpretation of the Geneva conference. . . . It is, however, not the interpretation of the President and not mine, and I don't think that it is the correct interpretation." Dulles and the president did not share "the view that the 'spirit of Geneva' meant acceptance of the *status quo* or the perpetuation of current injustices—especially the division of Germany—. . . . Above all, we have the firm intention to make German unification a touchstone."⁴⁵

In a conversation with the president, Dulles attributed Adenauer's pessimism to his age, to the difficulty of adjusting old views to new situations, and to his nervousness in view of his forthcoming trip to Moscow. "I [Dulles] said that it was difficult for a man of Adenauer's age—about 80—to adjust himself to a new line of thinking after he had been dedicated to another line for so long. I said I expected to write to Adenauer and also possibly ask Livie Merchant to go over and talk before he went to Moscow. I said that Adenauer obviously felt nervous about his forthcoming Moscow trip."⁴⁶

Although Dulles shared Adenauer's concern about the British and French tendency "to make a deal on the basis of the *status quo*,"⁴⁷ the differences of opinion between Washington and Bonn remained considerable. While Washington after the Geneva summit saw Moscow fighting a rearguard action and considered German reunification merely a matter of time, Adenauer continued to believe firmly in an unchanged Soviet plan of world domination. For him Moscow was interested in détente to gain some breathing space and was still trying to prise Germany out of the West.⁴⁸ Of course, one should not overlook the fact that Adenauer and Dulles were in general agreement concerning the basic questions of East-West politics and that they shared the same fundamental convictions. While under certain circumstances—especially at decisive political junctures—the German chancellor complained about their differences of opinion or deep misunderstandings, these complaints should

44. Adenauer to Dulles, August 9, 1955, 762.00/8–955, RG 59, NA; cf. Adenauer, *Erinnerungen, 1953–1955*, 478.
45. Adenauer, *Erinnerungen, 1953–1955*, 481–2.
46. Memo of conversation, President Eisenhower and Secretary Dulles, August 12, 1955, 762A.11/8–1255, RG 59, NA.
47. Dulles to Eisenhower, August 10, 1955, Ann Whitman File, Dulles-Herter series, Box 4, Dulles, John Foster, August 1955(2), DDEL. Cf. Felken, *Dulles*, 316.
48. Cf. Hans-Peter Schwarz, *Adenauer: Der Staatsmann, 1952–1967* (Stuttgart, 1991), 207–22.

be interpreted as political instruments skillfully used by Adenauer to underline German positions or to procure reassurances from the other side of the Atlantic. Without any doubt, the weeks between the summit and the chancellor's trip to Moscow were in Adenauer's judgment a decisive phase in East-West politics. Against this background, the chancellor's complaints had a clearly instrumental character. Crises of confidence have been part of the basic pattern of German-American relations since 1949, and no other German politician knew better how to make the most of these crises and to use them for German interests than Konrad Adenauer. Nevertheless, these diverging positions made the preparations for Adenauer's visit to Moscow even more difficult, especially since it had always been stressed that the negotiations in Geneva and Moscow were to be considered as one unit.

The Moscow trip, in September 1955, which was followed by the release of the last German prisoners of war in the Soviet Union, engendered like no other event the "Adenauer myth" in the eyes of the German public. Before the trip, a high percentage of Germans already approved of Adenauer's policy; after it, however, the rate of approval climbed even higher.[49] This was all the more surprising since the visit itself and especially the establishment of diplomatic relations between the Federal Republic and the Soviet Union basically confirmed the Kremlin's "two-states theory," and since German reunification—despite the September 14, 1955, letter concerning German unity ("Brief zur deutschen Einheit")[50]—obviously had been postponed to the distant

---

49. For a detailed analysis of opinion polls and statistical material, see Dietrich Thränhardt, "Wahlen und Wiedervereinigung," in *Adenauer und die Deutsche Frage*, 255.

50. Brief zur deutschen Einheit (letter concerning German unity) printed in Adenauer, *Erinnerungen, 1953–1955*, 550. In this letter, accepted by the Soviet leadership, Adenauer stated: "1. Die Aufnahme der diplomatischen Beziehungen zwischen der Regierung der Bundesrepublik Deutschland und der Regierung der UdSSR stellt keine Anerkennung des derzeitigen beiderseitigen territorialen Besitzstandes dar. Die endgültige Festsetzung der Grenzen Deutschlands bleibt dem Friedensvertrag vorbehalten. 2. Die Aufnahme diplomatischer Beziehungen mit der Regierung der Sowjetunion bedeutet keine Änderung des Rechtsstandpunktes der Bundesregierung in bezug auf ihre Befugnis zur Vertretung des deutschen Volkes in internationalen Angelegenheiten und in bezug auf die politischen Verhältnisse in denjenigen deutschen Gebieten, die gegenwärtig ausserhalb ihrer effektiven Hoheitsgewalt liegen." [1. Resumption of diplomatic relations between the Federal Republic of Germany and the Soviet Union does not entail mutually recognizing each other's current territorial assets. The final determination of Germany's borders will be decided in the peace treaty. 2. Resumption of diplomatic relations with the government of the Soviet Union will not change the legal position of the government of the Federal Republic to rep-

future. The Moscow visit of GDR prime minister Otto Grotewohl from September 17–20, right after Adenauer's return to Bonn, and the "treaty concerning the relations between the GDR and the USSR" of September 20 made this only too clear.[51] The indefinite postponement of reunification, of course, was much less grasped by the broad German public than by Bonn's political circles. The public cheered the return of the prisoners and—under the sway of the "economic miracle"—continued to come to terms with the division of Germany; only from time to time were there fits of bad conscience brought on by pondering the fate of one's "brothers and sisters in the zone." Marion Countess Dönhoff's editorial in *Die Zeit* on September 22, 1955, was as drastic as it was basically correct: "Diplomatic relations versus the return of prisoners of war means—if you use the method of just counting living people and not dead souls—that the freedom of the 10,000 has sealed the slavery of the 17 millions."[52] (The details of the Moscow trip and its results are beyond the scope of the present essay.)[53]

Diplomatic relations between West Germany and the Soviet Union became possible after Bonn had successfully placated Western Rapallo fears and related anxieties (concerning a German *Schaukelpolitik* between the two halves in order to achieve national goals)[54] in general by joining NATO and in particular by a careful policy of consultations, especially with Washington. Despite the harsh criticism of Charles Bohlen, U.S. ambassador to Moscow, who sensed a secret Soviet-German deal and who characterized the Soviet-German meeting as the USSR's biggest diplomatic triumph since 1945, Adenauer had the fullest American support both before and during his trip. A status report of the NSC Operations Coordinating Board treated the establishment of diplomatic

resent the German people in international relations and with regard to the political situation in those German territories presently removed from its effective jurisdiction.]

51. Cf. Verhandlungen zwischen der UdSSR und der "DDR" in Moskau vom 17–20 September 1955, in *Dokumente zur Deutschlandpolitik*, 352–82; for the text of the treaty, see 371–4.

52. *Die Zeit*, September 22, 1955.

53. Cf. Josef Foschepoth, "Adenauers Moskaureise 1955," in *Aus Politik und Zeitgeschichte*, B22/86, 30–46; Schwarz, *Adenauer: Der Staatsmann 1952–1967*, 207–22.

54. Cf. Renata Fritsch-Bournazel, "Frankreichs Ost- und Deutschlandpolitik im Zeichen der Genfer Gipfelkonferenz von 1955," in *Zwischen Kaltem Krieg und Entspannung*, ed. Thoss and Volkmann, 71–91; Axel Frohn, "Der 'Rapallo-Mythos' und die deutsch-amerikanischen Beziehungen," in *Deutschland in Europa. Kontinuität und Bruch. Gedenkschrift für Andreas Hillgruber*, ed. Jost Dülffer, Bernd Martin, and Günter Wollstein (Frankfurt/Berlin, 1990), 135–53.

relations between West Germany and the USSR without the slightest critical comment.[55] Of course, Adenauer regarded the establishment of these "normal" relations as a means of avoiding a return to the Potsdam negotiating table, and of course his trip also reflected at least a latent mistrust of Washington's Soviet policy and corresponding German fears of an American-Soviet bilateralism.

But, on the other hand, it was at least equally important, in view of the Western Rapallo trauma, for the chancellor to give West German–Soviet relations an undramatic, unspectacular character. For this reason it was not Hans Kroll, a recognized Soviet expert of the Weimar Republic and in the normal course of events the man predestined for the post, who was made the first Federal German ambassador to Moscow. To avoid reminders of the 1920s, Bonn in late 1955 sent to Moscow Wilhelm Haas, a man with much less profile, whom Kroll succeeded only in 1958.[56] Moreover, Adenauer in his Moscow talks avoided the issue of German reunification. He was not only alert to Western Rapallo fears, he also wanted to make sure that, especially in view of the forthcoming foreign ministers' conference, Germany as a whole remained the joint responsibility of the four powers. With regard to the foreign ministers' meeting Adenauer returned skeptical from the Soviet Union, and Grotewohl's visit to Moscow only confirmed his skepticism. At the beginning of October 1955 he told Luxemburg's foreign minister Bech that he had no hope that the foreign ministers' conference would produce any positive results.[57] Concerning the German question, Adenauer in Moscow had only been able to secure the minimal position that would allow the West to maintain the linkage between reunification and European security during the forthcoming negotiations. The "Letter concerning German Unity" (Brief zur deutschen Einheit) de jure prevented a premature closing of the GDR question and a border settlement.[58] The so-called Hallstein doctrine, developed by Adenauer's advisers on the way back from Moscow and presented to the German Bundestag on September 22, 1955, had basically the same objective. Its central message was that the FRG government would "in the future regard the establish-

55. Cf. Felken, *Dulles*, 325.

56. Cf. the memoirs of Ambassador Kroll: Hans Kroll, *Botschafter in Belgrad, Tokio und Moskau 1953–1962* (Munich, 1969), 129–34; Schwarz, "Die deutschlandpolitischen Vorstellungen," 32.

57. Cf. Rupieper, *Der besetzte Verbündete*, 457.

58. Cf. Wilhelm Grewe's statement, in *Entspannung und Wiedervereinigung*, 83.

ment of diplomatic relations with the GDR by third states with diplomatic ties to West Germany as an unfriendly act."[59]

Before and during the Geneva foreign ministers' conference, the West German government had to pursue two basically conflicting aims: it had to avoid, as far as possible, any recognition of the GDR while at the same time pushing Moscow for concessions in the matter of reunification. After the events of the summer, the latter aim had become completely unrealistic. What interest could Moscow have in abandoning the two-states theory and thereby destabilizing the GDR? Adenauer was quite aware of this. By 1955 the Soviet Union was in East Germany to stay. Adenauer also had to fight on the Western front, where he sensed the main danger to lie regarding the sensitive question of recognizing the GDR. Once again Adenauer found himself deeply worried about British plans for arms-control or inspection zones, because all such plans were based on the status quo of German division and thus carried with them the possibility of bringing in through the back door a recognition of this division and of the continued existence of two German states. In difficult intra-Western preliminary talks Bonn succeeded in relativizing these dangerous plans, thanks above all to American support. It was agreed that only the eastern border of a reunified Germany would become the demarcation line for possible arms-control agreements. In this way, disarmament was added as a third element to the package of reunification and European security.[60]

In October and November 1955, however, it became clear how quickly disarmament or arms-control agreements between East and West could lead to a consolidation of the status quo, and how dangerous and risky was the chancellor's insistence on the primacy of a universal, controlled disarmament.[61] Another question was how long Britain and France would be willing to compromise their genuine interest in détente and disarmament by respecting the premises of Germany's (Adenauer's) reunification policy. This question became particularly important in the case of Britain. The summit had made it very clear that German reunification would not lead to a European détente in the way Eden had hoped. Instead, it seemed that the package of German reuni-

---

59. *Stenographische Berichte des Deutschen Bundestags*, vol. 26, 5647 A; cf. Grewe, *Rückblenden*, 251–62.

60. Cf. Adenauer, "Wir haben wirklich etwas geschaffen" (30.9.1955), 594–7.

61. Cf. Kosthorst, *Brentano*, 81.

fication and European security represented a major obstacle to any form of détente. During the foreign ministers' conference the unity of the West could be maintained only with great difficulty. It was once again Soviet intransigence that prevented the complete breakdown of the precarious intra-Western compromises on the questions of Germany and of European security. The foreign ministers' meeting, in which in July everybody had placed such high hopes, ended without even a joint communiqué. Bonn was relieved, and even if official government statements repeatedly called for reunification, the time for concrete negotiations was over. After two Geneva conferences, the European status quo was much too fixed for sudden change to be achieved.[62]

Even if Bonn's political rhetoric continued to sing the cantus firmus of reunification, Adenauer and his advisers were well aware that after the events of 1955—Germany's NATO membership, the Geneva summit, Adenauer's Moscow visit, and the foreign ministers' conference—all political considerations now had to be based on the de facto existence of two German states, each of them firmly integrated in either the Eastern or the Western military alliance.[63] This did not mean that Bonn had accepted the status quo or even recognized it de jure. Discussions about Eastern and Western disarmament initiatives—which after 1955 shot up from the ground like mushrooms under the rubric of disengagement—showed Bonn still struggling to avoid formal recognition of the GDR and of Germany's division. The last attempt to find a negotiated solution for the German question took place at the 1959 Geneva foreign ministers' conference that was called in the shadow of Khrushchev's Berlin ultimatum. The 1959 Western peace plan, the so-called Herter Plan, was directly connected with the Western package proposals of 1955. This plan attempted in three phases to simultaneously solve the questions of German unity, European security, and international disarmament. But the diametrically opposed objectives of East and West foiled—as in 1955—any compromise. What interest should the Soviet Union have had in trading an East German satellite state, now firmly tied into the Eastern bloc, when the perspective was one of a united Germany very likely being a member of NATO? The building of the Berlin Wall in 1961 cemented—literally—the division of Germany. After 1959–1961 the issue of German reunification disappeared from the

62. Cf. the essays by Saki Dockrill and Antonio Varsori in this volume.
63. Cf. Grewe in *Entspannung und Wiedervereinigung*, 42.

East-West agenda for three decades. The real successes of détente in the 1960s and 1970s in the field of arms control and disarmament became possible, at least in part, because East and West had mutually accepted the European status quo and had agreed that the German question was not solvable for the time being.[64]

Those who look at 1955 or 1961 and consider Adenauer's reunification policy a complete failure, or even as untruthful from the start, are over-simplifying the matter. But it is also too simple to see the German unification of 1990 as a direct result of the first federal chancellor's policy. There was no direct pathway from Geneva 1955 to the Two-Plus-Four Talks in 1990. It was, however, important that German policy in the post-Adenauer years, even under the Social Democratic chancellors Brandt and Schmidt, did not give up the basic claim to reunification as stated in the preamble of the Grundgesetz. Thus the door was kept open for a possible future unification of the two German states, a solution that until 1989 seemed highly improbable, but never impossible.

64. Cf. Eckart Conze, "Vom Herter-Plan zum Genscher-Plan. Zum Zusammenhang von deutscher Einheit, europäischer Sicherheit und internationaler Abrüstung am Ende der fünfziger Jahre und heute," in *Europäische Rundschau*, 18 (April 1990), 65–77.

Open Skies and Closed Minds

American Disarmament Policy at the Geneva Summit

JOHN PRADOS

One of the significant proposals advanced by world leaders attending the Geneva summit was President Dwight D. Eisenhower's suggestion for an international system of aerial inspection, an offer that has come down in history as the "Open Skies" plan. In some ways Open Skies has come to connote the "spirit of Geneva," at least in terms of disarmament policy. It may therefore come as a surprise that Open Skies almost did not even make the conference. That the offer was introduced betokens President Eisenhower's personal commitment to it and his private knowledge of secret intelligence programs, as well as United States government efforts to fashion policies that could gain an edge in the cold war psychological and propaganda competition. To bring Open Skies to Geneva, Eisenhower found it necessary to maneuver among a number of his subordinate officials, since different segments of the American bureaucracy held far different views as to the purpose and meaning of the proposal. The ultimate rejection of Open Skies at the international level should not detract from Eisenhower's achievement in bringing it to the conference forum.

The present paper will outline the context that gave rise to Open Skies, which was essentially the need to respond to then-current disarmament proposals combined with the mechanisms within the United States government for generating disarmament policy. It will also examine Eisenhower's interest in a parallel stream of policy on psychological warfare, which evolved the specific proposal eventually tendered, as well as the president's private knowledge of intelligence programs that made him especially aware of the value of this type of proposal at this time. Finally, the paper will discuss the struggle to bring Open Skies to Geneva and briefly detail the presentation and reception of the proposal.

The Context

Early moves leading to the Geneva summit included Soviet approaches to the Austrian government in February 1955. At that time, as a result of proposals introduced by the British and French governments during the summer of 1954, the United States was attempting to work out its own position on the subject of general and comprehensive disarmament. The Departments of State and Defense had very different perspectives on the possibilities for agreement in this area. The Department of Defense (DOD) argued in January 1955 that the U.S. should press disarmament negotiations as a means of exposing the rigidities in the Soviet position, while assuming leadership on the Western side. Despite this putative willingness to negotiate, the Joint Chiefs of Staff (JCS), Eisenhower's most senior military advisers, and their DOD superiors were in agreement that the U.S. stood to gain more from ongoing weapons programs than from any attainable disarmament agreement.[1]

On balance, this military reticence in the face of potential agreements is understandable. The Eisenhower administration had adopted a military doctrine called the "New Look" which sought to control defense spending through greater reliance on nuclear and thermonuclear weapons. By 1955 several of the programs necessary to sustain this doctrine were reaching critical stages of development. For example, the B-52 bomber had begun deployment in air units, and the C- and D- models of this aircraft, which would fly in 1956, were in the engineering and prototype stages of development. The B-58, America's first supersonic nuclear bomber, was also in engineering development. The W25, W31, and W33 warheads, as well as the B28 bomb—all of which would be carried by the B-52 aircraft—were other key weapons programs. The U.S. nuclear testing program was at a critical phase as well. The TEAPOT series planned for 1955 at the Nevada Test Site included one nonnuclear and fourteen nuclear shots, among them DESERT ROCK 6, which involved the participation of Army troops maneuvering on the ground. In the Pacific on May 14 another nuclear test, WIGWAM, became the biggest shot America ever conducted at sea. Some of the most important data on nuclear weapons gathered by the United States would flow from

1. For a good summary of these viewpoints, see Kenneth W. Condit, *History of the Joint Chiefs of Staff*, Vol. VI: *The Joint Chiefs of Staff and National Policy, 1955–1956* (Washington, D.C., 1992), 79–83.

these and future planned tests. Disarmament schemes threatened these military programs.

Under Secretary of State John Foster Dulles, the State Department had a different range of concerns which nevertheless added up to a problem as far as comprehensive disarmament was concerned. At least the diplomats acknowledged that, with the nuclear balance of terror escalating as it was, disarmament would be preferable to a continuation of the arms race. But State argued that negotiating a comprehensive agreement would be too time-consuming and that no agreement could be put into place without an effective system for verification and inspection. Since, as State also conceded, no one could tell in advance of implementation how effective a system of inspection would be; and since State also recommended (as a first arms-control measure) a ban on nuclear fuel production, which could be among the most difficult controls to verify, this position amounted to rejection of the disarmament proposals on the table. Outside observers, who often viewed U.S. policy as an extension of Dulles's opinions, felt themselves justified in drawing pessimistic conclusions. Roscoe Drummond and Gaston Coblentz, for example, wrote of Dulles, "His penchant for extravagant anti-Communist rhetoric . . . contributed in large measure to a widespread European notion that the United States had become overly intransigent, self-righteous, and bent on prolonging the Cold War rather than on bringing it to an end."[2]

The interagency differences were aired before President Eisenhower at a National Security Council meeting on February 10, 1955. As the meeting record attests, Ike there revealed that he had misgivings of his own: "The President observed that every time recently that the subject of disarmament had come up in a conversation, he was reminded of the fate of Carthage. The Roman invaders had by false promises induced the citizens of Carthage to surrender their arms. The moment these arms were surrendered, the Roman Legions attacked the city. Even in its comparatively defenseless state, however, Carthage had resisted the invaders for the period of an entire year." The President now wished to link controls on nuclear and conventional forces, that is, he favored comprehensive disarmament. The major outcome of the meeting was

2. Roscoe Drummond and Gaston Coblentz, *Duel at the Brink: John Foster Dulles' Command of American Power* (Garden City, N.Y., 1960), 132.

agreement that a single individual, not from any of the interested agencies, would be appointed by the President to complete the arms-control policy review.[3]

Eisenhower reached beyond the lists of candidates submitted by the State and Defense Departments and the Atomic Energy Commission to select Harold E. Stassen as his special assistant for arms-control matters. Stassen, a former governor of Minnesota and director of foreign aid, had good Republican credentials and proved a passionate advocate of arms control. His policy review, however, stumbled over the same bureaucratic positions that had prevented interagency agreement earlier, and in addition Stassen fell afoul of personal animosity on the part of Dulles, who apparently feared Stassen might threaten his stewardship as secretary of state.

In the meantime, on 10 May the Soviet Union introduced a comprehensive disarmament plan of its own, a two-stage proposal that would have reduced conventional forces and military budgets, halted nuclear testing as of 1956, and installed an international inspection authority. The Soviet plan responded to proposals by France and the United Kingdom, and had features similar to those earlier Western plans. By this time also, arrangements for a multilateral summit at Geneva were rapidly falling into place, with a clear expectation that disarmament would figure among the subjects for the talks. An articulated United States position on disarmament had become more necessary than ever; an actual proposal would be even better.

Governor Stassen completed his policy proposals, terming them a "progress report" on his review, and brought them to the National Security Council on 26 May. Stassen referred to his proposal as a "first phase plan" and aimed it at "leveling off all armament efforts—nuclear, bacterial, chemical, conventional." The Stassen Plan would have established an "International Armaments Commission" that would carry out inspections "by land, sea, and air, with the aid of scientific instruments." A later addition to the report, submitted prior to NSC discussions, specified that the technical means contemplated for the verification processes included "radar, sonic devices, photographic

3. Because most of the key documents of this period have been declassified and published, citations here will be to the more accessible series *Foreign Relations of the United States*. In this case the source is a memorandum of discussion, 236th Meeting of the National Security Council, February 10, 1955, *FRUS, 1955–1957*, XX, 20–34.

equipment, radiation detection and measurement instruments, and other scientific instruments."[4]

True to previous U.S. bureaucratic experience, there was little agreement on the substance of the Stassen proposal. At the initial presentation at the NSC meeting of 26 May, President Eisenhower himself remarked that the scheme did not do enough to control means of delivery, such as bombers and missiles. The Atomic Energy Commission, at its own briefing by Stassen in mid-June, opposed a halt in nuclear testing and would go along with a halt in weapons production only if it could be done "in a manner which would not be to the disadvantage of the U.S." The JCS written opinion of June 16 now argued for comprehensive disarmament rather than Stassen's first-phase formula, reiterating their opinion in a memorandum to Secretary of Defense Charles E. Wilson on June 27: "The First Phase Plan . . . would not diminish those risks and is therefore not suitable as a United States proposal for control of armaments or as a basis for the United States position in international discussions on this subject." Secretary Wilson endorsed these objections in his own memorandum to the president the following day. The DOD felt that all political questions should be settled before any agreement was entered. The Department of State, according to Dulles's 29 June draft memorandum, agreed with the DOD premise that "the present and likely future position, in fact, gives greater protection than any plan that rested upon agreement and supervision."[5]

At the 253rd meeting of the National Security Council, which was held on 30 June, both Eisenhower and Dulles took exception to the Defense Department's all-or-nothing attitude regarding solution of political questions prior to a disarmament agreement. The glimmer of light in this torrent of pessimism had to do with verification. Secretary Dulles argued that in their traditional approach to disarmament the Soviets had always called for controls first and a solution of the inspection problem only afterwards. Dulles proposed to reverse this formula, and had argued in his memorandum on the Stassen plan that "the only phase

4. Assistant for disarmament, special staff study for the president, NSC action no. 1328, May 26, 1955, *FRUS, 1955–57*, XX, 101; assistant for disarmament, special staff study, IV, June 23, 1955, *FRUS, 1955–57*, XX, 131.

5. Atomic Energy Commission, informal notes of meeting of the special staff, June 15, 1955, *FRUS, 1955–57*, XX, 120; secretary of defense, memorandum to the president: "Progress Report on the Control of Armaments," June 28, 1955, *FRUS, 1955–57*, XX, 135; secretary of state, draft memorandum: "Limitation of Armaments," June 29, 1955, *FRUS, 1955–57*, XX, 141.

now to be developed in detail, for present use, should be a phase designed to test out in the most simple way possible the possibilities of limited mutual inspection." At the NSC, Secretary Wilson agreed that the "next step" in dealing with Russia ought to be that the "Iron Curtain should be cracked." One consequent outcome of the June 30 meeting was NSC Action No. 1419-d-1, which ordered Harold Stassen, in consultation with the bureaucracy, to "develop methods of inspection which would be deemed feasible and which would serve to determine what would be acceptable on a reciprocal basis to the United States."[6]

Origins of the Proposal

By virtue of the language regarding the inspection issue in his various progress reports, Harold Stassen can lay claim to being one originator of what became the Open Skies plan. There is another progenitor, however, and a distinct track that led even more explicitly to what Eisenhower presented at the Geneva summit. The proposals on this track in fact arose from American efforts to pursue another theme that was dear to President Eisenhower, psychological warfare.

From his first days in office Ike had been intensely interested in countering Soviet propaganda with positive United States efforts in the field. The issue was larger than mere propaganda, and indeed the Truman NSC had had a unit it called the Psychological Strategy Board (PSB). Eisenhower considered the PSB moribund and abolished it, but he also hired a special assistant, C. D. Jackson of Time-Life, to advise him on the same issues. Jackson left the administration at the end of 1954, at which time Ike appointed Nelson Rockefeller to this post, a position more or less equivalent to Harold Stassen's in disarmament matters. Rockefeller's mandate was to find ways to exploit Soviet vulnerabilities on information, ideology, and international issues, which naturally had a certain foreign-policy content. Rockefeller's role concerned John Foster Dulles, who was a fierce guardian of his own prerogatives as secretary of state.

In the months before the Geneva summit, Rockefeller's staff conceived and organized a "Vulnerabilities Panel" comprising social scien-

6. Secretary of state, draft memorandum: "Limitation of Armaments," June 29, 1955, *FRUS, 1955–57*, XX, 141; National Security Council, memorandum of discussion, 253rd meeting, June 30, 1955, *FRUS, 1955–57*, XX, 146; National Security Council, NSC Action 1419 (d) (1), June 30, 1955, *FRUS, 1955–57*, XX, 155 and n. 154.

tists and former officials under the chairmanship of Walt W. Rostow. The group met on the Marine base at Quantico, Virginia, between 5 and 10 June. It was on the second full day of the conference (7 June), Rostow recalls, that the idea of mutual aerial inspection was raised by academic and former CIA official Max Millikan as a possible option to include in the panel report. Millikan had heard a similar concept discussed at an arms-control seminar at Cambridge. Writes Rostow:

> [The idea] was quickly seized upon and put into our spectrum of proposals. But one member of the group, Hans Speier of RAND, was disturbed. He took [Stefan] Possony and me aside and said that the proposal was dangerous and he would have to inform air intelligence immediately that we were thinking of putting forward the idea. (Possony was a civilian working for air intelligence and also closely associated with Rockefeller's staff.) Neither Possony nor I thought the idea dangerous, even if, as Speier guardedly implied, the United States might be generating plans for unilateral aerial photography of the U.S.S.R.

Mutual inspection stayed in the panel report, albeit with the caveat of a footnote that such a measure would have to be considered carefully.[7]

The Quantico Panel's conclusions were briefed to Nelson Rockefeller and senior administration aides in the evening of 9 June. State Department representatives were conspicuous by their absence, though Rostow quotes telephone notes of Dulles's indicating that his brother, CIA director Allen W. Dulles, who was present at the meeting, had agreed to report back to the secretary on what transpired. Also in attendance was Colonel Andrew J. Goodpaster, President Eisenhower's efficient and ubiquitous staff secretary. The briefing marked the start of a period of several weeks during which Rockefeller sought to gain a hearing for his policy recommendations from the larger bureaucracy.[8]

The verification proposal headed the list of the Quantico Panel's recommendations for action to be taken during the forthcoming Geneva summit. The panel's summary report stated the United States should be prepared to initiate discussions of "a proposed agreement for mutual inspection of military installations, forces, and armaments, without limitations provisions," as well as "a convention insuring the right of aircraft of any nationality to fly over the territory of any country for

7. Walt W. Rostow, *Open Skies: Eisenhower's Proposal of July 21, 1955* (Austin, Tex., 1982), 30.
8. Rostow, *Open Skies*, 44–5.

peaceful purposes." This forerunner to the Open Skies plan, explicitly and in this form, was in circulation during the period in which the Stassen arms-control measures were under consideration in Washington. Though Rostow recalls the period prior to the NSC meeting on 30 June as a "rather sterile interval," it was during this interval that Secretary Dulles came to the conclusion expressed in his official response to the Stassen first-stage program, namely that limited mutual inspection should be the only disarmament measure to be developed in detail at this time. After the Security Council session, moreover, NSC Action 1419 had specifically ordered Stassen to develop his recommendations on feasible methods of inspection in more detail and then report back to the president.[9]

Eisenhower's Secret Knowledge

The disarmament policy debate proceeded within the administration as a whole. Various proposals were suggested to Eisenhower and a small circle around him who had knowledge of a wider range of U.S. government actions. In an exchange with Walt Rostow, Hans Speier alluded to one of the proposals: a covert effort to build the means to photograph Russia from the air. The idea had resonated among intelligence officials, who for years had wrestled with the headaches of an extensive but relatively limited peripheral collection program in Russia. In the space of a year (July 1954–July 1955) the United States had lost four planes in the Far East alone, most recently an RB-47 off Vladivostok. More than forty airmen had disappeared from the reconnaissance squadron rosters.

President Eisenhower also had another recommendation on his desk, from a panel of senior scientists advising on new defense programs. The Technological Capabilities Panel (TCP) reported in February 1955, much of its effort being devoted to such urgent subjects as missiles and air defenses. But one subpanel of this committee delved especially into intelligence matters and in late 1954 went privately to Eisenhower with a proposal for a high-altitude reconnaissance plane capable of flying right over Russia, not merely along its borders. The TCP, also known as the Killian Committee (its chairman was James R. Killian), would have tremendous impact on Eisenhower. The TCP report, titled "Meeting

9. Walt W. Rostow to Nelson D. Rockefeller, with attachment, "Summary of Recommendations Quantico Vulnerabilities Panel," June 10, 1955, *FRUS, 1955–1957*, V, 218; Rostow, *Open Skies*, 44.

the Threat of Surprise Attack," set a path the president followed for the rest of his administration. As the report put it, "We *must* find ways to increase the number of hard facts upon which our intelligence estimates are based, to provide better strategic warning, to minimize surprise in the kind of attack, and to reduce the danger of gross overestimation or underestimation of the threat. To this end we recommend adoption of a vigorous program for the extensive use, in many intelligence procedures, of the most advanced knowledge in science and technology."[10]

In seeking this goal, the Killian Committee made ten key intelligence recommendations, some of which have not been declassified to this day. One recommendation that is known, however, is the TCP's advocacy of Project AUTOMAT, the high-altitude reconnaissance plane also known as the U-2.

The plane would be built as a CIA project, through a special arrangement with Lockheed Aircraft, which set aside a secure plant for the purpose, which became known as the "Skunk Works." Lockheed offered to supply thirty U-2s for a cost of $35 million. Designer Clarence L. Johnson's design put the plane together from off-the-shelf components and plans originated for his earlier F-80 and F-104 aircraft. The Itek Corporation built the airborne cameras. Work on the first prototype elements got underway in September 1954 and was in full swing by late November, when, following Eisenhower's own approval, the interagency Intelligence Advisory Committee gave the program the green light. The biggest design difficulties with Project AUTOMAT revolved around the U-2's large wing surface (making stability a problem), and its high service ceiling (making engine restarts following high altitude flameouts another problem). Nevertheless, the engineering problems were gradually solved.

In the summer of 1955, with the Geneva summit approaching, Project AUTOMAT was in its final stage of prototyping. The U-2 airframe had been built and was being mated to its engines. In early July the initial aircraft was taken apart and shipped by air from the Skunk Works plant to a secret air-test range the CIA and Lockheed had acquired at Groom Lake in the Mojave Desert. It was reassembled there and static engine

10. Technological Capabilities Panel (Killian Committee) of the Science Advisory Committee, Report, "Meeting the Threat of Surprise Attack," February 15, 1955, *FRUS, 1955–1957*, XIX, 54.

test firings were first carried out on 29 July. Project AUTOMAT's first flight would be on 6 August and its first official flight test three days later.

This chronology is important because of the events leading up to the summit, which was to take place during the third week of July. Throughout the period of the design and prototyping of Project AUTO-MAT, President Eisenhower had been receiving regular briefings on the U-2 from Richard M. Bissell Jr., the CIA project manager. The president also had daily intelligence briefings from Andrew Goodpaster, who functioned as the White House contact for Project AUTOMAT and other matters. While the detailed record of president's consideration of the U-2 has yet to be declassified, and indeed may not exist on paper, standard practice would have been for Eisenhower to be briefed on the occasions of key milestones. These would have included the successful U-2 engine tests, the completion of the prototype, and Lockheed's affirmation that the U-2 was ready for flight testing. In particular, the CIA would have needed to apply for approval to move the aircraft test unit to Groom Lake, and that request would have come to Eisenhower in the same time frame as the National Security Council's deliberations on the Stassen proposals and Nelson Rockefeller's circulation of the Quantico Panel report. In the latter connection it is highly significant that Goodpaster, Ike's focal point on the U-2, attended the Quantico presentation of the option for mutual overhead reconnaissance. This evidence indicates that President Eisenhower had Project AUTOMAT at the back of his mind when the NSC was preparing U.S. arms-control positions for Geneva.

Eisenhower's actions during the last few weeks prior to the summit give the impression that the president was laying the groundwork for Open Skies. Ike had talked about missiles and bombers—nuclear delivery systems—at the first NSC presentation by Harold Stassen. At a July 6 news conference he mentioned that theme publicly, saying, "When you get to long-range bombing you need very large machines and very large flying fields from which they take off. Now, those can be detected." Similarly, the president declared, "I don't believe that you could take an extensive guided missile program and conceal it from any decent system of inspection."[11]

Shortly afterwards the president met in his office with Nelson Rocke-

---

11. Stephen E. Ambrose, *Eisenhower: The President* (New York, 1984), 258.

feller, who brought a new paper reiterating several of the Quantico panel's options for Geneva. The heart of this memorandum was an extended treatment of Open Skies:

> I believe that you should give serious consideration to the proposal on the part of the U.S. at the forthcoming conference for an agreement for mutual inspection of military installations, forces and armaments without limitations provisions. This proposal for testing an inspection system before limiting or reducing armaments seems to me to be a step in the direction of meeting all . . . points . . . I cannot see any aspect of it—even if the Soviets accept it, which is highly doubtful—which in any way seriously jeopardizes our security. Instead it would offer many advantages beyond the main one of testing to determine the practicability of an inspection system. Among the collateral advantages are the following:
>
> 1. Regains the initiative in disarmament negotiation; provides us a position in Geneva.
> 2. Helps break down the Iron Curtain.
> 3. Provides us intelligence.
> 4. Poses a difficult decision for the Soviets.
> 5. Focuses on a practical and immediate aspect of disarmament which people in general can understand.
> 6. Exposes the phoniness of the proposed Soviet inspection system—the Korean type that provides for international inspectors at ports, major airfields, etc.
> 7. Demonstrates first hand to the Soviets our greater war potential.[12]

Ike immediately called Foster Dulles and, according to the latter's telephone records, said that "he had just heard of an idea that might open a tiny gate in the disarmament fence." Though Eisenhower was here suggesting he had not previously known of the aerial inspection idea, he was a proven master at bureaucratic maneuvering and knew Dulles would be upset by any hint of prior collusion that had excluded the secretary of state. In any case, Dulles quickly agreed with the idea and promised to have it staffed out, hoping to get it included in the NSC paper on the upcoming summit.[13]

In spite of these conversations, when the Geneva paper (NSC-5524) was submitted to the council on 7 July, Secretary Dulles remained silent regarding the aerial inspection scheme, and the president did not

---

12. Nelson D. Rockefeller, memorandum to the president, July 6, 1955, reprinted in Rostow, *Open Skies*, 134.

13. John Foster Dulles, telephone memorandum, July 6, 1955, ibid., 46.

bring it up either. In the paper's subsequent version, NSC-5524/1 of 11 July, its entire entry on disarmament consisted of a single statement: "The current position of the U.S. with respect to U.S. policy on control of armaments is contained in NSC Action No. 1419." That decision, it will be recalled, taken at NSC on 30 June, had merely called for the bureaucracy to "develop" proposals for arms-control verification.[14]

In the meantime Secretary Dulles went on the offensive against Nelson Rockefeller, complaining to C. D. Jackson about "Rocky" at dinner on 11 July. The following day, when Rockefeller distributed a pamphlet his staff had put together on psychological strategy for Geneva, Dulles exploded: "I said to Mr. Rockefeller that I had grave questions as to the propriety of the President getting this kind of advice from sources outside of the State Department. I said that the Secretary of State was supposed to be the principal adviser of the President with relation to foreign affairs, but that if he was getting advice on the whole gamut of international issues from Mr. Rockefeller, that would put us into a competitive position." Some see Eisenhower as disciplining Dulles and Rockefeller by knocking their heads together like little schoolboys, but Ike refused to discard the Open Skies proposal, which he kept in his hip pocket. When he left for Geneva on 14 July, Dulles went with him; Rockefeller, Stassen, and Admiral Arthur Radford, chairman of the JCS, were sent to Paris, to be out of the way though available for consultation if necessary.[15]

Divorced from the histrionics of personality and historiography, the basic United States position going into Geneva was that mutual inspection should precede concrete measures of disarmament. That was the Americans' response to the Soviet comprehensive proposal of 10 May and was to be antecedent to attempts to negotiate the Stassen first-phase plan. For Dwight D. Eisenhower, inspection meant Open Skies. Secretary Dulles, the Joint Chiefs, Stassen, Rockefeller, and their aides all went on record favoring this option. The main question was presenting the option for maximum psychological advantage. Ike went on to handle that part of it quite well.

14. National Security Council, NSC 5524/1, "Basic U.S. Policy in Relation to Four-Power Negotiations," July 11, 1955, *FRUS, 1955–57*, V, 297.

15. John Foster Dulles, memorandum of conversation, July 12, 1955, ibid., 305; Michael R. Beschloss, *Mayday: The U-2 Affair* (New York, 1986), 99.

Presentation of Open Skies

Although the impression has come down through history that President Eisenhower sprang Open Skies upon the world as a cosmic surprise, in fact he seems to have worked up to the unveiling with considerable care. On Ike's first day in Geneva he hosted a luncheon for the British and French prime ministers and there alluded to his proposal. Eisenhower remarked that "he did not believe that disarmament could be disassociated from inspection," and though inspections alone could not verify nuclear weapons production, "other things could be observed, among these . . . the means of delivery of these weapons." Thus, "We might start off by devising a method of inspection that would be mutually acceptable." In his opening statement to the first plenary session of the summit on 18 July, Eisenhower spoke of "the possibility of frightful surprise attacks and the need for effective mutual inspection." Similarly, at a 20 July breakfast with Anthony Eden, Eisenhower told the British premier that "our Government had been giving very intensive thought" to disarmament and that "the very heart of any such arrangement lay in the efficacy of the inspection system."[16]

The key day for Eisenhower's Geneva deliberations on Open Skies was clearly 20 July. That morning, during the president's breakfast, Rockefeller and Stassen arrived from Paris and were briefed on conference developments. They then drove to Ike's villa, where they met with the president at 10:30 A.M. for almost an hour. Andrew Goodpaster was in attendance. Quite soon thereafter the president went on to host a luncheon for the Russians, and once more he built the stage for his proposal: "The President said a very specific and important question in the disarmament field was that of inspection." He mentioned airfields, long-range bombers, and factories producing guided missiles, and later pressed the point that it was "also necessary to convey a feeling of confidence to the people in general." Eventually returning to the last point, he declared that he "felt the necessary first step was to have a demonstrably effective system of inspection." When Eisenhower asked Soviet marshal Georgi K. Zhukov whether the world could look forward to

16. Department of State, memorandum of conversation at tripartite luncheon, July 17, 1955, *FRUS, 1955–57*, V, 365, 350; Department of State, delegation record of first plenary session, July 18, 1955, *FRUS, 1955–57*, V, 365; Department of State, memorandum of conservation at president's breakfast, July 20, 1955, *FRUS, 1955–57*, V, 400–1.

such a system of inspection, the Russian not only answered in the affirmative but, in response to a further question, said that such an approach would be "entirely possible" (i.e., politically feasible in the Soviet Union).[17]

Before and again after the afternoon plenary of the summit, President Eisenhower huddled with Dulles, Stassen, Radford, and Rockefeller to review the proceedings. The evening session was the vital one, with Ike sitting in an armchair by the fireplace, Dulles at his side. The discussion of Open Skies had now become explicit and detailed, especially with regard to the manner of presentation. Officials urged Eisenhower not to go beyond, even with the British and French, the general allusions to inspection he had already made prior to his formal presentation of Open Skies, for fear some leak might divulge the substance of the plan. Harold Stassen handed out a draft of a speech intended for Ike at the plenary, saying, "this proposal could constitute a splendid opening step in the move toward disarmament." Dulles "thought that from the standpoints of both drama and substance the proposal was very promising and should have a very great effect." Eisenhower remarked, in a 1964 oral history interview, that "the actual decision to make [this] proposal came right after a particular meeting during the Conference. . . . We knew the Soviets wouldn't accept it—we were sure of that. But we took a look and thought it was a good move." The next day, Thursday, 21 July, brought intense anticipation on the American side. One witness was the president's son, army major John S. D. Eisenhower, who was between postings and had been invited along on the summit trip. Major Eisenhower worked as an assistant to Andy Goodpaster, and was standing in Goodpaster's office that morning when Nelson Rockefeller came up to him. "You have *got* to be in the conference his afternoon," Rockefeller told him. "Your Dad is going to throw a bombshell!"[18]

At midmorning, seeking to prepare government subordinates for what was coming, Secretary Dulles sent Washington a cable, DULTE-26. President Eisenhower, Dulles wrote, "may refer to aerial photograph[y] as opening vast new possibilities and may state willingness of US

17. Department of State, memorandum of conversation at president's luncheon, July 20, 1955, *FRUS, 1955–57,* V, 412–3.

18. Office of the staff secretary (Goodpaster), memorandum for the record, July 20, 1955, *FRUS, 1955–57,* V, 428–9; Dwight D. Eisenhower Interview, July 28, 1964, John Foster Dulles Oral History Project, 43, Princeton University; John Eisenhower, *Strictly Personal* (Garden City, N.Y., 1974), 177.

to permit Soviet aerial photography of US provided Soviet willing to let us do same." As Dulles put it, "This challenge may be somewhat of a surprise and have spectacular appearance which will perhaps deprive the Soviet Union of their propaganda advantage in slogan 'ban the bomb.' "[19]

The afternoon plenary session began at the appointed time, 3:35 P.M., with Soviet premier Nikolai A. Bulganin presiding. Several pieces of other conference business were transacted before the Soviets introduced a draft resolution, the latest version of their 10 May disarmament proposal. Then President Eisenhower asked to speak.

In the gallery Nelson Rockefeller turned around and looked at John Eisenhower, who sat behind him. "Now listen. Here it comes," Rocky said. President Eisenhower recalled with surprise (given the importance of the proposal), "I decided to put forward the plan without delay, even without waiting for a final editing of the text." Ike's presentation was therefore partly extemporaneous. Working up to his theme, Eisenhower declared: "No sound and reliable agreement can be made unless it is completely covered by an inspection and reporting system adequate to support every portion of the agreement. The lessons of history teach us that disarmament agreements without adequate reciprocal inspection increase the dangers of war and do not brighten the prospects of peace. Thus, it is my view that the priority attention of our combined study of disarmament should be upon the subject of inspection and reporting." Poignantly, he went on, "I have been searching in my heart and mind for something that I could say here that could convince everyone of the great sincerity of the United States." Then, addressing the Russians directly, "I propose, therefore, that we take a practical step, and we begin an arrangement, very quickly, as between ourselves, immediately." Ike wanted each side to exchange "blueprints" of their military establishments, then the U.S. would provide "ample facilities for aerial reconnaissance, where you can make all the pictures you choose and take them to your own country to study." The Soviet Union would reciprocate. "The successful working out of such a system would do much to develop the mutual confidence which will open wide the avenues of progress for all our peoples."[20]

19. John Foster Dulles, Cable DULTE 26, July 21, 1954, *FRUS, 1955–57*, V, 434.
20. John Eisenhower, *Strictly Personal*, 177; Dwight D. Eisenhower, *The White House Years: Mandate for Change, 1953–1956* (New York, 1963), 619; Department of State, Cable SECTO 63, July 21, 1955, *FRUS, 1955–57*, V, 452–3.

In the audience, Nelson Rockefeller again turned to John Eisenhower, slapped him on the knee, "and gave a triumphant grin." Suddenly the lights flickered and went out. A thunderstorm had cut the power lines, but the delegates, ensconced in their private world of international relations, had been wholly unaware of he tempest outside. President Eisenhower was heard to comment, "Well, I didn't know I would put out the lights with that." It was 4:42 P.M. On the French side of the conference table, Premier Edgar Faure, who would be the next to present remarks to the assembly and who would take a very receptive view of the Open Skies proposal, was startled when the lights dimmed and the air conditioning whirred to a stop. He also recalled that a chair fell over at that instant. Faure turned to an associate and quipped, "These Americans are wonderful organizers—even making the lights go out!" Ike recalled in his memoirs, "As I finished, a most extraordinary natural phenomenon took place. Without warning, and simultaneous with my closing words, the loudest clap of thunder I have ever heard roared into the room, and the conference was plunged into Stygian darkness." Since Ike was a plains boy from Abilene, Kansas, where storms can be fierce indeed, this comment is an impressive gauge of his reaction.[21]

Soviet leader Bulganin made a few positive noises from the podium. Eisenhower quotes Bulganin as saying, "This is a very interesting suggestion. I assure you we'll study it very sympathetically." Of course, the Soviet response would be more important than any other, but this early Bulganin remark was not a good guide. Soon after Premier Faure's speech the delegates broke for the day, after which there was a cocktail party. Ike derided these daily drinking sessions as some kind of international substitute for the British custom of taking tea. Nikita S. Khrushchev, on the other hand, remembers the cocktails as an Eisenhower suggestion meant to end the day on a pleasant note, so that "if there had been any hard feeling or tensions aroused during the day's session, we could wash them away with martinis." At any event, it was during the cocktail hour that the real Russian reaction to Open Skies became evident.[22]

21. John Eisenhower, *Strictly Personal*, 177–8; Cable SECTO 63 (see note 35), July 21, 1955, *FRUS, 1955–57*, V, 452–3; Edgar Faure, "Remarks: Dwight D. Eisenhower and France," paper given at conference "Dwight D. Eisenhower As President," Hofstra University, March 30, 1984; Dwight Eisenhower, *Mandate for Change*, 620–1.

22. Dwight D. Eisenhower Interview, July 20, 1967, Columbia University Oral History Project, 58; Edward Crankshaw, *Khrushchev Remembers*, trans. and ed. Strobe Talbott (New York, 1971), 436.

Assistant secretary of state Robert R. Bowie was standing next to President Eisenhower at the cocktail hour, and they were talking in a group with Khrushchev, Bulganin, and Marshal Zhukov. Bowie recalled that Ike asked the Soviets what they thought of the proposal he had just made. In front of Khrushchev, Bulganin was now noncommittal. Ike then asked Zhukov whether during the war, knowing with certainty (due to such an inspection system) what weapons the enemy had would not have given him much greater confidence. Before Zhukov could answer, Khrushchev interrupted. "I don't agree with our chairman [Bulganin]," Khrushchev declared, "Your proposal is nothing but a spy thing, an intelligence mission, and we'll have none of it."[23]

Charles E. Bohlen, American ambassador to the Soviet Union, was also standing with the group. Bohlen recorded another version of the exchange in a memorandum that night. Except that it places Soviet foreign minister Vyacheslav Molotov in the circle in place of Bulganin, Bohlen's account confirms these retrospective recollections. Khrushchev was "extremely frank" and "polite throughout" but there was a hard edge to what he said. The Russians, reported Bohlen, "said it would not help the cause of disarmament or security at all but would merely mean that the intelligence services of the two countries would have confirmation of the present fragmentary information that they possessed."[24]

Khrushchev himself does not report any of these exchanges in his own memoirs. He does remember Eisenhower introducing him to Nelson Rockefeller during one of these cocktail hours. "There was nothing special about him," recalls Khrushchev. "He was dressed fairly democratically and was the sort of man who didn't make much of an impression one way or the other."[25] Khrushchev did not know that Rockefeller's propaganda suggestions had just scored heavily at his own expense.

Fragments of History

President Eisenhower did not use the term *Open Skies* in his presentation or indeed at the Geneva summit. The press and others soon en-

23. Eisenhower, Columbia Oral History, 58.

24. Department of State, memorandum of conversation at buffet, July 21, 1955 (USDel/ MC/15), *FRUS, 1955–57*, V, 456. Also see Bohlen's own account in Charles E. Bohlen, *Witness to History, 1929–1969* (New York, 1973), 382–9.

25. Eisenhower, Columbia Oral History, 60.

dowed the plan with the name that has come down through history. As expected, the Russians never accepted Open Skies, but the United States gained an advantage in world public opinion by offering to reveal its own military secrets through this mechanism. The major short-term gain was that the offer successfully supplanted discussion of other disarmament proposals at Geneva. Eisenhower recorded a further gain in knowledge, which was of direct benefit to him: The exchange with Khrushchev had revealed who was the real leader of the Soviet Union. Henceforth President Eisenhower constructed U.S. policy on the assumption that Nikita Khrushchev was the true interested party on the other side.

These gains were genuine enough, but they were also transitory. Yet the international situation, at least with respect to disarmament, was such that there existed potential for more lasting developments. The comprehensive disarmament proposals introduced by the West in 1954 and the Soviets in 1955 had the two sides at least talking the same language. Soviet testing of a thermonuclear weapon in 1955, bringing this technology to both sides in the cold war, helped energize peace movements. The agreement on the Austrian State Treaty, together with the "spirit of Geneva," opened a brief window of détente amid cold-war hostilities. It is unfortunate that this window was not used to float something of more enduring value than Open Skies.

One can argue that agreement on general, complete disarmament was not politically possible in the United States at this time. Certainly the U.S. military, in pursuit of its own programs, would have resisted real disarmament. In the throes of McCarthyism, there would have been difficulties securing agreement among the general polity as well. But the art of leadership lies in meeting such challenges. The basic fact is that general disarmament was not on the table in 1955 because of the Eisenhower administration's commitment to "rollback," a vision of cold war anti-Communism. Yet the difficulties the United States has encountered in recent years in reducing its military establishment, with the cold war over and no adversary in sight, makes it lamentable that the entrenchment of cold-war institutions was not curbed at a much earlier date. That is one tragedy of Open Skies.

On another level, the presentation of the Open Skies proposal at the Geneva summit represented a success for Dwight Eisenhower, the "hidden hand" president. Eisenhower succeeded in bringing forward a proposal for a confidence-building measure in spite of opposition from many quarters to those who had originated the concept. Ike also deserves some credit for offering the Russians an opportunity to do something (aerial photography) on a bilateral basis that he knew he himself was going to be able to do anyway, through the U-2, unilaterally. Asked in 1967 just who had crafted the Open Skies offer, the former president replied, "I think I was probably more responsible than anyone else."[26]

In spite of his own distaste for presidential special assistants Rockefeller and Stassen, John Foster Dulles also learned something from Open Skies. Later in 1955, complaining to his own staff of the seeming inability of the State Department to produce new ideas in foreign policy, Dulles held up Open Skies as an example of the kind of original thinking he wanted. This feeling may have had some impact on the secretary's receptivity three years later to proposals for a moratorium on atmospheric nuclear testing.

Perhaps the greatest real international benefit of Open Skies was its contribution to the spirit of Geneva. Despite the plan's origin as a gambit in psychological warfare, the simple idea that the United States might be willing to reveal secrets to reduce global tensions did build some confidence even though the proposal was never accepted or carried out. The Austrian State Treaty was undoubtedly a much greater component in building the "spirit," but Open Skies played a part as well. It remained to statesmen to capitalize on the results of the Geneva summit, an effort that would be crippled by the continuing international problems over the division of Germany.

26. Ibid.

East-West Trade at the Geneva Summit

ROBERT MARK SPAULDING

Introduction

As plans for a four-power summit meeting took shape in the spring and summer of 1955, anyone intimately acquainted with East-West trade policy debates as they had evolved within the United States, inside the entire Western alliance, and across divided Europe in the preceding years must have viewed the impending summit discussion of "East-West contacts," including trade, with some trepidation. Over the previous seven years, East-West trade questions had repeatedly demonstrated a singular ability to bring forth discordant views at every level: between East and West, within the Western alliance, and inside Western governments. Contrary to all expectations, however, East-West trade never developed as a substantive issue at the Geneva heads-of-government conference. This paper explains that unexpected scenario as the result of the power struggle in the Kremlin and uncertainty over the future course of Soviet economic policy. It concludes by setting the events of 1955 in the longer context of Soviet trade and trade policy viewed from the early 1950s into the early 1960s.

Managing Trade before the Geneva Conference

Unlike the core issues of military security, for which a widely perceived Soviet threat forged a trans-Atlantic consensus on the broad outlines of collective defense, the question of collective economic action against the Soviet bloc had not enjoyed any general agreement in the West prior to Geneva. The underlying and intractable source of difficulty lay in the fundamental divergence of Western European and American opinion on the extent to which exports from the West should be controlled. That story has been told often enough to require only a summary review here.[1]

In 1948–1949 the Western Europeans had willingly agreed to the establishment of a pan-Western export control program administered by the "Coordinating Committee" (CoCom). In the wake of Korean hostilities, the Western Europeans subsequently agreed to a significant expansion of the control program, in the autumn of 1950. By 1951 they felt that Western embargo policy had gone quite far enough, both in the extent of export controls and in the degree of pressure that the United States was exerting on Western Europe to further expand the program. In January 1951 the Danish deputy to NATO expressed his country's concern about Western moves "toward economic warfare." Six months later, Oliver Franks of the British embassy in Washington told the State Department the British were "understandably afraid of embarking on a 'slippery slope' of being called upon to take one action after another in this field."[2]

Four years later the British were still making the same point, that the "basic British position [was] averse to any extension [of] controls [that were] not [an] absolutely clear strategic necessity." Similarly, the U.S. State Department reminded Eisenhower's Committee on Foreign Economic Policy that "our major partners in East-West trade controls have always been most reluctant to adopt measures which they would regard as being in the nature of economic warfare against the peoples of the Communist bloc."[3]

As a further complication, neither the Truman nor the Eisenhower administrations, both of whom were deeply divided on this issue, could offer a consensus response to Western Europe's cautious and limited cooperation. In the Truman administration, Commerce Secretary Sawyer headed a hard-line group favoring greatly expanded Western European controls on trade with the Soviets. In the first term of the Eisenhower presidency, opponents of East-West trade gathered in Charles Wilson's

1. For accounts of export control policy in these early years, see Robert Mark Spaulding, "Eisenhower and Export Control Policy, 1953–1955," *Diplomatic History*, XVII (Spring 1993), 223–49, and the literature cited therein.

2. Spofford (U.S. deputy special representative on the North Atlantic Council) to secretary of state, 18 January 1951, *FRUS, 1951*, I, 1006; Perkins (assistant secretary of state for European affairs), memorandum of conversation, June 5, 1951, ibid., 1087.

3. Aldrich, telegram from U.S. embassy in U.K. to Department of State, 28 June 1955, *FRUS, 1955–57*, X, 238; Thorsten Kalijarvi (assistant secretary of state for economic affairs), memorandum, July 12, 1955, ibid., 243.

Department of Defense and in Allen Dulles's CIA. As late as February 1955 Joseph M. Dodge, chairman of the Council of Foreign Economic Policy (which Eisenhower hoped would emerge as the interdepartmental forum for policy decisions on East-West trade), argued that when trading with the Soviet bloc "any contribution through trade to improved living standards, no matter what its nature, becomes a direct contribution to military power and the industrialization that supports it."[4] That hard-line view was heartily supported by the deputy director of intelligence at the CIA, Robert Amory Jr., who agreed that "anything, e.g., a textile spinning frame or shoe machine equipment, which contributes to their [Soviet] industrial potential contributes to their military potential and any finished product frees their basic machinery to make end-items enhancing their military potential." Similar views were expressed by Deputy Assistant Secretary of Defense for International Security Affairs A. C. Davis, who thought it "clear that the entire communist economy should logically be considered in any free world policy aimed at limiting the expansion of military power in the communist bloc." As a result of this line of analysis, Davis urged "increased rather than relaxed, efforts" in bringing about "any delay in Soviet industrial expansion."[5] These were the voices that did indeed desire to lead the Allied governments down the slippery slope of economic warfare against the entire economy of the full Soviet bloc.

On the other hand, both administrations contained articulate East-West trade moderates willing to consider somewhat less stringent export controls if these would ensure genuine Western European cooperation on the issue. In the Truman years, Dean Acheson advanced this difficult argument, often with disappointing results. After 1953 it was the president himself who insisted on greater understanding for the Western European position and, over the initial objections of many NSC members, initiated a "moderate relaxation" of Western export controls. Even after Eisenhower's initial successes in this area, U.S. and Western European views remained incongruous. Differences over exports of gen-

4. Dodge (chairman of Council on Foreign Economic Policy), memorandum, 7 February 1955, *FRUS, 1955–1957*, X, 216. Dodge's hard-line views on East-West trade diverged sharply form those held by Eisenhower, and this divergence played no small role in Dodge's being replaced as CFEP chairman by Clarence B. Randall in July 1956. Not surprisingly, Randall's CFEP subsequently endorsed Eisenhower's more relaxed policies on East-West trade.

5. Memorandum from the deputy director of intelligence, Central Intelligence Agency, 10 February 1955, *FRUS, 1955–1957*, X, 218; memorandum from the deputy assistant secretary of defense for international security affairs, 23 February 1955, ibid., X, 222.

erators and copper wire as well as the appropriate degree of shipping
controls remained specific issues of Western European dissatisfaction in
the spring of 1955.[6]

In the United States, congressional action made bureaucratic debates
on East-West trade policy more complicated and more emotional for
both the Truman and Eisenhower administrations. Although the Truman administration had adopted new, more rigorous East-West trade
policies with the approval of NSC 104/2 in April 1951, Congress felt
compelled to make its own statement by passing the Kem amendment
and the Battle Act in June and October 1951. These acts directly linked
continued U.S. economic aid for Europe to Western European compliance with American wishes in export-control policy. The legislation
changed the export-control debate and further complicated the task of
persuading the Europeans to accede to U.S. requests. Congress, with its
emotionally charged voice, became a de facto participant in negotiations, and public sensitivity to the East-West trade issues increased dramatically in both Europe and America. Congressional action unleashed
a storm of indignation in Western Europe that never fully subsided.[7]

Thereafter, both administrations spent considerable time and energy
fending off congressional actions perceived as intrusions into presidential direction of foreign policy. In March 1955 the CFEP warned the NSC
that if executive departments did not use extreme caution in explaining
economic defense policies to the Congress, then "the executive may
find the legislative branch responding to an unintended but implicit invitation to pronounce policy for the executive in the very field of gov-
ernmental operations in which such rigid and insensitive formulation
of policy is most to be avoided." Subsequently, Undersecretary of State
Herbert Hoover Jr. characterized the hard-line and highly critical report
of the McClellan Permanent Subcommittee on Investigation into East-
West Trade in Strategic Materials as motivated by "election year politics, misunderstanding of the facts, or anti-foreign bias."[8]

6. These differences were not resolved by several exchanges between Foster Dulles and
Anthony Eden and between Harold Stassen (director of the Foreign Operations Administra-
tion) and Peter Thorneycroft (president of the British Board of Trade). See, for example,
State Department telegram to embassy in U.K., 23 February 1955, *FRUS, 1955–1957*,
X, 223.

7. See "Senator Kem's Monster," *Economist*, 10 June 1951. Throughout 1951, the *Economist, Neue Zürcher Zeitung, Le Monde, Wirtschaftsdienst*, and other leading European
papers published a steady stream of criticism of the Kem amendment and the Battle Act.

8. Report by the steering committee of the Council on Foreign Economic Policy, 24
March 1955, *FRUS, 1955–1957*, X, 232; memorandum from undersecretary of state, 2 April
1955, ibid., 324.

Cold-war congressional grandstanding spurred media sensationalism and a heightened public sensitivity to allegations that American corporations or Allied governments were trading with the Reds. Eisenhower described with considerable understatement the "seriousness" of "domestic political considerations" when approaching these issues, but he also referred impatiently to public "hysteria" as a major complicating factor.[9]

The lack of any way to demonstrate that these contentious Western policies were in fact retarding the war potential of the Soviet bloc nations provided a final element of frustration in the trade-policy debate. Even trade-policy hawks like Amory admitted that "it is hard to see how any control program can seriously impair Soviet might." Similarly, Allen Dulles concluded for members of the NSC that "current controls on trade between the West and the Soviet bloc did not impose any serious deterrent to the industrial growth or military capabilities of the Soviet bloc." In the State Department, Assistant Secretary of State for Economic Affairs Samuel Waugh chose to emphasize the "absence of satisfactory intelligence" and the resultant impossibility of assessing the contribution of individual commodities to the Soviet bloc's war or civilian economy.[10]

With so many crosscurrents of dissension, it is perhaps not surprising that the problems associated with formulating a common Western policy toward trade with the Soviet bloc brought forth responses that were far more emotional that those elicited by other, perhaps more critical, issues. After just one year in office, President Eisenhower began to show "great impatience and exasperation" with the topic; in July 1955 he moaned that "the topic of East-West trade seemed to him to arise at nearly every meeting of the National Security Council." Secretary of State John Foster Dulles characterized some aspects of the issue as "ridiculous." Secretary of Defense Charles Wilson, whose views on this subject Eisenhower had already labeled "absurd," admitted that the Defense Department was "a little emotional on this matter of East-West Trade" and that he himself was "burned-up" by the movement of some

9. Memorandum of discussion, 281st meeting of the National Security Council, 5 April 1955, *FRUS, 1955–1957*, X, 333.

10. Amory, memorandum, 10 February 1955, *FRUS, 1955–1957*, X, 218; discussion at 282d meeting of the National Security Council, 26 April 1956, ibid., 346; Waugh, memorandum, 21 February 1955, ibid., 220.

strategic commodities into the Soviet bloc. In sum, no issue had more severely vexed the American managers of the Western alliance in the years prior to Geneva than the "controversial, emotional, and important matter" of establishing a common Western program for controlling trade with the Soviets.[11]

Prospects for Geneva

The difficulties of managing East-West trade policy issues in the past meant that any discussion of these questions at the Geneva summit would involve significant risk for the Western governments, particularly the United States. But because the stated purpose of the meeting was to reduce international tensions, it was impossible to exclude a discussion of trade between the two systems. Commercial contacts had long been a classic method of building overlapping interests. Furthermore, as part of their materialist view of the world, the Soviets had traditionally asked for increased trade and trade credits as proof of peaceful intentions toward the USSR.

Criticism of Western trade controls had long since become a mainstay of Soviet cold-war propaganda. As the first summit meeting since the introduction of strategic export controls by the West, Geneva would provide the most visible platform to date for Soviet recriminations.[12] With trade policies rather unavoidably open for discussion, Western heads of state could expect at least a few paragraphs of Soviet accusations directed against the CoCom export control system. The foreseeable Soviet propaganda attack would be ostensibly supported by recent developments in Soviet foreign economic policies. Since 1952, when Moscow had hosted a "World Economic Conference," the Soviets had increasingly used selective trade actions in Western Europe, and even more so in the less developed world, to demonstrate the advantages of

11. Discussion, 188th meeting of the National Security Council, 11 March 1954, *FRUS, 1952–54*, I, 1108–16; discussion, 254th meeting of the National Security Council, 7 July 1955, *FRUS, 1955–1957*, X, 240; discussion, 281st Meeting of the National Security Council, 5 April 1955, ibid., 331–2; Steven Ambrose, *Eisenhower*, vol. 2, *The President* (New York, 1984), 39; executive secretary of the Commission on Foreign Economic Policy to the members of the commission, 15 December 1953, *FRUS, 1952–1954*, I, 1066.

12. Just prior to the Geneva summit, Molotov used the tenth anniversary meeting of the United Nations in San Francisco on 22 June 1955 to deliver another attack on western export controls. *New York Times*, 23 June 1955.

peaceful cooperation with the Soviet bloc.[13] In Western Europe, the Soviet trade offensive was particularly effective with the broad mass of pubic and business opinion, which knew very little about the structure and performance of the Soviet bloc economy.

Far more troubling than any Soviet trade tirade by itself was the clear possibility that Soviet criticisms of Western export restrictions might find some resonance with the British or French governments. Eisenhower was "sure" that East-West trade would come up at the conference and worried that this was a "problem where we had wide differences with our allies." At the 7 July 1955 meeting of the NSC, Eisenhower explicitly warned council members that at Geneva "in the area of East-West trade we might find ourselves on one side of the argument while our allies and the Soviets were on the other."[14] These concerns arose out of Eisenhower's acquaintance with trade issues as a long-standing point of controversy within the Western alliance.

Fortunately for the West, during a relatively brief period in the first half of 1955, U.S.-European differences over trade with the East had been at their lowest level in years. The most fundamental reason for this was that the economic argument for increased trade with the Soviet bloc had evaporated in the economic boom spreading across Western Europe. In West Germany, for example, both the foreign-policy bureaucracy and better-informed elements of the private sector (grouped in the Federal Association of German Industry's "Eastern Committee") had concluded that, from the economic perspective, the FRG did not need an economic agreement with the Soviets.[15] With West German industry

13. Dulles characterized Soviet actions as "raising hell with us by their purchase of surpluses from the underdeveloped countries." Discussion, 281st meeting of the National Security Council, 5 April 1955, *FRUS, 1955–1957*, X, 333. Between 1953 and 1957, virtually all elements of the U.S. foreign policy bureaucracy and corresponding elements in other western governments referred to a Soviet "economic offensive" or a "trade offensive."

14. Discussion, 249th meeting of the National Security Council, 19 May 1955, *FRUS, 1955–1957*, V, 184; discussion, 254th meeting of NSC, ibid., X, 240. For Dulles, who deeply feared "some slip of the allies" at Geneva, Eisenhower's warning must have produced no little anxiety; see C. D. Jackson's notes on dinner conversation with Dulles, 11 July 1955, ibid., V, 304.

15. Erhard stated that "the current economic situation [in the FRG] is characterized by full employment. With that, there is no economic motive for making concessions," Erhard to Adenauer, 25 August 1955, File 655, Bestand B 136, Bundesarchiv (hereafter, BA), B136/655. The West German foreign office offered a similar assessment: "In the short run, there is from the purely economic perspective no special interest in intensifying trade relations with the Soviet Union. In the long run, the Soviet Union could gain some importance as an 'evening-out' [of cyclic fluctuations] market." Report of 10 August 1955, File 96, Bestand 413.85.00, Politisches Archive des Auswärtigen Amts (hereafter, PAAA), 413.85.00/96.

operating at near capacity and at full employment, it was actually questionable whether significant Soviet orders for industrial equipment could even be accommodated.[16] Members of the Eastern Committee admitted that a significant increase in total exports from the FRG was not possible and that "a shift in trade relations to the detriment of new markets won since the war was not economically justified." A month later, industrial leaders acknowledged that the West German machine-building industry had additional industrial capacity for Soviet orders but that obtaining and holding the corresponding number of additional workers would be "exceedingly difficult."[17] A number of other Western European countries with labor shortages faced the same constraints.[18]

On the import side, West German industry had interest in Soviet raw iron, nickel, and manganese ores, timber, anthracite coal, and oil. Here, all Western European countries faced the question of how they might import substantially increased quantities of goods from the East without reducing the imports from the West, which ultimately was the means of securing foreign markets for European exports.[19]

Beyond these considerations, the failure of the Soviet market to develop after the "moderate relaxation" of Western export controls in 1954 had already aroused suspicions that the Soviet economy perhaps was not capable of greatly expanded trade with the West. In September 1953 the West German foreign office reminded its managers that well

16. Erhard noted that the "labor force and capacity limit our room for additional foreign economic activity. Trade agreements, except in special cases, must be seen as sacrifices or at least as concessions" (Erhard to Adenauer, 25 August 1955, BA B 136/655). Similarly, Scherpenberg stated on 8 August: "In the current economic circumstance of the Federal Republic, a large-scale economic agreement with the Soviets would require extraordinary exertions on the German side and would be by no means purely beneficial for us" (PAAA, 413.85/96).

17. Scherpenberg, Reinhardt, et al., meeting with the Eastern Committee on "Problems of Future Economic Relations with the Soviet Union," 18 July 1955, File 1, Bestand Ostausschuss, Archiv des Bundesverbands deutscher Industrie (hereinafter cited as BdI), OA/1; Lupin memorandum, 19 August 1955, PAAA, 413.85.00/110.

18. In 1953 British unemployment fell below 2 percent, and in the period after 1955 it hovered just above 1 percent; in 1954 unemployment in the Netherlands fell below 2 percent, and in 1956 it was below 1 percent; in Norway unemployment ranged from 2–3 percent for most of the decade. B. R. Mitchell, *European Historical Statistics, 1750–1970,* abridged ed. (New York, 1978), 67–8.

19. Carnap notes on meeting of Wolff et al. with members of the Foreign Office, 29 June 1955, BdI, OA/1; Maltzan on "The Question of East-West Trade," August 1954, BA B 136/7808. An additional concern was avoiding any significant degree of West German "dependence" on Soviet materials; see, for example, Hallstein's questions at the interministerial meeting of 2 August 1955, PAAA, 413.85.00/110.

before the embargo had begun to affect trade, Eastern Europe had not been able to deliver even half of the $3 billion in exports to the Western countries called for by the Marshall Plan. The "decline in agricultural production and the falling-off of earlier export possibilities," the "reckless industrialization and one-sided preference for heavy industry," and the "integration of the Eastern bloc countries" combined to drastically reduce Eastern European ability to trade with the West. Gradually the Germans and other Western Europeans came to realize that the "major difficulties" in East-West trade were not caused by the embargo rules, but rather by the "insufficient export abilities or export willingness" of Soviet bloc countries. Even "complete freedom of trade" after the embargo could not restore the old trade volume.[20] In the United States, Edward Doherty's Division of Functional Intelligence in the State Department reported shortly before Geneva that "there is evidence to suggest that the lack of foreign exchange may have inhibited USSR trade with the West as much as our export controls." Not surprisingly, earlier government and private-sector visions of a substantial revival of East-West trade had faded. Speaking for a number of leading West German industrialists in the Eastern Committee, Otto Wolff von Amerongen and Hans Reuter of the corporation DEMAG told Adenauer they approached East-West trade issues "without any great illusions about the scale or success of trade with the Eastern bloc."[21]

From the Western perspective, trade with the East grew at depressingly slow rates in the years immediately following the 1954 embargo revisions. For eight major Western European economies in the period 1947–1949, trade with Eastern Europe accounted for an average of 3 percent of total exports at this time and 4.4 percent of total imports. In 1956, trade with Eastern Europe made up only 2.8 percent of Western Europe's total exports and the same for imports, a meager increase of 0.3

20. Foreign Office commercial affairs department to all diplomatic officers, 9 March 1953, PAAA, 311.22/1; Maltzan to the Parliamentary Council for Trade Agreements, 19 January 1954, BA B 102/5933. Maltzan wrote similarly and at greater length in his draft article "On the Question of East-West Trade," August 1954, BA B 136/7808.

21. Memorandum . . . to . . . Armstrong, 24 June 1955, FRUS, 1955–1957, X, 237; Wolff to Direktor Carl Haiblen (Felten & Guilleaume) et al., 24 June 1954. BdI, OA/1. The similarity of Wolff's statement to Maltzan's formulation from August 1954 (that the federal government "has no illusions about the possibilities of a rapid increase" in East-West trade) shows the high degree of genuine consensus between the government and the private sector in evaluating the potential of the Eastern trade. See Maltzan's draft article "On the Question of East-West Trade," August 1954, BA B 136/7808.

percent for exports and 0.8 percent for imports since the peak of embargo in 1952.[22] Those numbers reflect how successfully the Western Europeans had reconstructed their export economies around Western Europe and the Americas. In the spring of 1956 Erhard remarked to a group of leading German industrialists that sales to the East were "interesting, but not necessary in order to achieve a healthy economic foundation."[23] With Western European hopes for increased trade with the Soviets diminished, the U.S. government understood very well that "except in the case of Japan, the objections of other friendly governments to the trade controls now are based primarily on political, rather than economic reasons."[24]

Politically, the first half of 1955 saw a relative muting of well-known U.S.–Western European differences over trade policies, which occurred between two periods of rather contentious intra-alliance exchanges on these issues. Serious friction with the Western Europeans had been relieved just recently with Eisenhower's initiative for a "gradual and moderate relaxation" of export controls, as the CFEP's steering committee noted in March 1955: "Concerning Eastern Europe, we are now relatively free of outside pressure for change in the controls. As already noted, the revisions just accomplished have relieved most of the international frictions that had been developing over control policy, and the Paris committees will be preoccupied for several months more with the disposition of residual problems of last year's review. The new enforcement measures are just taking hold, and are still being developed, and a period of experiences will be needed before stock can be taken of their adequacy."[25] The next serious crisis in the Western export control pro-

22. An average of the figures for Belgium-Luxembourg, France, West Germany, Italy, Netherlands, Denmark, Norway, and United Kingdom as given in Gunnar Adler-Karlsson, *Western Economic Warfare, 1947–1967* (Stockholm, 1968), 48–9, and United States Senate Committee on Foreign Relations, *A Background Study on East-West Trade*, 89th Cong., 1st Sess., April 1965, pp. 2–5. Both of these publications base their figures on United Nations data, primarily the annual *Economic Survey for Europe* and the *Yearbook of National Account Statistics*.

23. Erhard's assessment regarding the "Russian business" conforms almost identically with that of the German Chamber of Commerce, namely that it remains "interesting" even if "one has no illusions regarding it." German Chamber of Commerce (Altenburg) to Carnap, 8 June1954, BdI, OA/1.

24. Thorsten V. Kalijarvi, summary of a comprehensive review of economic defense policy by the CFEP's interagency task force, 12 July 1955, *FRUS, 1955–1957*, X, 243.

25. 24 March 1955, *FRUS, 1955–1957*, X, 230. Similarly, Kalijarvi felt these was no "immediate urgency" for changes in export controls (25 March, ibid., X, 234).

244 Robert Mark Spaulding

gram—that over the "China differential"—did not become acute until December 1955, when the British stated their intention to dismantle the differential unilaterally beginning in January 1956. Located between the 1954 friction over trade controls toward Eastern Europe and the 1956 crisis over controls toward the PRC, the first half of 1955 thus passed as a brief period of relatively little discord in this generally contentious field.

This mixed background of economic and political developments made it virtually impossible to envision how the East-West trade issue might play itself out at Geneva. Despite the negative risks associated with that uncertainty, at least some members of the U.S. delegation, Foster Dulles in particular, were eager to raise trade issues with Soviets. Convinced that economic difficulties underlay the Soviet desire to reduce tensions by meeting at Geneva, Dulles expected that promises of increased Western trade could be wielded by the United States with some success. Just before the summit meeting Dulles told the NSC that "it was his own feeling that our willingness to relax our trade controls was a strong negotiating card for us vis-à-vis the Soviets." According to Doherty at Functional Intelligence in the State Department, "other senior government officials consider Western trade controls a valuable trump card in the forthcoming negotiations"; he explicitly cited "senior officials in the departments of Commerce, Defense, and the Joint Chiefs of Staff." At its meeting on 7 July, the NSC debated whether the United Stated ought to offer increased trade in nonstrategic goods merely because the Soviets were also willing to increase this trade or whether instead the Soviets should be required to show willingness "to ameliorate the fundamental sources of tension between East and West." In Paris, the French government had expressed to the working group of Western governments the hope that an "expansion of East-West trade would play [an] important part in breaking [the] satellites from Soviet grip." A working-group subcommittee busily prepared a position paper on East-West trade.[26]

In contrast, Doherty's Functional Intelligence Division felt that "the Russians would be unwilling to make any but the most minor conces-

26. Discussion, 254th meeting of the NSC, 7 July 1955, *FRUS, 1955–1957*, X, 240. Doherty memorandum, 24 June 1955, ibid., 236; discussion, 254th meeting of the NSC, 7 July 1955, ibid., 239–40; U.S. delegation to Paris working group, telegram, 9 July 1955, ibid., V, 313. Dulles expanded on his comments at the NSC meeting at the State Department meeting of 11 August 1955. Ibid., 252 ff.

sions to obtain either a relaxation of Western trade controls or surplus agricultural commodities." Allen Dulles rated "expansion of East-West trade" as a "secondary issue" for the Soviets.[27]

Toward the end of preparations for Geneva, Eisenhower told the NSC that presenting the Soviets with a U.S. position on East-West trade issues would have to be "played by ear" at the conference. The president went on to conclude breezily that because East-West trade issues had been discussed so frequently by the NSC "there was not the slightest danger of making a mistake in this area."[28]

At Geneva

Oddly, East-West trade never emerged as a topic of extended discussion at Geneva. French premier Edgar Faure first raised the subject of "economic cooperation" in connection with disarmament in his opening statement on 18 July. On 22 July Eisenhower spoke directly to the East-West trade issue and export controls by suggesting that both sides ought to work to "create conditions in which unnecessary restrictions on trade would be progressively eliminated." Later that day Eden declared flatly that Britain would "welcome an expansion of the existing channels of trade between East and West."[29]

Predictably, Bulganin's opening statement criticized Western export-control policies as "artificial restrictions" on trade and went on to label them as "one of the serious obstacles to the relaxation of international tensions." Interestingly, although Bulganin urged the conference to "pay due attention to the problem of strengthening economic ties . . . and in particular to the development of trade," the Soviets never went beyond that initial general declaration.[30] Eden's statement had been a clear invitation for Soviet proposals on how acceptable trade might be expanded; Eisenhower had offered the possibility of loosened export restrictions. But the Soviet delegation declined to pursue these potential openings.

Because the Soviets did not respond to Western statements on trade,

27. Doherty, memorandum, 24 June 1955, *FRUS, 1955–1957,* X, 237; Allen Dulles, memorandum, 1 July 1955, ibid., V, 252.
28. Discussion, 254th meeting of the NSC, 7 July 1955, *FRUS, 1955–1957,* X, 239–40.
29. U.S. Department of State, *The Geneva Conference of Heads of Government* (Washington, D.C., 1955), 29, 64, 66.
30. Ibid., 42.

the issue was virtually excluded from immediate postconference assessments of the summit. Eisenhower barely mentioned the topic during his 25 July radio-television address, saying only "we talked about peaceful trade" and even this was an exaggeration.[31]

Assessing East-West Trade at Geneva

At present, we might best understand Soviet behavior regarding East-West trade at Geneva by viewing it in the context of two other sets of major international negotiations conducted with the Soviets in the middle of 1955: the Adenauer negotiations in Moscow in September and the second Geneva meeting, the conference of foreign ministers, in October and November.[32]

As Adenauer prepared for negotiations in Moscow, almost all elements of the West German foreign-policy bureaucracy thought that Soviets' economic difficulties played a major role in their desire to normalize relations with the FRG.[33] Adenauer himself was convinced that "the Soviet government endeavored to establish diplomatic relations with us in the special hope of thereby being able to expand their trade relations with us."[34] Because the Federal Association of German

31. U.S. Department of State, *The Geneva Conference of Heads of Government*, 86. On 9 August the State Department summarized to all diplomatic missions in Europe that "the specific subject of East-West trade was not discussed during the Conference of the Heads of Government in Geneva." *FRUS, 1955–1957*, X, 245.

32. As of this writing in December 1995, a host of problems in Moscow have limited Western attempts to explicate Soviet foreign economic policy decisions with new archival material from the trade policy section of the Foreign Ministry and from the Central Committee.

33. The foreign office briefing paper "German/Russian Economic Negotiations" (in Moscow) opened with a pessimistic assessment of the "economic situation in the Soviet Union" and went on to discuss at several points how the Soviets might use increased trade with FRG to improve their domestic economic conditions (PAAA, 413.85.00/96). Erhard mentioned the "difficult [economic] situation in the East" in his 25 August letter to Adenauer, offering thoughts on the interplay of "economic policy" and "political goals" in the upcoming negotiations (BA B 136/655). See also Khrushchev's own statements that in the mid-1950s Soviet machine tools were not of sufficient quality to develop the Soviet oil and gas industries and imports were needed (Nikita S. Khrushchev, *Khrushchev Remembers: The Glasnost Tapes*, trans. and ed. Jerrold L. Schechter and Vyacheslav V. Luchkov [Boston, 1990], 110–1).

34. Adenauer, *Erinnerungen, 1953–1955* (Stuttgart, 1966), 553. Quite possibly, Dulles had acquired his view on the importance of trade to the Soviets from Adenauer during the chancellor's June 1955 visit to the United States. In a 17 June conversation with Dulles on the upcoming summit, Adenauer urged Western leaders to "judge the Soviet situation in light of whether they will be able to overcome their economic and agricultural difficulties." *FRUS, 1955–1957*, V, 235.

Industry's "Eastern Committee" had been conducting informal trade negotiations with the Soviets for almost three years, it was widely assumed on the West German side that those economic negotiations would now fall in line with political discussions in Moscow. The foreign office saw the overlapping of commercial and political discussion as an opening for the use of economic diplomacy: "Within the framework of the other questions to be discussed [in Moscow], the conclusion of an [economic] agreement suitable to the Soviets is an important negotiating tool held by the Federal Republic."[35]

Detailed suggestions for the use of West German economic and financial strength to bring forth Soviet political concessions came from economics minister Erhard. He was convinced that "economic concessions . . . carry substantial weight" in Soviet calculations, and he understood that "our present state of economic development puts us in the position to offer significant economic compensation for important political concessions." Erhard suggested that Adenauer could offer "generous export credits, perhaps even in the form of transferable DM." In exchange, the FRG would demand the "fulfillment of genuine political demands in the direction of reunification"—specifically, free access to West Berlin in the form of international road and rail connections; creation of an all-German court for human rights; free circulation of books and newspapers; the right to travel between East and West Germany; and full freedom for the churches.[36]

Much to the surprise of the Germans, substantive trade talks with the Soviets never emerged in the course of the five-day Moscow visit. The Soviets offered the usual platitudes about the mutual gains that would result from closer economic relations but consistently refused to get involved in concrete discussions. On 10 September, Hallstein waved some economic bait in a short speech devoted to the advantages to be had from a "revival of the traditional trade between the Federal Repub-

---

35. Foreign Office report, 10 August 1955, 14, PAAA, 413.85.00/96. Although Scherpenberg admitted vaguely that "it cannot yet be determined at which level economic negotiations in Moscow will be conducted, rather this will be one point of the Chancellor's conversations in Moscow." Memorandum "Economic Negotiations with the Soviets," 8 August 1955, PAAA, 413.85.00/96.

36. Erhard to Adenauer, 25 August 1955, BA B 136/655. See also Hans-Peter Schwarz's earlier, undocumented report that Erhard and Mueller-Armack (in charge of economic policy) in the economics ministry advocated using economic incentives such as long-term loans as a means of gaining concessions from the Soviets. Hans-Peter Schwarz, *Die Ära Adenauer, 1949–1957* (Stuttgart, 1981), 274.

lic and the Soviet Union" and the need for discussions about the volume and composition of an exchange of goods. Khrushchev noted that the day's sessions had been "interesting," but he never directly responded to Hallstein's offer. The Soviets also ignored Adenauer's idea for the immediate establishment of a "Mixed Commission" to plan future economic contacts.[37]

A similar pattern developed at the foreign ministers' meeting in Geneva in October and November 1955, where the U.S. delegation arrived "prepared to take those actions toward facilitation of East-West trade which can be accomplished within the present legal and policy framework and which lie within U.S. power to halt or reverse." Molotov spoke repeatedly about the importance of trade in reducing tensions but refused to move beyond the rhetoric of criticizing the "artificially created barriers" and "discriminatory measures" of Western strategic trade controls. In the Committee of Experts, the Soviets offered not one suggestion for how a discussion of trade relations might proceed. Indeed, as both Dulles and Macmillan angrily pointed out, the Soviets refused to respond directly to Western suggestions for discussion of the ruble rate, patent protection, copyrights, or direct air links. Pressed by his Western counterparts on these points, Molotov squirmed, claiming "nobody here is prepared to raise the question of concluding any trade agreements either."[38]

What emerges from a review of these three sets of negotiations is an obvious Soviet unwillingness to negotiate an expansion of normal commercial relations between the two sides. In the West, several overlapping explanations circulated for this Soviet position.

Heinrich von Brentano, the new foreign minister in the FRG, told the Bundestag on 1 December 1955 that "the course of negotiations revealed that the Soviets were interested only in the end of the embargo for strategic goods, and not in peaceful trade." With a slightly different emphasis, Dulles concluded at the end of the foreign ministers' conference that there would be no agreement for increased trade "for the simple, now unmistakably evident reason that the Soviet Union remains basically opposed to developing a high level of trade between East and West." More cautiously, Albert Hilger van Scherpenberg (head of the

37. Bundesministerium für Gesamtdeutsche Fragen, comp., *Dokumente zur Deutschlandpolitik* (Frankfurt, 1961), Series III, vol. 1, p. 326; Adenauer *Erinnerungen*, 518.

38. Report, CFEP steering committee, *FRUS, 1955–1957*, X, 257; Dulles and Macmillan, statements of 14 November 1955, *Geneva Meeting*, 248 ff., 254, 256 ff.

Trade Policy Division at the West German foreign office) had concluded from his unofficial talks with Soviet trade representatives in Moscow, including Foreign Trade Minister Kumykin, that the Soviets had made a "political decision at the highest level" not to engage in "concrete" economic negotiations at this time.[39]

The development of Soviet foreign trade from the middle through the end of the decade supports Scherpenberg's view that Soviet disinterest in concrete economic negotiations was a short-term phenomenon ("at this time") of the period 1955–1956 rather than a long-term "basic opposition" as Dulles had concluded. From 1952 through 1954 the Soviets had been quite active expanding their commercial contacts outside of the Communist bloc as part of their economic offensive. They had, for example, energetically pursued an agreement with West German industrialists, negotiating a draft agreement for expanded trade between the two sides. In October 1954 meetings in Geneva, the Soviets offered manganese, chromium, soft timber, pitprops, cellulose, asbestos, and oil for delivery against German ships and machinery with a goal of 500 million rubles in two-way trade.[40] The contrast with Soviet tactics of avoidance in 1955 could hardly be greater. The Soviet economic offensive in that period had produced material results: 1954 Soviet imports from outside the Soviet bloc had increased 20 percent from 1952 levels, and imports from Western Europe were up 12 percent in this period.[41]

This early phase of Soviet trade activity fell off suddenly and dramatically at the beginning of 1955. The Soviets canceled a January 1955 follow-up meeting in Bern with the West Germans and then went through the major negotiations of 1955 refusing to engage in the type of substantive trade talks they had pursued one year earlier. Total Soviet imports slumped almost 4 percent from their 1954 level. In the first three quarters of 1955, Soviet purchases from nineteen nonbloc European countries fell 9 percent from their levels a year earlier, with sharp reductions in Soviet imports from Belgium, Denmark, Italy, the Netherlands, Norway, Portugal, and Sweden. In that period, the Soviets ac-

39. *Dokumente zur Deutschlandpolitik*, III, 1, 750; *Geneva Meeting*, 260; Scherpenberg to the Parliamentary Council, 28 September 1955, BA B 102/5933 H.2.

40. Zahn-Stranik memorandum, 20 October 1954, PAAA, 413.22/3. In the 1953 Geneva discussions, the Soviets had proposed two-way trade of 500 million rubles, a figure that apparently continued to serve as the basis for discussions in 1954. PAAA, 413.85.00/96.

41. *United Nations Statistical Papers*. Series T. *Direction of International Trade*, vol. VII, no. 6 (Geneva, 1956), 185.

quired a trade surplus with the West of almost $100 million.[42] Not until the spring of 1957 did the Soviets return to actively pursuing increased trade with the West.

Ironically, Eisenhower may have unknowingly offered the best explanation for the manner in which East-West trade issues played out at Geneva. The president had explicitly warned Dillon Anderson and other members of the NSC that they underestimated the "conspicuous confusion in the Russian dictatorship" since Stalin's death. The president analyzed the overall situation of the uneasy Soviet collective leadership, saying that "the struggle for power in the ruling group in the Kremlin" essentially precluded "a clear direction to Soviet policy." If this general analysis had been applied to East-West trade issues in 1955, the Western governments would have achieved a much better understanding of Soviet actions in that year. Further, a better understanding of the motives behind uncooperative Soviet positions on trade issues in 1955–1956 would have allowed the Western governments to recognize that short period as uncharacteristic of the long evolution of Soviet trade from the early 1950s to the early 1970s.[43]

Viewed over the course of a decade and beyond, Soviet commercial policy in the 1950s was headed toward significantly increased trade with the West. In that long-term development, 1955–1956 was a hiatus caused by the great uncertainty over the direction of Soviet economic policy that prevailed from the end of 1954 through the spring of 1957. That uncertainty stemmed from the many genuine problems affecting the Soviet industrial planning and agricultural production and from the final phase of the power struggle between Khrushchev and his rivals, which centered on domestic concerns. The economic issues facing Soviet leaders in the mid-1950s were perennial and defining in the inherited Stalinist economy: production of means of production versus production of consumer goods, and managing collectivized agriculture

42. Data on total Soviet imports from Mitchell, *European Historical Statistics*, 308; data on Soviet imports from Europe in the first three quarters of 1955 from United Nations Department of Economic and Social Affairs, *Economic Survey of Europe in 1955* (Geneva, 1956), B-9; data for Soviet imports from individual countries from the latter source as well as *United Nations Statistical Papers*, Series T, *Direction of International Trade*, vol. VII, no. 6 (Geneva, 1956), 185. Revealingly, Soviet exports to China declined in 1955, 1956, and 1957, meaning that reduced Soviet trade with the West at that time cannot be attributed to increased obligations to China; see B. R. Mitchell, *International Historical Statistics: Europe, 1750–1988* (New York, 1992), 628–9.

43. Discussion, 254th meeting of the NSC, 7 July 1955, *FRUS, 1955–1957*, V, 270.

in the face of peasant resistance. Khrushchev's plans for addressing these issues pitted him against Malenkov, Molotov, and Kaganovich. The result was a lengthy struggle over economic-development strategies that produced a confusing stream of conflicting announcements on the future of Soviet industrial policy. The twists and turns of that struggle cannot and need not be reviewed here. Rather, let us recall that the greatest period of uncertainty over economic policy began in January 1955 with Shepilov's attack on Malenkov's "New Course" and ended only in the spring of 1957, as Khrushchev finally ousted his old rivals and launched a new economic strategy.

In other words, precisely at the time when external affairs offered the Soviets an opportunity to negotiate an expansion of nonstrategic trade in 1955, the internal power struggle, now focused on economic policy, precluded any meaningful response to that opportunity. To cite one example, the Soviets canceled their January 1955 meeting with the West German industrial delegation because the trade attaché in Bern, Kurepov, was recalled to Moscow for consultations, almost certainly in conjunction with Malenkov's impending demotion and Mikoyan's resignation as minister of trade.[44]

Epilogue

Not until the spring of 1957 could Khrushchev implement a new economic strategy for the USSR based on greater incentives for agriculture and a decentralized reorganization of the Soviet economy with the new regional economic councils (*sovnarkhozy*). With a new—though ultimately unsuccessful—economic strategy in place, the Soviets returned to the active commercial policy they had followed between 1952 and 1954. In the Soviet system, any move toward decentralization spurred increased imports as end users of imported products gained influence on trade-policy decisions. Khrushchev's decentralization meant dramatically increasing imports from major Western trade partners. Increased Western imports implied negotiating a normalization of trade relations with the FRG.

A fresh Soviet offer for trade negotiations with the Federal Republic appeared in February 1957, at the same time Khrushchev first outlined

44. Mikoyan resigned as minister of trade on 24 January 1955. Bulganin replaced Malenkov as chairman of the council of ministers at the 8 February 1955 session of the Supreme Soviet.

his plans for economic decentralization to the Plenum of the Central Committee. The West German trade treaty was concluded in February 1958 and played no small role in the rapid rise of Soviet imports from the West in the final years of that decade.[45] The evolution of Soviet trade under Khrushchev now contradicted Dulles's belief that the Soviets were "basically opposed to developing a high level of trade between the East and the West."

The Berlin crises subsequently demonstrated that East-West merchandise exchanges could be resilient enough to survive short-term political problems. That stability must have played a role in Soviet thinking when they opted for a strategy of "import-led growth" in the 1960s. Developments at the end of the 1950s opened the door on the era of rapid Soviet–Western European trade growth that began in the early 1960s and ran through the mid 1970s. A decade after Geneva, expanding trade was the centerpiece of the extensive new "contacts between East and West" that characterized détente.

45. Total Soviet imports were up 40 percent between 1958 and 1961, with huge increases from some West European suppliers in that period: Britain up 55 percent, Belgium-Luxembourg up 46 percent, Sweden up 70 percent, Italy up 237 percent, and the Federal Republic up 80 percent (Statistical Office of the United Nations, *Yearbook of International Trade Statistics, 1962* [New York, 1964], 696). Soviet trade with China also recovered beginning in 1958 with both imports and exports showing huge increases in 1958 and 1959 (Mitchell, *International Economic Statistics: Europe,* 629).

From Good Breakfast to Bad Supper

John Foster Dulles between the Geneva Summit and the Geneva Foreign Ministers' Conference

RONALD W. PRUESSEN

"Hope is a good breakfast, but it is a bad supper."
—Francis Bacon

1955 was an especially complicated year in the history of the cold war, with rapid zigzags of mood and diplomatic activity. Purely coincidentally, shifts were synchronized with the seasons. During the winter months that began the year, long-frigid relations showed every sign of being immutable. If change were at all in the offing, it seemed possible only with respect to worsened hostilities: Moscow, for example, was issuing shrill warnings about the consequences of West German participation in NATO, and Beijing-Washington conflict over offshore islands like Quemoy and Matsu was growing worse by the day. Spring brought hints of a cold-war thaw, however, and the term "détente" began to dot discussions of the international scene. Soviet leaders began to move toward normalized relations with Bonn and Belgrade, and the long-delayed Austrian State Treaty was signed with great fanfare. By summer, hopes for an end to the cold war were climbing as high as the Swiss mountains that surrounded the first four-power summit conference held since Potsdam. But autumn and the return of winter saw the evaporation of the "spirit of Geneva." Follow-up negotiations of the substantive issues identified but not discussed at the summit proved almost entirely fruitless—especially during the foreign ministers' meetings held in October and November. If tensions did not quite return to the bitter level that had marked the beginning of the year, few continued to talk about "the end" of the cold war. And the Eastern European and Middle Eastern crises of 1956 made it doubly clear that the spirit of Ge-

254 Ronald W. Pruessen

neva had been either extremely fragile or extremely limited in the first place.

Such zigzags must have bewildered both average citizens and many government leaders in 1955—and they can still bedevil the efforts of historians trying to understand the special dynamics of this important moment in cold-war history. Confusing processes sometimes become clearer if an effort is made to trace the experiences of a single individual. What can be learned, for example, by following John Foster Dulles through the complex course of 1955—in particular, his movement from the hopeful breakfast of the Geneva summit through the disappointing supper of the foreign ministers' meetings later in the year?[1]

Dulles's thoughts and experiences can indeed serve as an especially useful focus when contemplating this period:

a. As secretary of state, he was a key player throughout 1955's dramatic events. Although not as overpoweringly significant as once imagined, the archival records of the period—now more fully available—do clearly demonstrate his striking influence on the shaping of American policies. His role within the time frame of autumn 1955, moreover, may even have been somewhat greater than usual, given Dwight Eisenhower's heart attack and extended recuperation.[2]

b. Dulles was a more complex figure than once imagined, and his behavior during 1955 provides some interesting illustrations of this. Furthermore, sensitivity to his specific complexities sets the stage for an overall reconsideration of what often seem to be the simplistic traditional images of international developments during this period.

c. More complex than once believed or not, Dulles was not completely unique. There were, for example, intellectual and psychological linkages with Eisenhower of quite fundamental significance, and many important connections to major protagonists like Harold Macmillan, Antoine Pinay, and Konrad Adenauer. A portrait of Dulles—and perhaps a portrait of any secretary of state—must always be to some degree a group portrait. At the very least, therefore, insights into the behavior of others can be gained through an examination of Dulles's interactions with them.

1. For a related discussion of Dulles's thought before and during the Geneva summit, see Ronald W. Pruessen, "Beyond the Cold War—Again: 1955 and the 1990s," *Political Science Quarterly*, CVIII (1993), 59–84.
2. See, for example, Stephen E. Ambrose, *Eisenhower: The President* (New York, 1984), 270–81.

I

In spite of the sour and vociferously obstructionist images often associated with him, John Foster Dulles came away from the Geneva summit in a positive and optimistic frame of mind. He did identify certain "problems" that had emerged. He believed, for instance, that cordial meetings with Moscow leaders had inevitably contributed to some "breaking down or . . . blurring of the moral barrier between the Soviet bloc and the free world." This might make it a little more difficult than previously to maintain Western unity—because of the way it would weaken "a cement compounded of fear and a sense of moral superiority." Nevertheless, Dulles was convinced that the overall results of the summit conference were "very much on the plus side for the West." The United States had known in advance that certain Soviet gains were bound to be made in Geneva, but Dulles had also foreseen "that the meeting could be made to create opportunities." If Washington remained both imaginative and diligent, he maintained, those opportunities could now be turned into solid achievements.[3]

Dulles had two especially appealing "opportunities" in mind—as he had previously had in the months leading up to the summit. First, he believed that German reunification was "in the air." As he put it to Konrad Adenauer, this goal could "be achieved in a couple of years if we are stout." For his part, Adenauer was nowhere nearly so optimistic, but Dulles was convinced that the chancellor had simply "not yet adjusted himself to the new possibilities which [Dulles] felt made more likely than ever before the unification of Germany." In a conversation with Eisenhower, the secretary of state said "it was difficult for a man of Adenauer's age—about 80—to adjust himself to a new line of thinking after he had been dedicated to another line for so long."[4]

Second, Dulles was also excited about Eastern European possibilities. Could the Kremlin retain tight control over its satellites much longer? Meeting with the Senate Foreign Relations Committee immediately after returning from Geneva, Dulles speculated about the prospect of Moscow's power being rolled back to the Soviet Union's own borders: "I would not want to put a date on it," he said, "but the way things are going, I think within 5 years there is a very good chance that will happen." In other settings, Dulles elaborated on his readings of Eastern Eu-

3. *FRUS, 1955–1957*, V, 534, 552.
4. *FRUS, 1955–57*, V, 546, 549–50.

ropean horizons. He was intrigued, for instance, by the potential ramifications of Soviet-Yugoslav détente. As he explained his thinking to Eisenhower on August 11:

> I said I rather foresaw that Tito now had the ambition to make himself the leader of a group of Communist states and attract them away from Moscow. I had particularly in mind Hungary, Rumania, and Bulgaria. I said that Tito had stood for the Bukharin brand of Communism which believed that you would have Communism on a national basis and that Communist countries need not necessarily be under the iron discipline of the Soviet Communist Party as the leader of the world proletariat.
>
> I said that if this was his ambition, it was one that we could afford quietly to countenance.[5]

Some facets of Dulles's summer expectations deserve further attention, because they proved significant to medium-range prospects for the spirit of Geneva. His estimates of time lines are important in this regard. German reunification might come in two years, he speculated, and freedom for the satellites in five. Although such scenarios were positive, the secretary was clearly not envisioning immediate additional progress. In respect to the diplomatic schedule, this meant that he did not see further negotiations in 1955—including the upcoming foreign ministers' sessions—as likely to yield stunning results. Dulles made this implicit cautionary note more explicit in a message to Adenauer midway through the second Geneva gathering: "I know neither of us expected to bring about German reunification at this particular conference," he wrote. "We did hope to create conditions so that we would thereafter be able to move in that direction and I think we are in a good way toward doing that."[6]

It is worth noting that this is another example of the many consistencies between Dulles's pre- and postsummit thoughts. Earlier in 1955, he had had reservations about the potential pitfalls of using the specific mechanism of a summit conference as a diplomatic tool. Problems like the future of Germany were too profoundly complex and significant to allow what he called "quicky" solutions. Heads of

5. Transcript, Executive Sessions of the Senate Foreign Relations Committee (Historical Series), vol. vii, 84th Congress, 1st sess., 1955 (Washington, D.C., 1978), July 25, 1955; *FRUS, 1955–57*, XXVI, 660–1.

6. *FRUS, 1955–57*, V, 681.

government were "not miracle men" and there might be unfortunate political and public-opinion consequences if too much attention were focused on the question of speed. So too with Dulles's approach to the foreign ministers' meetings in the fall of 1955. Further efforts in Geneva might help the discussions move toward desirable goals, but the secretary viewed such efforts as only one additional step in a considerably longer process.[7]

Another noteworthy facet of Dulles's mid-1955 perspective is the way positive expectations emerged from negative appraisals of the Soviet Union's state of health. Well before the summit, Dulles came to believe that dramatic changes were beckoning in Central and Eastern Europe because Moscow had become seriously overextended. Soviet leaders, he argued, were likely either to voluntarily change their behavior because they were "desperately looking for a respite" or to have their power curtailed by "restive" and "squirming" satellite populations. The conference itself only reinforced this judgment. Dulles returned to Washington more firmly convinced than ever that Moscow's interest in détente was "born not out of its strength, but out of its weakness; not out of its successes, but out of its failures." Extreme Soviet sensitivity regarding the future of East Germany, for instance, was clear evidence of the fact that leaders were "nervous" about the potential for a free fall of liberation dominoes throughout Eastern Europe. Internal Soviet problems remained severe as well:

> [T]he Soviet Union faced a heavy task in seeking to maintain a vast military establishment, both in terms of footsoldiers and in terms of modern weapons and means of delivery. The burden can be appreciated when it is recalled that the industrial base of the Soviet Union is less than one-third of the United States and that its agricultural production is not keeping pace with its population growth. The Soviet leaders have been attempting to expand rapidly, even sensationally, their industrial base through vast capital expenditures. This has accentuated the diversion of economic effort away from consumer goods, manufactured and agricultural. This has not produced a crisis, but it was an economic distortion which could not be endured indefinitely. Apparently, Soviet policies needed to be adjusted to

7. Sir G. Jebb to Foreign Office, July 15, 1955, Foreign Office 800/670/132480; record of meeting at the United States embassy in Vienna after dinner on May 14, 1955, Prime Minister's Office 11/893/110169, Public Record Office, London.

what the West, two years earlier, had defined as the need for a "long haul" basis.[8]

If Moscow's predicaments created exciting opportunities, however, Dulles did not deem it sufficient to simply sit back and wait for satisfying results. Faithful to a policy preference that often surfaced during his years as secretary of state, he concluded that promising circumstances needed to be molded—or pushed. Almost immediately after the Geneva summit, he thus began to urge the necessity of maintaining pressure on the Soviet Union. If Moscow's pragmatic calculations or frazzled nerves had led it to make what Dulles called "prepayments" in the spring—the Austrian treaty, for example—then he believed "it is possible that they will pay something more" in order to breathe yet fuller life into détente. In any event, it was necessary to explore the possibility. As he put it to Adenauer in mid-August, "How much they will yet pay remains to be seen. But it is certainly the intention of the United States to press them in this respect."[9]

In particular, the United States would insist that any continuation of the spirit of Geneva required an end to "injustices" like "the partition of Germany" and "satellite rule." At best, pressure along these lines would yield splendid and speedier breakthroughs. But even at worst, as Dulles explained to some of his key advisers, progress might at least be nudged further along. If the Soviets only made small concessions—offering what they themselves might believe was only a temporary dose of "the classic Communist maneuver known as 'zig zag' "—"it is possible that what the Soviet rulers design as a maneuver may in fact assume the force of an irreversible trend."[10]

Dulles's reactions to the summit and his desire to take advantage of what he saw as both real and increasing opportunities became readily apparent very soon after his return from Geneva. The thoughts and reactions quoted here, in fact, emerged almost entirely in the short period between late July and mid-August. It is important to note, however, that this frame of mind seems to have remained thoroughly consistent dur-

8. *FRUS, 1955–1957*, II, 253–4; *New York Times*, July 8, 1955, p. 4; Walt W. Rostow, *Open Skies: Eisenhower's Proposal of July 21, 1955* (Austin, 1982), 161; June 14, 1955 memorandum, White House Meetings Series, John Foster Dulles Papers, Mudd Library, Princeton University; *FRUS, 1955–57*, V, 548, 551; July 25, 1955, transcript, Telephone Conversation Series, John Foster Dulles Papers, Princeton University.

9. *FRUS, 1955–57*, V, 548–9.

10. Ibid., 552.

ing the two additional months preceding the regathering of the foreign ministers.

Records of the elaborate preparations for the foreign ministers' meetings contain implicit evidence of Dulles's ongoing expectations and policy preferences. The secretary of state took an early hand in designing such advance work and then remained personally involved at regular intervals. As early as August 1—only days after returning from the summit—he met with the British and French ambassadors in Washington to outline his thoughts about ways in which the three Western powers could "maintain the initiative." He was particularly "thinking of the desirability that the West be prepared to table fairly specific papers on Germany and European security." (These were the items purposefully twinned in the first lines of the "Directive" issued at the conclusion of the summit conference.) By August 15, this inclination had been incorporated into an official statement of "United States Post-Geneva Policy"; by August 31, Western discussions of various draft papers had already begun. Both individual meetings at senior levels and day-to-day efforts of various working groups in Washington, Bonn, and Paris were then a constant feature in September and October.[11]

One example of Dulles's regular involvement might be used to demonstrate his serious engagement and genuine expectations. On September 28, he met with British, French, and West German representatives in New York to review a "European Security" proposal prepared by a working group. In a purely quantitative sense alone, his comments on the draft were numerous and specific—in no way like those of a senior policy maker simply going through motions or double-checking matters of no personal significance. And the tone and thrust of his remarks make this doubly clear. At one point, for example, Dulles argued for less initial precision regarding an American pledge to "engage itself on the side of the Soviet Union in the event of a war in Europe." He was quite prepared to undertake "an engagement of such magnitude," he said, but it was too important to "peddle" or "cheapen . . . at the beginning." The Senate might go along with such "very serious language," but only if something like German reunification and German membership in NATO were part of a larger package. As a result, Dulles favored an approach which would feel out Soviet intentions first; if signs were encouraging, as he put it, "we would then be prepared to come to a text

11. Ibid., 542, 551–4, 613–4.

like the present one."[12] Such precise and weighty words betoken a mind deeply concerned with the issues at hand.

In addition to these various forms of implicit revelation, Dulles could also make his seriousness and expectations quite explicit during September and October. Again, just one example: a "Secret and Personal" October 3 letter to Adenauer, commenting on the chancellor's report of his recent experiences in Moscow. As Adenauer had done in his letter, Dulles freely and fascinatingly speculated about the nature of a new and significant moment in East-West relations:

> I am by no means sure whether the Russian leaders themselves have firmly settled precisely what it is that they want and the best means of going about it. There is no doubt that their country has undergone, and continues to undergo, profound changes, and that decisions made now, with regard to the opportunities of choice that confront them, will greatly affect the future of their country. Although Soviet diplomacy in recent months has moved with considerable skill with respect to limited objectives, I think that in the larger questions, relating to the fundamental choice between peace or war and the organization of their internal economy, the Soviet leaders are to a certain extent feeling their way.

Dulles did believe Kremlin leaders were likely to move in one of two alternative directions: one in which "the national objectives of the Great Russian state" would predominate or one in which devotion to "international Communism" would serve as the source of policy decisions:

> I think we do have an opportunity in the present situation to make it clear to the Soviet leadership and to the world at large that by one course of action, which would serve the legitimate interests of the Russian state, the Soviet leaders can obtain the advantages of peace abroad and a respite for the completion of necessary tasks at home, whereas by the other course of action they will merely cement and reinforce the defensive measures of the free world which they profess to fear. I conceive that our principal task in the coming negotiations is to make this choice clear to the Soviets. I think our principal line of action at Geneva should be, while continuing to oppose the program of international Communism in any of its forms, to hold out to the Russians the possibility of reaching peaceful settlements if the understandable objectives of the Russian state become uppermost in the minds of Soviet leaders.[13]

12. Ibid., 598–9.
13. Ibid., 610–3.

There is no facile optimism in this particular letter, to be sure. Nevertheless, and perhaps more impressively, there are signs of genuinely probing rumination and anticipation.

II

As John Young's discussion of the October–November foreign ministers' meetings makes clear, those who had developed optimistic expectations in the immediate aftermath of the Geneva summit were in for a rude awakening.[14] How did Dulles's behavior—and American foreign policy more generally—contribute to this collapse of hope? What responsibility did he and other U.S. leaders have for turning a good and hopeful breakfast into a bad supper?

The argument here will be that American policy in 1955—strongly influenced by Dulles—significantly undercut opportunities for either generalized détente or meaningful improvements in a troubled European environment. This was an ironic, even tragic, dénouement for the eager expectations and serious engagement which characterized Dulles in the months between the summit and the foreign ministers' meetings, but it is a fact of 1955 life nonetheless. The Soviet Union was certainly not totally free of responsibility for the disappointing results ultimately generated by the "spirit of Geneva," although early Western postmortems that castigated Moscow alone now seem absurdly incomplete. Nor should the inclinations and actions of men like Harold Macmillan and Antoine Pinay be left out of a fuller portrait of failure. It can be argued, however, that something more might have emerged if it had not been for the specific priorities and approaches most adamantly represented by Dulles—and represented by Dulles with Eisenhower's full support. This something more that might have been possible—as far as other key players were concerned—might not have amounted to the kind of full-fledged détente that some hopeful souls were looking for in 1955, but it would have been a promising step or two closer than the disheartening results that actually emerged.

What aspects of Dulles's policies proved to stand in the way of a genuine relaxation of cold-war tensions? Although this is a large and complicated question, two broad features of Dulles's behavior seem the most significant. One of these concerns the American approach to a substan-

14. Ibid.

tive issue that figured prominently in 1955's negotiations; the other pertains more to matters of overall mind-set and style.

The issue might be better described as *the* issue: the future of Germany. In 1955, as so often before, the so-called "German Question" or "German Problem" more or less overshadowed any number of important matters in the minds of American and other policy makers. In the period leading up to the foreign ministers' conference, Dulles made it clear that he considered German reunification to be "the touchstone" of U.S. policy. To a greater or lesser degree, for him the other agenda items passed on from the summit paled in comparison. For example, disarmament questions were important, but because work was "proceeding in the United Nations Subcommittee [on Disarmament]," Dulles thought they "might be disposed of in a perfunctory way" by having the leaders simply take note of developments there. Nor was interest in "East-West Contacts" likely to produce much more substantive progress. Three weeks before the Geneva sessions were set to begin, Dulles was still wondering "when the Department [of State] would come up with a position on East-West trade"—but wondering only in an offhand fashion that carried no implication of pressure regarding clarification of an important policy issue.[15]

"European Security" matters were closer to being a true priority concern for the secretary of state. When that issue was paired with "German unification," as it had been in the summit's final communiqué, Dulles told the National Security Council that this was "the most urgent and difficult" item on the foreign ministers' agenda. But the pairing was crucial and his own very specific approach was to insist on dealing with the substantive details of a European security system only after the "German Question" had been resolved. As he put it to the British and French ambassadors in August, "we should contemplate putting forward a definitive proposal for the reunification of Germany at the Geneva meeting and . . . discussion on European Security should take place only within this context of German reunification." While it would be desirable to have detailed security proposals ready for the foreign ministers' meetings, Dulles was not overly concerned about dotting every "i" and crossing every "t": "it might possibly prove unnecessary at Geneva to put forward specific proposals on European security," in fact, "since the Soviet Union might not move past the ini-

15. *FRUS, 1955–57*, V, 549, 565, 609.

tial premise of the Western position"—i.e., German reunification as a first step.[16]

It is also important to recognize that American policy incorporated very specific desiderata regarding the meaning of reunification. One of these was that reunification come in one fell swoop, with no intermediate steps or institutional hybrids delaying full-scale democratic elections. Nor should there be any restrictions on a newly sovereign Germany. While a European security agreement might eventually provide Moscow with various reassurances against the revival of some kind of German threat, there should be no question of Germany's being allowed to opt for total membership in NATO. Dulles was categorical about these matters. For instance, as preparations for the foreign ministers' negotiations proceeded, he strongly resisted British drafts on security, which proposed a large Central European region in which all military forces would be limited and inspected. Even though he himself had earlier been intrigued by the prospect of a quasi-demilitarized zone, he thought the timing was both premature and a little dangerous because "it would be interpreted by the Russians as meaning that the question of European Security could be developed apart from the reunification of Germany. A second drawback was that such a project would have to be conducted under conditions of a divided Germany, thereby encouraging the Germans to feel that we accepted the division of Germany as a more or less permanent fact." Perhaps a "pilot project" involving Norway or Turkey might be developed as an alternative, Dulles suggested.[17]

It should be noted here that American adamance regarding the achievement and definition of German reunification received emphatic encouragement from West Germany. Adenauer regularly pressed Washington about the need to avoid half-steps or concessions. For example, it was Bonn's insistence even more than U.S., British, and French inclinations that was responsible for the total lack of formal participation by either German government in the Geneva foreign ministers' conference. As Federal Republic foreign minister Heinrich von Brentano put it, Bonn preferred to give up a Geneva role for itself rather than risk anything that might bring "this non-existent state [the German Demo-

16. Ibid., 560, 564, 616.
17. Ibid., 563. See also Douglas Dillon to Secretary of State, October 13, 1955; John Foster Dulles to Jacob Beam, October 13, 1955; and John Foster Dulles to Jacob Beam, October 14, 1955, Decimal File 762.00/10–1355, Record Group 59, National Archives.

cratic Republic] into international discussions." Even Dulles pressed
von Brentano on this, to make sure he understood the precise nature of
the extreme Federal Republic position. In the end, however, Washington, London, and Paris all accepted Bonn's approach and agreed to carry
on only "private consultation" with their NATO ally during the foreign
ministers' meetings. (One contingency was discussed: the possibility of
reconsidering Bonn and Pankow participation in Geneva discussions if
the early stages of negotiations produced a satisfactory reunification
plan. If such an unlikely development came to pass, Adenauer was willing to alter his otherwise intransigent policy—as Dulles put it, "In other
words, you are willing to invite the GDR to its own funeral.")[18]

This all-or-nothing approach to German reunification was profoundly
significant in undercutting the potential for genuine détente by the end
of 1955. Washington's and Bonn's adamance on this touchstone issue
turned it into a "tombstone" issue instead. Dulles, Adenauer, and others regularly argued that it was Soviet obstructionism that short-
circuited progress on German reunification by the end of 1955—but
such contentions simply ignored the heavy measure of American and
West German responsibility for failure. In fact, Moscow's approach to
the German question had gone through significant and impressive
stages during 1955. There was no readiness to immediately accept a reunified Germany in which democratic elections and NATO membership were prominent features, but the Soviets were open to any number
of more limited but still promising steps. They had formally recognized
the Federal Republic of Germany and had negotiated a prisoner-of-war
agreement that even Adenauer felt he had to accept. Perhaps even more
significantly, Washington and Bonn recognized the significant shifts
taking place in Soviet policy. Adenauer returned from his September
visit to Moscow impressed by the fact that "at no time did [the] Soviets
propose that [the] Federal Republic should leave [the] Atlantic Pact":
Khrushchev's and Bulganin's chagrin concerning an expanded NATO
was made clear, but they also admitted that they now saw this as "an
unpleasant reality." Dulles agreed that new Moscow policies were "indeed a far cry from the Soviets' public professions of even twelve
months ago."[19]

By the fall of 1955, Moscow seemed ready to go on taking measured

18. *FRUS, 1955–57*, V, 600–1.
19. Ibid., 585, 611.

but potentially significant steps regarding outstanding German problems. In particular, Soviet policy emphasized the logic of fostering contacts between the two German governments. Given Bonn's and
Washington's more extreme positions, however, further 1955 progress
proved impossible. And since complete German reunification was a
U.S. precondition for movement on the European security front, the end
of that road was reached as well.[20]

Why was Dulles—among others, of course—willing to turn the
touchstone issue of German reunification into the tombstone of 1955
negotiations? He seems to have been inclined to do so primarily because
the future of Germany was an issue of transcendent significance to
him—so much so that even modest compromise with what he considered necessary policies was inconceivable. Germany—or just the Federal Republic of Germany, if necessary—had to be firmly attached to the
United States and the West; there was just no way around it.

Several strands of concern and conviction intertwined to produce this
thick, tough rope of policy for Dulles. Some are familiar, others less so:

a. Dulles was a major proponent of the well-known cold-war calculations common to overall American thinking throughout the 1940s
   and 1950s—and common in policy analysis elsewhere too, of course:
   i.e., the sense that Germany was a locus of such inherent economic
   and/or military significance that its loss to the Soviet Union (or to
   "Communism") was simply too horrible or dangerous to contemplate.[21]

b. He was also prone to calculations based on readings of pre-cold-war
   developments: i.e., the sense that Germany itself needed to be contained at least as much as the Soviet Union—and that NATO and
   other multilateral structures provided the surest means of bridling
   the German warhorse. Dulles was an early and consistent advocate
   of what Thomas Schwartz has referred to as the policy of "dual containment." As the secretary of state freely expressed it to Bonn's ambassador in Washington, "There are three choices: either a united
   Germany integrated with the West; a Germany identified with the

---

20. Ibid., 575–7, 584–5.
21. Ronald W. Pruessen, *John Foster Dulles: The Road to Power* (New York: Free Press,
1982), Chapters 12–3; Pruessen, "Beyond the Cold War—Again," 68–76; Pruessen, "Cold
War Threats and America's Commitment to the European Defense Community: One Corner of a Triangle," *Journal of European Integration History*, II (1996), 53–7.

East, or a Germany endeavoring to stand in between. The last was unthinkable, and would moreover be a contributing cause of conflict. . . . If anyone tried to block [Germany's] choice of the West, the most that could happen would be to drive Germany into the dangerous third position of trying to balance between East and West."[22]

c. The Dulles-Adenauer relationship doubtless influenced his thinking, perhaps in complex ways. While the U.S. secretary of state would almost surely have moved essentially as he did under almost any circumstances, there was emphatic reinforcement for specific policy inclinations in the close relationship he developed with the Federal Republic's chancellor. Much has been made of this connection—of the friendship that blossomed between two rigid old cold warriors with a shared taste for stern denunciations of godless Communism. It may be that the relationship was more limited and complex than this, involving respect on both sides, certainly, but some stiffness as well. It may also be that both Dulles and Adenauer displayed a measure of readiness to play or to use a partner in a fashion reminiscent of a marriage of convenience. At the very least, however, the secretary of state and the chancellor shared policy preferences and goals in a way that had great significance for each of them. Adenauer's visceral anti-Communism made him a very appealing German ally. His ambivalence about his own countrymen made him even more so. Given the "dual containment" premises of Dulles's policies, how much more appropriate a partner could there have been than a chancellor who worried about controlling his "carnivorous sheep"?[23] This was a chancellor whose worries led him to emphatic enthusiasm for the integrationist mechanisms which were similarly significant to Dulles. One of Adenauer's first reactions to the Geneva summit conference was to indicate his belief in the need "to revive or strengthen [the] European idea." Dulles, for his part, speculated on August 28 about the desirability of communicating to Moscow the seriousness of American views on European integration: "perhaps the strongest rational appeal was that the peace of Europe can only be founded upon greater European unity. The separateness of the European na-

22. Thomas Schwartz, *America's Germany: John J. McCloy and the Federal Republic of Germany* (Cambridge, Mass., 1991), 130; Pruessen, "Cold War Threats and America's Commitment to the European Defense Community," 57–69; *FRUS, 1955–57*, V, 557–8.

23. The fascinating phrase "carnivorous sheep" was attributed to Adenauer by Richard Nixon (*Leaders* [New York, 1982], 156).

tions was in large part a cause of past wars."[24] (These Dulles words suggest an aspect of the 1955 environment that deserves further attention from those exploring the course of the cold war and the overall dynamics of post-1945 international relations: the more-than-coincidental way in which leaders like Dulles—and Adenauer—were juggling negotiations on both old cold-war questions and new European economic relationships at precisely this point. Among other things, this combination provides a further indication of the way cold-war and pre-cold-war concerns were equally important elements in the 1955 landscape—or of the way in which post-cold-war calculations were evident in some quarters on both sides of the Atlantic.)[25]

All in all, Adenauer shared so many fundamentally significant policy inclinations with Dulles that he became the virtually indispensable designated German associate. Any temptation to waver from the toughest policies on German reunification—to consider the possibility of fostering relations between the two German governments as a transitional measure, for example—would have been stopped short by the chancellor's adamance on such a question. Even if there had been an inkling of a feeling that some more moderate approach might be worth trying, the possible loss of Adenauer's support on a full range of major issues—or fear of the collapse of Adenauer's leadership in West Germany—would have made the experiment seem much less worth pursuing.

Dulles's insistence on the importance of the issue of German reunification was clearly a product of substantive policy considerations. But at least in part, it was also affected by the particular circumstances or atmospherics of 1955. Moreover, the secretary of state's mind-set and personal style are relevant to an estimation of American responsibility for the demise of many 1955 hopes. In this regard it is especially important to appreciate the impact of Dulles's exhilaration and optimism concerning the predicaments of the Soviet Union. This was a secretary of state whose personality and perspectives were never as sullen or bleak as once imagined; he had enormous energy and an overwhelmingly positive sense of his ability to devise solutions for problems. Even granting this, however, it is necessary to take further note of the fact

24. *FRUS, 1955–57,* V, 538, 557.
25. See, for example, Pruessen, "Cold War Threats and America's Commitment to the European Defense Community," 57–69.

that his mood in mid- and late 1955 was characterized by a special measure of excited expectancy.

Unfortunately, heady moods can be dangerous as well as incredibly enjoyable. For policy makers as well as mere mortals, exhilaration can threaten logic and balance. Dulles had a real problem when it came to keeping a reasonable rein on his enthusiasm in 1955. Instead of calm and measured judgments, he demonstrated a worse-than-usual tendency to get carried away. Calculations regarding both short-term tactics and longer-range objectives were made in a far less prudent and judicious manner than would have been desirable. And in the end, distorted judgments led to the sacrifice of the possible in pursuit of the unattainable.[26]

As far as tactics were concerned, Dulles's sense of dramatic possibilities encouraged him to be doubly attached to a diplomatic style that emphasized pressure rather than negotiations. We must keep "pushing and pushing on the German unification issue," he told Bonn in August. "This continual reiteration technique" was "a major factor in the successful conclusion of the Austrian treaty," he assured the British and French. The greater the focus on reunification, "the more pressure to that end is exerted on the Soviets." He thought it was equally necessary to push Moscow on the satellite front. The voices of "squirming" populations were to be amplified by U.S. attention and assistance. Although Dulles's and other pronouncements generally cited American interest in "peaceful" liberation, Moscow might be excused if it had a hard time appreciating the charms of the caveat. (Then again, since pressure was the name of the game in Washington, it was Moscow's discomfort that was precisely the objective.) An extra turn of the Eastern European screws, it might be added, came with Dulles's flying visit to Tito on November 6—during a weekend break in the very midst of the Geneva foreign ministers' sessions.[27]

A tactical preference for pressure, as opposed to negotiations, emerged perfectly logically—if unfortunately—from the ambitious goals at which Dulles was aiming in 1955. Put baldly, his expectations led him to spurn the prospect of a cold-war thaw in favor of a cold-war victory. Why negotiate with Moscow when it was on the ropes—or

26. Pruessen, "Beyond the Cold War—Again," 76–82.
27. *FRUS, 1955–57*, V, 542, 546–7, 551–4, 555; *FRUS, 1955–57*, XXVI, 680–97.

close enough to the ropes to make its defeat conceivable? Why consider give-and-take regarding Germany or compromise in Eastern Europe when you believed that firmness and patience in those quarters would bring all that could be desired? Just before the summit conference, Dulles used a metaphor for his policy prescriptions that perfectly captured this focus on triumph rather than détente: "We have come such a long way by being firm, occasionally disagreeably firm, that I would hate to see the whole edifice undermined in response to a smile. . . . We are in the situation of being prepared to run a mile in competition with another runner whose distance suddenly appears to be a quarter mile. At the quarter mile mark, the Russian quarter miler says to the American miler, 'This is really a quarter mile race, you know, and why don't we call it off now?' "[28] At no point in the summer or fall of 1955 did Dulles conclude that the United States was any less likely to win the race.

If heady moods can be both enjoyable and dangerous, a thirst for victory can be both energizing and counterproductive. The actual rather than the hoped-for circumstances of 1955 nudged results toward the more problematic of these possibilities. While the Soviet Union was indeed at a difficult moment in its history, it was not so difficult a moment as to foreordain the full collapse of its power in Eastern Europe or Germany. Shrewder American or Western diplomacy might have been able to make more of Moscow's troubles—and of the flexibility and imagination that the troubles were to some degree generating. Pressure tactics, on the other hand, especially when paired with extreme positions on issues of profound significance to both the Soviet Union and the West, were destined to backfire.

Two somewhat parenthetical points can be added here. First, Dulles and Eisenhower regularly demonstrated this tendency to rely on a policy of pressure in pursuit of goals that turned out to be far too ambitious. Developments surrounding the 1955 summit and foreign ministers' conferences offer especially interesting and rather extreme examples, but they fit into a quite consistent larger pattern. It is a more complex pattern than can be sketched here, to be sure, involving counterpoint with the more temperate policy making often emphasized by so-called Eisenhower revisionism. Nonetheless, the more aggressive

28. Rostow, *Open Skies*, 160.

and irrational side of the Dulles-Eisenhower behavior does warrant recognition.[29]

Second, this Dulles-Eisenhower tendency to let appetite overpower judiciousness is also a feature of post-1945 U.S. policies more generally. The role of diplomacy and compromise, the question of prioritization, the problem of accurately gauging the weaknesses of both your enemies and yourself: all these are issues significant in the analysis of leaders from Franklin D. Roosevelt and Harry Truman to George Bush and Bill Clinton. This is, in fact, one of the reasons why the specific experiences of 1955 seem so worthy of attention.

Conclusion

As so often, John Foster Dulles turns out to be a complex figure in the aftermath of the Geneva summit. On the one hand, he was enthusiastically engaged and optimistic in a way that belies his usually dour and obstreperous images. On the other hand, the specific thrust of his energized expectancy significantly interfered with efforts to breathe stronger life into tentative hopes for détente. His extreme positions and ambitions, in tandem with a thoroughgoing resistance to genuine negotiations or compromise, were emphatically counterproductive. He was certainly not solely responsible for the stalemate that became 1955's bad supper, but he does seem to have been more directly responsible than most other leaders.

29. Attention to "the aggressive and irrational side of Dulles-Eisenhower behavior" is evident in various works. See Richard H. Immerman, ed., *John Foster Dulles and the Diplomacy of the Cold War* (Princeton, 1990); Robert J. McMahon, "Eisenhower and Third World Nationalism: A Critique of the Revisionists," *Political Science Quarterly*, CI (1986), 453–73; Richard A. Melanson and David Mayers, eds., *Reevaluating Eisenhower: American Foreign Policy in the Fifties* (Urbana, Ill., 1987); and Stephen G. Rabe, "Eisenhower Revisionism: A Decade of Scholarship," *Diplomatic History*, XVII (Winter 1993), 97–115. I have discussed the issue myself in "The Predicaments of Power," in *John Foster Dulles and the Diplomacy of the Cold War*, ed. Richard H. Immerman, 21–45, and "Beyond the Cold War—Again," 76–82. See also the Bischof essay in the present volume.

The Geneva Conference of Foreign Ministers, October–November 1955

The Acid Test of Détente

JOHN W. YOUNG

Introduction

The July 1955 Geneva head-of-government conference, featuring America's Dwight D. Eisenhower, the USSR's Nikita Khrushchev, Britain's Anthony Eden, and France's Edgar Faure, was the first East-West summit since Potsdam and represented the high point of détente in the mid-1950s. However, it was the foreign ministers' meeting three months later, among the same four countries, that—as Eisenhower said—provided the "acid test" of the "spirit of Geneva." This scheduling resulted from extensive planning in the spring of 1955 by leaders hopeful that they were engineering a means of maintaining and strengthening détente. When the British foreign office reviewed its policy on East-West relations before proposing a leaders' meeting to the Americans, it made an important decision: rather than holding a foreign ministers' conference *before* a summit meeting (the method that had been advocated beforehand), it was preferable to have an "exchange of views" at the leaders' level first. This would lead to more detailed talks among foreign ministers, to be held some months later.[1]

Hitherto, although Western foreign ministries had been skeptical about the value of summits (especially given the unfortunate precedent of Yalta ten years before), public opinion was heavily in favor of such meetings; even in McCarthyite America, about 70 percent of people

I am grateful to the British Academy for providing a Small Personal Research Grant that funded research for this paper, which is a variation of a paper prepared for the October 1995 conference in New Orleans on the 1955 Geneva summit. I am also grateful to Mrs. Janet Smith for typing the paper and to Dr. Jan Melisse for his valuable comments regarding it.
1. *Public Papers of the Presidents: Dwight D. Eisenhower, 1955* (Washington, D.C., 1959), 175.

consulted in Gallup polls pronounced themselves in favor of summits, a similar percentage to that measured in Western Europe. In May 1953 then British prime minister Winston Churchill had declared himself in favor of a summit but the British, American, and French foreign ministries all preferred to work toward a lower-level foreign ministers' meeting. This would avoid the dangers of leaders like Churchill pursuing personal diplomacy of the sort that many believed had given rise to the acceptance of a divided Europe and a Communized Eastern Europe at the end of the war. Foreign ministers, advised by their expert officials, would—it was hoped—be more knowledgeable about foreign policy, less likely to seek unwise settlements with Moscow, and less susceptible to the pressures of public opinion. Two foreign ministers' conferences were held between the four powers in 1954, in Berlin (to discuss Germany and European issues) and Geneva (to discuss the Far East). Nonetheless, a summit meeting remained a popular idea among the public, and by spring 1955 the British foreign office believed the West was in a position to "negotiate from strength" with the Soviets, since West Germany had just joined NATO and the Soviet leadership appeared divided.

The foreign office did, however, stress the need for the prospective summit to be held before rather than after another foreign ministers' conference. The hope was that such a process would reduce the risk of inflated public expectations surrounding the summit. The argument was that if the talks moved from the foreign ministers' level up to the crescendo of a summit, then the growth of public expectations would either pressurize the Western leaders to make unwise concessions or else, if the summit failed, provoke a deep popular demoralization accompanied by fear of a "hot" war. On the other hand, an ultimate failure at the foreign ministers' level would be far less dangerous. As it happened, the Geneva summit in July appeared successful partly because it did not examine in great detail such vexing questions as disarmament and the reunification of Germany. These issues were brought up but no agreements were reached. And the leaders were easily able to agree that foreign ministers' talks should be held to build on the apparent success of the summit. Indeed, all the usual difficulties in organizing an East-West meeting—such as the level of talks, membership, date, venue, and agenda—were quickly overcome on this occasion.[2]

2. H. Macmillan, *Tides of Fortune, 1945–1955* (London, 1969), 583–6. On the problems of organizing negotiations, see G. R. Beridge, *Diplomacy: Theory and Practice* (London, 1995), 119–34.

Therefore, a conference at the level of foreign ministers was to be held among the U.S., USSR, Britain, and France in Geneva (a neutral venue at the heart of Europe) before the end of October. There they were to "continue" discussions on three topics begun at the summit: first, "European Security and Germany"; second, disarmament; and third, the development of "contacts between East and West." Disappointingly, however, the foreign ministers' conference turned out to produce no agreement on any of the three areas of the agenda, ending instead with a short, factual communiqué that did not even set a date for a further meeting. It was evident that the newfound desire for détente had little substance. For historians, the significance of the arid debate between the foreign ministers lies in the evidence it provides that, even if the Soviets and Western powers were now talking to one another, they remained rigidly divided on fundamental issues. Even if public animosity between the two sides had lessened, the cold war was still very much alive. For those interested in investigating the process of diplomacy, the conference provides an interesting case study of complete deadlock in multilateral negotiations, despite the ease with which it was planned and the favorable environment created for it by the spirit of Geneva.[3]

In fact, the likelihood of failure in the foreign ministers' talks was always present. All the subjects on the agenda were set to produce deadlock. Neither singularly, nor as a whole, did the topics for discussion provide any scope for a "formula" settlement that might be accepted by both sides. The first item, European security and German reunification, was, of course, actually two subjects, but they were seen as too closely interlinked to allow separation. The Western powers would have preferred to put Germany alone at the head of the agenda, since it was a subject on which they believed they could put the Soviets on the defensive, especially in the public eye, by pressing the liberal-democratic case for free elections leading to an all-German government which could then join the Atlantic alliance. German unity "in freedom" was unlikely to appeal to the Soviets since it would mean surrendering their hold on East Germany only to see a reunited Germany enter NATO. Thus they preferred instead to shift the focus away from the process of German reunification to the wider issue of European security, hoping to create a system on the continent, or so they argued, in which a revived

3. Noble Frankland, ed., *Documents on International Affairs, 1955* (London, 1958), 48–9, 88. The communiqué of the summit is easily consulted in this volume.

Germany was no longer a threat to them or anyone else. The security question might include discussion of a nonaggression pact, limited arms zones, or a full-fledged "security pact for Europe." But there were always Western fears that such discussions would actually be exploited by the Soviets to go far beyond their stated aims and destroy NATO while leaving no effective security mechanism to take its place, thus enabling the Soviets, dominant as they were in Eastern Europe, to intimidate the whole continent and to influence a German settlement on their own terms. One technical complication for the Western powers was that, although European security and the German issue were lumped together as one item, the European security element was listed first, allowing the Soviets to argue that it should also be treated first in the foreign ministers' discussions.

Other items on the agenda were less important. On disarmament at least there was never much chance of a breakthrough; the summit communiqué only asked the foreign ministers to consider an initiative on disarmament in line with developments in the UN's Subcommittee on Disarmament. Since talks in the subcommittee had become calm by October, and were not due to be taken up again until the new year, there was no progress to be made at the foreign ministers' level either.

The last item for foreign ministers' discussion held, on the face of it, more scope for agreement. "Developments of Contacts between East and West" embraced two major subthemes, "free communications and peaceful trade."[4] These subjects had been raised at a late stage in the summit conference, so late in fact that there was only time for U.S. and French views to be stated at a plenary meeting on 23 July. President Eisenhower expressed an interest in easing the flow of ideas, people, and "peaceful goods" between East and West as a way of reducing tension. Edgar Faure was rather more concrete in his ideas for normalizing contacts while recognizing, in the short-term, the division of Europe; academic and artistic exchanges, tourism, freedom of broadcasts, a European investment fund, and even common organizations for transport and power figured in the French repertoire. However, British ideas were only introduced in a memorandum, and Soviet views were not set out at all.[5] Although "Development of Contacts" was then put on the

4. Again see the summit communiqué cited above. On the arguments over Item 1 of the agenda, see especially *FRUS, 1955–1957*, V, 503–12; on Dulles's expectation that disarmament would not take up much time in October–November, see 565 of the same volume.

5. *FRUS, 1955–57*, V, 574–8. For the French memorandum, see 526. The British memorandum is quoted in U.S. State Department, *The Geneva Conference of Heads of Government, July 18–23, 1955* (Washington, D.C., 1955), 64–6.

foreign ministers' agenda, there remained suspicions that both sides differed fundamentally on the issue. The West naturally had a desire to break down the Soviet limits on Western broadcasts and other ideological penetration into the Communist bloc, with the long-term purpose of spreading liberal ideals and dissolving Marxism; such had been a long-standing aim of the American psychological warfare program and had also figured in Churchill's desire for détente in the early 1950s. And in 1953 Churchill and Eisenhower had been particularly keen to use expanded Western trade (though only in "peaceful goods") with the Soviets to improve what Churchill called "peaceful infiltration" behind the Iron Curtain and to make the USSR vulnerable to Western pressure in times of crisis.[6] But the Kremlin could have little enthusiasm for such a policy unless it brought some large-scale reward for their side; as the foreign ministers' conference would show, the principal Soviet aim was to increase their trade in strategic goods with the West—the very goods which all Western leaders were determined should remain restricted.[7]

Western Planning for the Foreign Ministers' Meeting

As at the summit meeting (and as in many multilateral negotiations in which a group of countries seek to act in unison), the Western side faced the problem of producing a common position for the October conference, which necessitated some compromises between them. There were inevitably differences of emphasis between the three Western powers on some issues, and the very process of having ironed these out made the Western position rather inflexible when talks with the Soviets began. One major aim of the Americans, British, and French was, after all, to maintain a united front and prevent any Soviet "wedge-driving"; it was difficult to compromise with the Soviets on issues in which the West's position itself had only been decided after considerable debate. Furthermore, it is clear that an important element in any East-West talks (and this was true for both sides) was to expose contradictions,

6. Churchill's motives and policies and his differences with the U.S. regarding aims for cold-war fighting are fully discussed in John W. Young, *Winston Churchill's Last Campaign: Britain and the Cold War, 1951–5* (Oxford, U.K., 1996).

7. East-West trade limits have already generated a surprising body of research. See, for example, G. Adler-Karlsson, *Western Economic Warfare, 1947–67* (Stockholm, 1968); P. Funigiello, *American-Soviet Trade in the Cold War* (Chapel Hill, 1988); and, especially, T. E. Forland, *Cold Economic Warfare: The Creation and Prime of COCOM* (Ph.D. dissertation, University of Oslo, 1991).

supposed injustice, and any evidence of weakness in the other's position. The negotiating process was therefore largely an exercise in psychological warfare, the purpose being to convince one's own public, and the court of world opinion, of the rectitude of one's particular case.

Thus in an initial talk with the British and French ambassadors to Washington about the conference, John Foster Dulles argued that the West must keep the initiative by introducing "fairly specific" proposals on Germany and European security built on the ideal of German "unity in freedom." The secretary of state believed that by attacking the Soviets on the future of East Germany, the West could "further threaten the Soviet position" in all of Eastern Europe by undermining the faith of local leaders in the Kremlin, perhaps even achieving his most-cherished aim of destroying the Kremlin's hold on its satellites. The U.S. State Department believed that Soviet leaders had only appeared to be friendly at the Geneva summit because their previous "tough" policies had failed to intimidate the West and because military spending was becoming a burden to the USSR's economy. Geneva was dismissed as part of a Soviet "zig-zag" tactic (an American concept which allowed any change in Kremlin policy to be interpreted as merely a new manifestation of malicious intent). The summit had given the Soviets the appearance of "moral and social equality" with the West, allowing them to spread doubt among Western citizenry about the Kremlin's real intentions. But, the State Department argued, as long as the West maintained its unity and strength, it might turn the Geneva process into "an irreversible trend" which would eventually undermine the Soviet system, by removing the Soviets' sense of threat from the West, eliminating barriers to "normal contacts," and encouraging independence of the East European satellites.

The key question in summer 1955 was how far Moscow would allow such a process to go, and the foreign ministers' meeting would "provide a significant opportunity to gain insight as to this." Later documents confirm that the Americans were—without any recognition of the irony involved—planning a strategy similar to that which they saw the Soviets pursuing; the cold war was still being fought, but with the public appearance of moderation, the purpose being to exploit propaganda points and win over world opinion while sapping and exploiting breaches in the Communist position. Thus Dulles's special assistant William H. Jackson, in discussing Eisenhower's desire for East-West contacts, was adamant that U.S. policy was "designed to change conditions" in Eastern Europe and did not imply "acceptance of the status quo" in Eastern Europe. The West could gain specific advantages from East-West contacts (although the declassified version of the paper has the relevant section deleted, this presumably involved propaganda and espionage) and should try to push the Soviets so far on "the elimination of barriers to freedom of information and communication" that the process would become impossible to reverse. Yet Jackson (despite the apparent contradiction with Western liberal ideals) was not enthusiastic about freedom of travel between East and West because of the benefits this provided for KGB spies. Dulles was pleased with this paper and keen that at the foreign ministers' conference the West should try to deal separately with "contacts" and trade. On the trade issue, he recognized that the Soviets would be the ones pressing hardest for concessions, in an attempt to lower Western controls on goods with military potential.[8]

Before setting out for Geneva, Dulles issued a public statement that "security for Russians is not inconsistent with justice for Germans," but he warned the National Security Council on 20 October that the Soviets were unlikely to accept any deal that involved the abandonment of East Germany, and that they would instead harass the West on the issue of European security. The Americans recognized that in that area they would be on potentially weak ground. While prepared to contemplate a Europe-wide security treaty (including a nonaggression clause and limitation of armaments) the U.S. was determined not to sign such a pact until after a reunited Germany was brought into NATO.[9]

This led to some differences with the British, who, as so often in the recent past, seemed ready to consider a more moderate policy toward the Soviets. In late August the British sent a memorandum to Washington in which German membership in NATO was not made a prerequisite for a European security pact. The British view was that German "reunity in freedom" meant just that: a "free" Germany might decide not to join NATO (even if Britain, like America, hoped that it would join). Also, the British chiefs of staff drew up a "pilot scheme" for a zone of limited armaments in Central Europe, which could be put into operation even if Germany remained divided. Dulles pointed out to the Brit-

8. FRUS, 1955–57, V, 542–4, 551–4, 602–4, 605–10, 630–1.
9. Ibid., 616–20; Geneva Meeting, 11. In this article I have chosen to refer mainly to the published U.S. records of the conference, rather than to the French records (see n. 13 below) or the British (see n. 28).

ish minister in Washington, Sir Robert Scott, that such a scheme might be taken to imply Western recognition of the long-term division of Germany, and could thereby upset the German public. But in London, permanent undersecretary of the foreign office Ivone Kirkpatrick complained to a U.S. visitor that American views of European security were too grudging to be accepted by the Soviets and might themselves provoke public dismay. Kirkpatrick also expressed an abiding Western fear when he declared "if we do not succeed in obtaining unification for the Germans, they will one day set out to obtain it for themselves." The undersecretary's view was that the West should offer enough "icing on the cake" to induce the Soviets to agree to German reunification.[10] In this he merely reflected a long-standing British tendency; it was at the Geneva summit that the prime minister, Anthony Eden, had first launched the British idea for a limited armaments zone in Central Europe as a "practical test" of the principle of joint inspection of such zones, and as tangible evidence from both sides of a desire to reduce tensions.[11] When, in late August, he saw an American memorandum setting out their postsummit policy, Eden was very disappointed, reflecting that the U.S. itself seemed "fearful" of agreement and arguing that Britain should adhere to its own, more hopeful policy. The British, well aware of their vulnerability to a Soviet military attack and with a strong tradition of balance-of-power diplomacy (rather than any notions of "ideological crusade"), had long had differences of emphasis with the Americans on cold-war fighting, and the British public were less skeptical than Americans about the "spirit of Geneva."[12]

Yet the scale of these differences should not be exaggerated. Although after the summit Eden had told the cabinet that Soviet leaders "seemed genuinely anxious to secure a relaxation of international tension," the foreign secretary, Harold Macmillan, had expressed doubts "whether the foreign ministers, at their meeting in October, would make much progress towards the unification of Germany." British views on a European security pact were actually not that far removed from America's. They centered on a nonaggression undertaking and limited armaments

10. *FRUS, 1955–57*, V, 560–6, 572. On the danger that Germany might not join NATO, see the memorandum in PRO, FO 371/118253/1341 (n.d.), PRO.

11. Eden's plan is reproduced in Frankland, ed., *Documents*, 41–3. For a brief discussion, see A. Varsori, "Le gouvernement Eden et l'Union soviétique, 1955–1956," *Relations Internationales* 71 (Autumn 1992), 284.

12. PREM 11/1077 (23 and 31 August 1955), PRO.

zones, and were put forward largely in the hope of inducing the Soviets to agree to a German settlement on Western terms. London, like Washington, was well aware of the psychological importance of such proposals, arguing that even if the Soviet side rejected them, they would gain approval in world public opinion.[13]

Moreover, many British officials took a skeptical view of the foreign ministers' conference. William Hayter, the ambassador to Moscow, argued that the "Soviet leaders want a relaxation of tension. . . . But they are not prepared to pay for this by the sacrifice of any essential Soviet interest" either in Eastern Europe in general or in East Germany in particular. "They have ceased to think they can bully us; but they are not likely to let us bully them," and so, reasoned Hayter, the offer of security guarantees to the Soviets was only "a useful exercise from the point of view of Western public opinion." Furthermore, as the conference approached, the British became increasingly concerned about Soviet activities in the Middle East, where there were close Communist links to the Egyptian government. Twice in October Eden sent written complaints to Moscow about the Czechoslovakian decision to sell arms to Egypt. Just before the conference, there seems to have been a toughening of the British position. A special meeting of ministers on 19 October, under Eden's chairmanship, agreed with the U.S. view that concessions to the Soviets on European security should be dependent on their concessions on Germany and while there was interest in the idea of greater trade and contacts, there was also concern over the potential use the KGB could make of freer travel to the West.[14] When Macmillan arrived in Geneva he even pressed Dulles about "how long . . . we should be toyed with by the Russians" at the conference, given the increasing difficulties in the Middle East. Macmillan wished to end the conference by 19 November at the latest. It was Dulles who then struck a moderate tone, expressing his reluctance to take a tough line with the Soviets, which could upset world opinion.[15]

13. CAB 128/29, CM (55) 26 (26 July 1955), PRO. British proposals and arguments are most easily consulted in *DDF*; see 1955, II, 263–71.

14. PREM 11/899 (4 and 19 Oct.), PRO; CAB 128/29, CM (55) 36th (20 Oct.), PRO. On growing Anglo-Soviet tension in the Middle East, see FO 800/684 (27 September–30 October), PRO.

15. Dulles wanted Britain and France to take the initiative if it became necessary to break off the conference. He was affected by the fact that Eisenhower was ill and the public were likely to blame any tough policy solely on the supposedly uncompromising secretary of state. This also explains why, in the early phases of the conference, Dulles let Macmillan

Like the British, the French were somewhat keener than the U.S. to reach agreements with Moscow in 1955. Beset by problems in North Africa, the French knew it was in their best interest to lower cold-war tensions. Yet Paris had also long wished to keep West Germany firmly tied to the West and had little interest in German reunification, which could only recreate a strong potential menace on the French border. Earlier in the year the French had seemed very interested in a deal on disarmament, arguing that savings from the arms race could be used to tackle underdevelopment in the third world, and, as mentioned above, at the summit it was Edgar Faure who put forth the most far-reaching proposals on East-West contacts. After the summit, however, foreign minister Antoine Pinay was at pains to make clear to French ambassadors that the spirit of Geneva did not amount to much. There had been a change in atmospherics but not in Soviet positions on key subjects, and there was therefore no reason for the West to offer any concessions to the Kremlin. Roland de Margerie, director-general of political affairs in the French foreign ministry, took a view similar to that of the Americans and British when he argued in August that the Soviets were unlikely to agree to German reunification in the foreseeable future, and that they would use a European security pact to destroy NATO; therefore, the West should only agree to a security pact if the Kremlin were ready to move on the German problem. However, De Margerie was perhaps nearer to the British than to the Americans when he argued that the only genuinely practical areas of advance were either a limited armaments zone in Central Europe or East-West contacts. Jean le Roy, the French chargé d'affaires in Moscow argued at this time that, given the new dynamism and flexibility of the post-Stalin Kremlin, a Soviet change in policy on Germany and Europe could not be ruled out. But officials in Paris, like their counterparts in Washington and London, believed that the Soviets were simply seeking to achieve their old aims through new tactics, which were designed to fool the Western public into believing that Moscow was now a moderate, positive force in world politics. Therefore, while the French had certain differences of emphasis from America and Britain on certain subjects of East-West discussion, they can be said to have shared a broad Western consensus which

---

and Pinay make the key speeches: *FRUS, 1955–57*, V, 619–21, 631–2. On earlier U.S. fears that the British might even favor recognition of the Communist regime in East Germany, see 164–5.

saw the Soviets as continuing an antagonistic policy. The West was determined to stick to existing policies on West German integration into
the Atlantic alliance, but was ready to put forward concessions in certain clearly defined areas, partly in order to convince the public of their
leaders' pacific intent.[16]

This broad consensus was shared by the West Germans, who, although not formally represented in the talks, inevitably had an important impact on the views of Washington, London, and Paris. One of the
major events that followed the Geneva summit was the visit of Chancellor Konrad Adenauer to the USSR in September, when diplomatic relations were established between Moscow and Bonn. This visit did not,
however, make Adenauer any more confident about Soviet intentions.
Indeed, the Kremlin had simultaneously made new commitments to
the East German regime which made German reunification, and a
proper West German–Soviet settlement, less likely. Adenauer in turn
was determined to remain closely linked to the Western alliance and
(like the Americans) to reject any agreement that suggested that the division of Germany was permanent. Neither of these attitudes improved
the chances of agreement with the Soviets. Although the Western preparations for the foreign ministers' conference were largely handled on a
three-power (U.S.-British-French) basis, the Germans were allowed
some input and could be satisfied with the overall tactical approach: the
Western powers would, if only for the sake of public relations, appear
positive, but it was doubtful that sufficient concessions could be made
to induce the Soviets to agree to German "unity in freedom." Therefore,
the conference should be brought to an amicable end within two or
three weeks, and the NATO alliance, with West Germany a member,
should be preserved intact.[17] The German foreign minister, Heinrich

16. *DDF*, 1955, II, 165–9, 178–9, 187–8, 235–6. Also see the discussion in E. Calandri,
"La détente et la perception de l'Union Soviétique chez les décideurs français du printemps
1955 à fevrier 1956," *Relations Internationales*, LXXIII (Summer 1993), 176–7.

17. See the report of the tripartite working group that met in Washington on 19–23 September in *DDF*, 1955, II, Annexes, 325–44. Separate discussions were held, between 16 September and 13 October, in Bonn (including German representatives) on detailed
arrangements for German reunification; see *FRUS, 1955–57*, V, 613. The Western position
on disarmament was discussed in Washington, but a fully agreed-upon position was impossible to achieve; see *DDF*, 1955, II, Annexes, 426–9. Draft position papers were discussed
by Dulles, Macmillan, and Pinay on 27 September and a final tripartite position was settled
in Paris talks between 10 and 20 October (*DDF*, 1955, II, Annexes, 300–8, 378–425). Final
position papers on European security and Germany were discussed by Dulles, Macmillan,
and Pinay on 24 October (*FRUS, 1955–57*, V, 622, n. 2); for these final proposals, see *Ge-*

von Brentano, twice met Dulles, Macmillan, and Pinay in the weeks before the Geneva Conference to discuss European security and the German question. On both occasions von Brentano underlined his
government's absolute abhorrence of anything suggesting diplomatic
recognition of East Germany. The East Germans should only be brought
into talks on a "technical" level if the Soviets agreed to free all-German
elections; in such a situation, Dulles nicely put it, East Germany would
have been invited "to its own funeral." Von Brentano was also extremely skeptical of Eden's idea for a limited "joint inspection" area in
Central Europe. Like the Americans, Adenauer believed that such a
scheme might be taken to imply Western recognition of the status quo
in Germany. Yet Bonn did see the need to offer the Soviets some icing
on the cake if they were to accept German reunification; in a meeting
on 24 October, von Brentano suggested offering a concession whereby,
if the Soviets withdrew from East Germany, NATO forces would undertake not to enter it. Dulles feared that such an offer would create a
power vacuum in the East, or else lead the Soviets to demand a reciprocal NATO withdrawal from West Germany, thus undermining the alliance's whole forward defense strategy—but a version of von Brentano's
suggestion was adopted when German reunification was finally accomplished thirty-five years later.[18]

The Geneva Meeting

When the Soviet and Western foreign ministers began their talks on 27
October, they quickly settled final arrangements regarding the agenda,
dates of meetings, and the writing of a communiqué. The three Western
ministers all made statements suggesting the possibility of a deal on European security and German reunification, although they insisted that
these two complex issues be viewed as inseparable. They were not
hopeful about reaching an early agreement on disarmament, but all
three stated their faith in the benefits of greater East-West contacts.
Dulles argued that it was possible to tackle areas which "do not seri-

---

neva Meeting, 27–33. The three Western ministers met with Molotov in September at the
UN and settled various technical points about the Geneva Conference (DDF, 1955, II, Annexes, 307–13).

   18. FRUS, 1955–57, V, 596–601, 621–30; DDF, 1955, II, Annexes, 316–20. On German
criticisms of Eden's inspection plan, see Konrad Adenauer, Erinnerungen, 1955–59 (Stuttgart, 1967), 34–5.

ously involve the security of either side and which . . . assure reciprocal benefits''; Pinay went somewhat further in stating that a rapprochement between the two sides could gradually lead to "a united Europe" in which "our Western European ideal of cooperation may be extended to the whole of Europe," although he also (and without explaining the apparent contradiction in this) argued that the West did not seek the destruction of the Communist system. In making the conference's opening speech, Pinay pleaded for a more constructive approach than had characterized other meetings since the war: "Too often, in the past, exchanges of view between the representatives of our Governments . . . have been nothing but an interminable sequence of alternating monologues."

Yet what transpired in the remainder of this first meeting hardly held out much hope of a constructive atmosphere, let alone agreements. For, faced by a united front among the Western delegates—all insistent that their desire for German unity in freedom and greater East-West contacts did not threaten the USSR—the Soviet foreign minister, Vyacheslav Molotov, set out a long, forthright statement that showed no sign of dynamic change in Kremlin policy. He contrasted recent pacific Soviet actions (such as the opening of diplomatic relations with Bonn) with the existence in the West of NATO, a web of U.S. bases, and a remilitarized Germany. To underline his desire to end the Atlantic alliance, he bluntly declared, "The Soviet Union is for the liquidation of military groupings." On all three subjects on the agenda he differed from the Western position. A European security arrangement should be achieved, he argued, independently of German reunification, which he saw as being possible only when the Western powers recognized the equal status of East Germany and West Germany, allowing those two countries to settle their own future. On disarmament he pressed the old Soviet aim of complete nuclear disarmament, a move which would destroy America's superiority in atomic weapons. And where East-West contacts were concerned he was interested not in freer information flow but, as expected, in the "unhindered expansion of international trade," an undisguised criticism of Western strategic trade controls. When these opening statements were finished Pinay tried to move on directly to the first item of the agenda, but Molotov opposed this. There then followed an hour-long argument before the meeting closed in disagreement on a technical point.[19]

19. *Geneva Meeting,* 14–25.

On none of the three agenda items did it prove possible to reach even a minor agreement over the three weeks of talks. The first item, European security and Germany, predictably absorbed most of the conference, dominating the plenary sessions down to 9 November. Both sides adhered closely to positions they had held for at least the past two years. Thus the Western powers had come armed with a variation of the "Eden Plan" (so-called not because Eden had devised it but because it had originally fallen to him to present it to the Berlin conference of foreign ministers in January 1954). This was based, as Macmillan explained on 28 October, on free elections in all of Germany, which would lead to a government that would most likely join NATO. The West believed that NATO membership would restrain any resurgence of militarist-nationalist ambitions on Germany's part, but they were nonetheless ready to offer extra security guarantees to the USSR if it accepted German reunification in freedom. Molotov for his part had arrived with a draft European Security Pact (first presented at the summit on 20 July) that would maintain the division of Germany, and he went on to propose the dissolution within two or three years of existing alliances like NATO, complete nuclear disarmament, and the withdrawal of all foreign troops (including U.S. troops) from Europe. Though there was little in this package to appeal to the West, Molotov defended it on 28 October as a way to end militarism—especially in Germany—and cut arms spending.[20]

The following day the foreign ministers, to Molotov's satisfaction, dedicated themselves to the European security issue. Western ministers accused the Soviets of wanting to destroy NATO while maintaining the Communist system in (and thus Soviet military domination of) Eastern Europe. Molotov accused his adversaries of subordinating everything to the inclusion of a rearmed Germany in a military bloc antagonistic to the USSR. At this point, Dulles suggested breaking off discussion on Item One of the agenda, a step the British (concerned over the likely public reaction) opposed.[21] Two days later, however, Molotov introduced a revised version of his security pact, which no longer demanded the dissolution of NATO and which made some positive proposals for a

20. Ibid., 33–45. For statements by Dulles and Pinay, see 48–55. On the Western and Soviet proposals, see Frankland, ed., Documents, 31–4, 50–3.
21. Geneva Meeting, 55–74. On Dulles's desire to break off discussions, see FO 371/118253/1339 (31 Oct.), PRO.

zone of limited armaments in Central Europe.[22] But, as Dulles wrote to Eisenhower, the prime defect in these new ideas was that Molotov still wished to keep Germany divided and wanted to see the West recognize East Germany. Indeed, he proposed on 2 November that both Germanies should now join in an "All-German Council," which would put the freely elected Federal Republic on an equal basis with the Communist East. This the Westerners refused to do, and talks over the next two days proved to be largely repetitive and utterly fruitless exchanges regarding the first item.[23]

Dulles, who believed he had Molotov on the defensive (and saw the latter's revised security pact as proof of this), was determined now to expose the Soviets publicly for using European security as a "smokescreen" to prevent German reunification. The talks recessed from 5 to 7 November, when Molotov returned to Moscow, and there was considerable speculation among the Western delegations about whether he would bring some new proposal back. But no one expected radical alteration of the Soviet view on Germany, and when the talks were renewed on 8 November, Molotov made the most negative statement to date of the Soviet position. The next day debate on the first item was adjourned. Molotov attempted on 15 November to renew it, but without success. He was still eager to see a European security arrangement that recognized East Germany's separate existence, and he accused the West of offering Moscow only "paper guarantees." But the Western powers refused even to discuss security until the USSR was ready to hold meaningful talks on German reunification.[24]

As mentioned above, it was never likely that a breakthrough would be possible on Item Two of the agenda, disarmament. The main problem here was that—as had been made embarrassingly clear in recent UN meetings—the U.S., Britain, and France lacked a united position and never seriously intended to engage in detailed talks with Molotov. The French were concerned to maintain a united Western front if possible, but the British were afraid that if the Western powers tried to paper

22. *Geneva Meeting*, 75–82. For Western foreign ministers' fears that Molotov might also press for German neutrality—a move which might have put them on the defensive, see *FRUS*, V, 652–3.

23. *FRUS, 1955–57*, V, 660–1, 687–8; *Geneva Meeting*, 82–136. Also see *DDF*, 1955, II, Annexes, 464–6.

24. *FRUS, 1955–57*, V, 676–8, 680–1, 700–11; *Geneva Meeting*, 137–52, 153–72; Frankland, ed., *Documents*, 56–7.

over their differences, it would be easy for a seasoned campaigner like Molotov to expose that fact. Dulles, Macmillan, and Pinay therefore agreed that their best approach, from the viewpoint of public opinion, was to press for the principle of inspection in any disarmament agreement and also to repeat Eisenhower's Open Skies proposal. These were both questions on which, given past experience, Molotov would be entirely negative. A coherent, detailed Western position need not be defined until the new year, when the UN's Subcommittee on Disarmament was due to meet once more.[25] On 10 November, when the conference shifted its attention to disarmament, the foreign ministers duly divided on predictable lines. Dulles pressed for the principle of inspection, Pinay and Macmillan criticized Soviet plans for complete nuclear disarmament, and Molotov attacked Open Skies as a way to extend U.S. espionage that did nothing to end the arms race. Two more days of argument on the same themes simply led to an agreement that at least the differences of the two sides had been clarified.[26]

Item three of the conference was perhaps the most interesting, not because it resulted in any breakthrough—it did not—but because it involved an item which had not previously been discussed with any thoroughness by the two sides in the cold war. The development of peaceful contacts between East and West could be seen as an obvious and relatively painless way of building trust between them. Yet, as seen above, Western planners actually viewed contacts as a method of cold-war fighting: by opening the USSR up to the penetration of liberal ideas, the West could hope to undermine the Communist system, and by freeing Western broadcasts to the Soviets, the West could help its own propaganda agencies which were already well established as a cold-war weapon. For its part, the Soviet Union too was only interested in freeing East-West contacts in order to achieve certain specific aims—such as securing the import of technological and strategic goods from the West—and had no intention of allowing the capitalist powers to break down its policies of information control. The differences between the two sides were immediately apparent when the foreign ministers had an initial discussion of this item on 31 October.

25. *DDF*, II, 629–30; *FRUS, 1955–57*, V, 636–8, 670–1. For other Western discussions of tactics, see *FRUS, 1955–57*, V, 715–8 and 741–3. For a Western memorandum presented at the conference that largely confirms the work of the UN, see Frankland, ed., *Documents*, 57–9.

26. *Geneva Meeting*, 177–99, 201–25; *FRUS, 1955–57*, V, 757–8. On vain attempts to write a four-power declaration on disarmament, see *FRUS, 1955–57*, V, 754–7, 780–3.

Pinay, followed by Macmillan and Dulles, minimized the significance of strategic export controls as an impediment to trade (the volume concerned was certainly not large) and called for a freer flow of individuals, information, and ideas between the Communist and capitalist worlds as a way, they said, to promote "an atmosphere of confidence among states and a better understanding among peoples." They put forward a memorandum setting out seventeen specific ways to achieve this, including the elimination of censorship and "jamming" of broadcasts; exchanges of publications; the opening of information centers in capital cities; cultural, scientific and sporting visits; the end of restrictions on diplomatic travel; and an extension of tourism and air transport links. The low level of East-West trade was squarely blamed on Communist economics. In his reply, Molotov argued that Soviet policies were designed to protect its people's interests and that the West must respect the principle of noninterference in the internal affairs of others. He introduced a paper whose first point was the elimination of "existing obstacles and restrictions in international trade between East and West," which also wished to "broaden international scientific . . . relations, particularly in the field of the peaceful uses of atomic energy," and which asserted the right of all states to participate in such international agencies as UNESCO and WHO (a right which, of course, could be exploited by Communist states, like East Germany, which the West did not recognize).[27]

After this unpromising initial discussion, and in line with the decisions of the July summit, the issue of contacts was turned over to a group of experts, whose first meetings on 2 and 3 November were no more hopeful than that between the foreign ministers had been. The Soviet representative, Sergei Vinogradov, began by attacking the Western memorandum of 31 October and repeating the arguments already deployed by Molotov; the Western representatives refused either to focus the discussion on trade or to accept that all states had a right to enter UN agencies. It was decided to set up two expert study groups, one to look at trade, the other at general contacts. Once again, however, progress on the procedural side belied the fact that there was no meeting of minds on substantial issues. Over the next week officials in the study groups repeatedly talked past each other, with each side accusing the other of intransigence, although the atmosphere seemed to have been

27. *Geneva Meeting,* 228–48.

one of intense frustration rather than heated argument. On 10 November the experts had little option but to agree to disagree on every question before them.[28] Four days later, when the foreign ministers again looked at Item Three, the discussion did become "heated," at least in its later stages.[29] Molotov accused the West of restricting international trade and of wishing to conduct propaganda and espionage through the relaxation of information and travel controls (the second point, at least, was true); the Western ministers accused the Soviets of obstructionism and of showing little interest in the expansion of peaceful trade (which was also true). Dulles rightly pointed out that it was preposterous of Molotov to argue that East-West contacts should not affect the internal policies of states, since they inevitably did so.[30] In a final, barren discussion on 15 November, the two sides could not even agree on a joint statement about Item Three. The Western powers subsequently issued their own, blaming the Soviets for creating deadlock on the subject. In the closing exchanges Molotov declared that the West had deliberately framed its proposals to ensure Soviet rejection, while Dulles asserted that the Kremlin feared greater contacts because it knew that Communism was inherently weak. Both statements confirmed that, yet again, both sides came close to understanding the truth about the other's position but were incapable of acknowledging the truth about their own.[31]

As early as 7 November Dulles warned Eisenhower that, although the British and French delegations did not want the conference to "mark a break" with the Soviets, it was difficult to see the discussions "recording enough progress to justify holding a new conference." When Molotov exhibited such an uncompromising mood about Germany upon his return from Moscow, Dulles could see even less evidence that a future meeting with him would be useful. Pinay seemed to agree, but, Dulles complained, Macmillan "seemed to have been softened up, presumably by Eden." Eisenhower's response was to warn his secretary of state that it was essential for the West always to appear "reasonable." Subsequently, in a meeting on 9 November between the three Western foreign

28. *FRUS, 1955–57*, V, 661–3, 668–9, 682–7, 690–2, 711–5, 722–5, 728–34, 760–4.

29. According to Dulles; ibid., 776. See 768–9 for a bilateral Dulles-Molotov meeting.

30. At this meeting Pinay introduced a Western draft declaration on the relaxation of contacts. *Geneva Meeting*, 248–67; *FRUS, 1955–57*, V, 771–5.

31. *Geneva Meeting*, 269–79. For Macmillan's statement, see *Command Papers*, no. 9633, *Documents relating to the Meeting of Foreign Ministers . . . Geneva, October 17–November 16, 1955*, 161–2. For the Western declaration, see Frankland, ed., *Documents*, 66–9.

ministers and von Brentano, when the German minister suggested that the conference immediately be broken off, Dulles himself opposed this suggestion. The American's aim was to ensure that there be no further fruitless conferences, but not at the expense of provoking an immediate breach with the Russians. On this occasion, however, both Macmillan and Pinay were ready to consider a further conference with Molotov. They still adhered to this view on 14 November, but the eventual communiqué of the conference made no firm declarations about more talks.[32]

In their set-piece closing statements on 16 November, all four foreign ministers made predictable defenses of their overall positions. Once again, the Western ministers spoke with similar voices. Dulles argued that they had prepared for the conference in good faith, but that the Soviets were not really interested in agreement on the first and third items. Pinay was keen to underline the point that Moscow did not seem interested in real security guarantees in Europe, but rather wished to keep Germany divided, hold on to Eastern Europe, and destroy NATO. Macmillan feared that "at the worst we have taken a step backward," because rather than being concerned about East-West tensions "the Soviet delegation do not seem to mind our failure." At one point Macmillan repeated a point that Winston Churchill had made on several occasions: in rejecting contacts with the West the Russian government showed that it "fears our friendship more than our enmity," because a lowering of tension would make it harder to maintain the climate in which Communism thrived. In his own statement, Molotov was unapologetic, taking one last opportunity to criticize his Western colleagues because they wished to remilitarize Germany, maintain the arms race, and interfere in Soviet internal affairs.[33]

Conclusion

In reporting to their respective governments, both Dulles and Macmillan were clear that the turning point in the conference had been the stiffening of Molotov's position after his visit to Moscow in early November. The message was that the Soviets were not in any way ready to compromise their position in Eastern Europe as the price of agreement

32. *FRUS, 1955–57*, V, 699–700, 725–7, 776, 791–4, 802; *DDF*, 1955, II, Annexes, 469–72.

33. *Geneva Meeting*, 284–304.

with the West. In London, Macmillan now expected the Kremlin to devote its full attention to the Middle East—an area that had not figured in the foreign ministers' talks, since none of them had wished to add another contentious issue to their agenda, preferring to concentrate on established problems for which they had well-prepared positions. Even Anthony Eden did not seem perturbed about the failure of the foreign ministers' talks, writing to Eisenhower on 17 November, "It was hardly to be expected that our summer weather could have continued into the winter." In reply, the president was confident that, on the German question, the West had scored the most vital psychological point: "we have made clearer to everyone that . . . Soviet policy concerning Germany is designed to preserve [East Germany] as the keystone of their satellite position" rather than to protect the USSR's security. It is difficult to disagree with the judgment of one historian that, on the issue of Germany and European security at Geneva, Molotov made the "West's dilemma . . . so simple . . . that its statesmen had little opportunity to deviate."[34] Indeed, he was too intransigent to sow divisions among his opponents.

For their part, Western representatives seem genuinely to have believed, at times, that their offer of security guarantees to Moscow really was enough to induce the Soviets to accept German reunification on the basis of free elections and NATO membership.[35] But this was surely no more reasonable than Molotov's hope that the West would recognize East Germany. As a result, the Geneva meeting did not progress any further than had the 1954 Berlin foreign ministers' meeting. In 1955 the two sides in the cold war felt themselves too closely balanced for one to give way to the other; moreover, they had only recently begun to negotiate after the diplomatic freeze of Stalin's last years, and both inevitably approached talks with an attitude of suspicion and caution. Nikita Khrushchev may have been prepared to take a more dynamic course than Molotov, as with the sudden signature of the Austrian treaty (which had been delayed for eight years) in May 1955, but he had done so with specific pro-Soviet purposes in mind. He was not in the business of surrendering positions for inadequate gains. And, in the aftermath of the Geneva conferences his flexibility was seen not in concessions but

34. *FRUS, 1955–57,* V, 747–9; CAB128/29, CM (55) 41st (17 November), PRO; PREM 11/899 (17 November), PRO; Eisenhower to Eden, 19 November 1955, *The Diaries of Dwight D. Eisenhower* (microfilm, Frederick, Maryland, 1986); R. Goold-Adams, *The Time of Power* (London, 1962), 196.

35. For example, PREM 11/899 (15 November), PRO.

in the continued development of a more imaginative policy toward the "third" world, as he sought to build an alliance between Communists and former colonial states. As for the Western powers, they were content to continue the policy of building their strength as a prelude to more successful negotiations. That policy had not (as the British foreign office had hoped it might) forced the Kremlin to come to a settlement. In the long term, however, it might yet succeed and there seemed no real alternative.

The foreign ministers' meeting had at least raised the possibility of carrying the two sides away from cold-war enmities: talks, tourism, and trade had been discussed as a way to create a better international atmosphere. But it would be twenty years before the Soviets were ready to sign the Helsinki Agreements of 1975, in which they accepted greater contacts with the West in return for Western acceptance of the postwar territorial settlement in Eastern Europe. In 1955, during the first experiment with détente, such a dramatic "formula" for a cold-war settlement in Europe was impossible, and even a limited area of agreement on details proved elusive. Indeed, the very process of negotiation was used, not so much as a meaningful attempt at diplomatic progress, but as an exercise in psychological warfare. Both sides sought to impress public opinion with their own reasonableness, to highlight any unreasonable positions held by their opponents, and to do so without conceding the slightest material point. Although it would take a long time to be thoroughly tarnished, by mid-November 1955 the spirit of Geneva had failed Eisenhower's acid test.

Contributors

Colette Barbier is a graduate of the Paris Institute of Political Sciences and the Sorbonne. She has been a researcher in the French group of the International Nuclear History Program.

Günter Bischof holds a Ph.D. from Harvard University and is professor of history and associate director of the Center for Austrian Culture and Commerce at the University of New Orleans. He is coediting the series Contemporary Austrian Studies (Transaction) and Eisenhower Center Studies on War and Peace (LSU Press), for which he coedited the volumes *Eisenhower and the German POWs: Facts against Falsehood* (1992), *Eisenhower: A Centenary Assessment* (1995), and *The Pacific War Revisited* (1997). His *Austria in the First Cold War, 1945–55: The Leverage of the Weak* (1999) is the first volume to appear in Saki Dockrill's Cold War History Series (Macmillan/St. Martin's). He has taught as guest professor at the Universities of Munich, Innsbruck, Salzburg, and Vienna.

Eckart Conze holds a Ph.D. in history from the University of Erlangen-Nürnberg and is assistant professor of history at Tübingen University. He is author of *Die gaullistische Herausforderung: Deutsch-französische Beziehungen in der amerikanischen Europapolitik 1958–1963* (1995) and articles in *Vierteljahrshefte für Zeitgeschichte*.

Saki Dockrill holds a Ph.D. in history from the University of London and is senior lecturer in War Studies at King's College, University of London. In 1988–89 she was John M. Olin Fellow at Yale University. She is author of *Britain's Policy for West German Rearmament* (1991) and *Eisenhower's New-Look National Security Policy, 1953–61* (1996), and edited *Controversy and Compromise: Alliance Politics between Britain, West Germany, and the United States* (1998). She is codirector of the Cold War Programme in Europe, general editor of Macmillan's Cold War History Series, and a member of the editorial group for the *Cold*

War History Journal, published by Frank Cass. She is currently working on a book on the Wilson government's global policies during the Vietnam War.

Richard H. Immerman holds a Ph.D. in history from Boston College and is professor of history at Temple University. He is author of *The CIA in Guatemala: The Foreign Policy of Intervention* (1982; a Spanish edition is forthcoming) and *John Foster Dulles: Piety, Pragmatism, and Power in U.S. Foreign Policy* (1999), and coauthor with Robert Bowie of *Waging Peace: How Eisenhower Shaped an Enduring Cold War Strategy* (1998). He is also editor of *John Foster Dulles and the Diplomacy of the Cold War: A Reappraisal* (1990).

Ernest Richard May holds a Ph.D. in history from the University of California at Los Angeles and is Charles Warren Professor of History and director of the Charles Warren Center for American History at Harvard University. He has authored or edited numerous books, including *Thinking in Time: The Uses of History for Decision-Makers* (1986); *American Cold War Strategy: Interpreting NSC 68* (1993); and *Strange Victory: Hitler's Conquest of France* (2000).

John Prados holds a Ph.D. in history from Columbia University and writes in the Washington, D.C., area. He is author of, among others, *Keepers of the Keys: A History of the National Security Council from Truman to Bush* (1991), *Hidden History of the Vietnam War* (1995), and *The Ho Chi Minh Trail* (1998). He is also a prolific designer of war games.

Ronald W. Pruessen holds a Ph.D. in history from the University of Pennsylvania and is professor of history at the University of Toronto. He is author of *John Foster Dulles: The Road to Power* (1982) and *To the Nuclear Brink for Asia: The Quemoy-Matsu Crises of the 1950s* (forthcoming).

Robert Mark Spaulding holds a Ph.D. from Harvard University and is associate professor of history at the University of North Carolina at Wilmington. He was a postdoctoral fellow in the Ford Foundation program on Western European security at the Center for International Affairs at Harvard University. He is author of *Osthandel und Ostpolitik: German*

Foreign Trade Policies in Eastern Europe from Bismarck to Adenauer (1997). His articles on East-West trade and international political economy have appeared in *Diplomatic History* and *International Organization*. He is currently working on a project concerning the Rhine River.

Antonio Varsori is professor of the history of international relations and holds the Jean Monnet Chair in the History of European Integration on the Faculty of Political Sciences at the University of Florence, where he is also director of the postgraduate course in European Studies. He is author of *Il Patto di Bruxelles (1948) tra integrazione europea e alleanza atlantica* (1988) and editor of *La politica estera italiana del secondo dopoguerra (1943–1957)* (1993) and *Europe, 1945–1990s: The End of an Era?* (1995). Varsori is the Italian member of the Liaison Committee of Historians at the EU Commission and a member of the Editorial Board of the *Journal of European Integration History*. He is deputy editor of the journal *Storia delle relazioni internazionali*.

John W. Young holds a Ph.D. from the University of Cambridge and is professor of politics at the University of Leicester, where he has taught since 1993. He is author of *Britain, France, and the Unity of Europe, 1945–51* (1984), *France, the Cold War, and the Western Alliance, 1944–49* (1990), *The Longman Companion to Cold War and Détente, 1941–91* (1993), *Britain and European Unity, 1945–92* (1993), *Cold War Europe, 1945–91: A Political History* (1996), and *Winston Churchill's Last Campaign: Britain and the Cold War, 1951–5* (1996).

Vladislav Martin Zubok is a graduate of the Institute of U.S. and Canada Studies in Moscow and is currently a senior research fellow at the National Security Archives in Washington, D.C. He is coauthor of *Inside the Kremlin's Cold War: From Stalin to Khrushchev* (1996) and author of important articles on the Soviet Union in the cold war in *Diplomatic History* and the Cold War International History Program at the Wilson Center. He served as a principal consultant for a 24-part CNN documentary on the cold war.

Selected Bibliography

COMPILED BY MARKUS HÜNEMÖRDER

Primary Sources

Document Collections

Buchstab, Günter, ed. *Die Protokolle des CDU-Bundesvorstandes, 1953–1957.* Düsseldorf, 1990.

Command Papers. No. 9543. London, 1955.

Documents diplomatiques français, 1955. 2 vols. Paris, 1987, 1988.

Dokumente zur Deutschlandpolitik. Vol. III, no. 1, 5 May–31 December 1955. Berlin, 1961.

Frankland, Noble, ed. *Documents on International Affairs, 1955.* London, 1958.

Gehler, Michael, ed. *Gruber: Reden und Dokumente.* Vienna, 1994.

Historical-Diplomatic Division of the Ministry of Foreign Affairs of the USSR. *The USSR-PRC (1949–1983). Documents and Materials.* Vol. I., *1949–1963, Moscow.* Moscow, 1985.

James, Robert Rhodes, ed. *Winston Churchill: His Complete Speeches, 1897– 1963.* 8 volumes. New York, 1974.

Keesing's Contemporary Archives. Vol. IX of 32 vols., *1952–1954.* London, 1955.
———. Vol. X, *1955–1956.* London, 1957.

Mensing, Hans Peter, ed. *Heuss-Adenauer: Unserem Vaterland Zugute. Der Briefwechsel, 1948–1963.* Berlin, 1989.

Porter, Kirk H., and Donald B. Johnson, eds. *National Party Platforms, 1840– 1956.* Urbana, Ill., 1956.

Public Papers of the Presidents of the United States: Dwight D. Eisenhower, 1955. Washington, D.C., 1959.

Schilcher, Alfons, ed. *Österreich und die Grossmächte: Dokumente zur österreichischen Aussenpolitik, 1945–1955.* Vienna, 1980.

Statistical Office of the United Nations. *Yearbook of International Trade Statistics, 1962.* New York, 1964.

United Nations Statistical Papers. Ser. T, Vol. VII, No. 6, *Direction of International Trade.* Geneva, 1956.

U.S. Department of State. *Foreign Relations of the United States, 1951,* Vol. I,

National Security Affairs; Foreign Economic Policy. Washington, D.C., 1979.
Hereinafter abbreviated *FRUS.*
———. *FRUS, 1952–1954.* Vol. I, *General; Economic and Political Matters.*
1983.
———. *FRUS, 1952–1954.* Vol. II, *National Security Affairs.* 1984.
———. *FRUS, 1952–1954.* Vol. V, *Western European Security.* 1983.
———. *FRUS, 1952–1954.* Vol. VI, *Western Europe and Canada.* 1986.
———. *FRUS, 1952–1954.* Vol. VII, *Germany and Austria.* 1986.
———. *FRUS, 1952–1954.* Vol. VIII, *Eastern Europe; Soviet Union; Eastern Mediterranean.* 1988.
———. *FRUS, 1955–1957.* Vol. II, *China.* 1986.
———. *FRUS, 1955–1957.* Vol. IV, *Western European Security and Integration.*
1986.
———. *FRUS, 1955–1957.* Vol. V, *Austrian State Treaty; Summit and Foreign
Ministers Meetings 1955.* 1988.
———. *FRUS, 1955–1957.* Vol. X, *Foreign Aid and Economic Defense Policy.*
1989.
———. *FRUS, 1955–1957.* Vol. XIV, *Arab-Israeli Dispute, 1955.* 1989.
———. *FRUS, 1955–1957.* Vol. XVII, *Arab-Israeli Dispute, 1957.* 1990.
———. *FRUS, 1955–1957.* Vol. XIX, *National Security Policy.* 1990.
———. *FRUS, 1955–1957.* Vol. XX, *Regulation of Armaments; Atomic Energy.*
1990.
———. *FRUS, 1955–1957.* Vol. XXV, *Eastern Europe.* 1990.
———. *FRUS, 1955–1957.* Vol. XXVI, *Central and Southeastern Europe.* 1992.
———. *The Geneva Conference of Heads of Government, July 18–23, 1955.*
Washington, D.C., 1955.

Memoirs, Diaries, and Letters

Adenauer, Konrad. *Erinnerungen, 1953–1955.* Stuttgart, 1966.
———. *Erinnerungen, 1955–1959.* Stuttgart, 1967.
Blankenhorn, Herbert. *Verständnis und Verständigung: Blätter eines Politischen Tagebuchs 1949 bis 1979.* Berlin, 1980.
Bohlen, Charles E. *Witness to History, 1929–1969.* New York, 1973.
Boyle, Peter G., ed. *The Churchill-Eisenhower Correspondence, 1953–1955.*
Chapel Hill, N.C., 1990.
Colville, John. *The Fringes of Power: 10 Downing Street Diaries, 1939–1955.*
London, 1985. New York, 1985.
Crankshaw, Edward. *Khrushchev Remembers.* Trans. and ed. by Strobe Talbott.
New York, 1971.
Eden, Anthony. *The Memoirs of Sir Anthony Eden: Full Circle.* London, 1960.

Eisenhower, Dwight D. *The White House Years: Mandate for Change, 1953–1956.* New York, 1963.

———. The Diaries of Dwight D. Eisenhower. Microfilm. Frederick, Md., 1986.

Eisenhower, John S. D. *Strictly Personal.* Garden City, N.Y., 1974.

Faure, Edgar. *Mémoires.* 2 vols. Paris, 1982–84.

Ferrel, Robert H., ed. *The Eisenhower Diaries.* New York, 1981.

Grewe, Wilhelm G. *Rückblenden 1976–1951: Aufzeichnungen eines Augenzeugen deutscher Aussenpolitik von Adenauer bis Schmidt.* Berlin, 1979.

Griffith, Robert, ed. *Ike's Letters to a Friend, 1941–1958.* Lawrence, Kans., 1984.

Hughes, Emmet J. *The Ordeal of Power: A Political Memoir of the Eisenhower Years.* New York, 1975.

Khrushchev, Nikita S. *Khrushchev Remembers: The Glasnost Tapes.* Trans. and ed. by Jerrold L. Schecter and Vyacheslav V. Luchkov. Boston, 1990.

Kreisky, Bruno. *Zwischen den Zeiten: Erinnerungen aus fünf Jahrzehnten.* Vienna, 1986.

———. *Im Strom der Zeiten: Der Memoiren Zeiter Teil.* Vienna, 1988.

Kroll, Hans. *Botschafter in Belgrad, Tokio und Moskau 1953–1962.* Munich, 1969.

Macmillan, Harold. *Tides of Fortune, 1945–1955.* London, 1969.

Massigli, René. *Une comédie des erreurs, 1943–1956.* Paris,1978.

"Memuari Nikiti Sergeevicha Khrushcheva." *Voprosi istorii,* VIII–IX (1992).

Mendès-France, Pierre. *Oeuvres complètes.* Vol. III of 3 vols., *Gouverner c'est choisir, 1954–1955.* Paris, 1986.

Moch, Jules. *Une si longue vie.* Paris, 1976.

Resis, Albert, ed. *Molotov Remembers: Inside Kremlin Politics—Conversations with Felix Chuev.* Chicago, 1993.

Semjonov, Wladimir. *Von Stalin bis Gorbatschow: Ein halbes Jahrhundert in diplomatischer Mission.* Leipzig, 1994.

Spaak, Paul-Henri. *Combats inachevés.* 2 vols. Paris, 1969.

Secondary Sources

Books

Adler-Karlsson, Gunnar. *Western Economic Warfare, 1947–1967.* Stockholm, 1968.

Albrich, Thomas, Klaus Eisterer, Michael Gehler, and Rolf Steininger, eds. *Österreich in den Fünfzigern.* Innsbruck, 1995.

Allard, Sven. *Russia and the Austrian State Treaty: A Case Study of Soviet Policy in Europe.* University Park, Pa., 1970.

Ambrose, Stephen. *Eisenhower: The President.* New York, 1984.

Artaud, Denise, and Lawrence S. Kaplan, eds. *Dien Bien Phu: L'alliance atlantique et la défense du sud-est asiatique*. Lyon, 1989.

Ashton, R. A. *In Search of Détente: The Politics of East-West Relations since 1945*. London, 1989.

Bédarida, François, and Jean-Pierre Rioux, eds. *Pierre Mendès-France et le Mendésisme: L'expérience gouvernementale (1954–1955) et sa postérité*. Paris, 1985.

Beridge, G. R. *Diplomacy: Theory and Practice*. London, 1995.

Beschloss, Michael R. *Mayday: The U-2 Affair*. New York, 1986.

Bischof, Günter. *Austria in the First Cold War, 1945–55: The Leverage of the Weak*. New York, 1999.

Bischof, Günter, and Stephen Ambrose, eds. *Eisenhower: A Centenary Assessment*. Baton Rouge, 1995.

Bischof, Günter, and Josef Leidenfrost, eds. *Die Bevormundete Nation: Österreich und die Alliierten 1945–1949*. Innsbruck, 1988.

Bloch-Morhange, Jacques. *La grenouille et le scorpion*. Paris, 1982.

Blumenwitz, Dieter, ed. *Die Deutschlandfrage vom 17. Juni 1953 bis zu den Genfer Viermächtekonferenzen von 1955*. Berlin, 1990.

Bowie, Robert R., and Richard H. Immerman. *Waging Peace: How Eisenhower Shaped an Enduring Cold War Strategy*. New York, 1998.

Boyle, Peter G. *American-Soviet Relations: From the Russian Revolution to the Fall of Communism*. London, 1993.

Brands, Henry W. *Cold Warriors: Eisenhower's Generation and American Foreign Policy*. New York, 1988.

Broadwater, Jeff. *Eisenhower and the Anti-Communist Crusade*. Chapel Hill, 1992.

Carlton, David. *Anthony Eden: A Biography*. London, 1981.

Chang, Gordon H. *Friends and Enemies: The United States, China, and the Soviet Union, 1948–1972*. Stanford, Calif., 1990.

Colard, D. *Edgar Faure*. Paris, 1975.

Condit, Kenneth W. *History of the Joint Chiefs of Staff*. Vol. VI of 6 vols., *The Joint Chiefs of Staff and National Policy, 1955–1956*. Washington, D.C., 1992.

Cook, Blanche W. *The Declassified Eisenhower: A Divided Legacy of Peace and Political Warfare*. New York, 1981.

Craig, Gordon A., and Francis L. Loewenheim, eds. *The Diplomats, 1939–1979*. Princeton, 1994.

Cronin, Audrey Kurth. *Great Power Politics and the Struggle over Austria, 1945–1955*. Ithaca, 1986.

Divine, Robert. *Foreign Policy and Presidential Elections, 1952–1960*. New York, 1974.

Dockrill, Michael, and John W. Young, eds. *British Foreign Policy, 1945–1956*. London, 1989.

Dockrill, Saki. *Britain's Policy for West German Rearmament, 1951–1955.* Cambridge, 1991.

———. *Eisenhower's New-Look National Security Policy, 1953–1961.* New York, 1996.

———, ed. *Controversy and Compromise: Alliance Politics between Great Britain, the Federal Republic of Germany, and the United States of America, 1945–1967.* Bodenheim, Germany, 1998.

Drummond, Roscoe, and Gaston Coblentz. *Duel at the Brink: John Foster Dulles' Command of American Power.* Garden City, N.Y., 1960.

Dunn, David H., ed. *Diplomacy at the Highest Level: The Evolution of International Summitry.* Basingstoke, U.K., 1996.

Elgey, Georgette. *Histoire de la IV République.* Vol. III of 4 vols., *La république des tourmentes, 1954–1959.* Paris, 1992.

Eubank Keith. *The Summit Conferences, 1919–1960.* Norman, Okla., 1966.

Felken, Detlef. *Dulles und Deutschland: Die amerikanische Deutschlandpolitik, 1953–1959.* Berlin, 1993.

Foschepoth, Josef, ed. *Adenauer und die Deutsche Frage: Zwölf Beiträge.* Göttingen, Germany, 1988.

Funigiello, P. *American-Soviet Trade in the Cold War.* Chapel Hill, 1988.

Gabriel, Jürg M. *The American Conception of Neutrality after 1941.* New York, 1988.

Gaddis, John Lewis. *We Now Know: Rethinking Cold War History.* Oxford, U.K., 1997.

George, Alexander, Philip J. Farley, and Alexander Dallin, eds. *U.S.-Soviet Security Cooperation: Achievements, Failures, Lessons.* New York, 1988.

Gilbert, M. *Never Despair: Winston S. Churchill, 1945–1965.* London, 1988.

Girault, René, ed. *Pierre Mendès-France et le role de la France dans le monde.* Grenoble, 1991.

Goold-Adams, R. *The Time of Power.* London, 1962.

Greenstein, Fred. *The Hidden-Hand Presidency: Eisenhower As Leader.* New York, 1982.

Grosser, Alfred. *La IVᵉ République et sa politique extérieure.* Colin, 1972.

Haftendorn, Helga. *Sicherheit und Entspannung: Zur Aussenpolitik der Bundesrepublik Deutschland, 1955–1982.* Baden-Baden, Germany, 1986.

Heuser, Beatrice, and Robert O'Neill, eds. *Securing Peace in Europe, 1945–1962.* London, 1992.

Hilsman, Roger, and Robert C. Good, eds. *Foreign Policy in the Sixties: The Issues and Instruments.* Baltimore, 1965.

Höbelt, Lothar, and Othmar Huber, eds. *Für Österreichs Freiheit: Karl Gruber— Landeshauptmann und Aussenminister, 1945–1953.* Innsbruck, 1991.

Immerman, Richard, ed. *John Foster Dulles and the Diplomacy of the Cold War.* Princeton, 1990.

Kaenel, André, ed. *Anti-Communism and McCarthyism in the United States (1946–1954): Essays on the Politics and Culture of the Cold War.* Paris, 1995.

Kennedy-Pipe, Caroline. *Stalin's Cold War: Soviet Strategies in Europe, 1943 to 1956.* Manchester, 1995.

Knight, Amy. *Beria: Stalin's First Lieutenant.* Princeton, 1993.

Kohl, Wilfrid L. *French Nuclear Diplomacy.* Princeton, N.J., 1971.

Kosthorst, Daniel. *Brentano und die Deutsche Einheit: Die Deutschland- und Ostpolitik des Aussenministers im Kabinett Adenauers, 1955–1961.* Düsseldorf, 1993.

Kostyrchenko, Gennadi. *V Plenu u Krasnogo Faraona.* [Imprisoned by the Red Pharaoh.] Moscow, 1994.

Kovrig, Bennett. *Of Walls and Bridges: The United States and Eastern Europe.* New York, 1991.

Lacouture, Jean. *Pierre Mendès France.* trans. George Holoch. New York, 1993.

Lamb, R. *The Failure of the Eden Government.* London, 1987.

Larres, Klaus. *Politik der Illusionen: Churchill, Eisenhower, und die deutsche Frage, 1945–1955.* Göttingen, 1995.

Leffler, Melvyn S. *Preponderance of Power: National Security, the Truman Administration, and the Cold War.* Stanford, Calif., 1992.

Leonhard, Alan T., ed. *Neutrality: Changing Concepts and Practices.* Lanham, Md., 1988.

Marks, Frederick W., III. *Power and Peace: The Diplomacy of John Foster Dulles.* Westport, Conn., 1993.

May, Ernest R., ed. *American Cold War Strategy: Interpreting NSC 68.* Boston, 1993.

Melanson, Richard A., and David Mayers, eds. *Reevaluating Eisenhower: American Foreign Policy in the Fifties.* Chicago, 1987.

Mitchell, Brian R. *European Historical Statistics, 1750–1970.* New York, 1978.

Morsey, Rudolf. *Die Deutschlandpolitik Adenauers: Alte Thesen und neue Fakten.* Opladen, 1991.

Naimark, Norman. *The Russians in Germany: A History of the Soviet Zone of Occupation, 1945–1949.* Stanford, Calif., 1995.

Prados, John. *Keepers of the Keys: A History of the National Security Council from Truman to Bush.* New York, 1991.

Pruessen, Ronald W. *John Foster Dulles: The Road to Power.* New York, 1982.

———. *To the Nuclear Brink for Asia: The Quemoy-Matsu Crisis, 1954–1958.* New York, forthcoming.

Rauchensteiner, Manfried. *Der Sonderfall: Die Besatzungspolitik in Österreich, 1945 bis 1955.* Graz, Austria, 1979.

Richter, James. *Khrushchev's Double Bind: International Pressures and Domestics Coalition Politics.* Baltimore, 1994.

Rimbaud, Christiane. *Pinay.* Paris, 1990.

Rostow, Walt W. *Europe after Stalin: Eisenhower's Three Decisions of March 11, 1953.* Austin, Tex., 1982.

——. *Open Skies: Eisenhower's Proposals of July 21, 1955.* Austin, Tex., 1982.

Rupieper, Hermann-Josef. *Der besetzte Verbündete: Die amerikanische Deutschlandpolitik, 1949–1955.* Opladen, 1991.

Schmidt, Gustav, ed. *Ost-West-Beziehungen: Konfrontation und Détente, 1945–1989.* 3 vols. Bochum, 1993.

Schöllgen, Gregor. *Die Macht in der Mitte Europas: Stationen deutscher Aussenpolitik von Friedrich dem Grossen bis zur Gegenwart.* Munich, 1992.

Schwartz, Thomas Alan. *America's Germany: John J. McCloy and the Federal Republic of Germany.* Cambridge, Mass., 1991.

Schwarz, Hans-Peter. *Die Ära Adenauer, 1949–1957: Gründerjahre der Republik 1919–1957.* Vol. II of *Geschichte der Bundesrepublik.* Stuttgart, 1981.

——. *Adenauer: Der Staatsmann, 1952–1967.* Stuttgart, 1991.

——, ed. *Entspannung und Wiedervereinigung: Deutschlandpolitische Vorstellungen Konrad Adenauers, 1955–1958.* Vol. II, *Rhöndorfer Gespräche.* Stuttgart, 1979.

Spaulding, Robert Mark. *Osthandel and Ostpolitik: German Foreign Trade Policies in Eastern Europe from Bismarck to Adenauer.* Vol. I of Monographs in German History. Providence, R.I., 1997.

Steininger, Rolf. *The German Question: The Stalin Notes of 1952 and the Problem of Reunification.* New York, 1990.

——. *Deutsche Geschichte seit 1945.* Vol. II, *1948–1955.* Frankfurt, 1996.

Steininger, Rolf, Jürgen Weber, Günter Bischof, Thomas Albrich, and Klaus Eisterer, eds. *Die doppelte Eindämmung: Europäische Sicherheit und deutsche Frage in den Fünfzigern.* Munich, 1993.

Stourzh, Gerald. *Geschichte des Staatsvertrages, 1945–1955: Österreichs Weg zur Neutralität.* 3rd ed. Graz, 1985.

——. *Um Einheit und Freiheit: Staatsvertrag, Neutralität und das Ende der Ost-West-Besetzung Österreichs 1945–55.* 4th ed. Vienna, 1998. This is a substantially expanded and updated version of the preceding entry.

Thoss, Bruno, and Hans-Erich Volkmann, eds. *Zwischen Kaltem Krieg und Entspannung: Sicherheits- und Deutschlandpolitik der Bundesrepublik im Mächtesystem der Jahre 1953–1956.* Boppard am Rhein, 1988.

Van Oudenaren, John. *Détente in Europe. The Soviet Union and the West since 1953.* Durham, N.C., 1991.

Varsori, Antonio, ed. *Europe, 1945–1990s: The End of an Era?* London, 1995.

Young, John W. *Winston Churchill's Last Campaign: Britain and the Cold War, 1951–5.* Oxford, U.K., 1996.

——, ed. *The Foreign Policy of Churchill's Peacetime Administration, 1951–1955.* Leicester, 1988.

Zhai, Qiang. *The Dragon, the Lion, and the Eagle: Chinese-British-American Relations, 1949–1958.* Kent, Ohio, 1994.

Zubok, Vladislav, and Constantine Pleshakov. *Inside the Kremlin's Cold War: From Stalin to Khrushchev.* Cambridge, Mass., 1996.

Articles

Bischof, Günter. "The Anglo-American Powers and Austrian Neutrality 1953–1955." *Mitteilungen des Österreichischen Staatsarchivs,* XLII (1992), 368–93.

———. "The Making of a Cold Warrior: Karl Gruber and Austrian Foreign Policy, 1945–1953."*Austrian History Yearbook,* XXVI (1995), 99–127.

Brands, Henry W. "The Age of Vulnerability: Eisenhower and the National Insecurity State."*American Historical Review,* XCIV (1989), 963–89.

Calandri, E. "La détente et la perception de l'Union Soviétique chez les décideurs français du printemps 1955 à fevrier 1956." *Relations Internationales,* LXXIII (Summer 1993), 176–7.

Conze, Eckart. "Vom Herter-Plan zum Genscher-Plan: Zum Zusammenhang von Deutscher Einheit, europäischer Sicherheit und internationaler Abrüstung am Ende der fünfziger Jahre und heute." *Europäische Rundschau,* XVIII (1990), 65–77.

Dockrill, Saki. "Cooperation and Suspicion: The United States' Alliance Diplomacy for the Security of Western Europe." *Diplomacy and Statecraft,* V (1994), 138–82.

Gehler, Michael. "Kurzvertrag für Österreich? Die westliche Staatsvertrags-Diplomatie und die Stalin-Noten von 1952." *Vierteljahreshefte für Zeitgeschichte,* XLII (1994), 243–78.

———. "State Treaty and Neutrality: The Austrian Solution in 1955 As a 'Model' for Germany?"*Contemporary Austrian Studies,* III (1995), 39–78.

Immerman, Richard H. "Confessions of an Eisenhower Revisionist: An Agonizing Reappraisal."*Diplomatic History,* XIV (1990), 319–42.

———. "The United States and the Geneva Conference of 1954: A New Look." *Diplomatic History,* XIV (1990), 43–66.

Krone, Heinrich. "Aufzeichnungen zur Deutschland und Ostpolitik, 1954–1959." *Konrad-Adenauer-Studien,* Vol. III (1974), 134–201.

Küsters, Hanns Jürgen. "Wiedervereinigung durch Konföderation? Die Informellen Unterredungen zwischen Budesminister Fritz Schäffer, NVA-General Vinzenz Müller und Sowjetbotschafter Georgij Maksimowitsch Puschkin 1955/56." *Vierteljahrshefte für Zeitgeschichte,* XL (1992), 107–53.

Larres, Klaus. "Eisenhower and the First Forty Days after Stalin's Death: The Incompatibility of *Détente* and Political Warfare." *Diplomacy and Statecraft,* VI (1995), 431–69.

Larson, Deborah W. "Crisis Prevention and the Austrian Treaty." *International Organization,* XLI (1987), 27–60.

Mastny, Vojtech. "Kremlin Politics and the Austrian Settlement." *Problems of Communism*, XXXI (July–August 1982), 27–51.

Pearson, Lester B. "After Geneva: A Greater Task for NATO." *Foreign Affairs*, XXXIV (October 1955), 14–23.

Pruessen, Ronald W. "Beyond the Cold War—Again: 1955 and the 1990s." *Political Science Quarterly*, CVIII (1993), 59–84.

Richter, James G. "Reexamining Soviet Policy towards Germany during the Beria Interregnum." CWIHP working paper No. 3 (1992), 23–6.

———. "Perpetuating the Cold War: Domestic Sources of International Patterns of Behavior."*Political Science Quarterly*, CVII (1992), 271–301.

———. "Reexamining Soviet Policy towards Germany in 1953." *Europe-Asia Studies*, XLV (1993), 671–91.

Rupieper, Hermann-Josef. "Die Berliner Aussenministerkonferenz von 1954: Ein Höhepunkt der Ost-West-Propaganda oder letzte Möglichkeit zur Schaffung der deutschen Einheit?" *Vierteljahreshefte für Zeitgeschichte*, XXXIV (1986), 427–53.

Soutou, George-Henri. *The French Military Program for Nuclear Energy, 1945–1981.* Occasional Paper 3, Nuclear History Program, Center for International Security Studies at Maryland School of Public Affairs.

Spaulding, Robert M. "Eisenhower and Export Control Policy, 1953–1955." *Diplomatic History*, XVII (Spring 1993), 223–49.

Steininger, Rolf. "1955: The Austrian State Treaty and the German Question." *Diplomacy and Statecraft*, III (1992), 494–522.

Varsori, Antonio. "Alle origini della prima distensione: La Francia di Pierre Mendès France e la ripresa del dialogo con Mosca." *Storia delle relazioni internazionali*, VIII (1991), 63–98.

———. "Le gouvernement Eden et l'Union Soviétique, 1955–1956: De l'espoir à la désillusion." *Relations Internationales*, LXXI (Autumn 1992).

———. "Britain and the Death of Stalin." In Francesca Gori and Silvio Pons, eds., *The Soviet Union and Europe in the Cold War, 1943–53.* London, 1996, pp. 334–55.

Weathersby, Kathryn. "New Findings on the Korean War." *CWIHP Bulletin*, III (Fall 1993), 1, 14–8.

Young, John W. "Churchill's Bid for Peace with Moscow, 1954." *History*, LXXIII (1988), 425–48.

Zubok, Vladislav. "Soviet Intelligence and the Cold War: The 'Small' Committee of Information, 1952–1953." *Diplomatic History*, XIX (Summer 1995), 453–72.

Dissertations, Theses, and Papers

Angerer, Thomas. "Frankreich und die Österreichfrage. Historische Grundlagen und Leitlinien, 1945–1955." Ph.D. dissertation, University of Vienna, 1996.

Bischof, Günter. "Before the Break: The Relationship between Eisenhower and McCarthy, 1952–1953." M.A. thesis, University of New Orleans, 1980.

———. "Between Responsibility and Rehabilitation: Austria in International Politics, 1945–1955." 2 vols. Ph.D. dissertation, Harvard University, 1989.

Faughnan, Sean A. "The Politics of Influence: Churchill, Eden, and Soviet Communism." Ph.D. dissertation, Cambridge University, 1993.

Faure, Edgar. "Remarks: Dwight D. Eisenhower and France." Paper for the conference "Dwight D. Eisenhower As President." Hofstra University, 1984.

Forland, T. E. "Cold Economic Warfare: The Creation and Prime of COCOM." Ph.D. dissertation, University of Oslo, 1991.

Mongin, Dominique. "La genèse de l'armement nucléaire français, 1945–1958." Doctoral thesis, University of Paris I, 1991.

Pruessen, Ronald W. "The United States and European Integration in the 1950s." *Center for International Studies Working Paper.* University of Toronto.

Troyanovski, Oleg A. "Nikita Khrushchev and the Making of Soviet Foreign Policy." Paper for the Khrushchev Centennial Conference. Brown University, Providence, R.I., 1994.

Zubok, Vladislav. "Soviet Foreign Policy in Germany and Austria and the Post-Stalin Succession Struggle." Paper for conference "The Soviet Union, Germany, and the Cold War: New Evidence from Eastern Archives." Essen, Germany, 1994.

———. "Khrushchev and the Issue of Divided Germany, 1953–1964." Paper for the Khrushchev Centennial Conference. Brown University, Providence, R.I., 1994.

Index

Italicized page numbers refer to photographs and drawings.

McCarthyism, 9, 94, 126, 129–30, 232
McClellan Permanent Subcommittee on
  Investigation into East-West Trade in
  Strategic Materials, 237
Mendès-France, Pierre, 9, 46, 80–1, 94,
  98–106, 109, 148
Merchant, Livingston, 180
Messina conference, 95
Middle East, 253–4, 279, 290
Mikoyan, Anastas, 62, *156*, 196, 251,
  251*n*44
Millikan, Max, 221
Mollet, Guy, 108
Molotov, V. M.: and cooperation with
  Western Allies, 1; and Austria, 10, 123,
  124, 135–7, 140*n*50; on Germany, 10,
  93, 121–2, 183, 184; and Churchill, 44,
  57; power struggle with Khrushchev,
  57–9, 250–1; hardline European policies of, 60, 134, 135*n*39; and nuclear
  weapons, 60; and proposed summit,
  100, 150; compared with Eisenhower,
  125–6; on Khrushchev, 134*n*38; Khrushchev on, 135*n*39; photograph of,
  156; political cartoon of, *160*; at Berlin
  conference, 181; at Geneva Summit,
  183, 184; and Open Skies proposal,
  231; and East-West trade, 239*n*12, 248,
  287, 288; and economic policy, 251; at
  Geneva Conference of Foreign Ministers (1955), 282*n*17, 283–91. *See also*
  Soviet Union
Mongin, Dominique, 102–3, 108
Morocco, 116
Moscow summit (Austro-Soviet) of 1955,
  142–3, 142–43*nn*57–8
Mueller-Armack, Alfred, 247*n*36
Müller, Vinzenz, 203

National Security Council: and Eastern
  Europe, 17, 195, 202; and outcome of
  Geneva Summit, 17; NSC 68, 27, 28,
  29; NSC 162/2, 31, 41, 44, 131; Jackson's proposal to, 37; and Soviet policy, 43–4; on policy aims for Geneva
  Summit, 50, 52; NSC 38 on Austria,

119; and Austria, 132, 136, 140; and lo-
  cation of Geneva Summit, 150; NSC
  174 on Eastern Europe, 152; NSC 5501
  on Eastern Europe, 152; demilitarized
  zone in Germany, 202; and relations
  between West Germany and Soviet
  Union, 210–1; and disarmament, 217–
  20, 222, 224–6; Psychological Strategy
  Board of, 220; Geneva paper of, 225–6;
  and East-West trade, 237, 238, 240,
  244, 245, 250; and European security,
  262; and East Germany, 277
NATO: and European Defence Community (EDC), 7; and nuclear weapons,
  7–8, 31, 33–4, 187; West Germany as
  member of, 8, 9, 11, 14, 15, 33, 45, 50,
  65, 79, 99, 100, 106, 134, 146, 148, 164,
  185, 190–1, 213, 253, 263, 272, 290;
  and Soviet Union, 13, 63, 64, 65, 284;
  and rearmament versus country's economic and industrial strength, 20; and
  Lisbon force goals, 28; SACEUR of, 29,
  31, 164, 187; New Approach Group of,
  31, 33–4; Dulles on U.S. commitment
  to, 39; and Austria, 46; and demilitarized zone, 48; and united Germany,
  89, 178, 180–1, 188, 277; France in, 98,
  102; article 5 of NATO treaty, 171. *See
  also* North Atlantic Alliance
Naumov, Pavel, 71–2
Neiger, André ("Derso"), *160*
Netherlands, 7, 241*n*18
New Approach Group, 31, 33–4
Nitze, Paul H., 27
Nixon, Richard, 47
North Africa, 12, 98, 104, 112
North Atlantic Alliance, 12, 14, 18, 19,
  20. *See also* NATO
North Atlantic Treaty, 24, 171
North Korea, 24, 27–8, 32
Norway, 241*n*18
NSC. *See* National Security Council
Nuclear fallout, 18
Nuclear weapons: and NATO, 8, 31,
  33–4, 187; and France, 12, 102–3, 108;
  and Soviet Union, 14, 18, 25–7, 29, 33,

and Communism, 22–3; and Poland, 22; and Marshall Plan, 23; and Berlin blockade, 24; and atomic bomb, 25; and military-industrial complex of Soviet Union, 25; and Korean War, 27, 32; legacy of, 55–6, 61; Khrushchev on, 56, 58, 60; and Eastern Europe, 65; and Churchill, 76–7. *See also* Soviet Union
Starlinger, Wilhelm, 196n14
Stassen, Harold, 132, 218–20, 222, 224, 226–8, 233, 237n6
State Department, U.S.: on summit conference, 6, 105, 107; Soviet policy of, 6, 88–9, 107, 125, 195, 276; and arms control, 13; and policy aims of Geneva Summit, 109; and Austrian treaty, 120, 140, 141, 145–7; on Austria's relationship with Soviet Union, 125; and West Germany, 145–6; and European security system, 166; and Canute operation, 168–72; and Eden plan, 172–5; and disarmament, 217–9, 221; Dulles's criticisms of, 233; and East-West trade, 235, 238, 242, 244–5, 246n31, 262
Steel, Sir Christopher, 89
Steiner, Kurt, 139–40, 140n50
Stevenson, Adlai E., 35
Summit conferences: public opinion on, 271–2. *See also* Geneva Summit of 1955; and other summits
Suslov, Mikhail, 70–2
Sweden, 145, 252n45

Taiwan, 67–70
TCP. *See* Technological Capabilities Panel (TCP)
Technological Capabilities Panel (TCP), 222–3
Thompson, Llewellyn E., 46, 138, 138n46, 141, *159*
Thorneycroft, Peter, 237n6
Thoss, Bruno, 140, 144n60
Tito, 58, 61, 90, 151, 152, 193, 256, 268
Tocqueville, Alexis de, 21
Trade between East and West: at Geneva Summit, 16–7, 245–51; management

of, before Geneva Summit, 234–9; Soviet policy on, 234–52, 252n45; British policy on, 235, 244, 245, 252n45; and Coordinating Committee (CoCom), 235, 239; U.S. policy on, 235–9, 240, 240n13, 243, 246, 250, 262; and prospects for Geneva Summit, 239–45; and West Germany, 240–2, 240–41nn15–6, 246–8; and Eastern Europe, 242–3, 244; and China, 244, 250n42, 252n45; French policy on, 244; and Geneva Conference of Foreign Ministers (1955), 248, 274–5, 287–8
Troyanovsky, Oleg, 61, 62, 64
Truman, Harry S.: Soviet policy of, 23, 76, 94; defense policy of, 25, 26–8, 29; and Fair Deal, 26, 27, 29; and nuclear weapons, 26–7; and NSC 68, 27, 28, 29; in presidential election of 1952, 35; and Austrian treaty, 119; and East-West trade policy, 235–7; analysis of leadership of, 270
Truman Doctrine, 23
Turkey, 23, 55
Two-Plus-Four Talks (1990), 214

U-2 reconnaissance plane, 2, 223–4
UNESCO, 287
United Nations, 2, 10, 22, 89, 100, 171, 239n12, 262, 274, 286, 287
United States. *See* Dulles, John Foster; Eisenhower, Dwight D.; Geneva Summit of 1955; Truman, Harry S.; and government agencies and officials
USSR. *See* Soviet Union

Van Oudenaren, John, 75, 134
Van Zeeland plan, 165
Varsori, Antonio, 6, 9, 14, 187
Vienna Council of Foreign Ministers (1955), 149, 150
Vinogradov, Sergei, 105, 287
Von Brentano, Heinrich, 204, 248, 263–4, 281–2, 289
Von Eckardt (ambassador to UN), 204